Knowledge Management and Organizational Learning

Volume 15

Series Editors

Ettore Bolisani, University of Padova, Padova and Venice International University, Venice, Italy

Meliha Handzic, International Burch University, Sarajevo, Bosnia and Herzegovina

This series is introduced by the International Association for Knowledge Management (www.IAKM.net) with an aim to offer advanced peer-reviewed reference books to researchers, practitioners and students in the field of knowledge management in organizations. Both discussions of new theories and advances in the field, as well as reviews of the state-of-the art will be featured regularly. Particularly, the books will be open to these contributions: Reviews of the state-of-the art (i.e. syntheses of recent studies on a topic, classifications and discussions of theories, approaches and methods, etc.) that can both serve as a reference and allow opening new horizons Discussions on new theories and methods of scientific research in organisational knowledge management Critical reviews of empirical evidence and empirical validations of theories Contributions that build a bridge between the various disciplines and fields that converge towards knowledge management (i.e.: computer science, cognitive sciences, economics, other management fields, etc.) and propose the development of a common background of notions, concepts and scientific methods Surveys of new practical methods that can inspire practitioners and researchers in their applications of knowledge management methods in companies and public services.

This is a SCOPUS-indexed book series.

Aino Kianto • Slađana Čabrilo
Lina Užienė
Editors

Futurizing Intellectual Capital

Insights on Navigating Knowledge-Based Value Creation

Springer

Editors
Aino Kianto
Lappeenranta–Lahti University of Technology LUT
Lahti, Finland

Slađana Čabrilo
I-Shou University
Kaohsiung, Taiwan

Lina Užienė
Kaunas University of Technology
Kaunas, Lithuania

ISSN 2199-8663 ISSN 2199-8671 (electronic)
Knowledge Management and Organizational Learning
ISBN 978-3-031-80196-9 ISBN 978-3-031-80197-6 (eBook)
https://doi.org/10.1007/978-3-031-80197-6

This Springer imprint is published by the registered company Springer Nature Switzerland AG
The registered company address is: Gewerbestrasse 11, 6330 Cham, Switzerland

Foreword

For three decades I've written about the most important asset we can't see—intellectual capital. This intangible marvel continues to grow at an accelerated rate inside of organizations and nations. Yet, we continue to struggle with understanding the full extent of its power. This book aims to fill that void. In it, we learn about how to conceptualize intellectual capital in the future and, more importantly, how to leverage it for value creation.

In a world where change is the only constant, the value of intellectual capital has never been more critical. The ability to navigate and harness intangible assets is not just a competitive advantage but a necessity for survival in our modern, knowledge-intensive, business landscape. This book, *Futurizing Intellectual Capital: Insights on Navigating Knowledge-Based Value Creation*, is a timely and invaluable resource for individuals, teams, organizations, and nations seeking to understand and leverage the power of intellectual capital.

As we move toward three decades of cumulative academic research on the topic, intellectual capital has been considered by many, defined by some, understood by few, and empirically valued by practically no one. That's why we must continue the journey of learning more.

The chapters within this book provide a comprehensive exploration of various aspects of intellectual capital and its role in influencing firm performance and shaping the future. From understanding the fundamentals of its sub-components to exploring innovative strategies for its measurement and utilization, each chapter offers unique insights and practical guidance.

One of the key themes that emerge from this collection is the need for a shift in mindset—a move from viewing intellectual capital as a static asset to recognizing it as a dynamic force that can drive innovation and growth. This shift is particularly crucial in today's rapidly changing environment, where the ability to adapt and innovate is paramount.

The authors of these chapters are experts in their fields, drawing on years of research and experience to offer valuable perspectives and actionable strategies. Whether you are a business leader looking to unlock the full potential of your organization's intellectual capital or an individual seeking to enhance your personal knowledge assets, this book has something to offer.

As we navigate the complexities of the twenty-first century, the insights shared in this book will serve as a valuable guide, helping us not only to survive but to thrive in the face of uncertainty. I commend the authors for their dedication and expertise in bringing this important topic to light, and I am confident that their work will inspire and inform readers for years to come.

I hope that you find these chapters as enlightening and inspiring as I have. I'm positive that this book will have a prominent position on your bookshelf for years to come. May it serve as a beacon of knowledge and a catalyst for innovation in your own journey of futurizing intellectual capital.

Hamilton, ON, Canada Nick Bontis

Foreword and Future Hunting for Intellectual Capital

"To do the useful thing, to say the courageous thing, to contemplate the beautiful thing: that is enough for one man's life."
—T.S. Eliot & John Kjelldén 2024

This book covers many aspects of intellectual capital (IC). The forward-thinking scholars in their chapters deepen the understanding of IC. It is for the benefit of forthcoming researchers and practitioners in the field of intangible assets. Around 97% of our universe is still to be discovered, including the IC dimensions. Therefore, here I focus on finding signals of unknown and hidden values, challenging the traditional way of thinking and expanding the knowledge of IC.

What do you foresee in the future of the world around us? How is the role of intellectual capital changing? Is artificial intelligence the tool of the future? Relevant future skills might be less about the tools and more about the way of thinking, i.e., the rotating world and its signals.

As the grandfather of the IC subject, I am encouraged by the growing number of educational programs, publications, scholars, symposia, and prototyping and scaling of IC value. The number of cases to verify is increasing and the value of the stock market is increasing as well.

The recent IC paradigm, which emerges frequently in the context of knowledge management, is now expanding and is being offered among other ISO standards and developed in exploratory lab alliances such as the Japan Innovation Network.

Initiatives such as the Oracy Lab thinking touch on quantum physics "Sixth Sense." And it seems that the art of deep listening and discovering the almost hidden patterns different from other cultural paradigms deserves a place in the IC taxonomy.

As we know, the radiation spectrum is broad, of which our sight is only a small part. The James Webb Space Telescope (JWST) is designed to use the red portion of the spectrum. With 18 reflective plates carefully aligned, it can "see" remarkably small and distant items and patterns of items. JWST is a good metaphor for the new IC deep knowledge and knowledge navigational processes of deep and imaginative listening, seeing the incredibly small dynamic patterns in the background, and becoming aware of the clusters of insights sprinkled in the conversation for the new generation of IC universe with unarticulated IC value stars that form constellations of meaning and energy from "Thinking and Feeding Forward" or IC drilling of the

Next Generation. So let us highlight a few of the 18 plates in the JWST IC Lab, and live the message of Leonardo da Vinci "Saper Vedere," i.e., learning to see.

Many might try to simplify but lose the clarification perspective of the uniqueness of IC as a dynamic paradigm beyond the industrial era paradigm. The longitudinal understanding goes deeper. Perhaps, the AI might assist us in connecting the disciplines for cross-fertilizing IC bench learning.

Society 5.0 is in progress by Japan, under the leadership of Prof. Noboru Konno, in collaboration with Keidanren (JIN) and other futurizing pioneers. The core is the search for innovation policy for the Society of Tomorrow—a quest for a more intelligent value creation and economic regime. A key knowledge leader is Taka Sumita, now at Sumitomo Research Lab, Japan, in pioneering efforts with acknowledged knowledge gurus Prof. Ikujiro Nonaka and Prof. Noboru Konno, Exocyx Lab, Tokyo.

Where and how do you learn to think about the Future? For a long time, it has been about projection and visionary scenarios—like Jules Verne as well as research implemented by NASA. Today several research groups in various countries are doing experimental multi-team research on how to reach outer space. As human beings, we are limited to being in the gravitation space. The future thinking behind the space programs initially asked the core question: how to get beyond the Earth's gravity. It is a strong power of resistance.

Future skills are multi-team tasking—recently visualized by Nobel Prize in Medicine with RNA. Perhaps, the next question might be survival beyond Tellus. Recently, this has inspired a startup in Stockholm, Sweden. This is a knowledge navigation process. It starts with insights from Leonardo da Vinci's "Saper Vedere"—learning to see.

The Future IC Navigation skill is much more than driving a car. It is more like flying. It is a three-dimensional skill. The Future skill is also to connect the dots into a pattern, like qualified weather reporting. It goes beyond forecasting, onto anticipation skill—learning to look around the corner.

The implication of that challenge is to tap a multitude of sources of signals and data. That specific process might be labeled Oracy Lab conversation: in other words, deep listening for the inner voice and hidden signs. "Saper Vedere," as phrased by Leonardo da Vinci. But from another enlightening perspective.

Future of IC: Some Reflections on Feeding Forward

Let me list some quizzes for your mind stretch:

- Metrics development: Where is the metric of good connectivity between talents?
- Longitude metrics: How do we sketch the 3dd, with Avatar design?
- Going beyond the human resources: What is the value of an Avatar department?
- Integration into the ICT and AI: How will AI be smartening Nations? Cyber security? Societal Innovations?
- Bridging with culture and softer dimensions: What peace tools might be developed for conflict resolution?

- Mapping at both, macro levels such as NIC, as well as micro and nano levels of Green IC Health Innovation.
- Astropolicy as an emerging context for IC and societal politics.

Happy Future—begin to enjoy sensing beyond the noise of everyday life.

Stockholm, Sweden Leif Edvinsson

Contents

Introduction: Toward Futurizing Intellectual Capital Theory and Practice

Aino Kianto, Slađana Čabrilo, and Lina Užienė

Abstract

This editorial introductory chapter sets the stage for a forward-looking exploration of intellectual capital (IC) in both theoretical and practical contexts. It addresses the evolving landscape of IC in an era marked by rapid technological, institutional and socio-political disruptions and demonstrates the need for futurizing the field of IC. By providing a cohesive framework for the book's thematic sections, this chapter highlights the novel viewpoints and visions from leading experts concerning future directions for IC research and practice. It also summarizes the book's 16 main chapters and discusses how each of them pushes the boundaries of conceptual and empirical insights in the field of IC. This comprehensive introduction contributes to deeper understanding of the proposed new paradigms to align IC theory and practice with future economic, social, and technological changes.

The intellectual capital (IC) movement began approximately 30 years ago, with the fundamental realization that knowledge plays a crucial role in economic value creation. And what an influential realization that was!

A. Kianto (✉)
Lappeenranta-Lahti University of Technology (LUT), Lappeenranta, Finland
e-mail: aino.kianto@lut.fi

S. Čabrilo
I-Shou University, Kaohsiung, Taiwan
e-mail: sladjana@isu.edu.tw

L. Užienė
Kaunas University of Technology, Kaunas, Lithuania
e-mail: lina.uziene@ktu.lt

A. Kianto et al. (eds.), *Futurizing Intellectual Capital*, Knowledge Management and Organizational Learning 15, https://doi.org/10.1007/978-3-031-80197-6_1

Along with the advancement of information technology in the 1990s, companies began investing in knowledge management systems and tools, attempting to capture the valuable knowledge of their employees. Simultaneously, firms became interested in reporting their intellectual capital to promote their capabilities to external stakeholders. Concurrently, scholars were alerted to these new realities and began crafting the strategic perspective we now know as the IC school of thought. Indeed, the IC perspective gained momentum and spread globally, burgeoning into a legitimate scientific field of its own.

The initial idea for this book stemmed from our personal realizations that, although we have found the IC approach useful and inspiring in our work as scholars, educators, and work-life developers, the technological, institutional, ecological, and sociopolitical disruptions in recent years necessitate a more radical update to the IC school of thought than we had previously seen in either scholarly publications or practical applications.

Therefore, the vision of this book was to provide a platform for new thinking concerning what IC theory and practice should look like to address not only the current but, even more importantly, the future challenges of work-life and societies at large. When sending out the Call for Chapters to a targeted shortlist of potential contributors, we hoped to receive brave and courageous new ideas about the future of IC theory and practice.

We could not be more satisfied with what the authors have developed. The targeted call for chapters yielded 16 contributions from leading minds in the IC field worldwide, which together form a veritable wellspring of new avenues for IC research and practice. The chapters reveal pertinent changes and trends shaping the current business environment and their implications for IC theory, critically examining IC theory in light of associated opportunities and challenges. Keeping the future in focus and searching for answers to fundamental questions related to the development of IC theory and practice, which are essential for sustainable growth and social well-being, all chapters foresee novelties, such as new economic and societal models, new industries, and professions, and create novel understandings and viewpoints concerning the nature of IC, its effective management mechanisms, and the potential impact of IC on organizations and societies.

The book explains how emerging technologies and digitalization are changing the role of IC in organizations, how IC can contribute to solving sustainability challenges, which new risks organizations and managers face, and how to manage IC in an increasingly complex environment. The book advocates the adoption of a multi-level understanding of IC—a comprehensive approach that includes individual, team, organizational, national, and societal levels of IC—and emphasizes the interaction and dynamics between these levels. The thought-provoking chapters guide different interest groups on how to solve complex problems, inspire experimentation, and provide new perspectives for the development of IC theory and practice. Finally, the challenges discussed in the book expand the understanding of future individual, organizational, and national prosperity and open up new opportunities to strengthen IC as a dynamic driver of innovation, manage organizations and state institutions more efficiently, and improve public services and politics for global smart growth and peace.

This book offers a collection of 16 future-oriented chapters that present diverse insights from leading scholars and practitioners in the field of IC, providing readers with novel viewpoints and visions concerning IC theory and practice. The book is organized into four sections, each addressing a key area of future-proof IC research and practice. Although the chapters present individual narratives, they are gathered around a central theme to deepen the reader's comprehension of the subject matter.

In Part I, Intellectual Capital in Flux: Navigating Complexity, the authors challenge prevailing linear, static, and unidimensional thinking about IC and highlight a complex, dynamic, and multilevel structure of IC as essential to align and adapt the IC paradigm to global complexity. This section captures the essence of the holistic nature of IC and enhances our understanding of the dynamics of interactions between IC elements, IC levels, and a shared context in complex and multilevel IC ecosystems.

In the first chapter, "A Complexity Framework for Understanding Intellectual Capital," Constantin Bratianu demonstrates how IC is transforming from a potential form into a kinetic form through knowledge management as a moderator and presents the multiscale framework of IC (microscale, mesoscale, and macroscale) that includes rational, emotional, and spiritual capital at the individual level, social IC at the level of teams, and the basic triad structure of IC at the organizational level.

Addressing IC as a dynamic driver of innovation, Noboru Konno, in the chapter "Unleashing Intellectual Capital: Toward Dynamic Theory through the Humanization of Intellectual Capital," discusses IC within an ecosystem, underscoring the importance of "Ba" (dynamics of a shared context) and the humanization of the IC concept for sustainable growth in the era of advanced technology.

Tomi Hussi and Aino Kianto, in the chapter "Intellectual Capital as a Basis for Cash Flow and Renewal," adapt IC terminology for practitioners and introduce (human) energy, (organizational) platform, and demand (perceived and understood by the company) as a triad of organizational knowledge assets while also addressing IC dynamics by adding knowledge flows (offering, dialog, and reflection) that integrate knowledge assets and transform them into short-term value (cash flow) and long-term value (renewal).

In the chapter "Individual-Level Intellectual Capital—A Framework for Future Management and Reflection," Sanna Mari Alppivuori and Aino Kianto delve into individual intellectual capital and propose a model that includes five dimensions (human, structural, relational, renewal, and emotional capital), contributing to a multilevel IC theory and a more holistic understanding of the complex IC ecosystem from the perspective of the individual actors embedded therein.

The last chapter in this section, "The Liability of Tacitness in Intellectual Capital: Overcoming Research Challenges with Grounded Theory Designs," by Carla Curado and Tiago Gonçalves, emphasizes the critical role of tacit knowledge. The authors propose the concept of tacit IC, guide readers on how foundational principles of grounded theory (GT) may assist in addressing challenges in tacit IC research, and point to new theoretical and empirical directions in tacit IC research.

In Part II, Smart Societal Growth: Intellectual Capital in Sustainable Ecosystems, the authors address the role of IC in social ecosystems, illustrating the potential of IC in facilitating sustainable development and societal well-being. This section explores how IC extends beyond organizations and operates within public sectors, nations, and global communities. Three inspiring chapters examine the broader impact of IC on sustainable economic and societal growth, global competitiveness, and, most importantly, global community well-being.

Günter M. Szogs introduces intellectual companionship as a valuable paradigm to advance IC methods and approaches, and in the chapter "IC as Intellectual Companionship," he sets the stage for a discussion on the pivotal role that IC plays in achieving sustainable societal growth. He develops the concept of IC companionship to highlight how using holistic humanistic sources and focusing research on the interdependencies of disciplines and areas of interconnectivity may leverage IC's "treasures within" and facilitate a worthwhile and integral social transformation.

The chapter "Sustainable National Intellectual Capital (SNIC) and Its Applications" by Carol Y. Y. Lin presents an SNIC model and its applications that not only provide important guidelines to policymakers and decision-makers in international business but also propose an IC ecosystem that might serve as a foundation for future multilevel, multidisciplinary, and multicountry research on sustainable IC.

The final chapter in this section, "Relevance and the Future of Intellectual Capital Management in the Public Sector," completes the discussion on the role of IC at the societal level. Harri Laihonen and Paula Pusenius explore IC management in the public sector and propose how governments and public organizations can design policies to harness the full potential of IC for societal benefit and community well-being, as well as for building sustainable societies.

The chapters in Part III, Intellectual Capital Meets Artificial Intelligence: Reimagining the IC Landscape, explore the dynamic interplay between artificial intelligence (AI) and IC and examine how AI technologies are reshaping the IC landscape. Through three forward-thinking chapters, we delve into the implications for knowledge workers and organizations, innovation processes, and organizational strategies, offering insights into how AI can be harnessed to unlock the full potential of IC in the digital age.

First, Bror Salmelin in "Intellectual Capital and the Era of Raising AI" provides a snapshot of how AI is transforming the IC domain and management. Considering current AI to be "a semantic parrot, not more!" but also anticipating AI as the lifeblood of organizations and societies, the author emphasizes the humanized, tacit, and emotional aspects of IC and identifies "IC guardians"' to play an essential role in the AI era.

Second, Henri Hussinki and Josh Morton, in the chapter "From a Data-Driven to Information-Driven Management Paradigm: Reflections on Generative AI and Intellectual Capital Management," present a research agenda for Gen AI and IC management, along with research themes and illustrative research questions, to guide future studies in the field. The authors highlight the rich potential to unearth the nuanced interrelations and potential causal linkages between Gen AI, IC, operational efficiency, and complex problem-solving.

Finally, Susanne Durst in "IC-Related Risks and AI—Friends and Foes!" invites a more holistic and balanced thinking about positive and negative IC-related risks created or amplified by the increased use of AI. Viewing AI as both a complementary resource and a substitute will inspire further IC theory development and open up the scope for novel IC practices.

Part IV, Reenvisioning Intellectual Capital: Rethinking Economic Models, Value, and Progress in the Knowledge Era, delves into the transformative future of intellectual capital, offering visionary perspectives on how we can redefine and harness value and progress in an increasingly complex and interconnected world. Through a series of thought-provoking chapters, we explore alternative economic models, the morality of shared-value businesses, and the revaluation of success to facilitate the development of a foundational IC theory and the emergence of new paradigms that prioritize sustainability, social equity, and holistic well-being.

The first chapter in this section, "Considerations Towards the Development of a Foundational Theory of Intellectual Capital," by Anthony Wensley and Max Evans, provides a fundamental overview of IC research; discusses its historical development, boundaries, and commonalities with knowledge management; and critically reviews existing theories of the firm to provide valuable insights for developing a foundational IC theory.

Günter Koch, in "Futurizing Intellectual Capital: New Economic Models and the Venue of AI Requests for an Update," further illuminates alternative economic models and other aspects, such as natural capital accounting and AI, to address sustainability crises and proposes a renewed IC reporting (ICR) model that might help companies better communicate intangible assets related to sustainability.

Ante Pulic announces a new era called "knowlism" in his thought-provoking chapter, "The Future of Intellectual Capital in the Era of Artificial Intelligence: Analysis from the Perspective of Value Creation." This chapter highlights the complexity economy, AI as a part of structural capital, and entropy as a measure of work efficiency. It also presents an improved version of the well-known Value Added Intellectual Coefficient (VAIC) model as a suitable tool for multilevel IC measurement and optimization of value-creation processes in the knowledge economy.

In the chapter "Effective Intellectual Capital Management as the Enabler of Future Value and Success in a Knowledge Economy," Stefan Güldenberg challenges the outdated and backward-looking normative understanding of value and success by linking the IC framework with the attention-based view of the firm, system dynamics, organizational learning, and sensemaking and suggests new principles for IC measurement and management.

In the final chapter, "Being Critical about Intellectual Capital in 2024: Chocolate as a Manifesto for Social Change," John Dumay questions the morality of shared value business models in international business and ties together diverse discussions throughout the book about worthwhile IC research that contributes to the betterment of society and the environment. The Chocolate Scorecard serves as a manifesto for continued change in the way researchers conceptualize and undertake IC research to build a better society for everyone.

Our aspiration is that this book will pave the way for more future-proof IC research and practice and serve as a key reference volume for emerging and established scholars and practitioners in the field. We hope that it will inspire new thinking by breaking old patterns, making new connections, and gaining fresh perspectives on IC, thereby provoking future research impetus and offering ways forward with a revised understanding of IC and its role in organizational viability and global sustainability. Our hope is that this book will serve as a catalyst for future research, dialog, and concrete knowledge-based activities relevant to the future prosperity and well-being of knowledge societies.

This book is the result of wonderful intellectual companionship and a collective spirit and motivation to reenergize the IC community by sharing knowledge. We are deeply grateful to all the contributors for their exceptional work and dedication and their willingness to share their unique ideas and expertise, which makes this book a valuable resource for readers worldwide. We also want to acknowledge the outstanding and invaluable administrative assistance we received from Thanh Thuy Nguyen.

We hope that this book will also be a powerful tool for readers' personal and professional growth and an inspiration for forward thinking and exploration.

Thank you for embarking on this journey to the future of IC with us!

Part I

Intellectual Capital in Flux: Navigating Complexity

A Complexity Framework for Understanding Intellectual Capital

Constantin Bratianu

Abstract

The purpose of this chapter is to search for a possible answer to the future of intellectual capital by considering a complexity framework, able to reveal new aspects of both the content and the structure of it. Thus, the chapter will challenge the linear thinking of the canonical paradigm, its static nature, its rational content, and its mono-scale structure. Furthermore, the canonical model of intellectual capital, composed of human, structural, and relational capital, was designed for a generic organization. When it is applied at the level of individuals, it collapses to human capital, and when it is applied to ecosystems, it needs to be extended with new components. The canonical paradigm represents a static intellectual capital. We would like to demonstrate that intellectual capital is a dynamic entity, and it is transforming from a potential form into a kinetic form through the work performed by knowledge management. The final idea of this chapter is based on the multiscale representation of intellectual capital. At the microscale level, the structure of intellectual capital should consider the theory of knowledge fields, according to which we distinguish between rational knowledge, emotional knowledge, and spiritual knowledge. Thus, we will have rational intellectual capital, emotional intellectual capital, and spiritual intellectual capital. These components can be combined and scaled up to obtain any other model, including the classical one.

C. Bratianu (✉)
UNESCO Department for Business Administration, Bucharest University of Economic Studies, Bucharest, Romania

A. Kianto et al. (eds.), *Futurizing Intellectual Capital*, Knowledge Management and Organizational Learning 15, https://doi.org/10.1007/978-3-031-80197-6_2

1 Introduction

The paradigm of *intellectual capital* was constructed by the pioneers of this domain. The most significant contributions came from Edvinsson and Malone (1997), Stewart (1997), and Sveiby (1997). They remarked on the emergence of intangible resources as driving forces of companies' value creation, and they proposed different frameworks to evaluate those intangibles. The resulting paradigm that was accepted by most researchers is based on the triad of human capital, structural capital, and relational capital, although there were more variations on this subject (Andriessen, 2004). The *human capital* of a given organization contains the integration of all the information and knowledge people have within that organization. Here, we should include both explicit and tacit knowledge and the human intelligence that processes them. Also, we may define the human capital in terms of competencies all employees have at a given stage of organizational development. For the same generic organization, the *structural capital* component reflects the functional structure, the organizational culture, and all the information and knowledge contained in the regulations, databases, and intellectual properties. As Edvinsson (2002) remarked, structural capital contains all the intangibles which remain within organizations when all the employees leave for home. The *relational capital* reflects the internal and external relationships people and organizations may have with their stakeholders. On the whole, "Intellectual capital (IC) can be defined as all nonmonetary and nonphysical resources that are fully or partly controlled by the organization and that contribute to the organization's value creation" (Roos et al., 2005, p. 19).

The complexity of the new business environment, especially after the global crises generated by COVID-19, challenges researchers to enlarge the framework of the intellectual capital and to consider the new changes we witnessed in the last decade. As remarked by Kianto and Cabrilo (2022), "It is necessary to rethink the nature and content of intellectual capital along with novel theorizing of intellectual capital paradigms" (p. 611). The idea is developed further by Cabrilo and Kianto (2023), "It may be necessary to update the understanding concerning not only the essential knowledge resources but also the structure of intellectual capital and the way in which intellectual capital is related with new relevant organizational capabilities and aspects of organizational performance" (p. 178).

In a recent comprehensive analysis, Kianto et al. (2023) remark on the following main changes in the business environment, which request a paradigm change for *intellectual capital*: digitalization, remote work, gig work, open innovation and crowdsourcing, ethical leadership, sustainability, green IC, and organizational resilience. The authors bring in a series of arguments and define ten propositions for the reevaluation of human capital, structural capital, and relational capital. They argue for a larger perspective of understanding and explaining the concept of intellectual capital and its contribution to organizational performance and value creation. In our view, changing the paradigm should take advantage of the new paradigms designed for the concepts of *knowledge* and *knowledge dynamics* (Bratianu, 2011, 2023; Bratianu & Bejinaru, 2019a, 2020). These new developments are based on entropic thinking (Bratianu, 2019; Chalidze, 2000) nonlinear and systems thinking (Gharajedaghi, 2006; Senge, 1999), and probabilistic thinking (Taleb, 2007).

The purpose of this chapter is to explore *a complexity* approach to the construct of *intellectual capital* and to reveal new perspectives on understanding and explaining its nature, structure, and functionality within a multiple-scale semantic universe. We base our ideas on cognitive science (Friedenberg & Silverman, 2016; Kahneman, 2011) and complexity science (Bird, 2003; Gleick, 2008; Stacey, 2001; Stacey et al., 2000).

2 The Science of Complexity

Classical science is based on Newtonian logic that is linear, on deterministic thinking and reversible processes. Newtonian logic was at that time a genial simplification of reality and produced theories and laws, which allowed technology to develop and humanity to progress. Reality is not linear and not deterministic, and all processes are irreversible. To understand all these new aspects, scientists had to change many paradigms (Kuhn, 1970) and discover new horizons. A series of new paradigms have been integrated into the generic name of "Chaos Science" (Bird, 2003; Gleick, 2008) or "Complexity Science" (Stacey, 2001; Stacey et al., 2000), as shown by Gleick: "Relativity eliminated the Newtonian illusion of absolute space and time; quantum theory eliminated the Newtonian dream of a controllable measurement process; and chaos eliminated the Laplacian fantasy of deterministic predictability" (Gleick, 2008, p. 6).

The complexity logic incorporates *nonlinearity* as a fundamental characteristic of chaotic systems and as a consequence, these systems have a nonlinear behavior and "sensitive dependence on initial conditions" (Gleick, 2008, p. 23). From a practical viewpoint, small inputs may produce large outputs, creating the butterfly effect. For nonlinear systems, outcomes are not anymore proportional to the inputs, like for linear systems. Instead of linear correlations between outputs and inputs, we may have now polynomials, logarithmic functions, exponential functions, or trigonometric functions. For instance, the outcome of a change process is not proportional to the number of days needed to end it; it depends on the complexity of the change and on the effort of doing it. Also, learning some new procedures is not proportional to the number of hours put in that effort; it correlates with the motivation of people. Therefore, the level of intellectual capital as a result of learning is a nonlinear entity. Complex phenomena develop on multiple scales, displaying *self-similarity* of different patterns. Here we have to underline the dynamics between order and disorder and the *recursion* property, i.e., "pattern inside pattern" (Gleick, 2008, p. 103). This property is related directly to the fractals and their irregular patterns (Bird, 2003; Gleick, 2008). Complexity dynamics is characterized by the process of iteration (Stacey, 2001; Stacey et al., 2000). Iteration does not mean a simple repetitive sequence within a system, but a creative process. Self-similarity can be illustrated with the knowledge dynamics model developed by Nonaka and Takeuchi (1995) at individual, team, and organizational levels. *Socialization* generates new tacit knowledge that is transformed into explicit knowledge during the *externalization* stage. That explicit knowledge is amplified during the *combination* stage and transformed into tacit knowledge during the stage of *Internalization*. Intellectual capital is a result of this knowledge dynamics cycle.

Complex dynamic systems have a behavior that cannot be predicted by using analytical equations, as in the case of Newtonian systems. Their behavior can be described only from a macro-perspective and with respect to some attractors. According to the dictionary, *an attractor* is a state or behavior toward which a dynamic system tends to evolve (dictionary.com). An attractor can be represented by a point or by an orbit in the system phase space. When such an attractor generates states defining a fractal set, then it is called a *strange attractor* (Bird, 2003; Gleick, 2008; Pryor & Bright, 2007; Stacey, 2001). Because complex dynamic systems are based on irreversible processes, their behavior is related to the *entropy law* (Bird, 2003; Chalidze, 2000). Any transformation within such a system implies an increase in its entropy if that transformation is done naturally. Otherwise, the entropy may decrease if there is an organizing force, like management and leadership. Therefore, in organizations, we should be able to correlate the actions of managers with the consequence of decreasing or increasing the organizational entropy or the knowledge entropy (Bratianu, 2019; Chalidze, 2000). Knowledge entropy reflects the probability distribution of knowledge within an organization. When management enforces order like in the old paradigm of *command and control*, the knowledge entropy is low. The organizational intellectual capital is almost static and has very few changes for renewal. When managers change *the command and control* paradigm with a more relaxed and creative one, then there is a reverse trend of knowledge dynamics, and knowledge entropy increases. As a consequence, the organizational intellectual capital becomes more dynamic, and the innovation process is intensified.

3 Nonlinearity

Although *nonlinearity* is a fundamental characteristic of natural and social phenomena (Senge, 1999), from a linguist's point of view, the concept is conceived with respect to *linearity* (i.e., nonlinearity). Therefore, we need to explain the concept of *linearity* first and then, by negating its semantic dimensions, to explain *nonlinearity*.

Linearity is a social solution for understanding, explaining, modelling, and measuring complex phenomena and processes. The human mind has become almost linear, especially in cultures that have Greek and Roman roots (Nisbett, 2003; Ohmae, 1982). A linear system is defined as a system whose output is proportional to the input. If X is the input variable, Y is the output variable, and k is a process constant, then the behavior of the system can be described by a *linear equation* of the form $Y = kX$. The keyword here is the proportionality between the output variable and the input one. A system with linear behavior can be predictable and controllable. That explains why most of the people would like to work with linear systems. However, understanding linearity implies understanding the mathematical concept of *linear spaces*. Considering a mathematical space of scalars S, the following requirements are necessary to define a *linear space* (Bratianu, 2009, p. 416):

- If a and b are scalars in S, then $a + b$ is also a scalar in S.
- If c is a scalar in S, then ca is also a scalar in S.
- The scalar addition is *commutative*: $a + b = b + a$.
- The scalar addition is *associative*: $(a + b) + c = a + (b + c)$.
- There is *an identity element* such that: $a + 0 = 0 + a$.
- There is *an inverse element* such that: $a + (-a) = 0$.
- There is *distributivity* over scalar addition: $(a + b)c = ac + bc$.

The economic construct of *capital* is a measurable entity. Therefore, the result of measurement can be expressed in numbers. Let us consider the *money metric* and let us verify if the *capital* construct is linear or not. Let us consider the following: $a = 10$; $b = 15$; $c = 20$. Let N be the set of all natural numbers. Now, we check each requirement for its validity:

- $10 + 15 = 25$. The result 25 belongs to N.
- $20 \times 10 = 200$. The result 200 belongs to N.
- $10 + 15 = 15 + 10$. The addition is commutative.
- $(10 + 15) + 20 = 10 + (15 + 20)$. The addition is associative.
- $10 + 0 = 0 + 10$. There is an identity element.
- $10 + (-10) = 0$. There is an inverse element.
- $(10 + 15) \times 20 = 10 \times 20 + 15 \times 20$. The addition is distributive.

The validation of all requirements leads to the conclusion that the economic construct of *capital* is linear.

Linear thinking is powerful because people linearize all complex problems to make easier the process of finding solutions. Physical time is linear. One minute is equal to another minute, and one minute comes after the previous one ends. Our speech is linear. When we speak, one word comes after another and one sentence after another. The same happens with our writing. All measurements of the physical properties of objects and phenomena like length, area, volume, mass, temperature, and many others are linear. Budgetary salaries are linear because they are based on the multiplication of the number of worked hours by the quantum of money per hour. We may continue with other examples, but we have already shown how our education and everyday life contributed to the formation and development of our linear thinking. Therefore, linear thinking acts as a barrier to understanding and working with nonlinearity.

The concept of *intellectual capital* incorporated a semantic vulnerability from the very beginning (Bratianu, 2018) that created a barrier to its usefulness. It is the barrier of *linearity* that generates so many errors in understanding, using, measuring, and interpreting intellectual capital (Bratianu, 2009). The concept is based on a fusion between two other concepts: *intellectual* and *capital*. The concept of *intellectual* reflects an attribute of our mind and has a nonlinear nature. The concept of *capital* reflects a tangible object or stock of objects representing an asset of a company, and it has a *linear* nature, as shown above. In economic theory and practice, *capital* means "a large amount of money that is invested or is used to start a business" or "wealth or property" that is owned by a person or a company (Hornby, 2004). Therefore, the semantic fusion between a concept reflecting a tangible object and one that reflects an attribute of our mind created an ambiguity in understanding the nature of the resulting concept of *intellectual capital.* In our view, the new concept of *intellectual capital* should reveal a nonlinear entity, but it is not well understood by many researchers.

The root of the linearity error comes from the very definition of *intellectual capital* formulated by Stewart, one of the prominent pioneers of this construct: "Intellectual capital is the *sum* of everything everybody in a company knows that gives it a competitive edge", and "Intellectual capital is intellectual material—knowledge, information, intellectual property, experience – that can be put to use to create wealth" (Stewart, 1997, p. XI). The word *sum* clearly says that the definition refers to a linear entity because *summation* or *addition* is a linear operator. Dumay (2016, p. 169) revised the second formulation and changed "wealth" with "value," but keeping the idea that intellectual capital "is the sum of everything everybody in a company knows that gives it a competitive edge." Therefore, the linearity vulnerability remained in the minds of many researchers and academics.

Let us show that *intellectual capital* is not linear. We shall consider a set of concepts *C* and three elements belonging to this set: *a* = *stupid*, *b* = *stone*, and *c* = 100. If there is at least one requirement that is not valid for the linear space, then the new space of concepts is not linear. Let us consider the *summation* and the *inverse element* requirements.

- *a* + *b* = *stupid* + *stone* = *stupidstone*. The result is meaningless.
- a + (− a) = stupid + (non-stupid) = 0. The result is meaningless. Instead of getting zero, we get ambiguity.

The final result is that *intellectual capital* that contains knowledge (i.e., a set of concepts) is not linear. It is nonlinear. Therefore, in the very definition formulated by Stewart (1997), it is necessary to change the concept of *sum* with that of *integration.* Integration is not an addition and reflects the property of nonlinearity. That integration is performed by nonlinear organizational integrators, such as management, leadership, and organizational culture (Bratianu, 2013).

Unfortunately, all the metrics developed to measure intellectual capital are linear metrics based on different proxies which are linear. Measuring nonlinear entities using linear metrics can lead to catastrophic results. "These contemporary IC measurement frameworks are reifying IC in the same manner in which tangible assets are portrayed within accounting, which is akin to attempting to make the intangible tangible. This is what the author defines as an 'accountingisation' of IC" (Dumay, 2009, p. 205). An interesting case is that of designing the Knowledge Balance Sheet (KBS) for public universities in Austria (Federal Law Gazette, 2006; Habersham et al., 2013, 2018) and reporting them according to the law—Intellectual Capital Report Act (ICRA). The KBS is based on the canonical model of the intellectual capital composed of human, structural, and relational capital, and the purpose of ICRA is "presenting, evaluating and communicating intangible assets, performance processes and their consequences and serves as a qualitative and quantitative basis for generating and entering a performance agreement" (Federal Law Gazette, 2006). However, in defining the indicators to measure intangible assets, ICRA contains a series of proxies that are far away from the nature of intellectual capital. For instance, to measure the structural capital, ICRA used in its first version as an indicator of the "floor space" (in square meters) of the university, which represents a stupidity paradox (Alvesson & Spicer, 2016, p. X). A possible explanation of this phenomenon is offered by Albrecht (2003): "Western business thinking—particularly in America—as a codified in most widely circulated business magazines, business news broadcasts, management books, and conference programs, seems to have shifted steadily in recent years toward the impersonal and inhuman view of the enterprise. At the extreme of this view, assets are simply assets—including human beings" (Albrecht, 2003, pp. 4–5). When people realized the errors induced by such kinds of indicators, their number was reduced from 53 to 26 and finally to 24.

4 Dynamics

The first stage of using metaphors for explaining the concept of *knowledge* focused on physical objects and stocks (Andriessen, 2004, 2006, 2008; Barney, 1991; Bratianu, 2015). Physical objects and stocks are static concepts. As a consequence, intellectual capital, from this perspective, is static. As Kianto (2007) remarked, "The static asset approach adheres to the cognitivist perspective on knowledge, which assumes knowledge can be managed with tight procedures, policies, and defined action. It is also closer to the resource-based view of the firm, where the main interest is in acquisition and protection of valuable, rare, inimitable and non-substitutable resources" (p. 346). This static perspective was adopted easily by those working in accounting research and supported the idea of intellectual capital being a potential of integrated intangible resources (Bontis, 1999).

The second stage of knowledge metaphors is introduced as a reference concept like *fluids*, *flows*, and *stock-and-flow*, which reflect a dynamic perspective (Bolisani & Oltramari, 2012; Nissen, 2006). For instance, Nissen (2006) conceives knowledge as a fluid flow within the space of a company. The metaphor *stock-and-flow* incorporates both features of intellectual capital (i.e., static and dynamic). Knowledge stocks are considered in the nodes of the organizational knowledge network, while knowledge flows between nodes. The concentration or the level of intellectual capital in the network stocks can vary in time, creating local dynamics.

Kianto (2007) remarks that from a dynamic perspective, "knowledge is understood as emerging from the ongoing interactions between the organizational members and that the focus is not on the intangible *per se* but on the organizational capabilities to leverage, develop and change intangible assets for value creation"

(p. 344). Based on a critical literature review, Kianto (2007) identifies three interpretations of the intellectual capital dynamics:

(a) Dynamics are created by the social interactions of employees in the process of value creation.
(b) Dynamics due to organizational processes.
(c) Dynamics created by organizational changes.

The logic used by Kianto (2007) is clear: any variation of organizational knowledge generated by different activities and processes induces a variation in intellectual capital. More recently, Kianto et al. (2017) revealed a new aspect of intellectual capital dynamics that can be demonstrated if researchers evaluate the level of organizational intellectual capital over several years. The authors introduced the concept of *temporality* to underline the evolution of intellectual capital in time (years).

If we adopt a holistic perspective at the level of a generic organization, then we may conceive the dynamics of the intellectual capital as a transformation from its *potential* state into a *kinetic* one, like the transformation of potential energy into kinetic energy in Physics. In this perspective, the potential intellectual capital represents the result of the integration of all intangible resources at the level of organizations. Knowledge management (KM) acts as a force on that potential intellectual capital (PIC) and transforms it continuously into kinetic intellectual capital (KIC) that can create value. Kinetic IC is the active and dynamic component of the total organizational IC. Therefore, the value is created not by the potential state of intellectual capital but by its kinetic form, which makes sense from a practical point of view (see Fig. 1).

The logic of this transformation process produced by knowledge management is very simple. In a generic organization may exist a valuable potential IC (PIC). If the performance of knowledge management (KM) is low, then the kinetic IC (KIC) is low, and the value creation is low, although there is a high potential. For the same PIC, an intelligent KM can yield a high level of KIK, and thus, the value creation

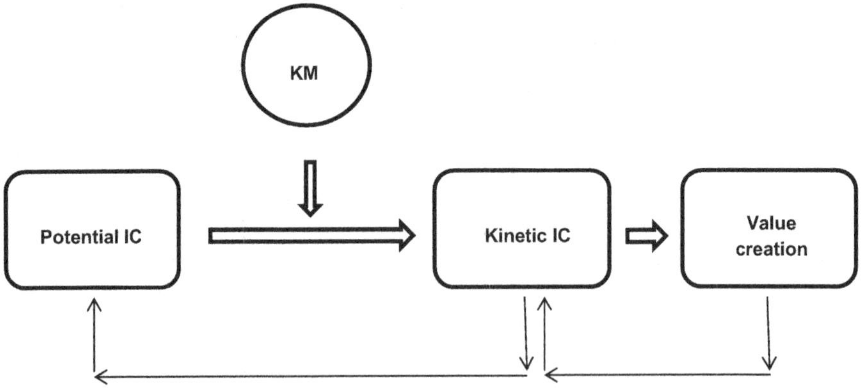

Fig. 1 The transformation of potential IC into kinetic IC

can be increased. KM acts like an external force if we consider the analogy with the transformation of potential energy into kinetic energy. All researchers who measure the relation between PIC and KIK and ignore the transformational role of KM cannot get reasonable explanations for the correlation between intellectual capital and value creation. The logic of ICRA based on static inputs could be an example of misinterpreting the value creation of the Austrian universities.

5 The Kernel Pattern of Intellectual Capital

The canonical model of intellectual capital, composed of human capital, structural capital, and relational capital, is conceived at the level of a generic organization (Andriessen, 2004; Ricceri, 2008). If we consider only one individual, then the model collapses and yields human capital. Therefore, the canonical model cannot be applied at the individual employee's microscale level. The question is if we may conceive a different pattern of intellectual capital to be meaningful at the individual microscale. The answer is given by the theory of knowledge fields created by Bratianu (2011, 2013, 2015) and further developed by Bratianu and Bejinaru (2019a, 2020).

The theory of knowledge fields is based on metaphorical thinking (Lakoff & Johnson, 1999) and the analogy with the concept of energy (Bratianu & Andriessen, 2008). The theory is constructed starting with three axioms derived metaphorically from the analogy with the concept of energy (Bratianu & Bejinaru, 2019a):

- Knowledge is a field.
- There are three basic knowledge fields: rational, emotional, and spiritual.
- Each field of knowledge can be transformed into any other field of knowledge.

Rational knowledge is the result of rational learning and is expressed by explicit knowledge. Thus, rational knowledge can be expressed using a natural or symbolic language. It is the result of rational learning and logical coherence (Baron, 2000). It is the knowledge used by system 2 of thinking, "the conscious, reasoning self that has beliefs, makes choices, and decides what to think about and what to do" (Kahneman, 2011, p. 21). The boundary of rational knowledge is given by the use of our consciousness and language. Education, science, and technology are all based on rational knowledge field. Even the knowledge management and intellectual capital domains developed with this implicit assumption in mind. Books and papers on knowledge management and intellectual capital discuss knowledge in terms of rational knowledge, like being the only way of knowing. This general implicit assumption constitutes a difficult barrier to overcome when considering emotional and spiritual knowledge.

Emotional knowledge is the result of experiential learning (Kolb, 2015) and the emotional states of human beings (Damasio, 1999, 2012; LeDoux, 1999; Hill, 2008). Experiential learning is what we learn when we do things by ourselves using our body and system 1 of thinking (Kahneman, 2011). As Nonaka and Takeuchi

(1995) remark, "In fact, the most powerful learning comes from direct experience. A child learns to eat, walk, and talk through trial and error; she or he learns with the *body*, not only with the mind" (p. 10). They call this learning result *tacit knowledge*, based on the idea of *the tacit dimension* of knowledge introduced by Polanyi (1983). Tacit knowledge incorporates emotional knowledge but is not identical to it. Emotional knowledge is wordless and can be expressed using body language (Ekman, 2003). If rational knowledge expressed in words and sentences has a linear property, emotional knowledge is nonlinear. The border between rational and emotional knowledge is given by the use of natural language (Pinker, 2008) and the conscious zone of the brain (Damasio, 2012). Emotional knowledge is subjective, and its intensity depends on the type of personality and context influence. Emotional knowledge constitutes the raw material to be processed by emotional intelligence (Goleman, 1995). Due to the complexity of the human brain, there is a certain overlapping between rational and emotional knowledge in constructing emotional thought (Frith, 2007; Gladwell, 2005; LeDoux, 1999).

Spiritual knowledge reflects our values and life principles. It is highly subjective, and it is focused on the purpose of our existence, life, and work (Zohar & Marshall, 2000, 2004). It is beyond the material existence and the emotional life. "We have to learn to see aspects of the world around us: stones, people, trees, sky. Equally, we have to learn to see meaning and value in the world around us, in our environment, in events, in human actions and lives" (Maxwell, 2007, p. 274). Spiritual knowledge is the main ingredient of wisdom and plays a critical role in developing a wise organization (Nonaka & Takeuchi, 2019). Spiritual knowledge implies a personal vision of self-development to attain a higher level of it (Kaiser & Martinez, 2023). Spiritual knowledge is bounded by an individual's culture and religion. When somebody changes his culture by deciding to live in another country or changing his religion, the boundary of spiritual knowledge changes. When somebody is working in a multinational company, the new working spirituality is influencing the domain of the initial spiritual knowledge. For people working in multicultural business environments, spiritual knowledge is processed by cultural intelligence (Bratinu & Paiuc, 2022; Soon & Van Dyne, 2015). Spiritual knowledge may have some overlapping with rational and emotional knowledge because its boundary is rather fuzzy. These characteristics influence the potential of intellectual capital and become critical for the kinetic intellectual as the result of working spirituality (Zohar & Marshall, 2004.

According to the third axiom, each form of knowledge can be transformed into another form of knowledge, generating continuous dynamics (Bratianu & Bejinaru, 2020). Unlike the SECI (Socialization, Externalization, Combination, Internalization) model proposed by Nonaka and Takeuchi (1995, 2019) for knowledge creation dynamics at the organization's level, the RESK (Rational, Emotional, Spiritual Knowledge) model proposed by Bratianu (2011, 2015) and refined further by Bratianu and Bejinaru (2019a, 2020) is conceived at an individual level. Knowledge dynamics based on thermodynamics transformation of one form of knowledge into another one impacts the process of decision-making (Bratianu et al., 2021; Hill, 2008; Kahneman, 2011). Although the classical decision-making theory is based on rational knowledge and the symbolic language of mathematics, in real

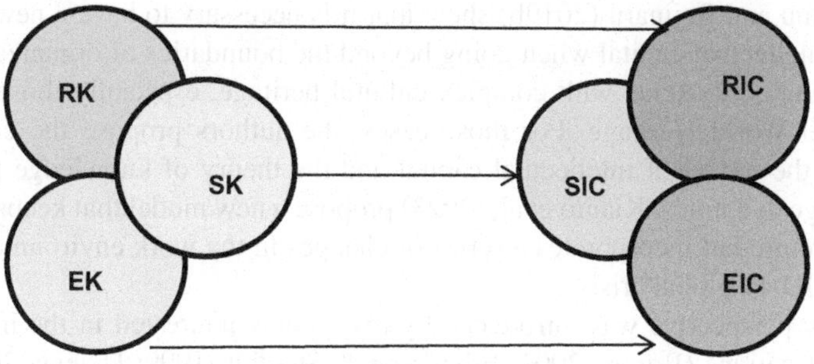

Fig. 2 The generation of the intellectual capital pattern at the individual level

life, this process is influenced as well by emotional and spiritual knowledge. Moreover, the emotional impact is faster than the rational one (Kahneman, 2011).

Individual intellectual capital represents the integration of all intangible resources given at a certain time. Therefore, its pattern should reflect the knowledge field structure. Rational knowledge (RK) generates rational intellectual capital (RIC), emotional knowledge (EK) generates emotional intellectual capital (EIC), and spiritual knowledge (SK) generates spiritual intellectual capital (SIC). Figure 2 illustrates the transformation of knowledge fields into intellectual capital fields.

6 The Multiple Scales Framework of Intellectual Capital

The canonical model of intellectual capital was conceived for a generic organization. When we change the perspective of analyzing intellectual capital, we learn that the canonical model no longer reflects the new environment. That explains the efforts of many researchers to change the model by reshaping it. Chen (2008) introduced the idea of creating a *Green intellectual capital* model composed of *green human capital*, *green structural capital*, and *green relational capital*. The new model crosses the boundary of the company and considers the participation of the external business environment in the extended relational capital component. Also, each component is extended by new features that reveal mostly cultural and ethical values. In other words, Chen (2008) is aware of the role of spiritual knowledge in the dynamics of intellectual capital and incorporates it not directly but through the influence of organizational culture and ethics. Schiuma and Lerro (2015) explored the extension of the canonical model of intellectual capital to regional development. They kept the structure of human, structural, and relational capital but considered an extension from *knowledge* resources to *knowledge asset* resources. "We define knowledge asset as any resource made of or incorporating knowledge that provides an ability to carry out a process or a function aimed at creating and/or delivering value. It can be a tangible or an intangible resource" (Schiuma & Lerro, 2015, p. 6). The authors induce this way the possibility for intellectual capital to contain tangible resources. That leaves open the door for defining indicators for measuring tangible objects, but it creates a semantic conflict with the concept of intellectual capital.

Bratianu and Bejinaru (2019b) show that it is necessary to have a new perspective on intellectual capital when going beyond the boundaries of organizations and considering ecosystems with complex cultural heritage, especially those declared UNESCO World Heritage. For those cases, the authors propose the connection between the model of intellectual capital and the theory of knowledge fields and knowledge dynamics. Kianto et al. (2023) propose a new model that keeps the basic triad structure but incorporates a series of changes in the work environment due to the COVID-19 global crisis.

A new perspective was introduced by researchers interested in the intellectual capital of nations (Bontis, 2004; Edvinsson & Stenfelt, 1999; Užiene, 2014; Yeh-Yun Liu & Edvinsson, 2008). The complexity of a nation comes from its scale and all kinds of ecosystems and organizations. The canonical model no longer fits such complexity. Therefore, researchers enlarged their evaluation framework, and after some trials, they designed a structure composed of *human capital*, *market capital*, *process capital*, and *renewal capital*. The national model of intellectual capital is measured using economic metrics like gross domestic product (GDP), which are linear metrics and use tangible proxies for evaluating intangible entities.

Figure 2 illustrates how the *individual intellectual capital* (IIC) is generated from the human knowledge fields. This is the *microscale* intellectual capital model, composed of rational intellectual capital, emotional intellectual capital, and spiritual intellectual capital. When a social context is created by several individuals, they interact through their knowledge fields and construct the *social intellectual capital* (SIC) of that context. Figure 3 illustrates how social intellectual capital is generated. It is generated at a higher scale because it involves relationships between people. Those relations are based on rational knowledge, emotional knowledge, and spiritual knowledge. Rational knowledge is exchanged through language (Pinker, 2008), while emotional knowledge manifests through body language (Gladwell, 2005). Spiritual knowledge is in the background and helps in constructing trust between people (Giacalone & Jurkiewicz, 2010).

Therefore, the model of social intellectual capital incorporates both knowledge and relationships and works at a larger scale that might be considered *mesoscale*. The model of social intellectual capital is composed of *rational social capital* (RSC), *emotional social capital* (ESC), and *spiritual social capital* (SSC), as shown in Fig. 3. From a practical viewpoint, this model can be applied to teams, which can be found in any organization, or in temporal groups of people, in different social contexts.

Organizations are composed of teams integrated into different managerial structures, with many complex relationships between them. Therefore, to analyze the intellectual capital at the organizational level, we need to move up to a *macroscale*. At this scale, intellectual capital is represented by the canonical model composed of human capital, structural capital, and relational capital. At the macroscale, we can analyze the interactions between a generic organization and its stakeholders or between different organizations within some networks. As a consequence, each component of the organizational intellectual capital incorporates rational social capital, emotional social capital, and spiritual social capital, which are composed of

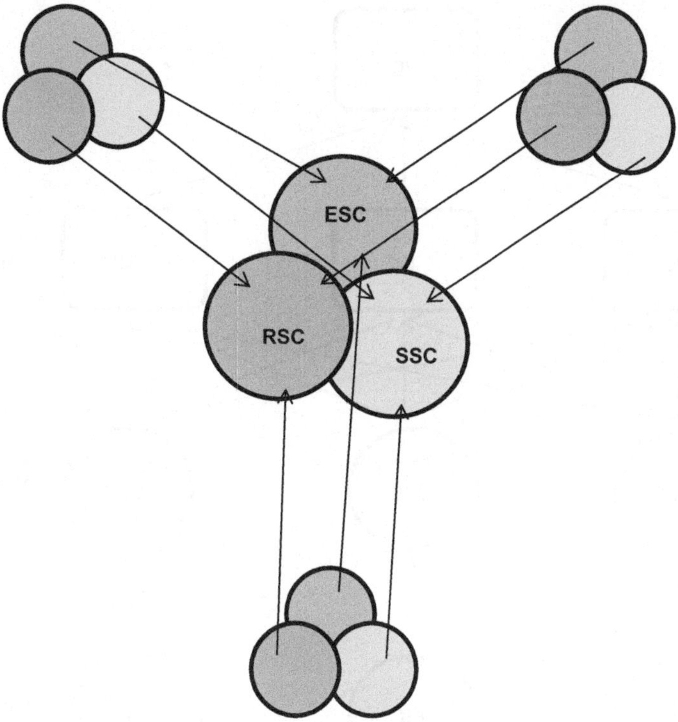

Fig. 3 Generation of the social intellectual capital (SIC)

the basic structures of rational knowledge, emotional knowledge, and spiritual knowledge. Figure 4 illustrates these structures.

Figure 4 represents a possible complexity framework of intellectual capital. It contains multiple scales representing intellectual capital and a recurrent pattern that is composed of rational, emotional, and spiritual knowledge. Also, we should add the fact that each entity is nonlinear and dynamic. In any real process, there are iterative influences between components operating at different scales because all of them exist in the same working time and space. At the team level, emotional and spiritual capital contribute to achieving synergy and trust which are driving forces for the team's performance.

The white color in Fig. 4 should be interpreted as a composed color resulting from the spectrum of all the other colors coming from the microscale and mesoscale elements. Figure 4 contains in the upper part the canonical model that incorporates all fields of knowledge, which generate the corresponding fields of intellectual capital (i.e., rational, emotional, and spiritual). At the organizational level, rational knowledge is represented by all regulations, working procedures, and software programs, including artificial intelligence applications, which support the decision-making processes. Emotional knowledge is integrated into the organizational culture and behavior codes which are specific for each organization. Emotional knowledge

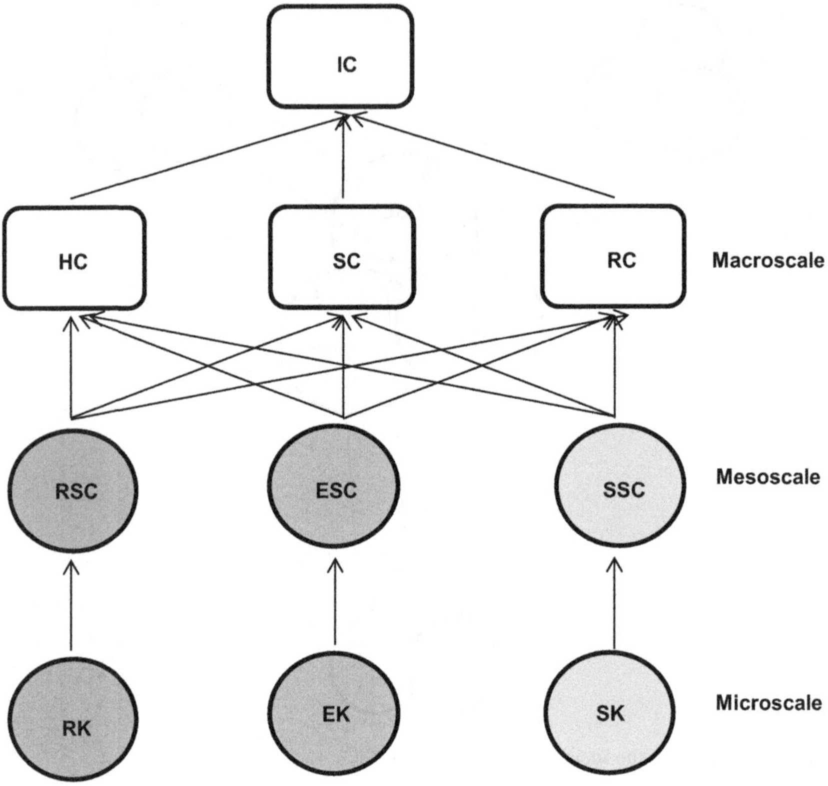

Fig. 4 The building blocks of the intellectual capital at the organizational level

is incorporated into the psychological climate and the motivational system. Spiritual knowledge is incorporated into the shared vision and mission of the company and contributes directly to creating the working spirituality.

The dynamics can be extended to the interactions between an organization and its stakeholders and between different organizations forming temporary or stable networks. When the analysis is going up to more complex structures, like nations, then we should introduce *megascales* and possible new components to reflect the whole system of systems.

7 Conclusions

The canonical model of intellectual capital designed by the pioneers of this research domain (Edvinsson & Malone, 1997; Stewart, 1997; Sveiby, 1997) is based on the triad of rational capital, structural capital, and relational capital. The model was designed for a generic organization, and its durability in time demonstrates the imaginative power of those pioneers. However, the model incorporated a semantic challenge from the beginning due to the synthesis between the economic concept of *capital* and the human attribute of being *intellectual*. The economic concept reflects a tangible and linear part of the business domain, while the human attribute reflects an intangible and nonlinear entity. The new concept of *intellectual capital* is supposed to reflect the hidden intangible resources (Andriessen, 2004; Bontis, 1999; Roos et al., 2005), which are nonlinear, but when it comes to measuring it, people use economic indicators and metrics that are tangible and linear (Dumay, 2009; Habersham et al., 2013). Thus, the results cannot stand for the true value of intellectual capital. Also, the new changes in the business environment generated by globalization, different crises, and new technological advances require a new perspective for understanding the nature and structure of intellectual capital.

The purpose of the present chapter was to reveal the main limitations of the intellectual capital canonical model and to suggest possible ways of overcoming them. Therefore, our analysis has shown how intellectual capital should be understood as a nonlinear entity and a dynamic one. That requires a real challenge in designing new metrics for the evaluation of intellectual capital. Adopting a complexity perspective, we were looking for a basic pattern that is recurrent in different configurations considered at the microscale, mesoscale, and macroscale levels. The recurrent pattern is emerging from the field structure of knowledge, and it contains rational intellectual capital, emotional intellectual capital, and spiritual intellectual capital. The canonical model constructed for organizations should be understood in a new light of the complexity of being composed of multiple scale elements, going down to the basic building blocks of rational knowledge, emotional knowledge, and spiritual knowledge.

The proposed complexity framework impacts futurizing intellectual capital practice by showing the importance of emotional and spiritual components in creating a shared system of values, behavioral codes, and motivational systems capable of improving the overall performance of the company, its agility, and resilience to find better solutions for new potential crises.

References

Albrecht, K. (2003). *The power of minds at work: Organizational intelligence in action*. American Management Association.

Alvesson, M., & Spicer, A. (2016). *The stupidity paradox: The power and pitfalls of functional stupidity at work*. Profile Books.

Andriessen, D. (2004). *Making sense of intellectual capital: Design a method for valuation of intangibles*. Elsevier.

Andriessen, D. (2006). On the metaphorical nature of intellectual capital: A textual analysis. *Journal of Intellectual Capital, 7*(1), 93–100.

Andriessen, D. (2008). Stuff or love? How metaphors direct our efforts to manage knowledge in organizations. *Knowledge Management Research & Practice, 6*(1), 5–12.

Barney, J. B. (1991). Firm resources and sustained competitive advantage. *Journal of Management, 17*, 99–120.

Baron, J. (2000). *Thinking and deciding* (3rd ed.). Cambridge University Press.

Bird, R. J. (2003). *Chaos and life: Complexity and order in evolution and thought*. Columbia University Press.

Bolisani, E., & Oltramari, A. (2012). Knowledge as a measurable object in business contexts: A stock-and-flow approach. *Knowledge Management Research & Practice, 10*(3), 275–286.

Bontis, N. (1999). Managing organizational knowledge by diagnosing intellectual capital: Framing and advancing the state of the field. *International Journal of Technology Management, 18*(5–8), 433–462.

Bontis, N. (2004). National intellectual capital index: A United Nations initiatives for the Arab region. *Journal of Intellectual Capital, 5*(1), 13–39.

Bratianu, C. (2009). The frontier of linearity in the intellectual capital metaphor. *Electronic Journal of Knowledge Management, 7*(4), 415–424.

Bratianu, C. (2011). Changing paradigm for knowledge metaphors from dynamics to thermodynamics. *System Research and Behavioral Science, 28*(2), 160–169.

Bratianu, C. (2013). Nonlinear integrators of organizational intellectual capital. In M. Fathi (Ed.), *Integration of practice-oriented knowledge technology: Trends and perspectives* (pp. 3–17). Springer.

Bratianu, C. (2015). *Organizational knowledge dynamics: Managing knowledge creation, acquisition, sharing, and transformation*. IGI Global.

Bratianu, C. (2018). Intellectual capital research and practice: 7 myths and one golden rule. *Management & Marketing. Challenges for the Knowledge Society, 13*(2), 859–879.

Bratianu, C. (2019). Exploring knowledge entropy in organizations. *Management Dynamics in the Knowledge Economy, 7*(3), 353–366.

Bratianu, C. (2023). Knowledge dynamics: Exploring its meanings and interpretations. *Management Dynamics in the Knowledge Economy, 11*(2), 100–111.

Bratianu, C., & Andriessen, D. (2008). Knowledge as energy: A metaphorical analysis. In D. Harorimana & D. Watkins (Eds.), *Proceedings of the 9th European conference on knowledge management* (pp. 75–82). Academic Conferences Publishing.

Bratianu, C., & Bejinaru, R. (2019a). The theory of knowledge fields: A thermodynamics approach. *Systems, 7*(2), 1–12.

Bratianu, C., & Bejinaru, F. (2019b). Intellectual capital of the cultural heritage ecosystems: A knowledge dynamics approach. In M. Handzic & D. Carlucci (Eds.), *Knowledge management, arts, and, and humanities: Interdisciplinary approaches and the benefits of collaboration* (pp. 215–240). Springer Nature.

Bratianu, C., & Bejinaru, R. (2020). Knowledge dynamics: A thermodynamics approach. *Kybernetes, 49*(1), 6–21.

Bratianu, C., Vatamanescu, E. M., Anagnoste, S., & Dominici, G. (2021). Untangling knowledge fields and knowledge dynamics within the decision-making process. *Management Decision, 59*(2), 306–323.

Bratinu, C., & Paiuc, D. (2022). A bibliometric analysis of cultural intelligence and multicultural leadership. *Review of International Comparative Management, 23*(2), 319–337.

Cabrilo, S., & Kianto, A. (2023). Futurizing the intellectual capital theory. In F. Matos & Rosa (Eds.), *Proceedings of the 24th European conference on knowledge management* (pp. 178–183). ISCTE – Instituto Universitario de Lisboa, Portugal., 7–8 September 2023.

Chalidze, V. (2000). *Entropy demystified: Potential order, life and money*. Universal Publishers.

Chen, Y. (2008). The positive effect of green intellectual capital on competitive advantage of firms. *Journal of Business Ethics, 77*, 271–286.

Damasio, A. (1999). *The feeling of what happens: Body and emotions in the making of consciousness*. A Harvest Book Harcourt.

Damasio, A. (2012). *Self comes to mind: Constructing the conscious brain*. Vintage Books.

Dumay, J. (2009). Intellectual capital measurement: A critical approach. *Journal of Intellectual Capital, 10*(2), 190–210.

Dumay, J. (2016). A critical reflection on the future of intellectual capital: From reporting to disclosure. *Journal of Intellectual Capital, 17*(1), 168–184.

Edvinsson, L. (2002). *Corporate longitude: What you need to navigate the knowledge economy*. Prentice Hall.

Edvinsson, L., & Malone, M. (1997). *Intellectual capital: Realizing your company's true value by finding its hidden brainpower*. Harper Collins.

Edvinsson, L., & Stenfelt, C. (1999). Intellectual capital of nations for future wealth creation. *Journal of Human Resource Costing and Accounting, 4*(1), 21–33.

Ekman, P. E. (2003). *Emotions revealed: Recognizing faces and feelings to improve communication and emotional life*. Times Books.

Federal Law Gazette of the Republic of Austria, issued on 15 February 2006, Part II, 63rd Regulation of the Federal Ministry of Education, Science and Culture on Intellectual Reports (Intellectual Capital Report Act – ICRA).

Friedenberg, J., & Silverman, G. (2016). *Cognitive science: An introduction to the study of mind* (3rd ed.). SAGE.

Frith, C. (2007). *Making up the mind: How the brain creates our mental world*. Blackwell Publishing.

Gharajcdaghi, J. (2006). *Systems thinking: Managing chaos and complexity. A platform for designing business architecture* (2nd ed.). Butterworth-Heinemann.

Giacalone, R. A., & Jurkiewicz, C. L. (Eds.). (2010). *Handbook of workplace spirituality and organizational performance* (2nd ed.). M.E. Sharpe.

Gladwell, M. (2005). *Blink: The power of thinking without thinking*. Back Bay Books.

Gleick, J. (2008). *Chaos: Making a new science*. Penguin Books.

Goleman, D. (1995). *Emotional intelligence*. Bantam.

Habersham, M., Piber, M., & Skoog, M. (2013). Knowledge balance sheets in Austrian universities: The implementation, use, and re-shaping of measurement and management practices. *Critical Perspectives on Accounting, 24*, 319–337.

Habersham, M., Piber, M., & Skoog, M. (2018). Ten years of using knowledge balance sheets in Austrian public Universities: A retrospective and prospective view. *Journal of Intellectual Capital, 19*(1), 34–52.

Hill, D. (2008). *Emotionomics: Leveraging emotions for business success* (Revised ed.). Kogan Page.

Hornby, A. S. (2004). *Oxford advanced learner's dictionary of current English* (6th ed.). Oxford University Press.

Kahneman, D. (2011). *Thinking, fast and slow*. Strauss, Giroux and Farrar.

Kaiser, A., & Martinez, H. A. (2023). Future path of knowledge management: How do spirituality, calling, and knowledge management fit together? In C. Bratianu, M. Handzic, & E. Bolisani (Eds.), *The future of knowledge management: Reflections from the 10th anniversary of the International Association of Knowledge Management (IAKM). Knowledge Management and Organizational Learning* (Vol. 12, pp. 113–129). Springer.

Kianto, A. (2007). What do we really mean by dynamic dimensions of intellectual capital? *International Journal of Learning and Intellectual Capital, 4*(4), 342–356.

Kianto, A., & Cabrilo, S. (2022). Challenging the intellectual capital theory: Suggestions for some ways forward. In: Cerchione, R. & Centobelli, P. (Eds.). *Proceedings of the 23rd European conference on knowledge management* (pp. 611–619). University of Naples Parthenope and University of Naples Federico II, Italy, 1–2 September 2022.

Kianto, A., Cabrilo, S., & Hussinki, H. (2023). Futurizing intellectual capital theory to uncover pertinent and explored horizons. In: Bratianu, C., Handzic, M., & Bolisani, E. (Eds.). *The future of knowledge management: Reflections from the 10th anniversary of the International Association of Knowledge Management (IAKM)* (pp. 67–90), Knowledge Management and Organizational Learning 12, Springer Nature.

Kianto, A., Inkinen, H., Ritala, P., & Vanhala, M. (2017). A temporal perspective to intellectual capital dynamics: How has IC changed in Finnish firms from 2013 to 2017? In: Tsui, E., & Cheung, B. (Eds.). *Proceedings of the 14th international conference on intellectual capital, knowledge management & organizational learning* (pp. 134–138), The Hong

Kong Polytechnic University, Hong Kong, 7–8 December 2017, Academic Conferences and Publishing International.
Kolb, D. A. (2015). *Experiential learning: Experience as the source of learning and development* (2nd ed.). Pearson Education.
Kuhn, S. T. (1970). *The structure of scientific revolution* (2nd ed.). The University of Chicago Press.
Lakoff, G., & Johnson, M. (1999). *Philosophy in the flesh: The embodied mind and its challenges to the Western thought*. Basic Books.
LeDoux, J. (1999). *The emotional brain: The mysterious underpinnings of emotional life*. Phoenix.
Maxwell, N. (2007). *From knowledge to wisdom: A revolution for science and the humanities* (2nd ed.). Pentire Press.
Nisbett, R. E. (2003). *The geography of thought: How Asian and Westerners think differently ... and why*. Free Press.
Nissen, M. E. (2006). *Harnessing knowledge dynamics: Principled organizational knowing & learning*. IRM Press.
Nonaka, I., & Takeuchi, H. (1995). *The knowledge creating company: How Japanese companies create the dynamics of innovation*. Oxford University Press.
Nonaka, I., & Takeuchi, H. (2019). *The wise company: How companies create continuous innovation*. Oxford University Press.
Ohmae, K. (1982). *The mind of the strategist: The art of Japanese business*. McGraw-Hill.
Pinker, S. (2008). *The stuff of thought: Language as a window into human nature*. Pinguin Books.
Polanyi, M. (1983). *The tacit dimension*. Peter Smith.
Pryor, R. G. L., & Bright, J. E. H. (2007). Applying chaos theory to careers: Attraction and attractors. *Journal of Vocational Behavior, 71*(3), 375–400.
Ricceri, F. (2008). *Intellectual capital and knowledge management: Strategic management of knowledge resources*. Routledge.
Roos, G., Pike, S., & Fernström, L. (2005). *Managing intellectual capital in practice*. Butterworth-Heinamann.
Schiuma, G., & Lerro, A. (2015). Identifying knowledge-based factors supporting regional development: Theoretical frameworks and system of indicators. In P. Ordóñez de Pablos & L. Edvinsson (Eds.), *Intellectual capital in organizations: Nonfinancial reports and accounts* (pp. 3–15). Routledge.
Senge, P. (1999). *The fifth discipline: The art and practice of the learning organization*. Random House.
Soon, A., & Van Dyne, L. (2015). *Handbook of cultural intelligence: Theory, measurement, and applications* (2nd ed.). Routledge.
Stacey, R. D. (2001). *Complex responsive processes in organizations: Learning and knowledge creation*. Routledge.
Stacey, R. D., Griffin, D., & Shaw, P. (2000). *Complexity and management: Fad or radical challenge to systems thinking?* Routledge.
Stewart, T. A. (1997). *Intellectual capital: The new wealth of organizations*. Doubleday/Currency.
Sveiby, K. E. (1997). *The new organizational wealth: Managing and measuring knowledge based assets*. Berrett Koehler.
Taleb, N. N. (2007). *The black swan: The impact of the highly improbable*. Penguin Books.
Užiene, L. (2014). National intellectual capital as an indicator of the wealth of nations: The case of the Baltic States. *Procedia-Social and Behavioral Sciences, 156*, 376–381.
Yeh-Yun Liu, C., & Edvinsson, L. (2008). National intellectual capital: Comparison of the Nordic countries. *Journal of Intellectual Capital, 9*(4), 525–545.
Zohar, D., & Marshall, I. (2000). *Spiritual intelligence: The ultimate intelligence*. Bloomsbury.
Zohar, D., & Marshall, I. (2004). *Spiritual capital: Wealth we can live by*. Berrett-Koehler.

Constantin Bratianu is Emeritus Professor of *Strategic Management* and *Knowledge Management*, UNESCO Department of Business Administration, Bucharest University of Economic Studies, Romania. He was invited as *Visiting Professor* to universities from the USA, Japan, Austria, Italy, Poland, Hungary, and Egypt. He was invited as Keynote Speaker at European Conference on Knowledge Management (ECKM), International Forum of Knowledge Assets Dynamics (IFKAD), Business Systems Laboratory Symposium (BSLab), International Conference on Business Excellence (ICBE), and some others. He is the former President of the International Association for Knowledge Management (IAKM). He is Editor in Chief of the international journal *Management Dynamics in the Knowledge Economy* and member of Editorial Board of *Journal of Knowledge Management, Knowledge and Process Management, Knowledge, Kybernetes, Business Process Management, Management & Marketing, and International Journal of Complexity in Leadership and Management*. He published over 45 books and over 250 papers and book chapters. He has been included by Stanford University in the top 2% of the most cited scientists in the world, starting from 2022. His main contributions to the domain of knowledge management are the *Theory of knowledge fields (TKF)*, the *Theory of knowledge dynamics (TKD)* based on thermodynamics, and *Emergent knowledge strategies*.

Unleashing Intellectual Capital: Toward Dynamic Theory Through the Humanization of Intellectual Capital

Noboru Konno

Abstract

Originally, intellectual capital (IC) was valued for its contribution to financial reporting, functioning as a searchlight for exploring the hidden aspects of balance sheets. However, in the current knowledge-driven innovation economy, IC should be further recognized and redefined as a vital force that fosters organizational innovation and growth. How does the integration of IC with knowledge assets (KA) influence the innovative capabilities of contemporary future-oriented organizations? Delving into this question, this chapter discusses the significance of IC as "potential capital" and as a dynamic driver of innovation. The relationship between IC and KA is examined as an analogy of a balance sheet. IC serves as a measure and mirror of KA for a firm: IC is generic and KA is specific. Here, the significant role of "ba" (a Japanese term for place; the context-sharing environment that fosters knowledge creation) and the human factors are highlighted. Additionally, leveraging and sharing "ba" across ecosystems is crucial for sustaining and driving growth. This can be discussed by considering the *humanization* of the IC concept.

1 Introduction

As the knowledge-based economy has progressed, which luminaries such as Peter Drucker (1993) foresaw, intellectual capital (IC) has been recognized as the basis of value, shifting the focus from tangible assets to intangible intellectual assets and knowledge. This endeavor of IC provided a framework for understanding the shift

N. Konno (✉)
Graduate School of Business Tama University, Tokyo, Japan
e-mail: noborukn@ecosyxlab.org

A. Kianto et al. (eds.), *Futurizing Intellectual Capital*, Knowledge Management and Organizational Learning 15, https://doi.org/10.1007/978-3-031-80197-6_3

in the economy. However, interest in this concept has waned compared to its wide adoption in the 1990s. The philosophy of IC has recently developed as variations of new intangible assets, such as human capital (HC) and environmental, social, and governance (ESG), and the understanding of IC has become part of today's common knowledge. The declining interest in IC as a term does not question its importance as an entity. However, revisiting the evolution of IC's role may be significant.

IC has evolved considerably since it was identified, first by Stewart (1991) and later by Edvinsson and Malone (1997). Their books marked the beginning of a global shift in our understanding of the importance of intangible assets. In the decade of these publications, especially from 1995 to 2005, interest in exploring and leveraging IC as a critical source of corporate value rapidly increased. Edvinsson and Malone highlighted the potential of IC beyond mere financial evaluation and paved the way for new perspectives.

IC was introduced during the era of the globalization of markets (Levitt, 1983). In the 1980s and 1990s, the world economy centered around developed countries and was on an upward trajectory. The value of IC was then verified as an increment that was reflected in metrics, such as market value. However, in the twenty-first century, the world economy saw an increase in the weight of developing countries; it began experiencing zigzag fluctuations, entering an era referred to as *global weirding* (Friedman, 2007). IC is not visibly linked to market value, except in some knowledge-intensive industries (such as pharmaceuticals). Therefore, it is necessary to consider how it relates to management.

IC is not merely an asset to be accounted for; instead, it is seen as a crucial element in the strategic development process of an organization. It encompasses various components, including HC; employees' skills, knowledge, and experience; relational capital (relationships with customers, suppliers, and partners); and structural capital (patents, trademarks, and organizational processes). In the contemporary business environment, intangible assets are increasingly recognized for their role in creating sustainable competitive advantages and driving innovation.

This essay revisits the significance and utilization of IC in today's knowledge and innovation economy and management from the knowledge management perspective.

The following three topics are discussed:

1. IC is the foundation of the corporate model in the knowledge-based economy. The IC and knowledge-based economy have been discussed concerning financial performance (Dženopoljac et al., 2016) and knowledge management (Jordão & Novas, 2017). We discuss the relationship between IC and KA as a combined model in this section.
2. The "ba" (place as shared context for knowledge creation) activates IC. The concept of ba was originally discussed by Nonaka and Konno (1998); it was more recently mentioned in the context of innovation (Nonaka & Takeuchi, 2019; Konno 2020). In this chapter, ba is highlighted as a crucial factor in creating knowledge and converting KA and IC.

3. The IC of ecosystems. As the ecosystem plays an increasingly important role in innovation, IC and value creation in ecosystems have become relevant topics (Iacuzzi & Pauluzzo, 2023). In this section, the IC of an ecosystem is discussed regarding knowledge creation.

2 IC as the Foundation of Corporate Models in the Knowledge-Based Economy

2.1 Intellectual Capital (IC) and Knowledge Assets (KA)

In the knowledge economy, knowledge is "the only meaningful resource" (Drucker, 1993) and the source of economic value, promoting sustainable growth through its creation and utilization (Romer, 1990). Unlike physical goods, knowledge does not diminish with use. It accumulates and becomes the foundation for long-term economic growth. Rather than viewing knowledge as static or materialistic elements, it should be understood as dynamic human actions. The knowledge creation management model places knowledge creation at the core of corporate value creation and realization, i.e., innovation. It integrates an organization that generates knowledge with strategies to achieve competitive advantage through knowledge creation (Konno & Nonaka, 1995).

Knowledge creation is a process through which organizations share, discover, and create value from new knowledge within firms, society, and the market. An epistemological base of the theory is Polanyi's concept of *tacit knowing* (1962). Furthermore, Hayek (1945) has explained that much of the knowledge in markets is tacit. Hayek's perspective on economic systems and Polanyi's epistemological viewpoint can be seen as complementary as knowledge creation spans both of their concepts of tacit knowledge. Therefore, the starting point of organizational knowledge creation is for members to gain tacit knowledge (tacit knowing) through shared experiences with their members and customers. Through this process, newly created knowledge is stored or formalized, becoming an asset for the organization. Thus, organizational knowledge creation can be modeled as the creation and utilization of knowledge assets (KA). Table 1 presents a framework to illustrate KA in organizations following the phases of knowledge creation with several examples.

KA and IC are closely related and often treated similarly; however, they can also be understood separately. KA is the specific element of knowledge an organization owns and can leverage for value creation (thus dynamic), and IC refers to the structural inventory of these assets (thus static). KA relates deeply to tacit or explicit knowledge corresponding to the knowledge-creation process; hence, they are often "sticky" (Prusak, 2006). IC is also generic and currency-like, providing a holistic view of how knowledge contributes to the value and success of an organization. Furthermore, IC as a concept transcends corporate boundaries and includes society and community IC. Thus, corporate IC and regional or urban IC can be considered as comparable common currencies.

Table 1 Knowledge assets (KA) based on the knowledge creation process[a]

Source of KA	Experiential KA	Cognitive KA	Coded KA	Facilitative KA
Market/customer	(Ex) Knowledge of customers and suppliers	(Ex) Brand reputation from customers	(Ex) Historical customer information and contracts	(Ex) Systems and tools to gain customer and partner knowledge
Organization	(Ex) Knowledge and competencies of professionals and employees	(Ex) Capacity for development and design and sense of quality	(Ex) Internal documents, manuals, and written manuals	(Ex) Educational training systems and tools for employees
Product/ technology	(Ex) Skilled knowledge about the product	(Ex) Product and service concept and product design	(Ex) IPs, copyrights, and licenses	(Ex) Social and legal systems for product knowledge
Corresponding knowledge creation process (not uniquely connected)	Socialization (tacit knowledge sharing and creation)	Externalization (converting tacit to explicit knowledge)	Combination (explicit knowledge formation)	Internalization (making explicit to tacit knowledge)

[a]Table columns indicate the qualitative patterns of knowledge assets corresponding to the knowledge creation process
Created by the author. Source: Konno (1998)

We hypothesize the relationship between the two by applying the *analogy* of the general accounting model between capital and assets:

$$[\mathrm{IC}]+[\mathrm{debt}]=[\mathrm{KA}](\text{intellectual capital}+\text{intellectual debt}=\text{knowledge assets}) \tag{1}$$

Table 2 presents the relationship between IC and KA, which are ambiguous and overlapping and often understood to have similar meanings. However, in this chapter, we intentionally separate the two and discuss their relationship using an analogy with general accounting principles. IC is the currency of knowledge, while KA is the utilized "net" intellectual resource. KA is an indigenous, sticky, and unique resource utilized by an organization.

In principle, assets are resources provided for business activities. Moreover, they are indispensable for profit generation and unique to companies. On the other hand, capital, such as money, is described generically. Companies try to develop human, relational, and structural capital (IC) to acquire, build, and utilize knowledge assets. The process of assets refers to knowledge creation and sharing activities of organizations (accumulation). Although IC is not represented in monetary terms, we value it in currency "C" for discussion. The management challenge is how effectively IC or "C" can be deployed for knowledge creation and the utilization of KA (C can also be indicated in monetary terms related to market capitalization, but the relationship is unstable because of market and environmental fluctuating factors).

Table 2 Intellectual capital, intellectual debt, and knowledge assets

Intellectual capital (IC)	Intellectual debt (ID)	Knowledge assets (KA)
IC encompasses intangible knowledge-related capital possessed by individuals and the entire organization, such as knowledge, skills, and experience. It can be classified into the following categories: 1. Human capital. 2. (Organizational) Structural capital 3. Relational capital. IC is measured by indicators based on the above classifications and represents the intellectual capital of the entire organization or ecosystem IC can be considered to be the currency of knowledge, represented by a common scale, but it does not significantly reflect the uniqueness of individual companies	ID represents knowledge-related liabilities or barriers that hinder an organization's ability to fully utilize its IC. In the equation, it is the negative counterpart to IC. Intellectual debt arises from factors such as: 1. Knowledge and skill gaps among organizational members. 2. Inefficient processes and systems that hinder the flow and utilization of knowledge. 3. Lack of innovation or an organizational culture that cannot adapt to changing market conditions. 4. Insufficient knowledge management leads to the loss of valuable knowledge assets.	KA are the net knowledge resources resulting from the combination of IC and ID. They represent the actual value-creating knowledge resources that an organization possesses and can utilize for competitive advantage. KA is acquired from different sources, ranging from tacit to formal levels and scientific to experiential knowledge. It is also organizationally shared as a product of the knowledge-creation process

Intellectual debts in Eq. (1) are counterparts of intellectual capital, and they represent the negative factors associated with an organization's intellectual activities and knowledge management. Specifically, intellectual debts include the following:

1. Obsolete knowledge and technology: Knowledge and technology that are outdated and no longer usable reduce an organization's competitiveness.
2. Inefficient business processes: Inefficient business processes waste time and money and reduce productivity.
3. Inadequate knowledge sharing and utilization: When knowledge is not properly shared and utilized within the organization, intellectual resources are wasted.
4. Low skill levels and lack of expertise: Employees' low skill levels and lack of expertise limit the organization's intellectual capacity.
5. Negative organizational culture: An organizational culture that discourages innovation will negatively impact intellectual activities.
6. Risk of intellectual property infringement: The risk of infringing on the intellectual property rights of others can lead to legal problems and loss of reputation.

Although the concept of intellectual debt is abstract, it has been argued in some areas, such as AI, that intellectual debt is growing rapidly, particularly because of machine learning.[1]

Managing and minimizing intellectual debts is critical for effectively leveraging an organization's intellectual capital and enhancing its competitiveness. This requires regularly updating knowledge (upskilling) and technology, improving business processes, promoting knowledge sharing, developing employee skills, and building an organizational culture that encourages innovation.

The knowledge creation process explains an organization's trial-and-error innovation activities. For example, ISO56002: Innovation Management System (IMS), which was published in 2019 by the International Standard Organization (ISO), positions the nonlinear trial-and-error process at the core of the management system (as innovation activities), identifying opportunities, creating concepts, validating concepts, developing solutions, and deploying solutions. This is synonymous with the knowledge-creation activity between tacit and explicit knowledge, also known as the Socialization, Externalization, Combination, and Internalization (SECI) model, which is linked to company performance, including growth and profit (Fig. 1). The degree of activity of knowledge transformation that comprises the SECI model increases the value-creation activities of an organization. Thus, the utilization of IC can be conceptualized as outlined in Fig. 1.

This "pipeline" involves activating HC, expanding relational capital, and designing structural capital as part of the knowledge creation process. This design and synthesis of tacit and explicit knowledge are driven by the vision and conceptual power of managers and organizations. The interaction between KA, which includes the organization's skills, experience, and knowledge, and IC creates synergies that promote innovation.

As Edvinsson et al. (2005) outlined, IC is the *capital in waiting*. In other words, regardless of how high potential IC is indicated using metrics, it will not produce effects unless utilized.

An approach linking IC and KA has been previously observed (Kianto et al., 2014). IC can be indexed and expressed according to its focus areas (human, relational, and structural capital); however, merely making it visible does not lead to its utilization. To utilize IC, an appropriate management system that is aware of the interrelationships between KA and KC must be in place. First, the transformation of

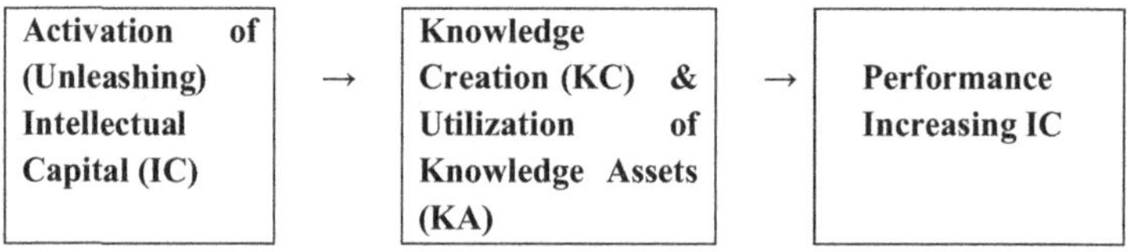

Fig. 1 A structural model of intellectual capital and knowledge assets

[1] Chapter 11 "Intellectual Debt With Great Power Comes Great Ignorance"; Part 2, The Cambridge Handbook of Responsible Artificial Intelligence, 2022, Cambridge University Press.

management principles is required to practice knowledge creation. Additionally, creating a ba (place-context) that activates IC by sharing tacit knowledge and its context, both inside and outside the organization, becomes crucial (Sect. 2). This approach leads to IC and KA in the ecosystem (Sect. 3).

2.2 The Era of Humanistic Management Principle: The Challenge of Japanese Management

The introduction of the IC concept coincided with the transition from a management model of industrial society characterized by labor-intensive management, which lasted until the late-twentieth century, to a knowledge-intensive management model (Konno & Nonaka, 1995). IC has existed in every company for some time. However, as business shifted away from the model based on tangibles, the importance of IC increased significantly.

Upon reflection, a question arises regarding what fundamentally underpins a company. IC originates naturally from humans and is attributed to human knowledge and capabilities. Hence, we ask whether a company is based on this human-based capital or whether it still primarily revolves around tangible goods and is founded on profit, productivity, and efficiency. This inquiry applies regardless of the industry and concerns the dimensions of the company's management system or principles (Fig. 2).

In Japan, the manufacturing sector still constitutes a significant portion of the economy compared with other countries, resulting in a deep-rooted manufacturing culture. Since the late twentieth century, amid the so-called lost 30 years, there has been a call for the revival of Japanese management through *monozukuri* (making things, in Japanese). However, during this period, Japan's position in the world by gross domestic product (GDP), the share of its manufacturing industry, and the number of manufacturing workers declined. Nonetheless, reports indicate that within Japan the manufacturing industry remains strong, as production values are maintained, and productivity is increasing despite the decrease in workforce numbers. Despite the growing narrative of a decline in manufacturing globally, Japan's production and manufacturing capabilities remain high, and certain sectors of

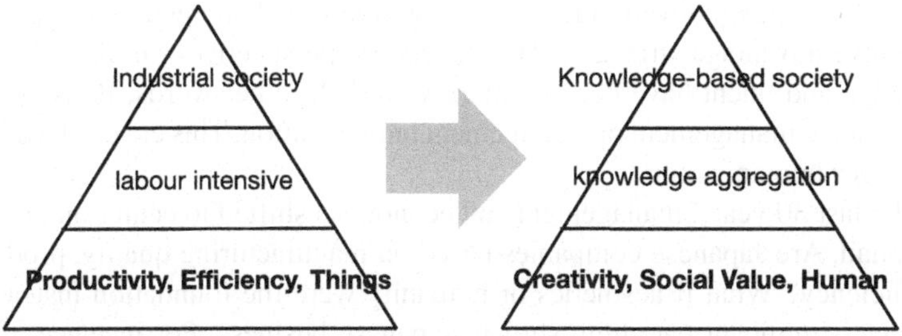

Fig. 2 What is the foundation of your company?

automobiles, parts, and materials industries are thriving. From the perspective of KA, it can be said that Japan still possesses considerable intellectual resources. However, the challenge is how these resources can be utilized in the knowledge economy.

The essential point is not the defensive debate regarding whether Japan's manufacturing industry excels in production or has high productivity (which has been declining in the long term compared with the global average). James Collins (2001), known for his book *Built to Last*, warns of the so-called competency trap, where focusing too much on one's strengths (e.g., technical competencies) can lead to losing sight of where best to apply efforts, even if capabilities exist. Being strong in manufacturing was optimal during the industrial age but may not fit the era of IC. The often-discussed question "Why can't Japan win despite superior technology?" centers excessively on technology and is inherently flawed.

Maintaining a traditional manufacturing model is unlikely to exploit these advantages. Konno (1998) previously proposed the concept of *knowledge manufacturing*, which involves rebuilding businesses around the knowledge behind physical production and creating valuable customer experience. Sticking to the traditional secondary industry will not escape obsolescence in the knowledge economy. Although there has been much discussion in Japan's manufacturing sector about solution business development based on goods and digital transformation (DX), success has not always been achieved. One reason is that a mindset based on "semantic value-added and solutions on goods (functional value)" alone does not yield the same profit volume as manufacturing businesses. If the mindset preserves the classical manufacturing management system, DX becomes a mere digitization of the old system. Therefore, a change in the mindset is necessary. As Paul Iske (2020), the Founder of the Institute of Brilliant Failures maintains, New Technology deployed in an old organization results in an expensive old organization ("NT + OO = EOO").

Figure 2 poses a question for the readers: What is the foundation of your enterprise? Is it goods, productivity, or efficiency, like a labor-intensive enterprise in an industrialized society based on tangible assets? Or is it humanity and creativity, based on IC, including HC? Incorporating IC is one way to change how a company exists.

Since the emergence of IC, there has been a significant shift in global management trends, particularly those marked by the 2008 Lehman Shock (bankruptcy of Lehman Brothers). Interest in dynamic knowledge creation and utilization has increased, focusing on knowledge creation theory, innovation management, design thinking, and open innovation rather than on traditional strategic management and competitive advantage strategies. Human-centric perspectives on the utilization of knowledge and talent have become more valued. In other words, IC is positioned under creative management or management humanization. This era can be described as an IC for humanization.

In the last 30 years, management and economics shifted to center on knowledge and human. Are Japanese companies based on manufacturing quality, productivity and efficiency? What if aesthetics or humanity were the foundation instead? This presents a significant paradigm shift in Japanese business. For instance, the term *ikumen* (involved fatherhood) has become a buzzword in Japan, indicating growing interest in men's participation in childcare. Indeed, the percentage of men taking parental leave has reportedly increased from a few percent to double digits over the last quarter-century, although the reality seems far from satisfactory.[2] While some major corporations actively promote this, many men still face pressure from their workplaces if they attempt to take leave for childcare purposes. However, the fundamental issue might not only be the consciousness and policies of individual companies but also the deeply ingrained male-centric values in Japanese society. These values, stemming from post-World War II efforts to recover through male-dominated labor and the male labor force-preferred industrialization values of the early twentieth century, are now being questioned. The COVID-19 pandemic has accelerated the shift in these values.

Industrial society was centered on male labor, with women managing household commodities. However, physical labor is not a prerequisite in a society that values knowledge; therefore, the gender gap is shrinking. In Japan, women tend to accomplish better academic achievements at universities.[3] The challenge lies in bridging the gap between this significant reality and the current situation in Japan. Broadly speaking, male participation in childcare not only reduces the burden on women but also increases productivity and opens possibilities beyond traditional male values, thereby potentially unlocking Japan's creative cultural potential for innovation. Therefore, new management principles must be tested.

Figure 3 shows an example of the new principles focusing on such knowledge creation and management.

1. Relationality based on empathy and intersubjectivity: Ba (the basic unit of intercorporeality)
2. Strategy and practice are the same (practical knowledge methodology)
3. The cycle of tacit and explicit knowledge is the core of innovation (knowledge creation theory)
4. Narrate one's own story, not others' (live the narrative)
5. Practical judgment based on purpose and means (practical syllogism)
6. Leadership of purpose, empathy, and ba (circle of prudence)
7. Dynamic organization (non-hierarchical organizational design)
8. Business model innovation in ecosystems (designing relationships)
9. Societal innovation (integrating market knowledge and technology)

Fig. 3 Principles of knowledge creation management. Created by the author. Source: Nonaka and Konno (2012)

[2] According to the Ministry of Health, Labor, and Welfare, the rate of male employees in companies taking maternity leave was 0.12% in FY1996. Since then, it has continued to rise, exceeding 5% in FY17 and increasing from 7.48% to 17.13% between FY 2019 and FY 2022. However, it is far from the target of 50% by 2025.

[3] In many countries around the world, girls tend to perform better academically than boys, according to the OECD's PISA survey and other studies. Japan shows a similar trend. That tendency is observed also in the universities: Yasuda, H. (2015) "Gender differences in fourth-year university student performance," Journal of the Tokyo University of Economics, No. 285. However, there have been barriers to higher education for women in Japan, although the percentage of women entering university has increased rapidly in recent years.

3 Ba for Synthesizing IC

3.1 Activating the Ba for Knowledge Creation

Next, we consider the efficacy of ba, a concept that originates from Japanese culture and philosophy. In knowledge creation, the context and ba shared among participants become critical (Nonaka & Konno, 1998), and enhancing the quality of ba facilitates knowledge flow among individuals. Ba is energized and supported by IC, aiding in transforming KA into actual value during knowledge creation. Organizations can leverage the power of ba to drive KA for knowledge creation.

Unlike information, knowledge depends on the context of its generation and transmission. Ba is defined as a "shared dynamic context or meaning" among participants in knowledge-creation activities shaped by time, space, and relationships. Ba, or place, is not just a functional or commercial space, such as an office, lab, museum, or theme park. Humans give various meanings to their surroundings and environments through their experiences; the totality of these meanings and relationships constitutes ba.

The concept of ba in knowledge creation was inspired by Japanese philosopher Nishida Kitaro (Nonaka & Konno, 1998). Nishida addressed establishing a Japanese (Oriental) ego based on his Zen experiences. This is summarized in the logic of the place of absolute nothingness. Plato had the concept of *topos* (which means place and topic in Greek) *of an idea*, but Nishida's place starts from a *place of nothingness,* such as Zen. We find the self through an awareness of the place of nothingness we reflect upon. Nishida posited that existence is not found as a separate thing as subject versus object but in a place of nothingness; moreover, we become aware of ourselves in this place through pure experience. This does not suggest a dualism that separates the I (subject) from you (object) but rather a world in which there is no separation between the subject and the object. In other words, we become aware of ourselves in a place (Nishida, 1921).

In knowledge creation, tacit knowledge is acquired from a place in a shared context, and new knowledge is created. An organization with ba encompasses multi-levels of dialogue, exchange, idea embodiment, hardware, software, and open hub functions.[4]

For managers, ba is similar to community IC and relational and structural ICs that create and share an organization's KA. Top management sees their organization as a living space or place, not just a tree of functions, which is fundamental to management. For example, management may see ba as a metaphor for the organization in the following ways:

- Open Relationships: A ba that promotes diversity (connects diverse knowledge) and nurtures relationships that connect people.

[4] There are four types of ba aligned with knowledge creation (Nonaka & Konno, 2018): originating Ba, socialization; dialoguing Ba, externalization; systemizing Ba, combination; and exercising Ba, internalization.

- Context for Value Sharing: A ba that evolves communication with the outside, where individuals connected to the company's vision and society create value, addressing a diversifying society.
- Business Platform: Top management recognizes the organization as a business platform in which they embody their business and management techniques.
- Information Space: Viewing the organization as an information space and creating an office environment that maximizes the power of information systems and knowledge workers to generate knowledge.
- Organizational or Management Systems: Viewing ba as a system that operates a company.
- By the author's interviews with the Future Center Alliance Japan (FCAJ).

The general incorporated association Future Center Alliance Japan (FCAJ, Tokyo, Japan), which promotes open innovation ecosystems, has been researching ba (place). Figure 4 shows an excerpt of the survey results from respondents working in Japanese companies. The survey asked respondents to evaluate their organizations and determine to what extent ba is recognized in each organization. In the process of knowledge creation, ba refers to the context in which the tacit knowledge of individuals within an organization is shared and created. This includes physical spaces as well as the relationships between the parties involved, supportive elements such as common software (including IT) and dialogue methodologies, and communication in virtual spaces. However, the fundamental basis of ba is co-experience based on physical and emotional empathy.

The survey's objective is to understand the relationship between innovation and ba.[5] Companies with high scores on 10 items related to software, hardware, systems, and culture concerning ba were discriminated against by other companies (Fig. 4a). Figure 4b compares the ease of conducting innovation and organizational culture between those with ba and those without.

The following characteristics were observed in companies where ba is recognized compared to those where ba is not recognized:

1. More opportunities for new projects.
2. Lower psychological barriers (to overcome silos).
3. More positive attitudes for the future in the organizations.

Therefore, ba is a fundamental condition (IC) for knowledge creation. In this ba, knowledge assets from different departments are shared, and new knowledge assets are created.

Companies with ba are characterized as being open, proactive, and cultivating an organizational culture suitable for innovation. The ba (shared dynamic context) generates intercorporeality and commitment through KA.

---

[5] Internet survey (Japan): (1) employees of private companies with at least 300 employees; (2) regular employees; (3) employees who have been with the company for 5 years or more. Number of samples 413 s in total. Period of the survey: Monday, December 3, 2012, (1 day).

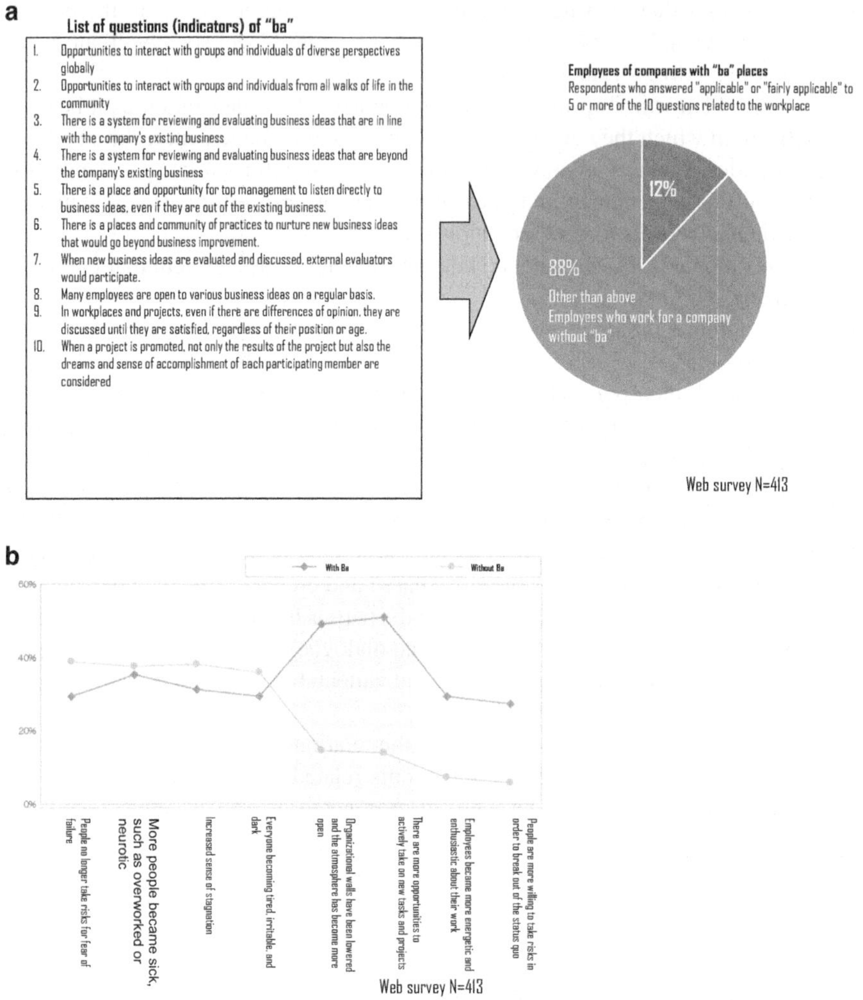

Fig. 4 Differences in awareness between companies with and without a ba (**a**, **b**). (**a**) Firms with/without ba. (**b**) Ba sets the situation for knowledge creation and innovation. The Future Center Research Group Survey, November–December 2012

Ba suggests a non-separated subject–object relationship, a sharing of context and meaning, which can be embodied in office spaces, specific locations, systems, programs, organizational norms, and cultures. The richness of these places increases psychological safety, making them places for knowledge creation (places are not just enablers but also capital for knowledge creation) and facilitating innovation.

3.2 Ba as the Intersection of KA and IC

We thus need to develop a framework that provides a solid foundation for innovation management. In this framework, reorganizing IC as a dynamic and essential resource for strengthening competitiveness and ensuring long-term success is vital. Effective management and personnel capable of utilizing KA are crucial for organizations to adapt to changing business environments and drive innovation and value creation. Furthermore, effective management and personnel capable of utilizing IC and knowledge activities are essential.

Here, the purpose becomes the driving force behind the IC and KA. The IC and KA complement each other only when a clear purpose is defined. Value realization comes from purpose-driven activities that provide direction and motivation for knowledge creation and innovation; this is particularly important in social and open innovation.

For example, Patagonia is an organization that focuses significantly on its purpose and place as an organizational entity to create advantages. Its strong environmental mission (purpose) forms an organizational place comprising HC, such as high reputation, employee loyalty, good customer relationships, and dedicated employees, as well as social capital, such as internal and external human relationships.

In 2019, FCAJ introduced the Evaluation Model for Innovation Centers (EMIC) framework as the world's first evaluation model for innovation places, benchmarking innovation centers both domestically and internationally. Various survey research, as well as innovation, ecosystems benchmarking, diagnostic services for companies, and concept book creation, have been developed based on this model (EMIC Report, 2019).

Innovation places are not merely workshop facilities; they are also the capital for practicing several innovation-related programs. The main reason for innovation failures is not a lack of ideas but a lack of infrastructure, resources, motivated personnel, supporting culture, and tangible and intangible incentives to support innovation activities. It is crucial to connect ideas within and outside the organization and coevolve through a series of programs and organizational functions.

The ISO 56002 (2019)[6] emphasizes the importance of innovation spaces/environments. Specifically, it describes creative environments, research and development (R&D) labs, maker spaces, simulation labs, and living labs as part of the infrastructure supporting innovation under "7. Support" (Clause 7.1.6.2). Thus, it is desirable to hypothesize how these relate to and interact with other innovation management factors and extract indicators for the expected objectives.

[6] Many of the causes of innovation failures are "contextual" requirements, such as the strategies that support them and the organizational capacity to realize them, rather than the innovation initiatives and activities themselves. ISO 56002 brings together the findings of these experiences to innovate as a system.

The innovation and knowledge-creation processes do not occur in traditional Taylorist offices as the right place and opportunities for innovation are essential. Moreover, they should not be limited to the boundaries of a single company.

The conditions for the success of innovation centers involve space design, which plays a significant role; however, merely enhancing hardware is insufficient. To activate innovation, it is important to ascertain whether the space functions as soft, hard, or systemic capital.

The EMIC framework is illustrated in Fig. 5. The left-hand side of Fig. 5a shows access to social resources, the right side shows access to the organization's internal resources, and the center is the specific innovation place element. Usually, these places (innovation centers, etc.,) are asked to describe their performance; however, this is a mistake. Such places (e.g., innovation hubs and centers) should be evaluated

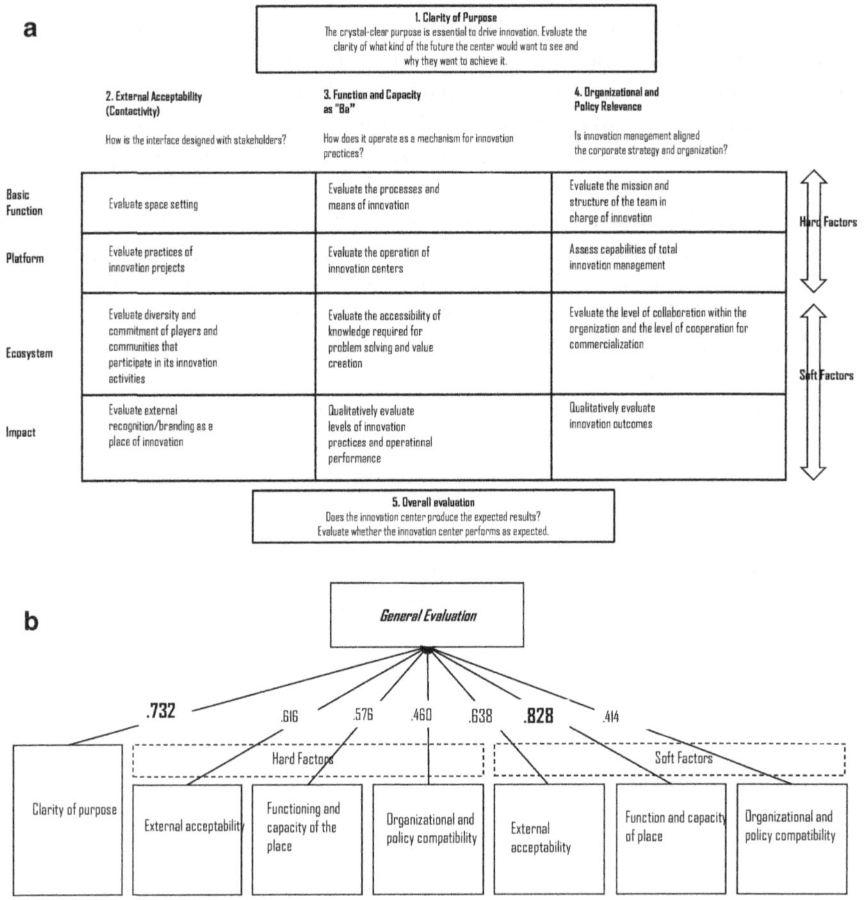

Fig. 5 Factors to form impact of innovation place (example). (**a**) EMIC for evaluating place as IC. (**b**) Contribution of each component to the overall evaluation. The EMIC Report, Future Center Research, 2019

regarding their contribution to the purpose or how effectively they link to social and internal resources. Figure 5b shows an example of the contribution of such field elements.

The functions of innovation centers and similar facilities are not workshops, event session locations, or training facilities; they are spaces for practicing companies' innovation strategies. Therefore, their outcomes should not be viewed as standalone entities but should be evaluated from the perspective of the following:

- Connecting internal (organizational) and external entities.
- Exchanging and creating knowledge (not just a hub).
- Equipped with appropriate hardware and software and assessed regarding their impact on the intended purpose.

4 IC of Ecosystems

4.1 IC and KA in Ecosystems

A model that promotes innovation through indigenous KA based on IC is not confined to a single-company framework. Instead, its effectiveness is recognized within the ecosystems formed by the gathering of diverse participants (Konno & Nonaka, 2018) (Fig. 6).

The management of knowledge assets based on intellectual capital represents a series of processes and practices that enable an organization to utilize its intellectual

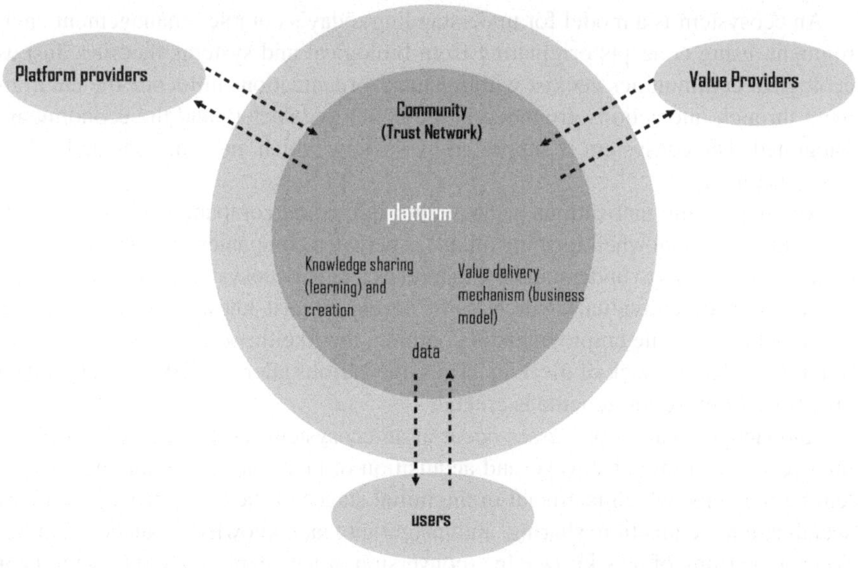

Fig. 6 Typical ecosystem model. Created by the author. Source: Konno and Nonaka (2018)

capital and link it to value creation. The most important factor is the "place" where organizational members work together to create knowledge.

Here, ecosystems and platforms should not be confused. An ecosystem is based on equal membership, and no person can control everything. First, the platform provider offers physical and virtual infrastructure for players in the ecosystem to effectively create, share, leverage, and reap the benefits of the ecosystem. Value providers (providers of products and services) and users utilize this value. The financial flows that make this ecosystem work are either user fees or the value providers that benefit from maintaining the ecosystem.

Ecosystems are important for various organizations, including Google, Apple, Facebook, Amazon, and Microsoft (GAFAM). In the past, manufacturing developed its business around the functional and symbolic values of things, such as product development, production, and marketing, and its own value chains. However, for users, this value is only part of the picture. For example, while the ability of an air conditioner to maintain a cool temperature may be a reason for its purchase, users are interested in the entire experiential offerings, including air quality, noise, environmental and energy cost, aesthetics, and the whole healthy living. From this perspective, manufacturing must provide products and conceive ecosystems and business models that encompass these aspects, that is not easy just for one firm.

Germany-led Industry 4.0, known for its concept of digitizing production sites or smart factories, is underpinned by rapid structural changes occurring outside the factory. Challenges faced by the industrial society, such as environmental impact, the complexities of globalization, and the digital revolution, are present. These changes indicate the limitations of the traditional worldview that treats customers merely as "consumers" and emphasizes the need for new business models as ecosystems.

An ecosystem is a model for understanding today's complex management environment, using concepts originating from biological and systems theories. Just as ecological communities coexist within nature, organizations influence the environment through interactions grounded in the belief that society and the economy are integrated. The ecosystem is supported by society, which, in turn, is made healthy by the economy.

Although many innovations occur within individual companies, horizontal collaboration is crucial when forming alliances between companies, governments, academia, and citizens to understand the market as a larger ecosystem. This requires the participation of individuals with varying levels of tacit knowledge. However, in Japan, where lifetime employment is common, the likelihood of knowledge depletion is high due to a lack of diversity. Thus, the various talents or HC are key, and an open social innovation scheme is crucial.

Knowledge creation processes occur at an ecosystem level (Fig. 7). This phase involves the sharing, discovery, and acquisition of tacit knowledge among ecosystem participants, which is crucial in the initial stages of the SECI process, such as socialization (acquisition, sharing, and insight into tacit knowledge) and dissemination and learning of new knowledge (conversion of new explicit knowledge to tacit knowledge). This process can occur in various forms.

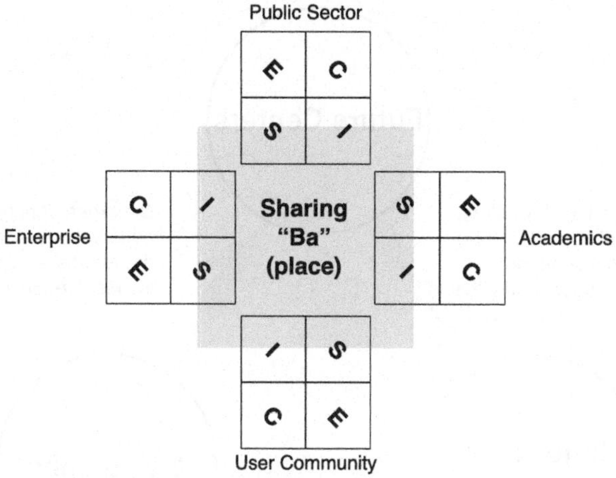

Fig. 7 Multiplayer knowledge creation. Created by the author. Source: Konno and Schillaci (2021)

Figure 7 depicts the starting point of the SECI process (Konno & Schillaci, 2021). Here, at Socialization (S), the sharing of a dynamic context occurs, and sharing places among parties is essential. Internalization (I) is a physical exchange between the involved parties and is important for sharing and implementing new knowledge. Thus, as depicted in this diagram, multiplayer knowledge creation aims to share the S and I positions in the quadruple-helix innovation (Leydesdorff, 2012). Here, IC is activated and knowledge creation in transversal projects is facilitated.

At least three place types can be considered in this framework and are interrelated in social innovation. For example, Fig. 8. includes Future Centers (FC), Innovation Centers (IC), and Living Labs (LL). The foundation of social and open innovation lies in their place (Fig. 8).

- *Future Centers* (FC) connect companies, governments/municipalities, communities/citizens, and educational institutions as boundary objects.
- *Innovation Centers* (IC) serve as places for open innovation, linking corporate technology with society.
- *Living Labs* (LL) are places for social experiments in prototyping, derived from the above.

The FCAJ advocates itself as the "Plural Sector," a social organization able to link these aspects of places. The term was originally coined by Henry Mintzberg. Mintzberg (2015) argued that a healthy society requires robust multi-sectors for rebalancing. Individual public and private sectors, such as companies, municipalities, and universities, cannot achieve transformation alone. Similar to the formation of the venture capital (VC) sector in the United States after World War II as a growth engine, there is a call for establishing a sector that plays a role in socioeconomic innovation in this era.

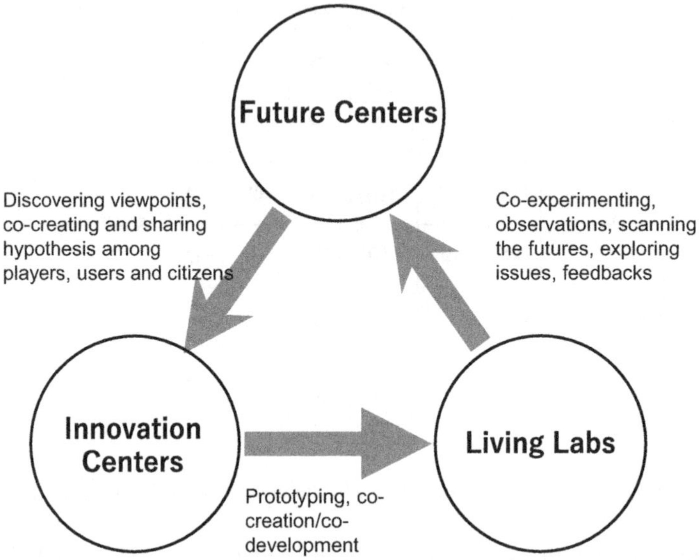

Fig. 8 Diverse players share knowledge creation (SECI) process through Ba. Created by the author. Source: Konno and Schillaci (2021)

Through these places, diverse players utilize KA and create new knowledge (assets), with IC forming these places. Simultaneously, these places can also be considered as shared relational IC.

Paul Romer, Professor at New York University and 2018 Nobel Laureate in Economics, presented a theory of long-term growth created by knowledge innovation. Knowledge (assets) does not diminish upon use (knowledge externalities), meaning that ideas or innovative technologies generated by individuals or organizations within a company are shared as social capital, propagated to other companies, and invested in R&D. Personnel (HC) and the volume of accumulated knowledge applied through innovation lead to the long-term growth of regions and nations.

This theory focuses on social capital and supports innovation. Industries, government agencies, municipalities, universities, research institutions, outstanding entrepreneurial communities, and citizens harmonize as knowledge ecosystems, demonstrating the strength of the socioeconomic system.

The external ecosystem and an organization's internal ecosystem are interconnected. Internal complexity is required to incorporate external complexity. Therefore, management must establish and practice an internal innovation ecosystem based on guiding principles. Innovation management involves exploiting the potential of social IC or the IC of society, that is, communities, cities, and regions related to ecosystems.

As Fig. 9 illustrates, Ba is the key to extracting human capacity and generating dynamics between IC and KA. External and internal ecosystems merge, mediated by the ba (place) where human capacities are drawn out. It illustrates the conceptual

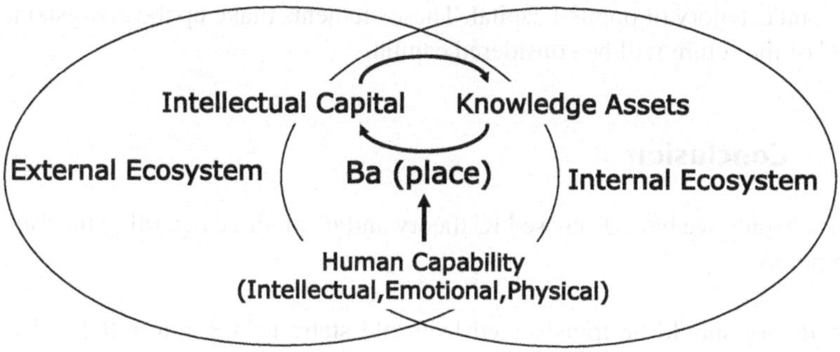

Fig. 9 Ba: Place of human engagement

links between elements such as Ba, internal and external ecosystems, and emotional IC.

4.2 People's Will Creates the Future of IC

The subjectivity of the people involved plays an important role in management systems. Traditional management, strategy, and organizational theories emphasize objectivity over subjectivity. However, in innovation, the starting point is often the innovator's will or righteous indignation or the stakeholders' emotions, doubts, and frustrations. These goals direct innovation, which is related to a purpose. Many start-up managers consider their purpose to be their starting point. Although these goals are generally clearly stated for new businesses in existing areas, it is difficult to set them for non-existing areas. Purpose and objectives differ in their subjective meanings and values. Innovation is a process in which individual subjectivity (e.g., tacit knowledge and purpose) is shared with organizational subjectivity and transformed into objective knowledge (e.g., formal knowledge and business models). Furthermore, innovation creates value that resonates with society and individuals. This aspects of humans and society is essential for innovation and should be part of or at the core of the IC.

For example, DX is presented to improve and enrich the inner human experience. Erik Stolterman, the first advocate of DX, argued that in a dramatically digitalizing society, humans must not be caught up in the wave (Croon & Stolterman, 2003). Rather, he defined DX as enriching internal experiences centered on aesthetic experiences and linking the impact of digitalization to a better social transformation. It regards transforming society and people's lives by reorganizing the knowledge of customers and organizations using digital technologies, including artificial intelligence (AI).

Customers and organizations must reaffirm this potential of emotional value as capital. The organization's capacity for empathy and the state of the individual's emotional state such as psychological safety in human and capital will be an important category of pointed capital. These elements make up the ecosystem; thus, the IC of the future will be considered capital.

5 Conclusion

In this chapter, we have discussed IC theory and IC practice regarding the following three points:

- IC theory should be transformed from old static to dynamic relational theory. The key to this is KA.
- IC theory must be connected to organizational reality. The key to this is the use of ba: place.
- IC theory must be further humanized. To do so, the physical and emotional elements of humans must be emphasized.

IC is often discussed in management, although its definition and measurement are not always clear with its outcome. As it is intangible and difficult to quantify, to determine its value, it has been attributed to various indicators such as market capitalization. The relationship between IC and performance remains uncertain, and it is important to understand how IC contributes to KA creation. A need for such a model has been proposed that links KA creation with the knowledge creation process and IC in this chapter.

At the microlevel, companies can convert IC into KA, which is essential for creating new knowledge. For example, in the sharing of tacit knowledge, it will be important to produce empathy and mutually shared physical experiences. In the formalization of tacit knowledge, a space for creative discussion will be necessary. In addition, in the consolidation of systematic knowledge, soft factors will be required, such as collaboration in virtual spaces using digital technology. The relationship between intellectual capital and knowledge assets can be seen from this perspective.

The concept of ba is crucial in this process; however, it can also be considered fundamental capital for the entire ecosystem when scaled up to encompass the organization and beyond. An ecosystem-based perspective is essential in modern management; therefore, ba should be considered an IC category.

Furthermore, the emotional aspects of IC have been overlooked in the literature. Traditionally, emotional value has been considered secondary in management within a logical-analytical context. "Place" is linked to human physical sensations and instincts, and the affective aspect is an emotional function. The term "intellectual" is related to the neocortex, but the future of IC should include the cerebrum, mesencephalon, and *medulla oblongata* (that is, the sixth sense). This corresponds to the age of AI when subjective and emotional capital will become increasingly important in the future management of the knowledge era.

In conclusion, companies need to recognize the importance of IC as fundamental capital within a humanized management system for knowledge creation, particularly in the knowledge era, where people's purpose and passion shared by place (ba) are critical factors in value creation. Such attempts lead us to consider IC as fundamental capital within a humanized management system for knowledge creation, namely, for innovation.

References

Collins, J. (2001). *Good to great*. Random House Business Books.

Croon, A., & Stolterman, E. (2003). *'Everyday aesthetics and design of information technology' Techne: Design aesthetics: Die Frage über Technik*. University of Barcelona.

Drucker, P. (1993). *Post capitalist society*. Harper Business.

Dženopoljac, V., Janoševic, S., & Bontis, N. (2016). Intellectual capital and financial performance in the Serbian ICT industry. *Journal of Intellectual Capital, 17*(2), 373–396. https://doi.org/10.1108/JIC-07-2015-0068

Edvinsson, L., & Malone, M. (1997). *Intellectual capital: Realizing your Company's true value by finding its hidden brainpower* (1st ed.). Harper Business.

Edvinsson, L., et al. (2005). Intellectual capital in waiting – A strategic IC challenge. *Handbook of Business Strategy, 6*.

EMIC Report (2019). *Evaluation model for innovation center*. https://futurecenteralliance-japan.org/activityen.

Friedman, T. L. (2007). The people we have been waiting for. *New York Times*, (2007–12–02).

Hayek, F. (1945). The use of knowledge in society. *The American Economic Review*.

Iacuzzi, S., & Pauluzzo, R. (2023). Looking for missing outcomes: Accounting for intellectual capital and value creation in ecosystems. *Journal of Management and Governance, 28*, 1117–1149. https://doi.org/10.1007/s10997-023-09688-3

Iske, P. (2020). Institute of brilliant failures: Make room to experiment, innovate, and learn. *Business Contact*.

Jordão, R. V. D., & Novas, J. C. (2017). Knowledge management and intellectual capital in networks of small- and medium-sized enterprises. *Journal of Intellectual Capital, 18*(3), 667–692. https://doi.org/10.1108/JIC-11-2016-0120

Kianto, A., Ritala, P., Spender, J.-C., & Vanhala, M. (2014). The interaction of intellectual capital assets and knowledge management practices in organizational value creation. *Journal of Intellectual Capital, 15*(3), 362–375. https://doi.org/10.1108/JIC-05-2014-0059

Konno, N. (1998). *Management of knowledge asset*. Nikkei Publishing.

Konno, N. (2012). *The grammar of knowledge creating management for prudent capitalism*. Toyo Keizai Publishing.

Konno, N., & Nonaka, I. (1995). *Intellectualizing capability*. Nikkei Publishing.

Konno, N. (2020) " The Innovation Catalog" Toyo Keizai Publishing (in Japanese).

Konno, N., & Schillaci, C. E. (2021). Intellectual capital in Society 5.0, by the lens of the knowledge creation theory. *Journal of Intellectual Capital, 22*(3), 478–505. https://doi.org/10.1108/JIC-02-2020-0060

Levitt, T. (1983). The globalization of markets. *Harvard Business Review*, May 1983.

Leydesdorff, L. (2012). *The Triple Helix of University-Industry-Government Relations* (February 2012). SSRN Working Paper Series.

Mintzberg, H. (2015). Time for the plural sector. *Stanford Social Innovation Review*, Summer 2015.

Nishida, K. (1921). *An inquiry into good* (English ed.) M. Abe & C. Ives (Translated by), 1990. Yale University Press.

Nonaka, I., & Konno, N. (1998). The concept of "Ba": Building a foundation for knowledge creation. *California Management Review, 40*(3), 40–54. https://doi.org/10.2307/41165942

Nonaka, I., & Takeuchi, H. (2019). *The wise company: How companies create continuous innovation*. Oxford University Press.

Polanyi, M. (1962). *Personal knowledge: Towards a post-critical philosophy*. University of Chicago Press.
Prusak, L. (2006). *Knowledge management and organizational learning*. Oxford University Press.
Romer, P. M. (1990). Endogenous technological change. *Journal of Political Economy, 98*(5, Part 2), S71–S102. https://doi.org/10.1086/261725
Stewart, T. A. (1991). Brain power: How intellectual capital is becoming America's most valuable asset. *Fortune, 3*.

Noboru Konno is a Professor (PhD in Management Informatics) at the Graduate School of Business of Tama University in Tokyo. He holds the roles of President of EcosyX Lab, President of Japan Innovation Network (JIN), and Founder of Future Centre Alliance Japan (FCAJ), and is a board member of the New Club of Paris. Konno's academic interests encompass knowledge ecology and ecosystems, focusing on knowledge creation theory, the concept of ba, design thinking, and innovation management systems. As an advisor to firms, he exercises theory and practices in numerous innovation projects. Konno has authored over 20 books, including *The Whole Innovation Catalog*. Furthermore, he has co-authored several articles with Dr. Ikujiro Nonaka, such as the widely cited pieces "The Concept of Ba" and "Intellectualizing Capability," which earned the Financial Times Global Business Book Award.

Intellectual Capital as a Basis for Cash Flow and Renewal

Tomi Hussi and Aino Kianto

Abstract

The discussion around intellectual capital (IC) has centered on organizational renewal and innovation, and the significance of IC for the effective execution of the current business model has been relatively overlooked. In this chapter, we claim that IC is equally relevant for both strategic goals and construct dynamic models portraying the role of knowledge assets and knowledge flows in the production of cash flow and renewal. We suggest that the IC-based dynamics of cash flow and renewal production are based on three types of knowledge assets (energy, demand, and platform), which interact through three knowledge flows (reflection, dialogue, and offering). The difference between cash flow and renewal processes lies in the direction of the dynamic process. We suggest futurizing IC theory and practice through an improved acknowledgment of the current cash flow perspective and the dynamics among IC components. Furthermore, we argue that it would also be wise to adjust IC terminology to make it more intelligible to the general, non-scholarly audience.

T. Hussi (✉)
Think Fellows, Espoo, Finland
e-mail: tomi.hussi@thinkfellows.fi

A. Kianto
LUT Business School, LUT University, Lahti, Finland
e-mail: aino.kianto@lut.fi

A. Kianto et al. (eds.), *Futurizing Intellectual Capital*, Knowledge Management and Organizational Learning 15, https://doi.org/10.1007/978-3-031-80197-6_4

1 Introduction

A vivid academic community has existed around the topic of intellectual capital (IC) for almost three decades. There are several highly esteemed scholarly journals in the field, such as the *Journal of Intellectual Capital* and the *Journal of Knowledge Management*, and numerous universities have established chairs, full professorships, and academic degree programs related to the field. Despite the vast academic interest, there seem to be few real-life business initiatives utilizing the IC approach (e.g., Nielsen et al., 2017). This is an interesting contrast with regard to the early phases, when the research was strongly rooted in the interests of practitioners (Bontis, 1996; Brooking, 1996; Darling, 1996; Edvinsson & Sullivan, 1996; Saint-Onge, 1996).

Bontis (1998) indicated the challenges related to the financial evaluation of IC and emphasized its strategic relevance. Since its beginning, such a strategic discussion around IC discourse has strongly emphasized the essential role of IC in organizational renewal and innovation. The crucial impact IC has on innovation performance and renewing an organization's offerings and operating methods has been well-established across the past decades (e.g., Buenechea-Elberdin, 2017; Inkinen, 2015; Subramaniam & Youndt, 2005). Recent reviews on the IC literature (Baima et al., 2021; Bellucci et al., 2021; Crupi et al., 2021; Demartini & Beretta, 2020; Paoloni et al., 2020) have demonstrated that the popularity of IC–innovation linkage as a research topic continues.

While renewal is an important method for survival in a rapidly changing business environment, a company must also be able to maintain the cash flow from its current business model; without a workable present, an organization will be unable to create its future. In this chapter, we claim that the IC approach can be useful not only for meeting the future expectations of the stock market and the ability to produce customer value in the long term but also for the current business operations, as a basis for aligning the human capital and other elements of IC into the current value creation.

In this chapter, we aim to enhance the practical dimension of the IC community. We assert that strengthening the cash flow perspective on IC can increase its importance for business managers, as it provides a clear framework for clarifying and communicating the logic of the company's business activities. IC can thus become a powerful tool for designing and communicating the business endeavors of an organization. Therefore, we argue that IC theory and practice should have a short-term focus on supporting a company's current activities and value capture from these activities to a much greater degree than it is doing today. A more balanced approach to IC, capable of charting out and clarifying all dimensions of value creation in both the short and long terms, can increase its adoption by practitioners.

This chapter contributes to futurizing IC theory and practice by developing a conceptual model that addresses the IC-based dynamics of cash flow (current business; short-term orientation) and renewal (future business; long-term orientation) production based on three types of knowledge assets (energy, demand, and platform), which interact through three knowledge flows (reflection, dialogue, and offering). The main theoretical contributions of the proposed model are an improved recognition of IC dynamics, as the model addresses the dynamics between IC components in an explicit manner, and a strengthening of the cash flow perspective on IC, which may improve IC relevance and legitimacy within business managers. From a practical perspective, this model may improve the synergy between IC theory and real managerial needs.

2 Identification of Knowledge Assets and Knowledge Flows

In their seminal book, Edvinsson and Malone (1997) suggested that value is created as an interactive outcome of various types of IC or knowledge assets, hence establishing the grounding for the IC field. Even though many other scholars have followed in their footsteps in building on the idea that value creation takes place at the intersection of IC components, there is relatively little understanding concerning the dynamics among knowledge assets. Overall, the understanding of the dynamic dimension of IC (Kianto, 2007; Kianto et al. 2017) has been relatively neglected in the literature, with very few studies explicitly addressing the dynamics between IC components (Bejinaru, 2018; Bratianu, 2008; Bratianu & Brejinaru, 2020; Giuiliani, 2015; Ståhle & Bonfour, 2008). The current chapter builds on the seminal ideas of Bratianu (2008, 2016; Bratianu & Bejinaru, 2020) and addresses IC dynamics as processes that integrate knowledge assets and transform them.

2.1 Knowledge Assets Form the Basis for IC-Based Value Creation

IC consists of the knowledge assets that an entity uses to produce value (Edvinsson & Malone, 1997). In terms of these knowledge assets, we extend on Edvinsson and Malone's original model (1997) and follow the traditional approach of dividing IC into three dimensions (Bontis, 1998; Edvisson & Malone, 1997; Sveiby, 1997; Youndt et al., 2004): demand (cf. relational capital), platform (cf. structural capital), and energy (cf. human capital) (Fig. 1). The choice of introducing a new terminology is based on the lack of practitioner adoption of the concepts developed in the IC literature. Human, structural, and relational capital are used in the academic literature but have been critiqued for being vague and indeterminate (Bontis, 1998; Spender & Grant, 1997). This is possibly due to the difficulties in grasping the essence of these concepts that real-life organizations are not using them practically at all. We introduce (human) energy, (organizational) platform, and demand (of the business environment as understood by the company) as concepts that are easier to comprehend.

In the three-dimensional classification of IC, human capital is mostly seen as the knowledge and competencies of an individual (Bontis, 1998; Edvinsson & Malone, 1997; Sveiby, 1997; Youndt et al., 2004). We take these elements into consideration

Fig. 1 Knowledge assets

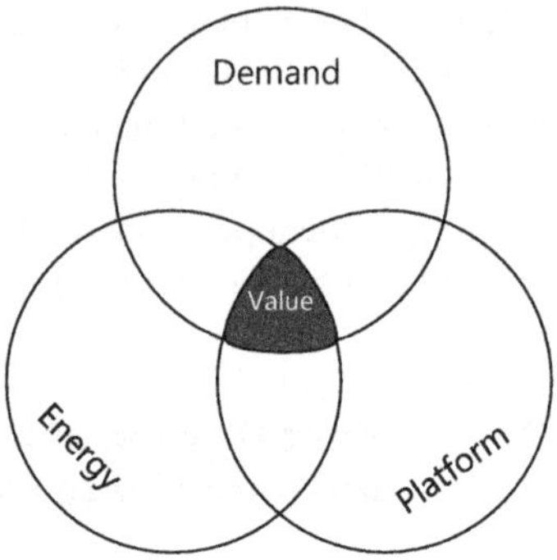

but also include motivation, functional capability, and health in our concept of human capital. In Finland, Hussi and Aura have conducted extensive research on the concept of personnel productivity (see, e.g., Ahonen et al., 2021; Aura 2021; Aura et al., 2015, 2018, 2020). In the model presented above, human capital is labeled *energy*. This is based on Aura and Hussi's (2024) definition that personnel productivity is a concept suitable for organization-level analysis, and its counterpart on the individual level is energy. The essence of discussing energy is that human capital also needs to be seen as a broad and holistic concept covering all aspects of the potential that lies in the personnel. As such, the competence and knowledge base are not effective if one does not have enough motivation and health-related capabilities to strive in their work tasks.

In terms of structural capital, Stewart (1998) emphasized systems, processes, and culture that enable effective and efficient functioning. Sveiby's (1997) idea of internal structure focuses on organizational elements that facilitate knowledge creation, sharing, and utilization within the organization. It is thus about organizational elements that are related to leveraging the knowledge of individuals. In this paper, we use the term *platform* instead of structural capital and internal structure to show features of structural capital as an organizational ability that enables the creation of offerings to meet the market's demand. This reasoning is in line with that provided by Youndt et al. (2004), who preferred organizational capital over structural capital. A platform enables an organization to combine all required resources so that an offering can be created. It also refers to the collective ability to crystallize individuals' views into organizational insights. It covers the managerial system, leadership, and organizational culture. The infrastructure for preserving and sharing knowledge is also included in the platform.

Relational capital emphasizes relationships and networks (Edvinsson & Malone, 1997; Sveiby, 1997). Relational capital and external structure are highly challenging concepts for practitioners to understand. Therefore, we adopted "demand," which refers to knowledge about markets and market needs, know-how to meet the market demand, and relationships that enable communication, information, and value exchange between the organization and the market. Fluency in understanding demand enables organizations to adapt to changing market conditions and customer preferences. As Sveiby (1997) put it, external relationships enhance the resilience of an organization in dynamic market environments.

2.2 Knowledge Flows as Dynamics of Value Creation

Inspired by Bratianu's (2008, 2016; Bratianu & Bejinaru, 2020) view of IC dynamics as transformational integrative processes, we examined the interaction of the knowledge assets explained in the previous section, by conceptualizing knowledge flows among them (Fig. 2).

At the intersection of demand and platform, we identify a knowledge flow called *offering*. It is the products and services that an organization provides to its customers to meet market demand. An offering is a crystallized understanding of how the organization can respond to the demand identified in the market as a business opportunity. Offering is a means of communicating value creation to the market and crystallizing the market's need into a specific set of products and services with which the organization aims to meet the demand.

Dialogue between the platform and energy is the interaction between the organizational structure and the employees. In this sense, the work community is also seen as a part of the platform, as energy refers only to the potential of individuals. Dialogue breathes life into a platform while forming the basis for the roles and responsibilities of individual employees. It emphasizes collaboration in an organization at various levels and in different contexts.

Finally, *reflection* is the interaction between energy and demand. It is the individual employees of an organization who make all observations about the changing demands and expectations of customers. In contrast, reflection refers to the impression and evaluation that the market makes about the personnel as actors fulfilling the tasks related to customer service. Reflection is a process that aims at changing one's view and thinking with regard to something, with analyzing and contemplating at its core.

As stated above, all three knowledge flows work in two directions: offering and reflection from the market into the organization and its employees, and vice versa. This means that knowledge flows are related to two larger processes, namely, cash

Fig. 2 Knowledge flows

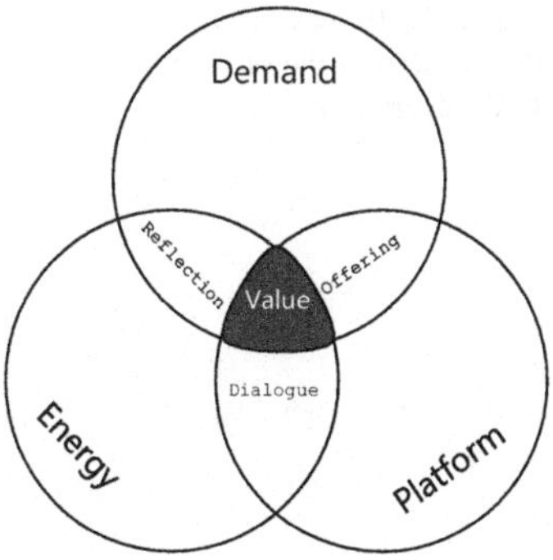

flow generation and an organization's renewal. Cash flow and renewal open up a new perspective on how IC is related to the current and future business activities of the company.

3 IC as the Framework for Understanding Cash Flow Generation

At the end of the day, the existence of a company is based on its ability to generate cash flow and thus sufficient funds to cover its operations costs. Cash flow provides insights into how much funds the company currently has and what the outlook looks like in the coming months.

However, in addition to just monitoring cash flow, it is also advisable to broadly share an understanding of the logic of how the company actually generates cash flow through its operations. A clear understanding of the ways in which a company adds value to its customers helps to focus on the right priorities. When the entire organization understands the basics of generating cash flow, executing the needed activities and processes and making decisions become easier. This is where the role of IC in shaping the success of the current business model stands out (Fig. 3).

There have been ideas in the IC literature related to current business activities, ranging from classics such as Sveiby's (1997) intangible balance sheet, where IC is seen as an entity that is strongly related to the market value of the company, to Ahonen's (2000; Hussi & Ahonen, 2002) division between generative and commercially exploitable intangibles and numerous empirical studies demonstrating the link between IC and a firm's market performance (e.g., Maditinos et al., 2011). However, these accounts do not reveal the mechanisms and role that IC plays with regard to current business activities. This chapter aims to mend this situation by demonstrating the logic of how IC is at the core of the process of running the current business model and thus creating cash flow.

When looking at IC in the cash flow direction, the analysis starts with demand. Demand is a need in the market that is identified by a company. It is a company's interpretation of the needs of its potential customers and where the company can provide added value through its products or services. This interpretation was created

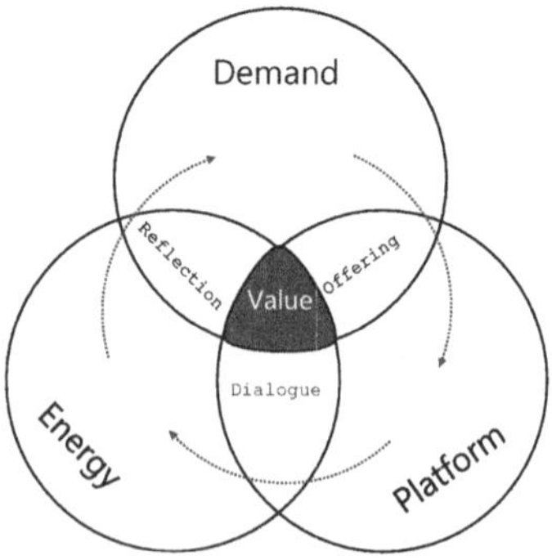

Fig. 3 IC framework for the virtuous circle of cash flow generation

because of the renewal process, which is discussed in the next section. The company's task is to respond to demand through its operations. Meeting customer needs is the foundation of business and, consequently, cash flow. Therefore, the company must be able to identify or create demand in its own market.

By offering solutions, the company addresses the identified market demand and provides a solution to customer needs. The offering also includes sales and marketing—how solutions are made known to customers and therefore available for purchase. The company itself forms a platform through which the offering is implemented. In terms of cash flow, the platform is the target of streamlining and optimization—how to ensure that the platform serves the implementation of the offering in the best possible way. Developing the platform is not just top-down bureaucratic management but is best achieved through community-driven approaches, incorporating the views of the entire organization.

The platform's operation requires the contribution of people in the organization, utilizing their available energy. The activities defined by the platform are organized within the organization through dialogue and assigning roles and concrete tasks to individuals. Expertise is the most crucial aspect of energy, i.e., human capital. However, expertise alone can accomplish little if the other components of energy are not in order. Motivation to act according to the organization's goals is needed to support expertise. Strong expertise and a burning desire are not enough if the person does not have sufficient functional capacity to meet the requirements of the role.

When a company operates efficiently and can respond to customer needs with its operations, it reflects on demand through customer satisfaction and loyalty. A well-functioning company's reputation in the market grows, attracting new customers, thus increasing demand through both repeat purchases from existing customers and an expanding customer base. The cash flow perspective on IC can thus be seen as a virtuous circle.

4 IC as the Framework for Understanding Organizational Renewal

The long-term survival of an organization requires renewal. When a company, in addition to creating cash flow, takes care of its ability to renew, it secures its future financial performance. With renewal, a company can respond to changes in its operating environment. Excessive focus on the current businesses that form the basis of the cash flow reduces attention to one's own current activities. Standing still is not sufficient in responding to the rapidly changing demands of the business environment; thus, current performance development is not sufficient for sustainable performance. Figure 4 portrays the role and dynamics of IC in renewal.

Renewal means sensitivity to detect changes in the demands placed on the company and the ability to react to them. The fate of Nokia's mobile phones is such a classic example that even ChatGPT mentions it as the first example of a company falling behind its competitors. Renewal requires the workforce to perceive and understand changes in the operating environment. In a well-functioning work

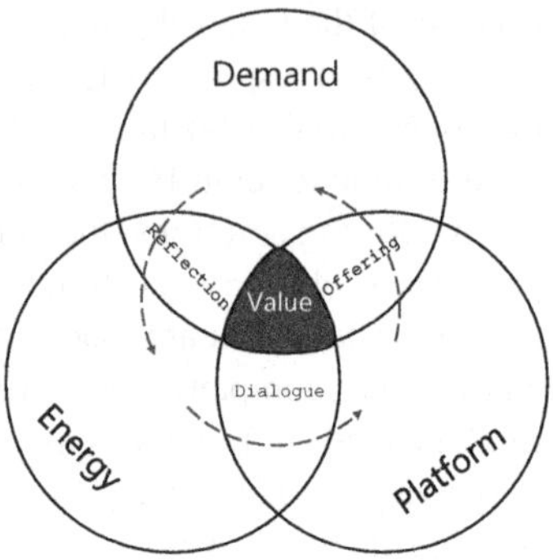

Fig. 4 IC framework for the virtuous circle of organizational renewal

community, these observations are condensed into a new type of offering that meets changed needs.

Energetic personnel are the root of renewal. The company itself does not perceive changes in the operating environment; a human is needed for that. The ability to perceive changes is based on a person's ability to think and make interpretations. There are usually various signals of change that are visible well in advance. However, there are almost endless signals around us that require a strong vision to pick up the messages that genuinely need a response. Not only does the perception of messages matter but there is also a need to understand the root causes of changes and their impact on one's own business.

Understanding the significance of signals does not come out of thin air; it requires a solid knowledge base. In addition to expertise, effective work also requires motivation and the ability to function amidst various, often conflicting, requirements. Thus, an energetic and genuinely well-being workforce is the most important factor in the ability to renew.

In a world saturated with various messages, relying solely on observations made by individuals does not get us very far. The significance of messages becomes clear only when individuals share their thoughts. By collectively pondering, observations gain depth and evolve into more structured perspectives. The most impactful choices about what actions to take based on observations are also made in collaboration.

The development of the platform by the company is based on jointly defined actions. The combination of refined services and practices is packaged into a renewed offering that responds to the changing market demand. Thus, the foundation of future cash flow is renewed.

Utilizing everyone's wisdom is the key. Renewal requires capabilities from both the personnel and the organization. In a psychologically safe community, everyone dares to express their views, which can be collectively developed further. The possibilities for influence and trust in the continuity of work also increase commitment to the company and its success. Sustainable performance development indicates the company's ability to sustain good financial results in the long term.

5 Futurizing IC Theory Through Cash Flow and Renewal Dynamics

In this chapter, we argue that IC theory emphasizes future-oriented renewal to the relative neglect of supporting the successful execution of the current business model. However, while renewal is undoubtedly an urgent topic in a rapidly changing business environment, a company must also maintain the cash flow from its current business model. Therefore, we claim that IC is relevant for both these perspectives and recommend a better acknowledgment of cash flow as an essential means to futurize IC theory. If IC discourse has to maintain—and, in effect, improve—its business relevance and legitimacy, it should address the real needs of practitioners. Since practicing managers tend to be more interested in the execution of current priorities than the development of future potentials, addressing the role of IC in generating cash flow and providing a model for addressing this issue may be important ways to sync IC theory with real managerial needs.

Building on and modifying the classical IC model by Edvinsson and Malone (1997), we propose that cash flow and renewal can both be approached from the perspectives of three types of knowledge assets: energy, demand, and platform. Energy represents the capabilities of a company's employees. The platform is the context created by a company, where individuals and company structures come together to realize the core of the business model. Demand refers to interpreting and being able to react to the expectations of the business environment.

The second key suggestion for futurizing IC theory is an improved recognition of IC dynamics—that is, knowledge flows among the knowledge assets. We argue that both cash flow and renewal are energized by the three knowledge flows that put the assets in motion: reflection, dialogue, and offering. Reflection refers to the interaction that the employees of a company have with the operating environment. Dialogue is the mutual interaction and information-sharing among a company's employees. Offering refers to the totality of products and services on which a company relies to meet market needs.

Cash flow and renewal share the same elements but differ in terms of the process direction (Fig. 5). The cash flow perspective starts with demand. A company identifies market demand, to which it responds with its offering. The platform is created

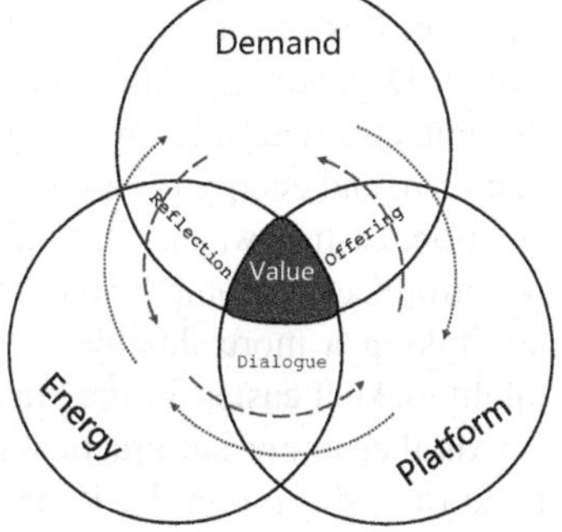

Fig. 5 IC-based dynamics of cash flow and renewal production

by the company to implement the offering in the best possible manner. The platform's operation sets requirements for the use of employees' energy. Through internal dialogue, requirements are structured into the roles and tasks of individuals. If the employees of the company can efficiently and effectively implement its offering, it is reflected in demand as good customer satisfaction and loyalty. This train of reasoning is in line with the service–profit chain model proposed by Heskett et al. (1997).

Renewal also relies on demand, energy, and the platform. Demand remains the starting point, but now the first knowledge flow is reflection. In renewal, reflection means that a company's employees observe changing and emerging needs in the operating environment. The energy of the employees, which includes their knowledge, motivation, and ability to act, significantly influences how sensitively the operating environment is monitored and assessed. In dialogue, observations made by individual employees are shared within the work community and developed into platform improvements, becoming a characteristic of the company. A new way of operating and solutions are crystallized into a new offering that better meets the market demand. The renewed offering maintains the company's competitiveness in the future. This sequence follows the phases contained in typical innovation process models (e.g., Tidd et al., 2005).

In summary, we assert that IC is relevant for both renewal and generation of current cash flow and recommend an increased emphasis on the latter. We also argue that understanding IC-based value creation through a dynamic perspective makes sense and propose a theoretical model for examining such dynamics through knowledge flows. We hope that future IC research will consider our suggestions and apply our theoretical models to examine empirical cases in real-life situations.

6 Futurizing IC Practice Through Cash Flow and Renewal Dynamics

Despite the widespread academic interest and established position of related core journals, such as *Journal of Intellectual Capital* and *Journal of Knowledge Management*, practical solutions based on IC are rare. As discussed earlier in this chapter, this might partly be due to the unclear and academic nature of the concepts used in IC discourse. To make the dimensions of IC more easily approachable, we chose in this chapter to use labels that are better understandable for the general public. Depending on the aspects that one wishes to highlight, it is worth limiting the concepts within IC by using more specific labels. Our choice of using demand, platform, and energy is based on the aim of emphasizing the two processes of value creation, cash flow, and renewal. We suggest that a broader array of concepts could be introduced to complement the traditional human, structural, and relational capital. Taking a more flexible and needs-driven approach toward conceptualization might make it easier for the practitioners to adopt the framework, too.

Another important practical implication of this chapter is the description of the logic of cash flow in the IC framework. Cash flow and renewal are often viewed separately. People responsible for business are typically more interested in cash flow, as their compensation and, in extreme cases, their employment depends primarily on the company's financial results. Renewal, in contrast, is particularly important for those working in development roles, as they are evaluated based on the effectiveness of their development efforts. However, the ability to play both the short and long games simultaneously is a prerequisite for the sustainable success of the company. Thus, this chapter suggests futurizing IC theory and practice by addressing both sides of this equation, also including the dynamics among energy, platforms, and demand.

The cash flow direction described in this chapter makes IC discourse more relevant to C-suite management. While having general responsibility over the business operations of an organization, a CEO is most heavily rated by the short-term performance of the company. The understanding of IC in a cash flow direction makes it more applicable to support the organization in achieving its short-term goals. We expect that a broader understanding of the various business implications of the IC framework will make it more meaningful and interesting for practitioners to adopt.

Through the clarified concept of cash flow generation, it is easier to communicate business logic to the entire staff in a similar manner. The fundamentals of business logic can be explained by deliberately discussing the assumptions and choices behind knowledge assets (energy, platform, and demand) and knowledge flows (dialogue, reflection, and offering). A clear and shared understanding of these assumptions makes them explicit and makes it possible to analyze and develop them further together.

Understanding the IC-based fundamentals of business also engages the staff, as they understand the significance of their actions and roles in business activities. A widely shared understanding of cash flow creation also strengthens employees' sense of psychological security. The conditions for continuing operations are in place, and jobs are not threatened. The renewal described in this chapter is a continuous process for which the company itself must take responsibility. This means that the leaders must actively set the direction and create a participatory organizational culture by leading with their own example. However, dialogue leveraging collective wisdom also shares responsibility with the entire workforce and utilizes everyone's potential to the fullest. This motivates employees and takes care of their well-being by increasing the meaningfulness of work. Therefore, community-driven approaches to IC are needed, where each member of the work community utilizes their capabilities in the best possible way for the achievement of common success.

A better understanding of the IC-based logic of value creation is also beneficial for individual employees because it makes the goals of the work clearer and thus creates a solid base for increasing meaningfulness. Understanding these objectives makes it possible to craft one's job. According to Harju et al. (2016), opportunities for job crafting reduce job boredom and increase work engagement. This creates a feedback loop to energy, as being inspired by the work is a key element in employees' energy.

The cash flow direction also creates a better basis for the renewal of the organization. Precise and trustworthy execution of the current business model strengthens the relationship between the organization and its customers. Enhanced trust deepens interactions with customers and increases openness in communication. This is highly valuable for bringing up even more sensitive topics in the functioning of the customer organization. The ability to share even delicate information makes it possible to react to changing expectations earlier and, thus, increases competitive advantage.

7 Concluding Remarks

In this chapter, we demonstrate that IC is relevant not only for an organization's renewal but also for its capability to run the current business model and thus create cash flow. Both these processes are based on the same knowledge assets and knowledge flows. It is the question of the direction that separates these processes.

We made a conscious decision of introducing new terminology to make it easier for practitioners to adopt the key contributions of the IC framework. The justification for these decisions has been presented above in this chapter.

We hope that our contribution to this chapter will give our readers new ideas and insights. This chapter is highly exploratory in nature. Hopefully, some of these ideas will also ignite interest in future research projects that could possibly validate our suggestions.

Acknowledgments Dr. Tomi Hussi would like to thank Mr. Jarmo Hyökyvuori for the collaboration in the process of creating the model that forms the core of this chapter.

References

Ahonen, G. (2000). Generative and commercially exploitable intangible assets. In J. E. Groejer & H. Stolowy (Eds.), *Classification of intangibles* (pp. 206–213). Groupe HEC.

Ahonen, G., Aura, O., Hussi, T., & Ilmarinen, J. (2021). The financial impact of management by self-determination – Empirical evidence from Finland. *European Journal of Management, 21*(1), 93–110.

Aura, O. (2021). *Henkilöstötuottavuuden johtaminen teollisuudessa – Työkaari kantaa – tuottavaa työhyvinvointia hankkeen seuranta-analyysien yhteenveto.* Ossi Aura Consulting.

Aura, O., Ahonen, G., & Hussi, T. (2015). *Henkilöstötuottavuus ja eurot – case rakennusala.* Keskinäinen Eläkevakuutusyhtiö Etera.

Aura, O., Ahonen, G., & Hussi, T. (2018). *Henkilöstötuottavuuden johtaminen Arjessassa 2015–2017.* Arjessa Oy.

Aura, O., Ahonen, G., Hussi, T., & Ilmarinen, J. (2020). *Itseohjautuvuuden johtaminen 2020.* Ossi Aura Consulting.

Aura, O., & Hussi, T. (2024). *Paremman johtamistyön manifesti.* Pro-Insight Finland Oy.

Baima, G., Forliano, C., Santoro, G., & Vrontis, D. (2021). Intellectual capital and business model: A systematic literature review to explore their linkages. *Journal of Intellectual Capital, 22*(3), 653–679.

Bejinaru, R. (2018). The key processes of knowledge dynamics and intellectual capital in organizations. *Challenging the Status Quo in Management and Economics,* 599.

Bellucci, M., Marzi, G., Orlando, B., & Ciampi, F. (2021). Journal of Intellectual Capital: A review of emerging themes and future trends. *Journal of Intellectual Capital, 22*(4), 744–767.

Bontis, N. (1996). There's a price on your head: Managing intellectual capital strategically. *Business Quarterly, 60*(4, Summer), 41–47.

Bontis, N. (1998). Intellectual capital: An exploratory study that develops measures and models. *Management Decision, 36*, 63–76.

Bratianu, C. (2008). A dynamic structure of the organizational intellectual capital. In M. Naaranoja (Ed.), *Knowledge management in organizations* (pp. 233–243). Vaasa University.

Bratianu, C. (2016). Knowledge dynamics. *Management Dynamics in the Knowledge Economy, 4*(3), 323–337.

Bratianu, C., & Bejinaru, R. (2020). Knowledge dynamics: A thermodynamics approach. *Kybernetes, 49*(1), 6–21.

Brooking, A. (1996). *Intellectual capital: Core asset for the third millennium enterprise*. International Thomson Business Press.

Buenechea-Elberdin, M. (2017). Structured literature review about intellectual capital and innovation. *Journal of Intellectual Capital, 18*(2), 262–285.

Crupi, A., Cesaroni, F., & Di Minin, A. (2021). Understanding the impact of intellectual capital on entrepreneurship: A literature review. *Journal of Intellectual Capital, 22*(3), 528–559.

Darling, M. (1996). Building the knowledge organization. *Business Quarterly*, Winter.

Demartini, M. C., & Beretta, V. (2020). Intellectual capital and SMEs' performance: A structured literature review. *Journal of Small Business Management, 58*(2), 288–332.

Edvinsson, L., & Malone, M. S. (1997). *Intellectual capital: Realising your company's true value by finding its hidden brainpower*. Harper Business.

Edvinsson, L., & Sullivan, P. (1996). Developing a model for managing intellectual capital. *European Management Journal, 14*(4), 356–364.

Giuliani, M. (2015). Intellectual capital dynamics: Seeing them "in practice" through a temporal lens. *Vine, 45*(1), 46–66.

Harju, L. K., Hakanen, J. J., & Schaufeli, W. B. (2016). Can job crafting reduce job boredom and increase work engagement? A three-year cross-lagged panel study. *Journal of Vocational Behavior, 95–96*, 11–20.

Heskett, J. L., Sasser, E., & Schlesinger, L. (1997). *The service profit chain: How leading companies link profit and growth to loyalty, satisfaction, and value*. The Free Press.

Hussi, T., & Ahonen, G. (2002). Managing intangible assets – a question of integration and delicate balance. *Journal of Intellectual Capital, 3*(3), 277–286.

Inkinen, H. (2015). Review of empirical research on intellectual capital and firm performance. *Journal of Intellectual Capital, 16*(3), 518–565.

Kianto, A. (2007). What do we really mean by the dynamic dimension of intellectual capital? *International Journal of Learning and Intellectual Capital, 4*(4), 342–356.

Kianto, A., Sáenz, J., & Aramburu, N. (2017). Knowledge-based human resource management practices, intellectual capital and innovation. *Journal of Business Research, 81*, 11–20.

Maditinos, D., Chatzoudes, D., Tsairidis, C., & Theriou, G. (2011). The impact of intellectual capital on firms' market value and financial performance. *Journal of Intellectual Capital, 12*(1), 132–151.

Nielsen, C., Roslender, R., & Schaper, S. (2017). Explaining the demise of the intellectual capital statement in Denmark. *Accounting, Auditing & Accountability Journal, 30*(1), 38–64.

Paoloni, M., Coluccia, D., Fontana, S., & Solimene, S. (2020). Knowledge management, intellectual capital and entrepreneurship: A structured literature review. *Journal of Knowledge Management, 24*(8), 1797–1818.

Saint-Onge, H. (1996, April). Tacit knowledge: The key to the strategic alignment of intellectual capital. *Strategy & Leadership, 24*, 10–16.

Spender, J. C., & Grant, R. M. (1997). Knowledge and the firm: Overview. *Strategic Management Journal, 17*(Special Issue, Winter), 5–9.

Ståhle, P., & Bounfour, A. (2008). Understanding dynamics of intellectual capital of nations. *Journal of Intellectual Capital, 9*(2), 164–177.

Stewart, T. A. (1998). *Intellectual capital. The new wealth of organisations*. Nicholas Brealey Publishing.

Subramaniam, M., & Youndt, M. A. (2005). The influence of intellectual capital on the types of innovative capabilities. *Academy of Management Journal, 48*(3), 450–463.

Sveiby, K. E. (1997). *The new organizational wealth: Managing & measuring knowledge-based assets*. Berrett-Koehler Publishers.

Tidd, J., Bessant, J., & Pavitt, K. (2005). *Managing innovation: Integrating technological, market and organizational change* (3rd ed.). Wiley.

Youndt, M. A., Subramaniam, M., & Snell, S. A. (2004). Intellectual capital profiles: An examination of investments and returns. *Journal of Management Studies, 41*(2), 335–361.

D.Sc. Tomi Hussi is an entrepreneur running his own company ThinkFellows. In his role as a practical professional, Hussi's assignments mainly focus on consultancy, business coaching, and training. He has yet also actively participated in different research projects even during the recent years. Hussi's research interests focus on intellectual capital, knowledge management, personnel productivity, and employees' well-being. The foundations for these interests were laid during the first half of Hussi's career when he worked for 10 years as a researcher and team leader in various research organizations. Hussi's articles have been published in journals like *Journal of Knowledge Management, Journal of Intellectual Capital*, and *European Journal of Management*. Hussi has also contributed to edited books such as Intellectual Capital Revisited and Work Health and Management Control. Hussi is a sought-after speaker and esteemed expert. He is working mainly with people in managerial roles in larger organizations and executive teams. Within the intellectual capital framework, Hussi is especially interested in the relationship between IC and business activities, human capital and organizational performance, and IC and organizational renewal.

D.Sc. Aino Kianto is Full Professor of Knowledge Management at the LUT Business School, Lappeenranta-Lahti University of Technology (LUT), Finland. She is the leader of the LUT Knowledge Management Team, one of the world's leading academic laboratories working on knowledge-related management topics and executing the Master Programme on Knowledge Management and Leadership since 2001. Prof. Kianto's research focuses on knowledge management, intellectual capital, and innovation, resilience, and organizational renewal. Her research on these topics has been published widely and acknowledged with several international awards. Her papers have appeared in, for example, *Journal of Business Research, Technovation, R&D Management, Human Resource Management Journal, Journal of Knowledge Management, Journal of Intellectual Capital, and Accounting, Auditing, and Accountability Journal*. Prof. Kianto has delivered keynote speeches and acted as a track chair in many international conferences and currently serves in the editorial board of four academic journals. She promotes the transfer of research-based insights to work life by collaborating with companies and public organizations in research projects and consulting, press interviews, lectures in industry events, and teaching MSc and MBA courses. In the intellectual capital field, she is especially known for advancing the dynamic dimension of intellectual capital and her studies addressing the intersection of intellectual capital and knowledge management, innovation, and organizational performance.

Individual-Level Intellectual Capital: A Framework for Future Management and Reflection

Sanna Mari Alppivuori and Aino Kianto

Abstract

Since individuals play an important role as both reservoirs and operational implementers of organizational knowledge, individuals' intellectual capital should be a central interest in intellectual capital theory and practice. However, this seems not to have been the case, as only a small niche of research publications has examined the intellectual capital (IC) of individuals. This chapter builds on previous literature and a qualitative interview study among knowledge workers to propose a model for individual IC. In the model, five dimensions are outlined: human, structural, relational, renewal, and emotional capital, which span individual employees' intellectual capital-related resources. The chapter takes IC theory forward by deepening knowledge on individual aspects of intellectual capital, thus paving the way for its more holistic and systemic understanding. For IC practice, the chapter provides insights concerning managerial applications of the individual IC model.

1 Introduction

According to the knowledge-based view of organizing, individuals have a fundamental role in productive activities. It is the individual employees in an organization that know and can do and use their knowledge and abilities to create, share, and

S. M. Alppivuori (✉)
Communications & Marketing, Customer Experience, Sustainability, Enfo Oy, Espoo, Finland

A. Kianto
LUT Business School, LUT University, Lahti, Finland
e-mail: aino.kianto@lut.fi

A. Kianto et al. (eds.), *Futurizing Intellectual Capital*, Knowledge Management and Organizational Learning 15, https://doi.org/10.1007/978-3-031-80197-6_5

apply knowledge for producing goods and services—or don't (Grant, 1996). Thereby, individuals are the primary carriers, users, and producers of intellectual capital (IC) of the organization. Since individuals play an important role as both reservoirs and operational implementers of intellectual capital, individuals' intellectual capital should be a central interest in IC literature.

However, while IC has been largely and widely discussed as a concept relating to companies (Edvinsson & Malone, 1997; Bontis et al., 1999), non-profit and governmental organizations (Guthrie & Dumay, 2015; Secundo et al., 2018), as well as more macro-level entities such as cities, regions, ecosystems, nations, and even cross-national entities (Bonfour & Edvinsson, 2005; Schiuma et al. 2008; Bontis, 2004), it seems that a fundamental level of analysis has been largely overlooked: that of individuals. This is both surprising and worrying, since, after all, it is the individual people who are the actors that both carry and utilize intellectual capital to produce goods and services (Grant, 1996). Furthermore, as individuals within organizations and other social systems differ, neglecting the individual level of analysis also risks overlooking essential contingencies that fundamentally impact collective-level behaviours and outcomes, as well as optimal management mechanisms. Thus, we propose the futurizing of IC research by widening its scope to individual-level aspects of IC.

The small niche of research publications that have so far examined individual-level IC have proposed the view that the role and inclusion of individuals in IC are pivotal and that it is important to take care of personnel members and their competence and networks (e.g. Wang & Chang, 2005; Tomé et al., 2014; Naidenova et al., 2015; Vetrenko et al., 2017). For individuals personally, intellectual capital plays a crucial role in their success in the labour market (Lasisi et al., 2023; Reich & Kaarst-Brown, 2003). Overall, there seem to be many analytical and practical benefits to be had from an improved understanding of individual IC.

Hence, we argue that the individual knowledge worker perspective should be much better acknowledged in IC research—and related practice. To contribute to furthering this cause, we develop a model of individual-level IC that encompasses five dimensions. Specifically, we first review the past research on individual intellectual capital to summarize the existing understanding of individual-level intellectual capital. In our systematic review, only 15 topical previous studies were found, exemplifying the relative lack of interest in this analytical level of intellectual capital research. Then, we build on this understanding and report on an empirical study conducted by interviewing eight knowledge workers and, based on our findings, propose an amended model of the components of individual-level intellectual capital. The chapter concludes by presenting a theoretical model of the components of individual-level intellectual capital and discussing its contribution to futurizing IC theory and practice.

2 Literature Review on Individual Intellectual Capital

Intellectual capital is a collection of intangible resources, information, experience, and knowledge assets that an organization, community, country, or society possesses and uses to create economic, social, or environmental or use value (Dumay, 2016, 169). Intellectual capital has been examined especially as an organizational-level issue and, to some extent, also at a more macrolevel (ecosystem, region, national level) (e.g. Roos et al., 2005; Hussinki et al., 2017). There has been very little research into the individual level.

According to a widespread understanding, intellectual capital is divided into three parts: human capital, structural capital, and relational capital. The first element of the three-part breakdown is *human capital*, such as skills, personal traits, attitude, tacit knowledge, level of education, experience, and personal networks. The second element is *structural capital*, which includes values, culture, atmosphere, processes, systems, technologies, codified information, and intellectual property rights. The third element is *relational capital*. It covers relationships with customers, suppliers, resellers, media, potential partners, community, and other stakeholders, as well as co-operation agreements, image, and brand (e.g. Roos et al., 2005, 73–81). The essence of intellectual capital has originally been examined as a static organizational resource, but a later parallel concept is that of the dynamic nature of intellectual capital, which means that the elements of intellectual capital develop and interact as a kind of flow (Kianto, 2007; Bratianu, 2007, 2008). This viewpoint suggests an interconnected and interactive relationship between the IC of individuals and that of the organizations they inhabit.

Synthesizing from the definitions by Wang et al. (2018, 1204; 2019, 896; 2020, 1107), we conceptualize individual IC as the sum of knowledge, skills, and abilities held by an individual, which the individual uses to succeed in their work. To examine the existing research knowledge concerning this topic, we made a search in the Scopus database and found 15 articles to examine in more detail. Table 1 demonstrates the conceptualizations and models of individual IC presented in the earlier studies.

The previous studies can be seen to have appeared in four waves. The very first articles start to identify and recognize the presence of the individual level in the more general realm of the IC topic at large (Bratianu, 2007, 2008; Reiche et al., 2009). Bratianu (2007, 2008) emphasized the dynamic nature of intellectual capital and the interrelationships between its constituent elements and examined individual IC implicitly, as integrated into the organization's intellectual capital through employee knowledge, intelligence, and values. Reiche et al. (2009), in turn, highlighted the role of individuals in the creation of an organization's intellectual capital, especially based on diversity and wealth of individuals' knowledge, but did not explicitly discuss individual IC.

The next wave of studies started to examine value creation from the individual's perspective departing from the typical threefold categorization of IC into human, structural, and capital dimensions. These studies examine an individual's IC in a more focused manner. This group includes, e.g. Mura's and Longo's (2013) study

Table 1 Definition and structure of individual intellectual capital, summary of articles

Researchers	Year	Definition of individual intellectual capital	A view of the structure of Individual intellectual capital
Bratianu, C.	2007	Not defining IIC	Individual knowledge Individual intelligence Individual values *as integrators for intellectual capital*
Bratianu, C.	2008	Not defining IIC	Individual knowledge Individual intelligence Individual values *as integrators for intellectual capital*
Reiche, B. S., Harzing, A. W., & Kraimer, M. L.	2009	"Specifically, we define individual intellectual capital as an assignee's overall stock of knowledge, and interunit intellectual capital as the sum of knowledge that is collectively held across two MNE units"	*Individual intellectual capital* Knowledge volume Knowledge diversity Knowledge richness
Mura & Longo	8/2013	Not defining IIC	Human capital: innovation, intrinsic work reflection, practical application Structural capital: group cohesiveness, communication, trust, contributionRelational capital: networking and employee's perception of customers and consumers
Arenas, Griffiths & Freraut	10/2013	"IC is a recipe for personal business success that the individual designs through leveraging his knowledge, skills, networks and sense for innovation to enable him to achieve sustainable benefits"	Human capital: competencies, attitude, intellectual agility Relational capital: job search channels, attitude of social networks, membership [of] sports teams, objective use [of) email, interpersonal communication Renewal and development capital: internal, personal business, current development work Happiness: internal, family, social, professional
Tomé, Naidenova & Oskolkova	2014	Not defining IIC	Human capital: competence Structural capital: Individual intellectual property (IPRs) Relational capital: image and networks

(continued)

Table 1 (continued)

Researchers	Year	Definition of individual intellectual capital	A view of the structure of Individual intellectual capital
Naidenova, Parshakov, Zavertiaeva & Tomé	2015	Not defining IIC	Human capital: competence Structural capital: Individual intellectual property (IPRs) Relational capital: image and networks
Sultanova, G., Svyatov, S. and Ussenbayev, N.	2018	"IC at the individual level covers competencies (human capital), intellectual property (structural capital) as well as image and networks (relational capital) of persons"	Human capital Structural capital Relational capital Problem solving, critical thinking, and creativity mentioned as competencies
Wang, Bu & Cai	2018	"We define intellectual capital as the sum of dynamic knowledge owned or controlled by an individual, which constitutes his/her competitive advantage in his/her organization"	Individual human capital (IHC): the objective knowledge accumulated in the process of learning and working, including their experience, skills, attitude, talent, and intellectual agility Individual structural capital (ISC): the total of subjective knowledge that one obtains during the thought and cognitive process, which includes an individual's principles, standards, and methods Individual relational capital (IRC): the sum of knowledge of actual and potential resources embedded within a network of relationships owned by an individual or social unit

(continued)

Table 1 (continued)

Researchers	Year	Definition of individual intellectual capital	A view of the structure of Individual intellectual capital
Wang, Liu & Cai	2019	"The sum of dynamic knowledge owned or controlled by an individual, which can be leveraged to perform his/her job"	Individual human capital: – Suitable work experience – Professional skills – Academic ability – Problem-solving skills Individual structural capital: – Good methodology to deal with the problems – Mature thinking way of dealing with the problems – Clear decision logic to face change – Efficient operation procedures Individual relational capital: – Good collaborating skills to handle problems with others – Used to learning from others in workplace – Good relationship with my stakeholders – Good at communication with different people – Maintaining of appropriate interactions with different people
Wang, Cai, Liu, liu & Meng	2020	"The sum of knowledge and skills owned or controlled by individual employees"	Human capital Structural capital Relational capital
Wang, Cui, Cai, Ren	7/2021	According to Wang et al., 2018 to the definition and structure	According to Wang et al., 2018 to the definition and structure
Bu, Zhang, Li, Zhang	8/2021	According to Wang et al., 2018 to the definition and structure	According to Wang et al., 2018 to the definition and structure
Aprile, Nicoliello & Durst	10/2021	Not defining IIC	Human Capital – Natural capital Structural Capital – Sports capital Relational Capital – Media capital

(continued)

Table 1 (continued)

Researchers	Year	Definition of individual intellectual capital	A view of the structure of Individual intellectual capital
Wang, Cui, Cai & Ren	2022	IIC definitions on element level in description of structure	Individual human capital: the sum of objective knowledge obtained in the process of individual learning and working, such as intellect, technology and experience Individual structural capital: the sum of subjective knowledge accumulated in the process of thinking and cognition in work, such as principle, standard, and method Individual relational capita: the sum of knowledge of interpersonal interaction skills, network construction, and resource allocation, which is formed in the process of communicating and interacting with others in work

on the assessment and performance of individuals' intellectual capital, where they developed the IGIA index (Internally Generated Intangible Assets Index) to assist managers in measuring and monitoring individual intellectual. As typical, these researchers use the standard threefold definition of IC in human, structural, and relational dimensions (Tomé et al., 2014; Naidenova et al., 2015). In contrast, Arenas et al. (2013), focused on value creation from the individual's perspective and studied how individual intellectual capital is defined and whether the management and identification of one's own intellectual capital leads to personal benefits for the individual. They modified the standard approach by switching structural capital for renewal and development capital and adding happiness as a fourth element of their model.

The third group of studies builds on the standard vocabulary of IC discourse and systematizes the structure of individual IC (IIC) as *individual human capital, individual relational capital,* and *individual structural capital* to specifically apply to intangible capital at the level of employees and individuals (e.g. Tomé et al., 2014, Naidenova et al., 2015; Wang et al., 2018, 2019). Research endeavours have focused on establishing the role of three-partite IIC as an antecedent to such work-related behaviours and outcomes as creativity, self-, and team reflexivity (Wang et al., 2020), innovativeness (Wang et al., 2022), and employability (Sultanova et al., 2018). Overall, these studies confirm the versatile impact IIC has on various facets of individual capacity and performance.

As the only representative of the fourth wave, the last article relevant to the topic concerned the application of the concept of individual intellectual capital to elite sports Aprile et al. (2021) present a framework in which the traditional three-part structure of intellectual capital—human capital, structural capital, and relational capital—is transformed into *natural capital, sports capital,* and *media capital* and their sub-elements. The case study and simultaneous observational unit is one top-level individual athlete. The article states that the examination of individual intellectual capital is suitable for fields such as elite sports and other fields, where image and celebrity play a role. Aprile et al.'s study (2021) diverged from the previous articles in that they customized the dimensions of individual IC to the world of top sports. The main takeaway from their paper is that the nature of IIC differs according to the work context.

3 Research Methods: Empirical Study

There was only a limited amount of existing research and literature available on the topic of individual intellectual capital. For this reason, our study represents basic research aiming to produce a clearer understanding of the phenomenon under consideration and its structure. The choice of method—a qualitative empirical study—was particularly based on the fact that we wanted to investigate individuals' personal views of intellectual capital so that we could compare and combine them with the ideas offered by theory. An interview study was decided as a suitable method to meet the need to obtain primary data directly from the target group, who were knowledge workers in this case. The target group consisted of eight consultants in the information technology sector in Finland. Our assumption was that intellectual capital is important for people working as consultants, and knowledge workers have the ability to discuss, reflect, and verbalize related matters and their significance.

We used semi-structured interviews to collect data. The interview questions were targeted at those things that, according to the interviewees, enabled them to succeed in their work. The interview protocol included some specifications concerning aspects of individual IC that have been identified in previous empirical studies (e.g. Mura & Longo, 2013; Wang et al., 2018; Aprile et al., 2021), but interviewees were allowed to negate those and to expand to other topics.

We followed an abductive logic in our reasoning and analysis. The data was analysed with content analysis, proceeding by reducing expressions, categorizing, and grouping them, summarizing observations, and finally linking those back to the theory by abstraction. The analysis process began by identifying and then reducing to 1–3 codes the interviewees' expressions that were related to the research question. A total of 552 expressions were produced. A thematic coding process was subsequently carried out, in which the coded expressions were categorized into inductively formulated, data-driven themes. This initial coding was then refined in another thematic coding, which resulted in 45 categories. Some of the categories were labelled according to IC categories from the previous literature, but some themes rose from the data.

Finally, we took a theory-based approach and utilized the sub-elements that had emerged from the previous theory of intellectual capital as a framework for examining the constructed categories. At this stage, the process of examining the component categories, forming compilatory concepts, and linking them to theory became merged. After the third thematic coding and the last theory-based linking stage, the result was a total of 30 sub-elements of individual intellectual capital mentioned by the interviewees, which can be organized along five theoretical components of individual IC.

4 Findings Concerning the Components of the New Individual Intellectual Capital Model

Based on the empirically emerged categories and dialogue with the literature, our final model of individual intellectual capital features five components of individual IC, constructed by 30 sub-elements. In the following paragraphs, we will address each of the five components of individual IC.

When processing the results, we used various questions to challenge the data concerning the sub-elements. This resulted in a 2 × 2 matrix (Fig. 1: Structure of individual-level intellectual capital). With the help of the matrix, we produced an understanding of the structure of individual intellectual capital and the location of each sub-element in this structure. The 2 × 2 matrix was formed with the following main questions:

- Is this type of intellectual capital immediately and freely available to the individual? Is using and accumulating it dynamic and swift from an individual's perspective? Or, alternatively, is the intellectual capital in question tied to something, and released slowly or through more difficulty, or does it take longer to acquire or achieve it?
- Where is the impact of this intellectual capital directed? Is the impact and use directly directed to the individual and their intellectual capital or rather outwards and towards their performance and results or other individuals?

Table 2 summarizes the five components of the model of individual intellectual capital and all its sub-elements, together with a short definition and the sources that influenced each sub-element. In the remainder of this chapter, each sub-element is individually discussed.

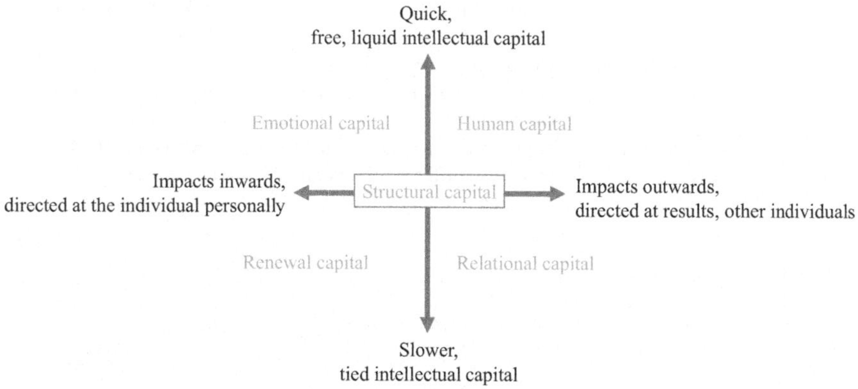

Fig. 1 Structure of individual-level intellectual capital

Table 2 Summary of the sub-elements of individual intellectual capital

Component	Sub-element	Sub-element description/ definition	Influential sources for sub-element
Human capital			
	Skills, competencies, and knowledge	A person's professional and academic skills, competence profile, abilities, and knowledge	Bratianu (2007, 2008), Arenas et al. (2013), Mura and Longo (2013), Wang et al. (2018, 2019), Tomé et al. (2014), Aprile et al. (2021)
	Personal traits and tendencies	Hereditary and accumulated tendencies and characteristics, traits, temperament, style of acting, and talent	Aprile et al. (2021)
	Experience	All the experience that a person has already accumulated and is constantly cumulating from different contexts	Wang et al. (2018), Tomé et al. (2014)
	Intellectual agility and thinking methods	Cognitive capability, attributes of thinking and intelligence, and mastered methods	Bratianu (2007, 2008), Arenas et al. (2013), Wang et al. (2018)
	Problem-solving skills	Ability to approach and solve different problems; decision-making logic	Wang et al. (2019)
	Wellbeing and recovering practices	A person's mental and physical wellbeing and recovering practices that support life management and coping at work	Arenas et al. (2013), Aprile et al. (2021)
	Attitudes	A person's attitudes and their impact on actions	Arenas et al. (2013), Wang et al. (2018)
	Creativity and development of ideas	Creative, participatory activities, brainstorming, insight, innovation	Mura and Longo (2013)
Relational capital			
	Personal networks and relations	The people a person knows, and the relationship network made up by them, the quality of relationships	Mura and Longo (2013), Arenas et al. (2013), Wang et al. (2019), Tomé et al. (2014), Aprile et al. (2021)
	Communication skills	Communication skills needed to achieve and maintain relational capital	Arenas et al. (2013), Wang et al. (2019), Tomé et al. (2014)
	Co-operation skills	Ability to act and adapt one's actions in different co-operative situations	Arenas et al. (2013), Wang et al. (2019)

(continued)

Table 2 (continued)

Component	Sub-element	Sub-element description/ definition	Influential sources for sub-element
	Networks as a source of information	The existing and potential opportunity to acquire and exchange information in a person's network	Wang et al. (2018)
	Participation and presence	Personal participation, input, and presence in each community, connecting to the community culture	Mura and Longo (2013), Wang et al. (2019), Tomé et al. (2014)
	Employee reputation	The perception, image and reputation formed of a person by others	Aprile et al. (2021), Tomé et al. (2014)
	Social media and publicity	Social media activity, media presence, media visibility, and publicity; has an impact on, e.g. reputation and networks	Aprile et al. (2021)
Structural capital			
	Working practices and methods	The practical means, processes, and methods for streamlining work developed by a person, such as time management, prioritisation, identification, and selection of the most suitable working methods, learning practices	Mura and Longo (2013), Wang et al. (2018), Aprile et al. (2021)
	Successes at work	Getting things done, finishing things, and making progress; highlights as well as more everyday results and outputs	Arenas et al. (2013), Aprile et al. (2021)
	Education	Education acquired by a person, including, e.g. degrees, courses, and more informal studies	Arenas et al. (2013), Naidenova et al. (2015), Vetrenko et al. (2017)
	Reflectivity	Ability to examine and assess one's own actions, strengths, development targets, and development	Mura and Longo (2013), Wang et al. (2020, 2021)
	Trust factors	Factors upholding trust, such as transparency, integrity, keeping promises, flexibility, personal approach, professionalism, consistent actions, and goodwill	Mura and Longo (2013)
	Tacit knowledge	Knowledge tied to the individual, often situation-specific; difficult to put into words and summarise, objective knowledge as a result of learning and working	Wang et al. (2018) (original definition by Michael Polanyi 1966)

(continued)

Table 2 (continued)

Component	Sub-element	Sub-element description/ definition	Influential sources for sub-element
	Codified information	In this context, information specifically documented and recorded by a person for their own use	Organisation-level models
	Values	Goal-oriented concepts and thinking models that guide an individual's actions and behaviour	Wang et al. (2018)
Renewal and development capital			
	Learning and development	Changes in thinking and actions, acquiring new information, knowledge, skills, competencies, and capabilities	Arenas et al. (2013), Wang et al. (2019)
	Resilience	Mental flexibility that is especially needed in situations involving change and adaptation and in recovering from them	Arenas et al. (2013)
	Career-thinking	Practical and business-oriented thinking and systematic approach related to one's career and how it is built	Arenas et al. (2013), Aprile et al. (2021)
Emotional capital			
	Emotions	Emotions and feelings experienced by an individual	E.g. Ekman (1992), Goleman (1999), Mayer et al. (2004), Sydänmaanlakka (2006), Volmer (2012), Fontaine et al. (2013)
	Recognizing emotions	Detecting one's own and others' feelings and emotions and the ability to name them	Goleman (1999, 2003), Mayer et al. (2004), Sydänmaanlakka (2006), Ashkanasy and Humphrey (2011), Kluemper et al. (2013)
	Managing emotions	Ability to manage impulses generated by one's emotions and to regulate one's behaviour and actions based on it	Mayer and Salovey (1993), Goleman (1999), Mayer et al. (2004), Sydänmaanlakka (2006), Kluemper et al. (2013)
	Utilizing emotions in action	Utilizing emotional knowledge in actions, ability to exert influence and produce desired reactions in others	Mayer et al. (2004), Goleman (1999), Sydänmaanlakka (2006)

4.1 Individual Human Capital

In the matrix of individual intellectual capital, human capital is located in the corner where capital is quickly and freely available and easy to realize. Its use is visible and impacts outwards from the individual to their performance and results. Individual human capital comprises eight sub-elements: *skills, competencies and knowledge, personal traits and tendencies, experience, intellectual agility and thinking methods, problem-solving skills, wellbeing and recovering practices, and creativity and development ideas*. The sub-elements have been formed by comparing and combining the views expressed in literature on individual human capital and the results of the empirical study.

The first sub-element of individual human capital is *skills, competencies, and knowledge*. They are an intrinsic part of an individual's intangible capital, and their necessity and presence in the model are very clear; this sub-element is mentioned in past models, both organizational- and individual-level ones. In the theory as well as the qualitative study, the sub-element of skills, competencies, and knowledge was one of the most frequently presented factors, and a relatively broad amount of vocabulary was attached to it, which is why the sub-element required a new summarizing title. This sub-element has been linked with words related to a similar element of capital expressed in eight source articles (Bratianu, 2007, 2008; Arenas et al., 2013; Wang et al., 2018, 2019, Tomé et al., 2014; Mura & Longo, 2013; Aprile et al., 2021), and the sub-elements have also been reflected organisation-level elements. Some of the words have been direct matches and therefore straightforwardly linked, and in addition to these, the words *practical application* (Mura & Longo, 2013) and *objective knowledge as a result of learning and working* (Wang et al., 2018) have been linked to this sub-element that brings together skills and competences. The sub-element has a strong link to on-the-job learning as well (e.g. Grönfors, 2010). Capabilities are also a sub-element typically mentioned at the organizational level.

In the theory, the second sub-element of *personal traits and tendencies* was for example called talent and original characteristics (Wang et al., 2018; Aprile et al., 2021). Talent and personal tendencies can partly be improved by their holder while partly being determined by the genome. In this sub-element, we also include the characteristics presented by Aprile et al. (2021). Talent and tendencies are closely linked to individuals. From the organization-level sub-elements of human intellectual capital, matching content has been merged with personal characteristics. The results from the empirical study introduced a view on how an individual's early interest in a certain field or subject matter may support intellectual capital. It is about tendencies, which are also linked to the sub-element of career-thinking in renewal capital. We regarded "talent" as a rather demanding term in the sense of vocabulary. Is everybody talented? The interviewees did not mention the word even once. For these reasons, we wanted to neutralize the title of the sub-element and, in the evolution of the results, we deliberately made it more easily approachable. Thus, our solution was the title personal traits and tendencies.

The third sub-element is *experience* (Wang et al., 2018), which we included in the model because of its relevance for the individual level. It persisted as an element from organization-level models and, in a way, went through the research process with no changes, which we consider natural and self-evident. Experience inevitably increases an individual's intellectual capital, and it is also included in organizational models. Another part of the experience can also be interpreted to be the diversity and richness of knowledge presented by Reiche et al. (2009, 514).

The fourth sub-element is *intellectual agility and thinking methods*. Intellectual agility has been presented by Arenas et al. (2013) and subsequently by Wang et al. (2018). Bratianu (2007, 2008) also highlighted intelligence as an integrator of individual intellectual capital. Aprile et al. (2021) present "original characteristics" as a sub-element of natural capital, which can be broadly interpreted as covering intellectual capacity and potential. The empirical study enriched this element, as the interviewees highlighted not only agility but also different approaches related to thinking (analytical, systematic, subconscious, etc.), which is why intellectual agility was complemented with thinking methods.

The fifth sub-element is *problem-solving skills* (Wang et al., 2019; Sultanova et al., 2018), which is not part of organizational human capital but appears as a significant resource at the individual level. Problem-solving skills (Wang et al., 2019) received a clear confirmation, especially from the knowledge workers who were the target group of this study.

The sixth sub-element is *wellbeing and recovering practices*. The interviewees highlighted the importance of taking care of oneself and having sufficient recovery as a counterbalance to the work. This sub-element resonates with Arenas et al.'s (2013) ideas on happiness as a dimension of IIC and Aprile et al.'s (2021) emphasis on wellbeing and lifestyle as IIC components. This sub-element is undoubtedly very important for non-knowledge workers as well. Balance and wellbeing are essential positive sub-elements of IIC.

The seventh sub-element is *attitudes*, inherited from the organizational level and presented at the individual level by Bratianu (2007, 2008), Arenas et al. (2013), and Wang et al. (2018). It is likely not possible to separate this element from an individual's actions.

The eighth sub-element is *creativity and initiative*. We first processed this sub-element under the title creativity and development ideas, but processing the individual level and the progress of the empirical study shaped the element of development ideas into the initiative. Keeping innovation, creativity, and development ideas—which were used as the foundation—as a separate sub-element would have created an unnecessary overlap. The empirical study confirmed the need for this element. The creativity and initiative presented for renewal capital at the organisational level (Hussinki et al., 2017) were included, and the innovation presented for individuals by Mura and Longo (2013) was merged with it. Sultanova et al. (2018, 119) present creativity as an individual's competence. Innovation is the ability to create new things and put them into practice. Our interpretation was that innovation manifests more as *activities* at the organizational level, and individuals are linked to it via their creativity and initiative-based development ideas.

4.2 Individual Relational Capital

The next component in the model of individual intellectual capital is relational capital. Relational capital has a particular outward impact on the individual, and it takes time to form it and unlock its potential. The accumulation and release of relational capital are tied to other individuals. This is why relational capital is placed in the bottom right corner of the model (see Fig. 1). Relational capital comprises seven sub-elements: *personal networks and relations, communication skills, co-operation skills, networks as a source of information, participation and presence, employee reputation,* and *social media and publicity*. In the theory, a large number of sub-elements were associated with relational capital, especially by Arenas et al. (2013), Wang et al. (2019), and Aprile et al. (2021). When preparing the model, we considerably summarised the sub-element potential offered by the theory.

The first sub-element of relational capital is *personal networks and relations*, the presence of which can be regarded as almost indisputable. Networks include current and former colleagues, customers, suppliers, different communities, and more. Relationships and networks as part of relational capital have been presented by most authors addressing individual intellectual capital (Arenas et al., 2013; Mura & Longo, 2013; Tomé et al., 2014; Wang et al., 2018, 2019). Reiche et al. (2009) researched individual intellectual capital from a social perspective. Relationships are also strongly highlighted in numerous models of organizational relational capital (e.g. Roos et al., 2005; Hussinki et al., 2017).

The second sub-element of individual relational capital is *communication skills*. These skills could also be regarded as part of the human capital component, but because they have such a strong outward-directed impact from the individual, require a recipient or another party to be realized, and enable the creation of relational capital, we have placed them as part of relational capital. This understanding is also consistent with authors who have previously addressed individual relationship capital (e.g. Arenas et al., 2013; Wang et al., 2018, 2019; Reiche et al., 2009). Communication skills are not usually expressed with this kind of precision at the organizational level, but for individuals, the role of communication skills in relational activities is undeniable and therefore constitutes a separate sub-element.

As the third sub-element, we present *co-operation skills*, which originate from Wang et al. (2019), who brought up the element of "good co-operation skills for solving problems with others". The benefits of relational capital are reaped in co-operation with others, and there are often various challenges and problems that require solving. In our view, communication alone is not enough for successful co-operation, but co-operation skills are additionally necessary as a separate sub-element.

Networks as a source of information is the fourth sub-element of relational capital. It contains the possibilities of new information and is in itself a description of the value of a network to its holder. An individual can benefit from their network in many ways and find satisfaction for various needs, but this study focuses especially on the information and resources needed in the context of business and work life. This sub-element combines, for example, the job search channels and memberships presented by Arenas et al. (2013) and the opportunities for information acquisition and exchange presented by Wang et al. (2018, 2019) and the opportunities for increasing the amount and wealth of information presented by Reiche et al. (2009). In addition, when widening the scope of interpretation, we can add the identification of new business opportunities, which Hussinki et al. (2017) presented as part of entrepreneurship capital. From the perspective of knowledge workers, a particular value of networks was the information potential that helps to carry out and solve a specific task or problem. In our view, it is important to understand information as a broad concept in the context of the model of individual intellectual capital. For example, in sales, information from a worker's network can help them identify what the customer really wants and needs, who makes the decisions, and what kind of offer the customer would appreciate.

As the fifth sub-element of individual relational capital, we present *employee reputation*. In this category, we condense reputation, image, and popularity, which have been presented as part of intellectual capital in several sources (Aprile et al., 2021; Tomé et al., 2014), and we bring it to the context of work. Based on the results, others' perception of a person, their reputation, and image—i.e. employee reputation—has an impact on assigned work roles and finding employment, for example. The next sub-element, *social media and publicity*, can strengthen employee reputation when used correctly.

The sixth sub-element is *social media and publicity*. Especially Aprile et al. (2021) strongly highlighted factors related to both reputation and public relations and the media as individual intangible resources. In the model of individual intellectual capital, we distinguish between employee reputation—the earned or assigned image associated with a person—and social media and publicity, i.e. a person's visibility in different public avenues. Individuals' opportunities and means for influencing these two sub-elements differ. An individual will have an employee reputation in their own network, even without publicity. Social media and publicity and their utilization are partly under the control of the individual, and these tools can either support or weaken the individual's capital.

The empirical study supplemented individual relational capital with a new sub-element that had not been mentioned previously in the theory. In the experience of the knowledge workers, individual relational capital requires *participation and presence* in order to be realized. This observation by the interviewees is good and important. Presence and participation are intangible, but individuals can personally regulate their quantity and quality. We considered the research findings essential and consistent with our model and included the element in the model.

4.3 Individual Structural Capital

Individual structural capital is placed at the centre of the model, having an impact in all directions. In the case of the individual, it forms a kind of platform where the individual can use the sub-elements of structural capital to strengthen and use their other components of intellectual capital. From past literature, we identified 13 sub-elements of individual structural capital, of which we filtered eight sub-elements into our model, supported by the results of the empirical study. The eight sub-elements are as follows: *working practices and methods, successes at work, education, reflectivity, trust factors, tacit knowledge, codified information, and values*. The elements are self-explanatory, and many of them can also be found at the organizational level. As a special feature, the individual level included the results, significance, and successes at work as well as reflectivity. Successes at work create a motivating experience for the individual and thus long-lasting structural capital. Management practices can also directly influence the empowerment of individuals in this area.

The first sub-element is *working practices and methods*, whose equivalent at the organizational level is processes, systems, and technologies (e.g. Roos et al., 2005, 73–81). In publications discussing individual structural capital, closely related concepts included standards, methods (Wang et al., 2018) and good problem-solving methodology, mature thinking, decision-making logic, and effective operational practices (Wang et al., 2019).

The second sub-element is *successes at work*. This sub-element, which expresses the positive and motivating experience base accumulated by an individual, was most strongly influenced by the victories and sports successes mentioned by Aprile et al. (2021) that drive an elite athlete forward. This sub-element includes results achieved at work and their direct and perceived significance. It can also be directly linked to the everyday life of knowledge workers. The selection of this sub-element was also reflected in the happiness factors used by Arenas et al. (2013), such as internal happiness and professional happiness, which are, however, more prominently reflected in the balance and wellbeing sub-element under the human capital component.

The third sub-element of structural capital linked to the individual, which typically takes an individual both time and energy to acquire and whose impact is released in several directions, is *education*. Education as such has previously been brought up at the individual level by Naidenova et al. (2015) and in the context of goal-oriented sports-related training by Aprile et al. (2021). The educational background tied to individuals has typically been included in organizational capital, and the inclusion of education in individual structural capital was almost self-evident.

The fourth sub-element is *reflectivity*, which was pioneered by Mura and Longo (2013) as part of their model of human intellectual capital at the individual level. Although Wang et al. (2019) did not include reflectivity in their model, they researched its important role as part of individual performance. In our view, it was natural to include this important separate ability as a sub-element of the model; after all, reflection as a kind of meta-ability helps the individual to assess and work on their intellectual capital. Through reflection, individuals can assess their own actions and identify their weaknesses, strengths, and development targets.

The fifth sub-element relates to trust—already highlighted by Mura and Longo (2013) in the first publication concerning the individual level—which we refer to as *trust factors*. Individual-level trust factors include consistent actions and goodwill combined with competence (e.g. Blomqvist, 1997, 282).

The sixth sub-element is *tacit knowledge*, which in itself is tied to individuals and which Wang et al. (2018) included under the title of subjective knowledge. However, we are reverting the title back to tacit knowledge, which has been commonly used in the organization-level model and thus links the examination of the different levels together.

The seventh sub-element of individual structural capital is *codified information*. Although the amount of codified information may be significantly lower at the individual level than at the organisational level, it should be mentioned as part of structural capital. Similar to tacit knowledge, this sub-element is inherited from organisational structural capital to the individual-level model. For knowledge workers, codified information appeared to have relatively small importance, which they justified with factors such as information becoming quickly outdated and the constant availability of searchable information. However, we would not exclude this sub-element from the model. The sub-element also has a reference point in the SECI model by Nonaka and Takeuchi, to which we have not gone in detail in this study (e.g. Nonaka et al., 2000, 12).

The eighth sub-element is *values*, in which we have combined the individual's principles presented by Wang et al. (2018), the individual values presented by Bratianu (2007, 2008), and the concept of value commonly used in organizational intellectual capital. In terms of values, an interesting finding from the interviews was the aspect of representativeness, which meant for the interviewees that if the values represented by the employer conflicted with their own values, they would not want to be involved.

4.4 Individual Renewal Capital

Individual renewal capital refers to an individual's ability to renew, develop, and change. Renewal capital first impacts the individual personally and the other components of their intellectual capital. It typically takes time and effort to accumulate, release, and implement the three sub-elements of renewal capital, *learning and development, resilience, and career-thinking*. These aspects are clarified by the additional questions used to construct the model. Renewal capital is placed in the bottom left corner of the model (Fig. 1). Organizations need to be able to renew, and Hussinki et al. (2017) outlined the elements of organization-level capacity for renewal as the acquisition of new information, a learning organization and creativity and initiative. Employees as individuals are poised to implement this with their own renewal capital, which impacts them personally while also indirectly impacting the organization's renewal development.

The first sub-element of renewal capital is *learning and development*, which was presented at an early stage by Arenas et al. (2013) under the title of development work. Wang et al. (2019) also refer to an element of learning from others. Knowledge workers involved in consulting are very willing to learn new things and develop. This feature is combined with career-thinking, in which the interests that people have from a young age steer them towards their field.

The second sub-element is *resilience*, the roots of which are in the internal capacity for renewal presented by Arenas et al. (2013), now named resilience to align more closely with the vocabulary currently associated with the subject matter. Resilience refers to mental flexibility that is especially needed in situations involving change and adaptation and in recovering from these situations. Resilience benefits individuals in adapting to changes in their operating environment and in achieving personal wellbeing.

The third sub-element is the *career-thinking* done by individuals. Its background is most directly influenced by the personal business presented by Arenas et al. (2013), which they used to describe career-related ambition and pursuit and reaping the economic results of one's own potential. A similar phenomenon was described by Aprile et al. (2021) in the context of elite athletes' professional choices, team choices, and competition choices. This sub-element was formed by combining past results and interview results and applying the sub-element as a concept suitable for the background of a knowledge worker. Although some of the interviewees reported that coincidence had had a fairly large impact, they felt that they had discovered their field by identifying their areas of strength, which later has facilitated career-thinking. For the knowledge workers, the deliberateness of career-thinking seemed to increase with age. Here we can note a clear link between the above and the sub-element of reflectivity included in structural capital. From these aspects and on the basis of a broader analysis of the sub-elements, we gave the sub-element the more generally applicable title of career-thinking.

4.5 Individual Emotional Capital

The fifth component of the model of individual intellectual capital is emotional capital. Previous research has ignored the existence of emotions as part of the intangible capital of individuals. A perceivable distant connection could be found in the thoughts about happiness by Arenas et al. (2013). For individual intellectual capital, the special value arises from recognizing the presence of emotions and emotional capital in individual intellectual capital and taking it into account as part of the entirety of an individual. At the same time, it offers an interface between the model of intellectual capital and the broad field of theory concerning emotions, linking these concepts together. In the future, this will enable more holistic and versatile discourse and the management of individual intellectual capital. It is about positioning and the fact that the consideration of organizational resource-based intellectual capital has previously ignored emotions. The four sub-elements of emotional capital are *emotions, recognizing emotions, managing emotions, and utilizing emotions in action*.

At the beginning of this section, we will briefly examine the field of emotions and emotional leadership in general. The background of this component has not been addressed in the past theory on intellectual capital, and it was only included in this study as it arose during the development of the model. Ashforth and Humphrey (1995, 97) have stated that emotions are an integral part of organizational life, and emotions are often beneficial to an organization. In an organization, emotions occur at several levels. For example, Ashkanasy and Humphrey (2011, 215–216) present five levels of occurrence: situation-specific within a person, emotional differences between persons, dyadic interactions between individuals, team and group level, and organization-wide.

As a basis for forming emotional capital, we use a combination of the classifications by Mayer et al. (2004) and Goleman (1999), and we summarize emotional capital to cover the *emotions* and emotional intelligence of an individual, which is divided into three parts: *recognizing emotions* (one's own and others'), *managing emotions,* and *utilizing emotions in action.* "Emotional intelligence is the ability to recognize and interpret one's own emotions and those of others and to utilize this knowledge in one's own thinking and actions and in interaction with others" (Sydänmaanlakka, 2006, 301). Emotions and experiencing them are the intangible property of an individual and thus part of individual emotional capital. However, emotions as such are not enough to be examined at the level of intellectual capital, and it is essential to link emotional intelligence with emotional capital. This emphasizes the individual's ability to influence the content of their emotional capital and its utilization. If, on the other hand, emotional capital was reduced to just emotional intelligence, one could ask why not link it to individual human capital (competencies/intelligence). Altogether, the above justifies the inclusion and placement of emotional capital in the model. Emotional capital is located in the corner of the model where individual intellectual capital is free and quick and has a primary and immediate impact on the individual personally. It is clear that when an individual's emotions cause actions, they also secondarily impact other people, such as other members of the work community. Behaviour creates behaviour (Juuti & Salmi, 2014, 97–99). Because emotions lead to different reactions, they also have a positive or negative impact on the individual's situation-specific ability to use the other sub-elements and resources of their individual intellectual capital.

In our model, individual emotional capital consists of the following:

- Emotions.
- Recognizing emotions (one's own and others').
- Managing emotions.
- Utilizing emotions in action.

The knowledge workers confirmed that emotions are strongly involved in their work and must be addressed, no matter how reluctantly. An individual's personal emotions have an acute impact on work efficiency and results, and everyone will also have to process others' emotions. According to the interviewees, these situations involve perceiving and receiving customers' emotions and supporting colleagues, for example. We noted that received emotions were more often described as negative or being related to frustration than positive feelings. On the other hand, the interviewees said that experiences of success are motivating. At the sub-element level, this is linked to the results, significance, and successes at work sub-element of structural capital, which again strengthens the understanding of the dynamic interaction of the sub-elements of intellectual capital.

5 Conclusions

IC has been studied intensively at organizational and macro levels for decades, but although individuals are the key carriers and the sole implementors of IC, their viewpoint has been left relatively more in the shade. This chapter addressed individual IC as the sum of knowledge, skills, and abilities held by an individual, which the individual uses to succeed in their work. A model for understanding the structure of individual-level IC was developed that specified the construct to include five facets: human, relational, structural, renewal, and emotional capital.

These five dimensions of IIC can be further classified according to their:

1. Rigid vs. dynamic nature.
2. Inwards vs. outwards influence.

Based on this elaboration, the full model of IIC is presented in Fig. 2. Human capital is placed as liquid capital with an outwards, dynamic impact on results. Relational capital, on the other hand, is outward-facing capital that impacts other people and is tied to networks, placed at the bottom right corner of the matrix. For individuals, relational capital is always directed outwards, either as an activity (e.g. networking) or related to impact (e.g. image, reputation), and it is thus always external. Renewal capital is a factor that impacts the individual and their actions and performance with some delay and thus belongs to the bottom left corner of the

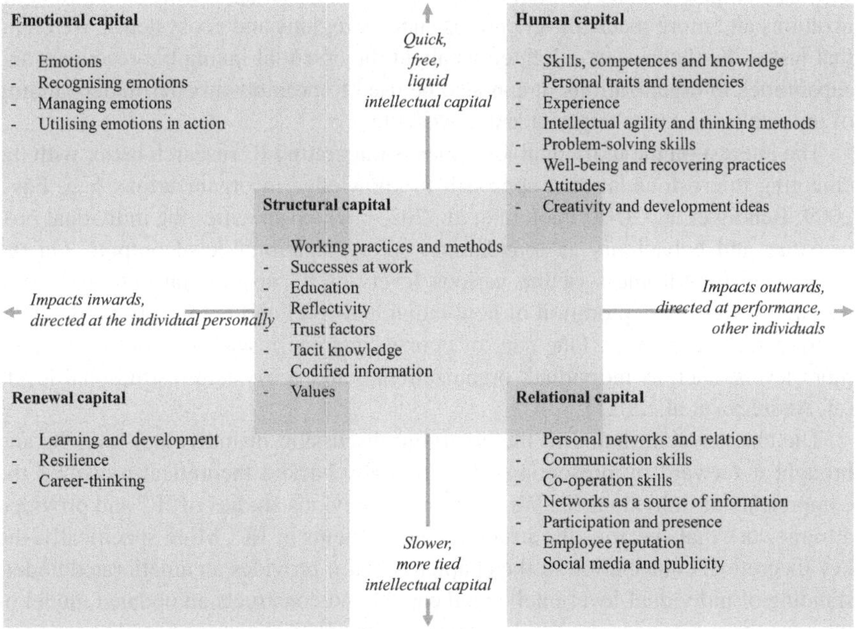

Fig. 2 New model of individual intellectual capital

matrix. Structural capital has an impact in several directions, and it also contains both tied and more free-moving elements. Therefore, its placement is at the centre of the matrix. Structural capital is a kind of platform for an individual's actions, acting as the foundation for building on and holding up the individual who uses the tools that structural capital makes available. The fifth component is free, quick, and inward-directed emotional capital. Emotions are within the individual and specific to the individual.

5.1 Contributions to Futurizing IC Theory

A significant part of intellectual capital is tied to individuals, but there has been very little previous research into individual intellectual capital, with neglect of individuals' perspective and hardly any consideration of its structure (e.g. Roslender & Fincham, 2001; Aprile et al., 2021). The study at hand addressed this research gap and produced new knowledge by examining individual intellectual capital from the employee perspective and by presenting a five-part model of the structure and components of individual IC. The overall contribution of our chapter for futurizing intellectual capital lies in emphasizing the necessity of better recognizing the level of individual propensities in IC research and practice. For IC theory, this means acknowledging the role of individuals more clearly.

Hence, we propose a future emphasis on employees for IC theory, as individual carriers and executors of IC, and their individual knowledge resources and abilities. This new emphasis will complement the more traditional approaches to IC in organizations and more macro-level entities such as regions and ecosystems. We claim that just as IC theory can enlighten us about the essential intangible resources and capabilities in organizations, it can also be used to promote a better understanding of individuals in knowledge-intensive worklife.

The interest on the individual level means integrating IC research better with the emerging micro-foundational approach to knowledge in organizations (e.g. Foss, 2009; Bendig et al., 2018; Paoloni et al., 2023), which specifies the individual propensities and behaviours as foundations of organizational-level outputs. On the other hand, mindfulness of the various levels of IC inspires an enticing future research direction: exploration of how individual-level and organizational-level IC interact with each other. One can, of course, imagine research models with even more levels, such as individual, organizational, and ecosystem/institutional levels (cf. Andreeva et al., 2021).

The chapter contributed to the emerging discussion of individual-level IC and brought it forward by presenting an empirically backed theoretical model of the components of individual IC. We built on the previous studies of IIC and provided a framework that specifies the structure and elements of IIC. More specifically, the key theoretical contribution of the chapter is that it provides an ameliorated understanding of individual-level intellectual capital and constructs an updated model of its constituent components. We demonstrated that IIC consists of five main components: individual human, relational, structural, renewal, and emotional capitals.

Furthermore, the new dimension of emotional capital was constructed and brought up as a novel element of IIC. This insight into integrating emotions into IC creates a new and exciting interface between academic discussions on IC and emotions. Also, renewal capital has been left in the shade in earlier works on IIC. A better acknowledgement especially of these two novel IIC dimensions will hopefully support the IC research to better acknowledge human beings in all their complexity as in the centre of IC, emotions, and all included. In the future, this will enable more holistic and versatile discourse in IC management.

Finally, as the management of IC can greatly benefit from being able to measure and monitor IC elements, the development of IIC metrics presents a potentially very fruitful future research avenue. The classification of IIC presented in this paper demonstrates the features of IIC to be operationalized into measurement indicators to assess the level of IIC. In addition, a 360-degree type of empirical approach involving information collection from a wider set of stakeholders could be used to complement the self-assessments in order to provide a more reliable evaluation of IIC. Finally, the model presented in this chapter can be implemented to examine IIC in various types of professions and organizations to validate its applicability and usefulness in different contexts.

5.2 Contributions to Futurizing IC Practice

This study also has several implications for futurizing IC practice. First, for practicing managers, it is essential to understand that individuals' knowledge, skills, and abilities are decisive for organizational value creation. Even if the interviewees in our study were knowledge workers in the information technology sector, we suggest that the IIC model itself is applicable also to freelancers, gig workers, key opinion leaders, and specialists in many types of fields and professions. After all, it is individuals who either use their IC for productive purposes and who either know and can do what they need at work - or don't.

The presented framework of five IIC dimensions guides to understanding what kind of knowledge and abilities are needed from individuals in dynamic knowledge-intensive worklife: technical skills and substance and knowledge, networks and collaboration skills, work methods and practices, resilience and development, and managing emotions. Having a deeper comprehension of the essential facets of individual IC is useful for both leadership and management of knowledge-intensive organizations.

The components of intellectual capital are strongly and dynamically interactive and create value for both their holder and their operating environments. The five-fold framework of IIC suggests taking the individual into account as a whole, not forgetting their emotions. The new element of emotional IIC suggests that acknowledging the role of emotions in the worklife and paying conscious management attention to them is useful also for knowledge-based operations. Thus, managers would be wise to include recognition and dealing with emotions in their activities.

Finding the right talents and identifying potential competence is essential for companies. The model of individual intellectual capital can be applied for example in recruitment, both for application profiling and as background material for interview frameworks. The codification of an individual's IC elements enables the analysis of the core competencies that are important for the success of a particular activity or profession, and the identification of these elements also provides opportunities for increasing equality (Tomé et al., 2014, 189).

From a managerial perspective, a deeper understanding of individuals' intellectual capital supports, for example, recruitment and personnel development investment decisions and activities. It can be applied to increase individual commitment and to fully capitalize on individuals' potential. When both management and employees are aware of the essence of IIC, it is possible to achieve more successful employment relationships, for example, through achieving congruence between the values of individuals and organizations (Edwards & Cable, 2009). This knowledge will help also to tie individual IC to organizational-level strategic management of IC (Vătămănescu et al., 2023).

From an individual employee's perspective, identifying one's own IIC can be seen as an exercise in reflection with a positive connection to performance (Wang et al., 2020). In a recruitment situation, the baseline is the IC the individual brings with them at the time of recruitment. Subsequently, IC can be developed in co-operation through workplace learning as well as training and development activities (Coyte, 2019; Noe et al., 2003).

Another important contribution of the model presented in this chapter is that it can be used to support both individual as well as organizational IC management by providing a tool for self-reflection. On an individual level, a knowledge worker may reflect upon the IIC elements that bring the most value to their work. The model can also be used as a template for organizing dialogue in the work group or organization to discuss the key facets of needed intangible resources in different work roles, acknowledging organizational strategy and other contextual contingencies.

In sum, practice-wise, the presented model of individual intellectual capital can be applied by organizations to better assess and manage the intangible resources of their current and potential employees and by individuals to reflect upon and strengthen their personal intellectual capital. This will benefit the overall relevance of the intellectual capital-based approach to management and organizing and work life in general.

References

Andreeva, T., Garanina, T., Sáenz, J., Aramburu, N., & Kianto, A. (2021). Does country environment matter in the relationship between intellectual capital and innovation performance? *Journal of Business Research, 136*, 263–273.

Aprile, R., Nicoliello, M., & Durst, S. (2021). Framing intellectual capital for elite athletes. *Journal of Intellectual Capital, 23*(7), 1–17. https://doi.org/10.1108/jic-05-2021-0126

Arenas, T., Griffiths, P., & Freraut, A. (2013, January). An individual-centred model of intellectual capital. In *Proceedings of the 10th international conference on intellectual capital, knowledge management & organisational learning* (pp. 46–54).

Ashforth, B. E., & Humphrey, R. H. (1995). Emotion in the workplace: A reappraisal. *Human Relations, 48*(2), 97–125.

Ashkanasy, N. M., & Humphrey, R. H. (2011). Current emotion research in organizational behavior. *Emotion Review, 3*(2), 214–224. https://doi.org/10.1177/1754073910391684

Bendig, D., Strese, S., Flatten, T. C., Da Costa, M. E. S., & Brettel, M. (2018). On micro-foundations of dynamic capabilities: A multi-level perspective based on CEO personality and knowledge-based capital. *Long Range Planning, 51*(6), 797–814.

Blomqvist, K.-M. (1997). The many faces of trust. *Scandinavian Journal of Management, 13*(3), 271–286. https://doi.org/10.1016/S0956-5221(97)84644-1

Bonfour, A., & Edvinsson, L. (Eds.). (2005). *Intellectual capital for communities*. Elsevier.

Bontis, N., Dragonetti, N. C., Jacobsen, K., & Roos, G. (1999). The knowledge toolbox: A review of the tools available to measure and manage intangible resources. *European Management Journal, 17*(4), 391–402. https://doi.org/10.1016/S0263-2373(99)00019-5

Bontis, N. (2004). National intellectual capital index: a United Nations initiative for the Arab region. *Journal of Intellectual Capital, 5*(1), 13–39.

Bratianu, C. (2007). An integrated perspective on the organizational intellectual capital. *Review of Management and Economical Engineering, 6*(5), 107–112.

Bratianu, C. (2008). A dynamic structure of the organizational intellectual capital. In M. Naaranoja (Ed.), *Knowledge management in organizations* (pp. 233–243). University of Vaasa.

Coyte, R. (2019). Enabling management control systems, situated learning and intellectual capital development. *Accounting, Auditing & Accountability Journal, 32*(4), 1073–1097.

Dumay, J. (2016). A critical reflection on the future of intellectual capital: From reporting to disclosure. *Journal of Intellectual Capital, 17*(1), 168–184. https://doi.org/10.1108/jic-08-2015-0072

Edvinsson, L., & Malone, M. S. (1997). *Intellectual capital: Realizing your company's true value by finding its hidden brainpower*. Harper Business.

Edwards, J. R., & Cable, D. M. (2009). The value of value congruence. *Journal of Applied Psychology, 94*(3), 654.

Ekman, P. (1992). Are There Basic Emotions? *Psychologist Review, 99*(3), 550–553.

Fontaine, J. J. R., Scherer, K. R., & Soriano, C. (2013). Components of emotional mean-ing: A sourcebook. *Oxford University Press*. https://doi.org/10.1093/acprof:oso/9780199592746.001.0001

Foss, N. (2009). Alternative research strategies in the knowledge movement: From macro bias to micro-foundations and multi-level explanation. *European Management Review, 6*(1), 16–28.

Goleman, D. (1999). *Tunneäly työelämässä.* (Working with emotional intelligence.) Keuruu. Otavan Kirjapaino Oy.

Grant, R. M. (1996). Toward a knowledge-based theory of the firm. *Strategic Management Journal, 17*(S2), 109–122.

Grönfors, T. (2010). *Työssä oppiminen – avain tuottavuuteen*. Kauppakamari.

Guthrie, J., & Dumay, J. (2015). New frontiers in the use of intellectual capital in the public sector. *Journal of Intellectual Capital, 16*(2), 258–266.

Hussinki, H., Ritala, P., Vanhala, M., & Kianto, A. (2017). Intellectual capital, knowledge management practices and firm performance. *Journal of Intellectual Capital, 18*(4), 904–922. https://doi.org/10.1108/jic-11-2016-0116

Juuti, P., & Salmi, P. (2014). *Tunteet ja työ. Uupumuksesta iloon*. PS-kustannus.

Kianto, A. (2007). What do we really mean by the dynamic dimension of intellectual capital? *International Journal of Learning and Intellectual Capital, 4*(4), 342–356.

Kluemper, D. H., DeGroot, T., & Choi, S. (2013). Emotion management ability: Predicting task performance, citizenship, and deviance. *Journal of Management, 39*(4), 878–905. https://doi.org/10.1177/0149206311407326

Lasisi, T. T., Lazareva, E. I., Abramyan, G. A., Gavrilova, J. V., & Murzin, A. D. (2023). Intellectual capital and technology as factors of career success: Role of income inequality. *Economies, 11*(2), 63.

Mayer, J. D., & Salovey, P. (1993). The intelligence of emotional intelligence. *Intelligence, 17*(4), 433–442. https://doi.org/10.1016/0160-2896(93)90010-3

Mayer, J. D., Salovey, P., & Caruso, D. R. (2004). Emotional intelligence: Theory, findings, and implications. *Psychological Inquiry, 15*(3), 197–215.

Mura, M., & Longo, M. (2013). Developing a tool for intellectual capital assessment: An individual-level perspective. *Expert Systems, 30*(5), 436–450. https://doi.org/10.1111/j.1468-0394.2012.00650.x

Naidenova, I., Parshakov, P., Zavertiaeva, M., & Tomé, E. (2015). Look for people, not for alpha: Mutual funds success and managers intellectual capital. *Measuring Business Excellence, 19*(4), 57–71. https://doi.org/10.1108/MBE-11-2014-0039

Noe, R. A., Colquitt, J. A., Simmering, M. J., & Alvarez, S. A. (2003). *Developing intellectual and social capital.* The organizational frontiers series, 209.

Nonaka, I., Toyama, R., & Konno, N. (2000). SECI, Ba and leadership: A unified model of dynamic knowledge creation. *Long Range Planning, 33*(1), 5–34. https://doi.org/10.1016/S0024-6301(99)00115-6

Paoloni, P., Massaro, M., Dal Mas, F., & Bagnoli, C. (2023). Microfoundations of intellectual capital. Evidence from Italian small accounting firms. *Knowledge Management Research & Practice, 21*(4), 725–737.

Reich, B. H., & Kaarst-Brown, M. L. (2003). Creating social and intellectual capital through IT career transitions. *The Journal of Strategic Information Systems, 12*(2), 91–109.

Reiche, B. S., Harzing, A. W., & Kraimer, M. L. (2009). The role of international assignees' social capital in creating inter-unit intellectual capital: A cross-level model. *Journal of International Business Studies, 40*, 509–526.

Roos, G., Pike, S., & Fernstöm, L. (2005). *Managing intellectual capital in practise*. Elsevier.

Roslender, R., & Fincham, R. (2001). Thinking critically about intellectual capital accounting. *Accounting, Auditing & Accountability Journal, 14*(4), 383–399. https://doi.org/10.1108/09513570110403425

Schiuma, G., Lerro, A., & Carlucci, D. (2008). The knoware tree and the regional intellectual capital index: An assessment within Italy. *Journal of Intellectual Capital, 9*(2), 283–300.

Secundo, G., Massaro, M., Dumay, J., & Bagnoli, C. (2018). Intellectual capital management in the fourth stage of IC research: A critical case study in university settings. *Journal of Intellectual Capital, 19*(1), 157–177.

Sultanova, G., Svyatov, S., & Ussenbayev, N. (2018). Transmitting competencies at universities in Kazakhstan: intellectual capital of teachers. *Journal of Intellectual Capital, 19*(1), 112–134. https://doi.org/10.1108/JIC-04-2017-0058

Sydänmaanlakka, P. (2006). *Älykäs itsensä johtaminen. Näkökulmia henkilökohtaiseen kasvuun.* (Intelligent self-leadership: Perspectives on personal growth.) Helsinki. Talentum.

Tomé, E., Naidenova, I., & Oskolkova, M. (2014). Personal welfare and intellectual capital: The case of football coaches. *Journal of Intellectual Capital, 15*(1), 189–202. https://doi.org/10.1108/JIC-06-2013-0064

Vătămănescu, E. M., Bratianu, C., Dabija, D. C., & Popa, S. (2023). Capitalizing online knowledge networks: From individual knowledge acquisition towards organizational achievements. *Journal of Knowledge Management, 27*(5), 1366–1389.

Vetrenko, P., Chernysheva, E. A., Levitina, I. Y., Voronkova, O. V., & Mikheeva, D. G. (2017). Encouraging employees to increase the labor intellectualization level as a factor of evolution of the intellectual capital. *European Research Studies, 20*(4A), 568–577.

Volmer, J. (2012). Catching leaders' mood: Contagion effects in teams. *Administrative Sciences, 2*(3), 203–220. https://doi.org/10.3390/admsci2030203

Wang, W. Y., & Chang, C. (2005). Intellectual capital and performance in causal models: Evidence from the information technology industry in Taiwan. *Journal of Intellectual capital.*

Wang, Z., Bu, X., & Cai, S. (2018). Core self-evaluation, individual intellectual capital and employee creativity. *Current Psychology (New Brunswick, NJ), 40*(3), 1203–1217. https://doi.org/10.1007/s12144-018-0046-x

Wang, Z., Cai, S., Liu, M., Liu, D., & Meng, L. (2020). The effects of self-reflection on individual intellectual capital. *Journal of Intellectual Capital, 21*(6), 1107–1124. https://doi.org/10.1108/JIC-03-2019-0043

Wang, Z., Cui, T., Cai, S., & Ren, S. (2021) Team reflexivity, individual intellectual capital and employee innovative behavior: A multilevel moderated mediation. *Journal of Intellectual Capital*, Ahead-of-print No. ahead-of-print. https://doi.org/10.1108/JIC-11-2020-0362

Wang, Z., Cui, T., Cai, S., & Ren, S. (2022). Team reflexivity, individual intellectual capital and employee innovative behavior: A multilevel moderated mediation. *Journal of Intellectual Capital, 23*(6), 1276–1295.

Wang, Z., Liu, D., & Cai, S. (2019). Self-reflection and employee creativity. *Chinese Management Studies, 13*(4), 895–917. https://doi.org/10.1108/CMS-09-2018-0683

M.Sc., BBA, Sanna Mari Alppivuori is Senior Vice President, Marketing and Communication, Customer Experience, and Sustainability, and a member of the executive team of Enfo Oy, an established Finnish IT service company. Alppivuori has decades of experience in change leadership, business development, and personnel management, especially focusing on the areas of strategy, communication, customer relationship management, sales management, and customer experience. She holds a diverse background in external and internal communication and marketing operations. Alppivuori has carried both consultant and in-house executive roles. She has supplemented her knowledge with master's studies in knowledge management at LUT University. During her studies, she especially familiarized herself with the intangible capital of individuals. Alppivuori is an inspiring speaker, facilitator, and mentor, and she is interested in combining individual IC theory, models, and practice in business life for both individual employee-level and company-level success.

D.Sc. Aino Kianto is a Full Professor of Knowledge Management at the LUT Business School, Lappeenranta-Lahti University of Technology (LUT), Finland. She is the leader of the LUT Knowledge Management Team, one of the world's leading academic laboratories working on knowledge-related management topics and executing the Master Programme on Knowledge Management and Leadership since 2001. Prof. Kianto's research focuses on knowledge management, intellectual capital, and innovation, resilience, and organizational renewal. Her research on these topics has been published widely and acknowledged with several international awards. Her papers have appeared in, for example, the *Journal of Business Research, Technovation, R&D Management, Human Resource Management Journal, Journal of Knowledge Management, Journal of Intellectual Capital, and Accounting, Auditing and Accountability Journal*. Prof. Kianto has delivered keynote speeches and acted as a track chair at many international conferences and currently serves on the editorial board of four academic journals. She promotes the transfer of research-based insights to work life by collaborating with companies and public organizations in research projects and consulting, press interviews, lectures at industry events, and teaching MSc and MBA courses. In the intellectual capital field, she is especially known for advancing the dynamic dimension of intellectual capital and her studies addressing the intersection of intellectual capital and knowledge management, innovation, and organizational performance.

The Liability of Tacitness in Intellectual Capital: Overcoming Research Challenges with Grounded Theory Designs

Carla Curado and Tiago Gonçalves

Abstract

Tacit intellectual capital (IC) gathers non-explicit organizational knowledge stocks that contribute to supporting business intelligence. This chapter addresses the challenges in tacit IC research and proposes a situational roadmap adaptable to various scenarios to facilitate a deeper understanding of tacit IC. Organizational stocks of knowledge are accumulated through knowledge-flow activities over time. Tacit IC gathers tacit components of intellectual, human, relational, structural, and renewal capital. However, tacit stocks of knowledge are difficult to define. We suggest using Grounded Theory to overcome the research challenges of addressing tacit IC. We propose that Grounded Theory offers a broad and flexible methodological toolbox useful for building a better understanding of tacit IC. This chapter contributes to tacit IC theoretical development and provides practical ways of advancing tacit IC research gap-spotting, the tacit IC literature review process, and tacit IC research coding processes and data analysis; all these advances will benefit our understanding of tacit IC. We believe that such research development will reveal and clarify practical implications. We conclude by offering future IC research tips and presenting forthcoming tacit IC practices that will support a sustainable competitive advantage.

C. Curado (✉) · T. Gonçalves
Advance/CSG, ISEG – Lisbon School of Economics and Management, Universidade de Lisboa, Lisbon, Portugal
e-mail: ccurado@iseg.ulisboa.pt; tgoncalves@iseg.ulisboa.pt

A. Kianto et al. (eds.), *Futurizing Intellectual Capital*, Knowledge Management and Organizational Learning 15, https://doi.org/10.1007/978-3-031-80197-6_6

1 Introduction

Nonaka (2007) posits that knowledge transformation from tacit to explicit, and vice versa, creates the foundations of business intelligence. Business intelligence regards dynamic capabilities that firms can use to create leading-edge knowledge in a dynamic setting (Shafiee, 2022). In such a context, failing to consider tacit organizational knowledge can have harmful consequences. The stock of organizational knowledge is captured in an organization's intellectual capital (IC) (Curado et al., 2011; Dahiyat et al., 2023). Given such dependence upon organizational knowledge, we propose that special attention be paid to tacit organizational knowledge. The influence of tacitness in IC is significant (Venkitachalam & Busch, 2012). Intellectual capital is a complex phenomenon (Cosa et al., 2023) in which components (e.g., human, relational, structural, and renewal) are interdependent (Buenechea-Elberdin et al., 2017; Dahiyat et al., 2023) and supplied by tacit knowledge (Kucharska, 2022). Tacit knowledge is quite inaccessible, non-standardized, and challenging to recognize, use, and share (Attaran, 2022). Therefore, it is important to understand the role of tacit knowledge in IC and how it drives its components (Kucharska, 2022).

The degree of knowledge tacitness affects relationships between the components of IC and innovation performance (Buenechea-Elberdin et al., 2018). As a result, it is relevant to overcome research challenges regarding the responsibility of tacitness in IC. This chapter highlights an approach based on Grounded Theory (GT) to overcome the liability of tacitness in IC research by presenting advice about data-collection methods, data coding, and analysis strategies that should be considered to ensure quality GT research. Additionally, it presents an integration of research using mixed methods GT to overcome qualitative limitations surrounding GT. This chapter contributes to the theoretical and empirical development of tacit IC research by suggesting research to support the usage of GT (Gonçalves, 2022).

IC refers to "the stock of knowledge at a particular time, which has been accumulated through knowledge flow activities" (Dahiyat et al., 2023: p. 18), so that "all the stocks and flows of knowledge that can be leveraged to create value and competitive advantage" (Ritala et al., 2023; p. 3). IC has a positive impact on business intelligence, competitive advantages (Shafiee, 2022), and innovation (Cabrilo et al., 2018; Ganguly et al., 2019; Ritala et al., 2023). Several components of IC are frequently considered, including human, structural, relational, and renewal capital (Kucharska, 2022).

Knowledge sharing stimulates the flow of new knowledge, which can contribute to organizational efficiency and effectiveness (Wang et al., 2014). The stock of organizational knowledge is a relevant asset (Goswami & Agrawal, 2018) and can be classified into two types: tacit and explicit knowledge. Tacit and explicit knowledge stocks contribute to tacit and explicit IC. Tacit knowledge stocks are based on actions, commitment, and involvement in a context. Explicit knowledge stocks, on the other hand, are based on codified knowledge, which can be formally expressed and transmitted systematically (Polanyi, 1966). Tacit knowledge is intangible; explicit knowledge is tangible.

Tacit knowledge is invisible, nonverbalized, intuitive, abstract, complex, and unarticulated; therefore, it is hard to codify and difficult to disseminate. Tacit knowledge incorporates skills that are contextual-specific and are captured in experience (e.g., know-how and know-why). It is difficult to communicate; because it resides in people's minds and memories, it is highly personal. Tacit knowledge is shared when trust, motivation, reciprocity, and organizational culture support it; it can appear when there is fear of losing individual power. Tacit knowledge is an asset of inter-organizational collaboration, it is very relevant to innovation, and it is revealed by its performance and achievements. Explicit knowledge, on the other hand, is visible and resides in books, documents, databases, manuals, rules, and guides. Explicit knowledge exists in symbolic or written forms, and it comprises facts, theories, and instructions. It is objective and relatively simple to codify and disseminate; therefore, it is easily communicated and can be captured in know-about. Explicit knowledge is stored in organizational repositories; therefore, it can be easily accessed and imitated. Explicit knowledge can be transferred by procedures, formal language, handbooks, and information systems (Kucharska, 2022; Sikombe & Maxwell, 2019).

Tacit knowledge is positively associated with human, structural, and relational capital; explicit knowledge is not associated with relational capital. Tacit knowledge is positively associated with organizational performance; explicit knowledge is positively associated with financial performance (Wang et al., 2014). In this chapter, we address the scarcity of literature related to tacit IC to advance research (cf. Kianto et al., 2023) and our understanding of the role and value of tacit IC. We propose methodological paths to advance tacit IC research gap-spotting, the tacit IC literature-review process, and tacit IC research-coding processes and data analysis, in the benefit of tacit IC understanding.

2 Tacit Intellectual Capital

IC is most relevant in the context of tacit knowledge sharing and creation (Venkitachalam & Busch, 2012). Considering that tacit knowledge sharing significantly contributes to its components (human, structural capital, relational, and renewal capital) (Paoloni et al., 2023; Buenechea-Elberdin et al., 2017; Kucharska, 2022), we must recognize the relevant contribution of tacit knowledge in IC research.

IC refers to the stocks of organizational knowledge at a particular time (Dahiyat et al., 2023). We accordingly propose that tacit IC refers to stocks of tacit organizational knowledge. We believe that IC is a form of hidden, intangible resources (Mouritsen & Larsen, 2005). Therefore, tacitness is at the heart of IC. Conceptualizing tacit knowledge requires recognizing shared meaning amongst people in professions or communities of practice (Håkanson, 2007). As tacit knowledge is embedded in actions, taking place within a context and subjected to interpretations, it cannot easily be codified, retrieved, or shared (Peet, 2012). Even so, it is positively associated with IC components (Wang et al., 2014). Tacit IC gathers the tacit components of IC (i.e., human, relational, structural, and renewal capital). Tacit knowledge influences decision-making, time management, quality, and competitiveness

(Ganguly et al., 2019) and shapes organizational behavior. Each one of the primary components of IC assumes a different form of tacit knowledge:

Tacit human capital captures human-embodied knowledge (Dahiyat et al., 2023). It gathers tacit knowledge: the individual knowledge stock of an organization and the individual mindsets, assumptions, beliefs, and biases of that organization's members. It is embedded in employees' competencies, knowledge, skills, innovativeness, attitude, commitment, wisdom, and experience. Their intuition, perspectives, beliefs, and values result from their experiences and form a mental grid to support decision-making (Saint-Onge, 1996; Wang et al., 2014; Karimi et al., 2023). Tacit knowledge sharing positively influences human capital (Kucharska & Rebelo, 2022). Tacit knowledge is accessible solely via person-to-person interactions; consequently, human capital is mostly tacit (Buenechea-Elberdin et al., 2018) (i.e., it is non-organizational embodied knowledge).

Tacit structural (or organizational) capital encompasses organizational culture, norms, and shared patterns of behavior. It is made up of collective mindsets and filters that shape how organizational members see the world and react to it. Such organizational values, principles, and "ways of doing things" remain largely implicit (i.e., unspoken and taken for granted) (Saint-Onge, 1996). Tacit structural (or organizational) capital refers to the valuable intangible assets that employees do not take away when they leave the organization; those assets are embedded in organizational capabilities, organizational culture, routines, and procedures (Wang et al., 2014).

Tacit relational (or social) capital includes the collective perceptions of meaning and value and intangible organizational networks (Saint-Onge, 1996). It consists of the value and knowledge that reside in connections with stakeholders (Inkinen et al., 2017; Oliveira et al., 2020). It is intangible and can be found in networks, norms, trust, and communication among employees that facilitate the flow and subsequent integration of knowledge (Dahiyat et al., 2023). As a result, organizational social networks are closely related to knowledge creation and sharing; intense social network interactions can lead to increased tacit knowledge sharing (Ganguly et al., 2019).

Tacit renewal capital regards organizational learning capabilities and facilitates organizational creativity and innovation (Kianto et al., 2010; Buenechea-Elberdin et al., 2017; Kucharska, 2022). It includes a climate of learning and a tolerance for mistakes and fosters tacit knowledge sharing. As a result, it supports innovation (Kucharska, 2022). Renewal capital relies on the resources of a firm to refresh knowledge; it involves the ability to acquire new information and develop skills and learn (Cabrilo et al., 2018). Therefore, it comprises proactive and organizational knowledge creation. Tacit renewal capital emphasizes the tacit dimension of knowledge and skills development to serve innovation performance (Ritala et al., 2023).

Another component of IC has recently surfaced in the literature: entrepreneurial capital. Entrepreneurial capital refers to tacit aspects of IC, like employees' ability to identify business opportunities, take risks, and make complex decisions. This component also has a positive effect on innovation performance (Cabrilo et al., 2018). Hence, research on the tacit dimension of IC is of immense potential value; it influences IC disclosure, and it impacts organizational business intelligence and competitive advantage. It also presents a challenge in the development of research strategies that can address individual phenomena embedded within tacit knowledge. Other less-frequently considered components of IC (e.g., social tacit knowledge and financial tacit knowledge) can also influence the disclosure of IC (Karimi et al., 2023).

Given that tacit knowledge is easier to observe than it is to describe (Kucharska, 2022), we suggest an approach to research that tackles systematic and iterative data collection that generates theory grounded in data (Qureshi & Ünlü, 2020). We suggest focusing on the use of alternative methodologies to conceptually refine the tacit component of IC. We propose how to address the tacitness of IC to benefit IC research that can deliver relevant results by using GT.

3 Applying Grounded Theory to Understand Tacit Intellectual Capital

Grounded Theory describes a general research methodology that develops a constant comparative method. It combines tenets that merge positivist traditions of research with a symbolic interplay of human behavior and interactions (Glaser & Strauss, 1967). According to Corbin and Strauss (1990), the use of GT as a methodological toolkit should pursue the scientific narrowing of disciplines grounded in social sciences by providing specific logics and ensuring careful and rigorous control over qualitative research.

Grounded Theory is well-suited for investigating relatively poorly explored social phenomena (Fendt & Sachs, 2008). Tacit IC presents a current conceptual and empirical challenge, often described as a complex web of tacit or intangible resources difficult to outline (Bamel et al., 2022; Dumay & Cuganesan, 2011; Roos, 2017). Although previously discussed in the literature, the use of narrative data or more symbolic-driven research methods can help shed light on IC phenomena (Dumay & Cuganesan, 2011; Dumay & Cai, 2015). Nevertheless, a review of current publications related to IC (cf. Bamel et al., 2022) suggests that the use of GT-related tenets is still rare.

Recent studies have emphasized the importance of integrating thematic maps and using narrative principle-based approaches to understanding IC (Abhayawansa et al., 2018; Dumay & Cai, 2015; Dumay & Cuganesan, 2011; Dumay & Roslender, 2013). According to Dumay (2009), the wide recognition of IC as an organizational asset in dire need of management can be better understood by exploring the measurement of intangible factors. Such focus in a research effort beyond positivist traditions echoes an effort to pursue research that can deeply explore complex dynamics of value creation, that recognizes questioning, and that addresses the "how" of IC (Dumay, 2009; O'Donnell et al., 2006). Furthermore, the social reality of IC components (Dumay & Cai, 2015) suggests the need to understand subjectivity and social interactions pertaining to IC's phenomenology and conceptualization. Therefore, the complex nature of related research questions requires effective gap-spotting. Research gap-spotting falls into three basic modes (Sandberg & Alvesson,

2011), which applied to tacit IC research identify ways of constructing research questions related to tacit IC from reviewing existing literature:

Confusion spotting: identifies research questions on competing explanations for tacit IC.

Neglect spotting: identifies research questions on overlooked areas, under-researched areas, or research areas lacking empirical support for tacit IC.

Application spotting: identifies research questions for extending and complementing the existing literature in tacit IC.

By combining the basic modes of research gap-spotting and the features of GT, we describe the research potential of each option in Table 1.

Numerous research efforts have addressed the need to understand IC with the support of GT. Spender (2006) argues that the socially constructed views of several theories shaping IC (e.g., institutional theory) are adequate for exploring intellectual phenomena using constructivist processes and are furthermore aligned with more recent schools of thought shaping GT (Charmaz, 2006). Nevertheless, the rethinking of models supported by GT is a continuous concern of IC (Holland, 2017) that requires additional development. Given such scarcity in the literature, we

Table 1 Articulation between tacit IC research gap-spotting and the features of GT

Gap-spotting basic modes	Research focus	Relevant GT feature	Research potential
Confusion spotting	• Defining IC (Dumay & Cai, 2015). • IC *as an* intangible asset *versus* IC *as part of* intangible assets (Dabić et al., 2021). • Quality *versus* quantity of IC (Dumay & Cai, 2015).	Theoretical sampling, comparison, memoing, theoretical sensitivity	Importance of investigating different settings to create a dense theory; explanation through the reorganization of empirical data
Neglect spotting	• Theoretical insufficiency to explain social contracts pertaining to IC (Abeysekera, 2006). • IC disclosure among contextual differences ((Dabić et al., 2021).	Comparative, processual, theoretical sensitivity	Understanding of the underlying social reality; the importance of social construction coming from actors that might challenge the theory
Application spotting	• Context units that delineate the scope of IC (Beattie & Thomson, 2007). • Combination between human capital and IC (Dabić et al., 2021; Nahapiet & Ghoshal, 1998).	Theoretical sampling, comparative, coding, core categories, memoing, and saturation	Developing investigations exploring different settings; allowing for the construction of theory from the combination of existing social practices

build on previous work discussing the need to develop content analysis approaches to better understand the complexities of IC (Dumay & Cuganesan, 2011; Dumay & Cai, 2015).

This chapter offers useful perspectives on GT methodology and actionable guidelines that can enhance conceptual clarity in research and expand our current knowledge of tacit IC. It provides the necessary methodological support to answer qualitative research questions related to "what," "how," and "which." We provide an examination of classic GT (Glaser & Strauss, 1967), interpretivist GT (Corbin & strauss, 1990), and constructivist GT (Charmaz, 2006) by discussing and providing a methodological blueprint that can guide future research on tacit IC supported by the principles of GT.

Conceptual and empirical works focused on the IC field address a need for the delineation of categorical distinctions, contextual differences, and theoretical challenges (Dabić et al., 2021). Moghadam and Makvandi (2019), for example, suggest the addition of spiritual capital to the discussion of IC. Such a challenge to theoretical foundations is further explored by Amoozesh et al. (2024), combining a quantitative approach with a coding strategy to understand the proposed model through the exploration of determination factors. Such research design, compatible in its process with interpretivist GT, assumes theory as central to research, exploring the importance of the context of phenomena to guide research (cf. Fig. 1).

Similarly, extensive work by Dumay and colleagues on the use of a qualitative narrative discourse to understand IC (e.g., Dumay & Cai, 2015; Dumay & Cuganesan, 2011; Dumay & Roslender, 2013) suggests the importance of coding, complex inputs, and even actor-driven interpretation as key factors to advance existing knowledge of IC. Such an argument has parallels with the exploration of categories and overarching concepts found within various GT frameworks (Holton, 2010; Makri & Neely, 2021). The employment of a concurrent system that requires simultaneous data collection and analysis can aid in clarifying overlapping conceptual boundaries (Dunne, 2011). To achieve such theoretical development relying on data, one should consider using theoretical sampling techniques. Theoretical sampling techniques can contribute to data saturation and facilitate a thorough examination of the disparities within IC. Therefore, and as proposed by Holton (2010), research on tacit IC using the existing GT toolkits should:

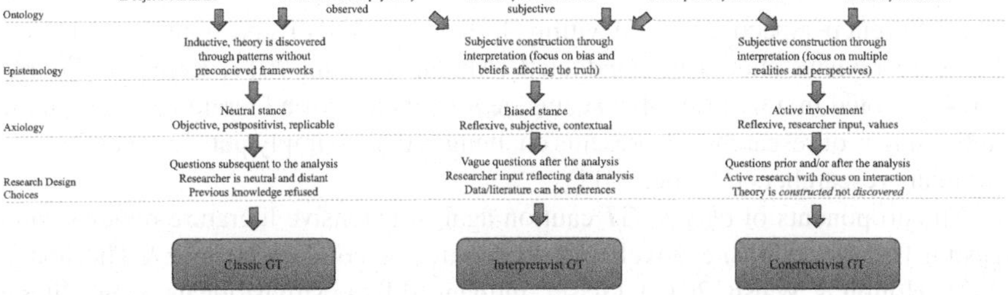

Fig. 1 Tacit IC research design considerations using different GT approaches

(a) Develop a coding system conducive to comparing aspects of tacit IC.
(b) Facilitate the emergence of categories pertaining to tacit IC.
(c) Enable comparisons between categories related to tacit IC.
(d) Evaluate emerging theories in light of the existing literature.
(e) Distinguish between substantive (local, cultural, situational) and formal (general) theory development within the realm of tacit IC and its dimensions.

The three GT perspectives presented here allow for a degree of perspective in their coding systems that should reflect a research choice deriving from knowledge necessity. For example, while classic GT allows for a coding strategy that supports the quantitative testing of findings due to its alignment with the positivist school, interpretivist GT relies on the role of interpretation and subjectivity of data (Glaser & Strauss, 1967; Glaser, 1992). On the other hand, Charmaz presents an alternative perspective that emphasizes the researcher's inherent bias stemming from the research environment (Charmaz, 2014). This pragmatic ontology diverges from both the distanced stance of classic GT (Glaser, 1992) and the action-oriented interpretation of interpretivist GT (Corbin & strauss, 1998).

Instead of prioritizing theory discovery, Charmaz advocates for theory construction (Charmaz, 2006), highlighting the researcher's influence throughout the data collection and analysis process. However, discrepancies in the underlying philosophies of the GT approaches give rise to tensions regarding two core principles: coding frameworks and the incorporation of existing literature in theory development (Alammar et al., 2019; Charmaz, 2006; Charmaz & Thornberg, 2021; Glaser, 1992; Kenny & Fourie, 2014; Corbin & strauss, 1998).

Subsequent sections explore these distinguishing principles and offer guidance tailored to each approach while considering some of the gaps in tacit IC research previously presented. Consequently, the delineation of research problems and questions varies across the three GT perspectives. Figure 1 provides a choice framework for the discussed GT perspectives, considering the ontological, epistemological, and axiological concerns that might arise during the choice of research designs pertaining to IC.

3.1 Abstaining or Postponing? The Relevance of the Literature Review Process

The different perspectives found within GT have sparked diverse opinions as to how literature reviews should be conducted (Alammar et al., 2019; Kenny & Fourie, 2014). Rooted in a tradition that seems *against* the use of a literature review in the initial stages of research, GT presents challenges that—simply put—are not feasible for many researchers (Dunne, 2011).

The proponents of *classic GT* caution against extensive literature reviews, suggesting that they might negatively impact research outcomes (Charmaz & Thornberg, 2021; Holton & Walsh, 2017). Glaser, influenced by positivist ideals, views literature review in GT as restrictive, fearing it could reduce creativity and further hinder theory development that derives from raw data (Kenny & Fourie, 2014). However, Glaser (2005) acknowledges the potential benefits of a literature review conducted outside the field at later research stages to offer support without biasing coding frameworks; such a review can foster the development of the original concept.

Interpretivist GT acknowledges the value of preliminary literature reviews for contextual understanding and supplementary data (Corbin & Strauss, 1998). This perspective recognizes that research builds upon existing knowledge (Sebastian, 2019). Such a perspective advocates for an adaptable approach wherein a literature review informs coding frameworks and connects substantial and formal theories (Kenny & Fourie, 2014). However, interpretivist GT leans toward a selective rather than exhaustive review process (Corbin & Strauss, 1998), consistent with a critical-realist approach seeking a deeper grasp of reality.

Constructivist GT adopts a pragmatic view of a literature review. Charmaz (2006) suggests that integrating existing theories can contribute to new theory without biasing data collection (see also Thornberg & Dunne, 2019; Charmaz & Thornberg, 2021). This approach encourages researchers to balance the use of literature review throughout all research stages while maintaining a degree of distance or even skepticism (Thornberg & Dunne, 2019; Charmaz & Thornberg, 2021). Charmaz (2006) argues that this balanced approach, coupled with deep immersion at the conclusion of the research, nurtures creativity by acknowledging that research operates within a broader context.

The evolution of GT perspectives suggests a nuanced compromise in more recent years that advocates for the restrained use of a literature review to preserve researchers' creativity. Focusing the discussion on the scope of tacit IC research, the use of a literature review tends to partially drive qualitative research (cf. Abhayawansa et al., 2018; Dumay & Cai, 2015; Dumay & Cuganesan, 2011; Dumay & Roslender, 2013). That situation confers a more flexible approach than interpretivist or constructivist GT approaches. Despite discrepancies, the conditional acceptance of a limited literature review by numerous classic GT scholars suggests a potential convergence among the three approaches in the development of theoretical refinement (Charmaz, 2006). Table 2 presents an overview of the literature review integration process and suggests a decision framework based on tacit IC research needs.

Hence, research approaches regarding the best research strategies for tacit IC should consider the following characteristics when one is designing a GT study:

(a) A literature review exploring prior knowledge of tacit IC should be reserved for after the final stages of data analysis, according to the classic GT method. This approach, rooted in post-positivism, demands detachment from prior knowledge to safeguard against bias in theory generation (Glaser, 1992). Such a position is suitable for scenarios where both neglect spotting and confusion spotting drive the research questions in IC research and there is an emphasis on new theoretical development of IC phenomena.
(b) Curate a selective (but not exhaustive) literature review consistent with Interpretivist GT practices. Researchers should avoid entering research on tacit IC with a "blank slate' (Corbin & Strauss, 1990). Prior research on tacit IC can

Table 2 The literature review process and data analysis integration using GT approaches

Philosophical standpoint	Literature review rationale	Common strategies	Operationalization
Classic	• The literature review process should be limited/is of little relevance. • Conducted *after* the research process.	• Need for the development of a coding strategy. • Theoretical saturation must be achieved in all positions. • Categorization is required for sensemaking of data. • Continuous comparison processes required.	The coding framework permits the development of new theory on tacit IC
Interpretivist	• The literature review process can be beneficial. • It should consider researcher experience and input. • Literature review as *secondary data*, complementary to the primary research process.		The coding framework allows for the discovery and subsequent refinement of existing theories on tacit IC
Constructivist	• Literature review to be conducted after codification of data. • Literature review as a facilitator of emerging themes and codes. • Literature review as immersive but requiring delaying the late stages of research.		The coding framework is open in its nature. Theoretical blocks are constructed upon and do not stem directly from data. Tacit IC is volatile and requires literature input for guidance

Adapted from Alammar et al. (2019), Charmaz (2006, 2008), Kenny and Fourie (2014), Sebastian (2019)

elucidate vague research problems and aid in the coding process without overshadowing originality.

(c) Embrace flexible literature review practices under constructivist GT (Charmaz, 2006). Researchers leverage their existing knowledge yet ensure that the review process does not dictate or alter the research trajectory. Instead, it serves as scaffolding for theory construction and can help increase the sophistication of the theory. A prior literature review on tacit IC is essential to ensure academic honesty and respect but should be considered only for the sake of research construction and theoretical edification (Charmaz, 2006; Stern, 2007).

3.2 On Sampling: Purposeful Data Sources

Achieving representative samples to address GT research design constitutes a challenge in qualitative research. Although largely broad in terminology usage, methods or reliable techniques that reflect data-gathering strategies are commonly defined as *purpose sampling* (Charmaz, 2006). On the other hand, both classic and interpretivist GT present a lack of discussion on sampling strategies, given the acknowledgment of *theoretical sampling*—a perspective that defends a need of more data based on concepts that emerge from the initial data analysis. Therefore, it comes as unsurprising that Glaser's dictum "all is data" (1998) represents a core standard of operation when considering sampling strategies in GT. By extension, Birks and Mills (2015) recommend the use of both qualitative and quantitative data in GT. Recommendations include:

- Interviews.
- Focus groups.
- Surveys and questionnaires.
- Documents (e.g., transcripts, letters, reports, grey literature).
- Artistic/other media outputs (e.g., music, artifacts, videos, blogs).
- Memos.

The initial stage of *purposive sampling* guides the gathering and/or creation of data following two approaches: that of extant data (guided by the researcher) and that of elicit data (already available) to the researcher (Birks & Mills, 2015). Researchers intentionally select participants and/or data sources capable of addressing their research question. Simultaneous data generation and/or collection alongside analysis form the cornerstone of GT research design. The researcher gathers, codes, and analyzes these initial data before proceeding with further data collection/generation. Purposeful sampling furnishes the initial dataset for analysis by the researcher. Subsequently, *theoretical sampling* (as part of the coding process; see Sect. 3.3) emerges from the codes and categories derived from the initial dataset (Charmaz, 2006).

Theoretical sampling can be used to pinpoint and pursue leads from the analysis, fill in gaps, clarify uncertainties, validate intuitions, and scrutinize interpretations as the study unfolds (Tie et al., 2019). According to Charmaz (2006), theoretical sampling further supports the subsequent/concurrent data-coding strategies and ensures that thematic representativity is achieved. Theoretical sampling can assume various forms and reflect the use of notes and memos complementary to the extant data collection; it can also rely on previously conducted interviews and documents fueled by the extant data collection and/or by the data-coding strategies. According to Charmaz (2014), there are several strategies that can be enforced to ensure theoretical sampling characterized by relevance and quality. Researchers should reflect on theoretical sampling considering:

(a) A contextual understanding of data (e.g., considering revisiting semi-structured interviews, changing the protocol after patterns emerge from participants).
(b) Theory development (e.g., documents that allow for further refinement of codes or categories).

(c) The degree of flexibility (e.g., a focus on less-rigid data-collection strategies that might limit the richness of insights).
(d) Data that can inform contradicting cases (e.g., clarifications, reassessment of existing codes, changes to data collections).
(e) Full disclosure of ethical challenges deriving from the time and resources required (e.g., planning ahead for all possible sources of data that might require ethical clearance, including instances of their contribution to theoretical sampling).

3.3 Constructing Meaning: Data Coding and Analysis Strategies

Coding frameworks pertain to the levels of data organization within GT research (Glaser & Strauss, 1967). The ways of conducting the data coding and analysis differ between different frameworks, but all of the frameworks operate on three common fundamental coding principles and strategies (Dunne, 2011; Holton, 2010):

Theoretical sampling involves comparing data to reveal emerging theories and the necessity for additional data. This strategy is useful for answering the "how?" of the data analysis. Grounded theorists frequently pursue disconfirming cases that may challenge aspects of the emerging theory, thereby enhancing the development of the theory (Pinnington et al., 2016). The theoretical sampling process represents the development of categories. This process should reflect two fundamental attributes: properties (what they represent for theory) and dimensions (specific/general) (Charmaz, 2006).

Constant comparison elucidates the conceptual underpinnings of data coding. Consequently, the data is categorized into emerging and core categories, thereby facilitating theory discovery (Holton, 2010). Adhering to the principles of GT, these mechanisms are imperative for revealing results and steering a research process anchored in empirical data (Glaser, 2005). To ensure robust analysis, GT relies on data-collection methods that prioritize open-ended information, aiming for comprehensive insights (Holton, 2010) (e.g., interviews, narratives, memos, documents, incidents, etc.).

Theoretical saturation denotes the point during the analysis at which no new data emerges. This term conveys meaning to "how much" data is sufficient. According to Glaser and Strauss (1967), theoretical saturation is achieved when no additional data is being found that can contribute to developing properties of the category. Similarly, Charmaz (2006) suggests that this process should consider more than the repetition of events and stories, but only when no novelty is observed. The extant criteria for saturation in GT are not defined but are instead often left in the hands of the researcher after redundant codes and categories are defined (Charmaz, 2006; Glaser & Strauss, 1967). Nevertheless, interviews still constitute a core source of data in GT research. Recent perspectives on GT have included constructivist GT, which recognizes the need to establish criteria to ensure research feasibility.

Numerous recommendations persist pertaining to how GT research can rely on interviews as data assets (Charmaz, 2006; Creswell & Creswell, 2018; Hennink & Kaiser, 2022; Vasileiou et al., 2018):

- Data saturation is an arbitrary post hoc criterion to achieve saturation in GT; recommendations suggest protocols (e.g., considering research proposal needs) considering, at least, 25 interviews (Charmaz, 2006).
- Including between 10 and 50 participants in qualitative research designs enables data saturation (Creswell & Creswell, 2018).
- Saturation is expected to be achieved after around 30 interviews; post hoc considerations ensure that flexibility can derive from complex phenomena and heterogenous participants (Vasileiou et al., 2018).
- Data saturation can be observed in as few as 17 interviews or in between 4 and 8 rounds of focus-group discussions (Hennink & Kaiser, 2022).

Following the points of convergence among the three positions discussed here, we propose that—beyond establishing *a priori* sampling choices (cf. Sect. 3.2)—researchers should consider best practices in qualitative research that can support theoretical saturation using both the *purpose sampling* and the *theoretical sampling* views of data collection. Consequently:

- Benchmarks should be considered in light of discipline traditions and brief overviews of previous similar research.
- Data triangulation must be concurrently conducted, considering the tenets of purpose and theoretical sampling.
- An overview of the skills of the research teams and the *a priori* availability of data should also be considered to be relevant criteria for attaining theoretical saturation.

Nevertheless, there are distinctions in coding strategies between GT methodologies; these strategies require detailed processes to ensure success.

Classic GT retains two core coding stages: *substantive coding* and *theoretical coding* (Holton, 2010). Rooted in principles of theory discovery, classic GT employs a flexible process aimed at minimizing researcher influence (Glaser, 2005). Substantive coding involves line-by-line data categorization, followed by the grouping of codes into concepts representing categories. According to Holton (2010), codes reflect one-to-two-word ideas labelled by the researcher; these verbs or actions segment the data in an abstract fashion. Categories reflect the products of constant comparisons of the data (i.e., incidents and concepts that emerge and saturate into categories). These codes and categories in turn undergo continuous comparison until a core category emerges (Holton, 2010). Subsequently, the core category is selectively coded; that process delimits and isolates it into a substantive concept through the comparison of selective information (Holton, 2010; Kenny & Fourie, 2014). The final stage, theoretical coding, focuses on analyzing relationships between substantive concepts to elucidate a new theory (Holton, 2010) (Fig. 2).

The *Interpretivist GT* coding framework is notably more intricate. It comprises three distinct coding stages, underpinned by paradigms and a conditional matrix guiding analytical decisions (Corbin & Strauss, 1990). While open coding in interpretivist GT bears a resemblance to its classic counterpart (Kenny & Fourie, 2014), it allows for the creation of subcategories characterized by greater abstraction. Corbin and Strauss (1990) advocate for coding categories based on their unique properties and dimensions; the latter encompasses aspects such as degree, frequency, intensity, and duration to establish an initial hierarchy of categories. In the open-coding stage, data is broken into smaller parts, and codes are developed in vivo directly from the data. Next, the similarities and differences of the data are analyzed (Corbin & strauss, 1990). Concepts and categories reflect higher- and lower-order phenomena. The following questions should be answered by an open-coding approach: what, who, how, when, why, whereby, and what for? We consider below an example of the problem of insufficiency to explain social contracts pertaining to tacit IC (Abeysekera, 2006):

- What?—Which dimensions of tacit IC are described? What forms of social bonding are reported?
- Who?—Who are the main relevant actors?
- How?—How are space, time, backgrounds, or contexts relevant?
- Why?—Is the data providing sufficient justification for the phenomena?
- Whereby?—Do different actors engage in different strategies?
- What for?—What commonality of consequences is observed?

After the open coding is complete, axial coding can be used with a subcategory labeling system to systematically examine the relationships between the emerging categories (Corbin & Strauss, 1990). This approach elevates the abstraction level, facilitating the emergence of a core category. Lingering concerns during this coding stage should reflect occurrences that develop the phenomenon, the related contexts,

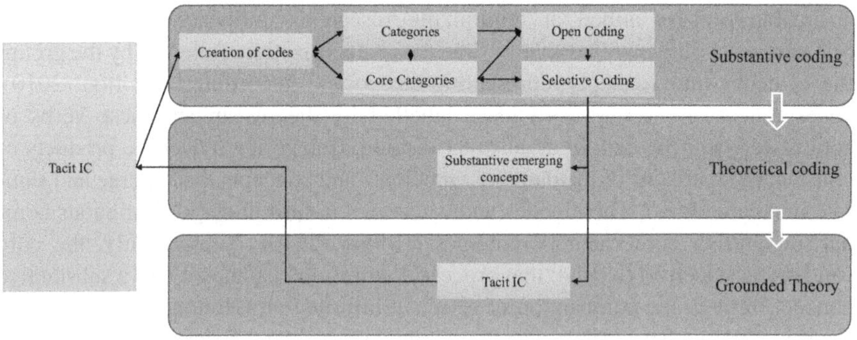

Fig. 2 Coding process within a classic GT approach (adapted from Holton, 2010)

the strategies that lead to the phenomenon, and the combination of actions to achieve the phenomenon (Vollstedt & Rezat, 2019).

After identifying a core category, selective coding can be used to reveal the nature of the phenomena in a conceptual manner. This process involves providing a descriptive overview and integrating it into a hierarchical structure supported by a paradigm. The properties and dimensions of the core category undergo reassessment, and the emergent theory resulting from selective coding is reconnected with existing data. Categories lacking refinement are further coded to ensure conceptual density (Corbin & Strauss, 1990).

Such a meticulous breakdown of the coding framework enables a cycle of refinement that can bolster the discovery of a theory (Sebastian, 2019). Additionally, a fourth level of analysis is introduced to clarify the conceptual subject's extent that relies on a conditional matrix. This matrix aids researchers in comprehending actions, interactions, and levels (individual versus collective; national versus international, etc.). Such a matrix can shed light on substantial or formal theories (Corbin & Strauss, 1990).

Strauss' coding framework, characterized as extreme or even destructive (Glaser, 1992), is acknowledged for its specificity and density (Fig. 3). The rationale behind the coding process depends on a thoroughly interconnected approach that takes into account the complexities of data codification; such codification can be troublesome for researchers less familiar with the GT toolkit. Nevertheless, subsequent studies have favored a more flexible approach aligned with constructivism and accordingly focused on relaxing the coding framework (Kenny & Fourie, 2014; Sebastian, 2019). Such trends have also been observed in recent IC-related research using the GT toolkit (e.g., Amoozesh et al., 2024; Chen et al., 2023).

On the other hand, constructivist GT, as advocated by Charmaz (2006, 2008), emphasizes a more flexible and malleable coding process. Here, the researcher's

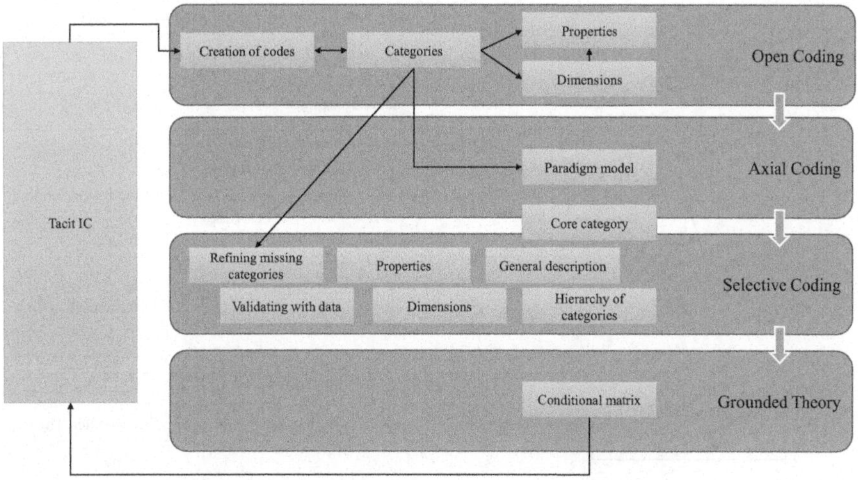

Fig. 3 Coding process within an interpretivist GT approach (adapted from Strauss & Corbin, 1990)

interpretative influence and engagement with participants shape the coding framework. This approach involves open or line-by-line coding initially. However, challenges can arise when theoretical cues dominate the themes, blurring the distinctions between them (Charmaz, 2006; Charmaz & Thornberg, 2021). Feelings, interpretations, and verbal cues are integral to the coding process and reflect a dynamic relationship between the researcher and the participant. This situation is referred to as in vivo coding (Charmaz, 2006). Subsequently, the initial codification is refined in a second stage using the core GT principles of memo writing, theoretical sampling, and theoretical saturation (Fig. 4).

The paradigms discussed—classic GT, Straussian GT, and constructivist GT—offer different approaches to data coding. Each paradigm has distinct implications for achieving conceptual clarity (Kenny & Fourie, 2014). The flexibility to blend these approaches, as noted by Kenny and Fourie (2014), fosters creativity without compromising methodological integrity. This flexibility is particularly relevant when investigating complex phenomena across philosophical stances—from post-positivism to pragmatism. Examples of such complexity are reflected in current research gaps that persist in the discussion of IC (cf. Table 1). Understanding both context units that delineate the scope of IC (Beattie & Thomson, 2007) and the challenges pertaining to combining human capital and IC (Dabić et al., 2021; Nahapiet & Ghoshal, 1998) requires methodological designs that could benefit from the articulation of various GT principles; constructivist GT is particularly relevant in this context.

Building on the previously identified gaps in tacit IC research (Table 1), we propose a decision-making grid to address the theoretical development and refinement of tacit IC research that makes use of different GT perspectives. Table 3 summarizes points to consider during data coding. Similarly, Fig. 5 expands on the rationale previously presented by summarizing the data-coding strategies relevant to each of the gaps noted previously (cf. Table 1).

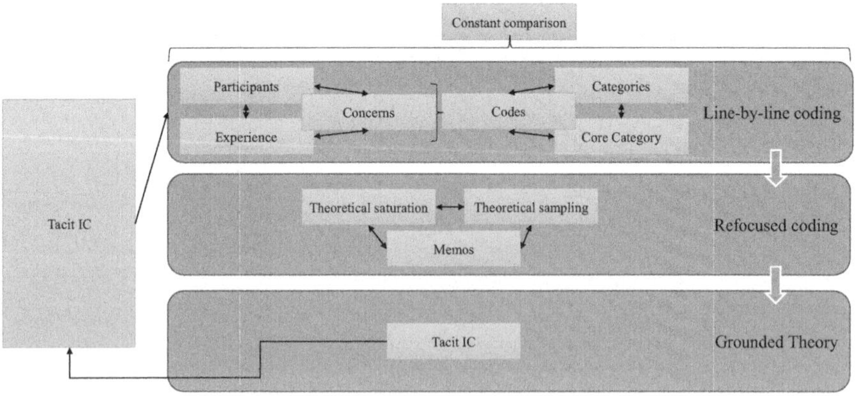

Fig. 4 Coding process within a constructivist GT approach (adapted from Charmaz, 2006)

Table 3 Tacit IC research goals and GT data coding rationales

Tacit IC research goal	Coding rational	Interpretations from the data
Clarify tacit IC	Coding after occurrence	Causes, conditions
Tacit IC mechanisms	Coding after processes	Phases, stages, predictors
Levels of tacit IC	Coding after degrees	Elements, dimensions, self-image, identities
Frequency and quality of tacit IC	Coding after dimensions	Intensity, continuity, self-image, identities, relationships
Consequences of tacit IC	Coding after goals	Consequences, ends, goals, purposes
Tacit IC in context	Coding after culture	Values, beliefs, emotions, sentiments, culture, social inputs
New theoretical drivers of tacit IC	Coding after theories	Scope, integration, relevance, Fit

Adapted from Vollstedt and Rezat (2019)

After the coding process is complete, it is advisable to determine the relationships between categories and draw them together into higher-order dimensions (i.e., second-order dimensions and aggregated dimensions). The content analysis of the coded data should be reliability tested to ensure that it remains constant in all variations of the measurement process (Krippendorff, 1990). The work of different coders should be compared to ensure that coding adheres to data to from the study's context to develop the first order concepts, in the spirit of Gioia's methodology (Clark et al., 2010; Gioia et al., 2010, 2012; Nag et al., 2007). The first-order categories can then be associated to form the emergent second-order dimensions (Gioia et al., 2010); intercoder agreement analysis can also be conducted to ensure agreement.

3.4 Bypassing the Bias: The Integration of Mixed Methods in Grounded Theory

The debate between strict and flexible approaches inherent to GT frameworks has raised concerns about this framework's perceived lack of structure and subjectivity. That situation has been particularly evident in management research, where criticism has highlighted issues such as a paucity of GT studies and issues of mislabeled data (Makri & Neely, 2021). Scholars have responded by proposing solutions to bolster the methodological robustness of GT; they have advocated for systematic literature reviews, detailed research protocols, and the integration of mixed methods research (Tranfield et al., 2003; Charmaz, 2014; Johnson et al., 2010).

According to Johnson and Onwuegbuzie (2004), mixed methods research is often referred to as the third major research paradigm. It has experienced an exponential increase in interest in recent years in fields such as social sciences, management, and health sciences (Guetterman et al., 2017). Three frequent core research designs arise from mixed methods processes; these designs are backed by the

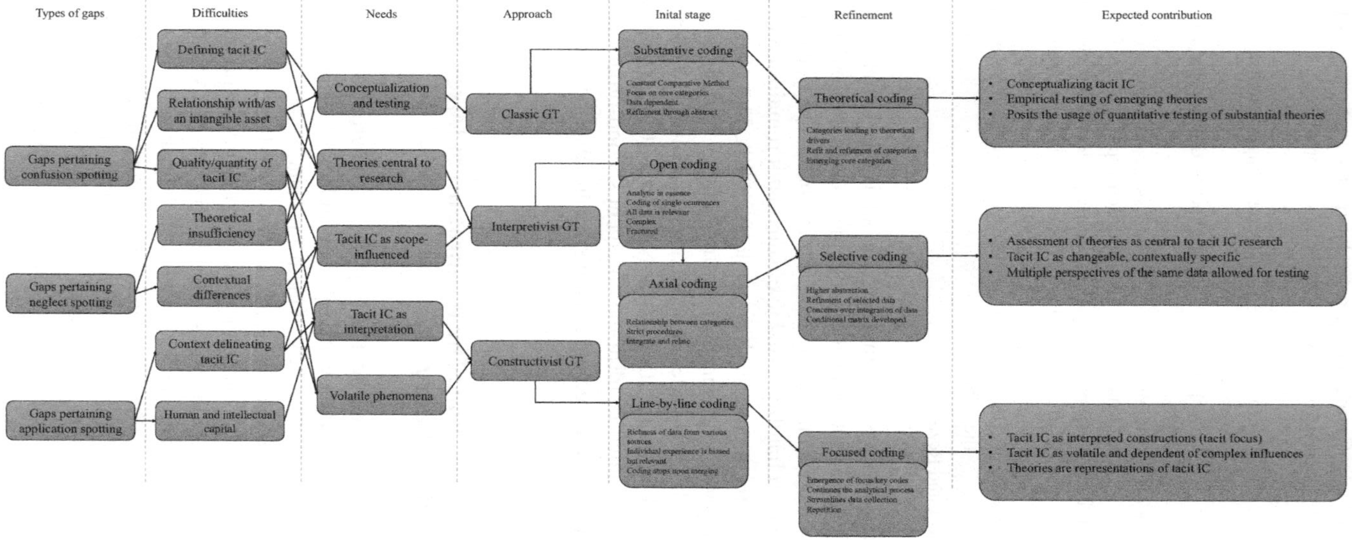

Fig. 5 Suggested uses of coding frameworks in GT approaches for tacit IC research (Adapted from Gonçalves, 2022)

pragmatic school (Creswell & Plano Clark, 2018) of *convergence*, *explanation*, and *exploration*.

- *Convergence* designs tend to combine quantitative and qualitative studies conducted in an independent manner. The integration of findings justifies the etymology of this design, enabling stronger inferences (e.g., complementary research methods) or the integration of data during the analysis.
- *Explanatory* mixed methods studies tend to follow an explain-expand structure of reality. In such a research design, an initial quantitative strand of research is followed by a qualitative research strand to enrich the findings and provide insights into possible complexities limited by quantitative designs alone.
- Lastly, *exploration* mixed methods designs explore a similar sequential approach. However, where the qualitative strands precede the quantitative strands of research to build a theory and test it—an aspect that draws parallels to data theory building defended by GT principles (Charmaz, 2006).

Therefore, it comes as unsurprising that integration, a core feature of mixed methods research (Creswell, 2015; Guetterman et al., 2017), also represents principles that echo those pertaining to GT (i.e., merging of findings and data, interconnectedness, and theoretical building) (Fetters et al., 2013; Shim et al., 2021).

A mixed methods approach to tacit IC research makes it possible to overcome the limitations of single-method studies by adopting a comprehensive methodology that combines quantitative and qualitative research options. Quantitative and qualitative research approaches should be judged and evaluated according to different criteria (Bryman & Bell, 2003). However, such approaches should guarantee research quality because they follow the principles of trustworthiness and authenticity in the spirit of constructivism (Guba & Lincoln, 2005). Trustworthiness encompasses four criteria that are equivalent to those in quantitative research (Bryman & Bell, 2003): credibility (which parallels internal validity), transferability (which parallels external validity), dependability (which parallels reliability), and confirmability (which parallels objectivity).

Authenticity (Guba & Lincoln, 2005), in turn, encompasses four other criteria: ontological authenticity (producing and offering IC specialists actionable models), educative authenticity (merging contributions from practitioners and scholars to provide diverse perspectives on the phenomenon), catalytic authenticity (providing feedback to the participants in the research), and tactical authenticity (offering support to IC managers wishing to address tacit IC).

The integration of quantitative and qualitative methodologies into GT is not entirely new; the practice aligns with GT's pragmatic roots (Guetterman et al., 2017). This synthesis has sparked discussions within the GT community focused on developing a more inclusive research paradigm. The rise of the mixed methods movement has reinvigorated debates on combining methodologies to revolutionize qualitative inquiry in GT research (Walsh, 2015). Johnson and Walsh (2019) suggest that mixed methods GT research should retain key features and uphold the core principles of GT while maximizing data analysis through the combined use of quantitative and qualitative methodologies. In particular, mixed methods GT researchers should:

- Consider both the inductive/exploratory views of GT and the deductive methods to address theory building.
- Acknowledgement literature reviews as relevant to guide the initial stages of design, the development of modelling questions, and the shaping of the first formative models (c.f. Guetterman et al., 2017).
- Embrace traditional forms of data validation (e.g., causation, validity, fits, indices, etc.) as complementary to the research design.
- Create numerous research products that can be used to develop a more robust theoretical model.

Despite its potential, mixed methods GT remains relatively underexplored; there are, however, ongoing efforts to refine its theoretical and methodological frameworks (Guetterman et al., 2017). Recent research has applied mixed methods GT principles to theoretical modeling, particularly when exploring phenomena related to organizational knowledge (Ngulube, 2020). To the best of our knowledge, applications of mixed methods research have been practically nonexistent in the realm of IC (e.g., Sadangharn & Joungtrakul, 2018); they are often the by-product of exploratory rationales found in doctoral dissertations (c.f. McGill, 2006; Chen, 2012). Applications of GT in this context are still developing. However, notable examples have focused on capturing and diffusing tacit elements that affect theory building (e.g., Shim et al., 2021). Nevertheless, while applications of GT in this domain remain underdeveloped, recent research efforts have focused on addressing its potential to fill gaps. One example is the development of ecosystem-dependent models for IC (Chen et al., 2023) and the validation of newly proposed dimensions of IC that test substantial theories (Amoozesh et al., 2024). Table 4 adds presents an overview of suitable legitimation strategies (Guetterman et al., 2017; Howell Smith et al., 2020) that should be encouraged in the development of mixed methods GT in IC research. By extension, Fig. 6 builds on the initial research questions developed in this chapter (cf. Sect. 3; Table 1) to guide IC-focused research according to the flexible principles of integrative mixed methods GT.

In conclusion, mixed methods GT confers a versatile approach for theory development by combining core GT principles with diverse research methodologies and stances (e.g., confirmatory, descriptive, exploratory). Continued exploration of mixed methods GT has the potential to advance our understanding of complex phenomena and drive innovation in tacit IC qualitative research practices. However, the complex toolkit of mixed methods research paired with GT tenets necessitates caution when developing research.

Recent studies addressing the state of IC research have focused on a need for innovative research in IC and, in particular, tacit IC (cf. Cuozzo et al., 2017; Dumay & Guthrie, 2017). Such advances are important given the increased prevalence of intangible assets in business reporting (Cuozzo et al., 2017). As suggested by the authors, "Finding an implied disclosure is like finding a needle in the proverbial

Table 4 Overarching considerations of mixed methods GT for tacit IC research design quality

Mixed methods GT considerations	Examples
On sampling	• Quantitative-qualitative interaction in tacit IC should consider the same pools for testing.
On behavior and language	• Consider the influence of emic (behavior) and etic (language) in the development of models/measures/theories on tacit IC.
On design weaknesses	• Common research on mixed methods GT considers a sequential exploratory design to respect interpretivist principles. • Development of measures for tacit IC should consider limitations that are incompatible with quantitative exploratory factor analysis (e.g., Howell Smith et al., 2020).
On literature reviews	• Consider the nature of the research question surrounding tacit IC to support a GT paradigm choice. • Include a preliminary literature review on tacit IC to define the first formative model. • Cite relevant sources on GT methodology (e.g. Charmaz, 2006). • Cite relevant sources on mixed methods methodology (e.g. Creswell & Plano Clark, 2018). • Cite relevant sources on mixed methods GT discussions (e.g., Guetterman et al., 2017; Creswell, 2015).
On data curation	• Document and address multiple sources of data that allow not only for exploration *but also* for causality (experimental data, idiographic, monothetic documents, etc.)
On validation	• Ensure that data pools are able to withstand feasible validation (e.g., protocols, saturation, discriminant validity, causality, etc.) when addressing tacit IC. • Clearly identify the GT processes being used (sampling, coding strategies). • Use engagement, triangulation, coding richness, researcher bias, and debriefing strategies to enhance contributions. • Delineate strategies for generalization and/or contextual/cultural/identity-related limitations and specifications.
On reasoning	• Develop procedural diagrams/design flows that justify using both mixed methods and GT design. • Approach the relevant strategies of mixed methods research design (convergence, explanation, exploration) to justify the study rationale. • Clearly describe the model-development process.
On standards	• Address guidelines for good reporting of mixed methods studies. • Address guidelines for good reporting of GT studies. • Allow for and explicate formative, middle-level, and meta-level models pertaining to tacit IC.

Adapted from Johnson and Onwuegbuzie (2004), Howell Smith et al. (2020)

haystack, because the term 'intellectual capital' is absent from contemporary corporate reporting outside IC reports, which arguably no longer exist" (p. 23). Such discourse challenges the traditional qualitative discourse of exploring phenomena related to tacit IC, paving way for an argument that, paired with the technological capabilities to process text data, motivates the need for a combined quantitative approach.

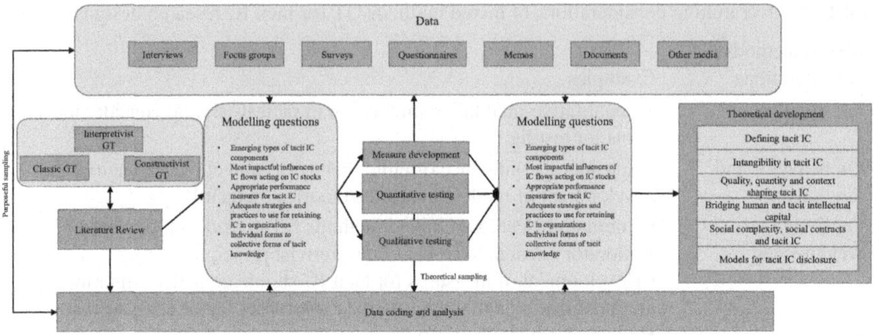

Fig. 6 Suggested mixed method GT research designs for tacit IC research (Adapted from Gonçalves, 2022)

The primary tenets of mixed methods GT enable innovative improvement of tacit IC by allowing for abductive and pragmatic philosophies of research aimed at exploring social and technological models applicable to tacit IC (cf. Howell Smith et al., 2020). Mixed methods GT can build on the research potential discussed above in several ways. Therefore, combining theoretical sampling with quantitative testing can support the development of measurement and quantitative testing in different sectors and promote new and existing theoretical models of IC for tacit disclosure (cf. Fig. 6).

Mixed methods GT also represents a potential route for identifying knowledge gaps in tacit IC. Such a proposal supported is supported by a growing technological capacity that allows for the processing of multiple sources of data; such a capacity respects not only the core feature of mixed methods GT (Johnson & Onwuegbuzie, 2004) but also the need for innovation in tacit IC research (Cuozzo et al., 2017). Similarly, the testing of possible IC applications by permitting complementary and integrated methods in data triangulation additionally supporting the need for an application gap that still presents a degree of subjectivity between tacit IC measurement and reporting (Paoloni et al., 2023).

4 Concluding Remarks

The foundational principles of GT are broad in scope and yet constitute a flexible methodological toolbox useful for building a better understanding of tacit IC. However, the extensive array of options and symbolic interactions inherent to GT can pose challenges to inexperienced researchers. To provide a structured approach amidst this complexity, this chapter offers a framework for advancing research. It encourages scholars to critically evaluate how GT methodologies can address persistent inconsistencies in the study of tacit IC. Through exemplified approaches drawn from research, we lay the groundwork for future theory-building grounded in cohesive data synthesis. We propose a situational roadmap adaptable to various scenarios to facilitate a deeper understanding of tacit IC.

Our recommendations reflect philosophical stances that remain subject to debate. Focusing on three prominent GT approaches—classic, interpretivist, and constructivist—we explore their similarities and differences in scientific literature development. Methodological weaknesses inherent to these approaches prompt us to consider using Mixed Methods to integrate quantitative designs into GT. Nonetheless, this chapter articulates the core principles that can serve as guides for future research, to leverage the diversity of GT to refine theories of IC.

The framework outlined here can aid in research decisions by simplifying complex ontological approaches into digestible components. Grounded theory demands a comprehensive methodological arsenal aimed at theoretical exploration and refinement. As emphasized by Alammar et al. (2019), GT's tolerance for ambiguity fosters nuanced perspectives shaped by continuous questioning and exploration. That situation echoes a necessity that can further contribute to and inspire research to challenge current knowledge and point to new conceptual and empirical directions to shape tacit IC.

Proper integration of GT mixed methods studies into the IC discourse will contribute to improving tacit IC research design quality; that situation will hold true for classic, interpretivist, and constructivist approaches. This chapter makes original interrelated contributions to tacit IC theoretical development. These contributions can be summarized as follows:

(a) Dense theory development will emerge from the adequate match between tacit IC research gap-spotting and the features of GT.
(b) Theory creation will result from the tacit IC literature review process and data analysis integration supported by suitable GT approaches.
(c) Tacit IC research coding processes and matching GT approaches will promote theoretical clarification and new theoretical drivers of tacit IC.
(d) Tacit IC research goals and appropriate GT data coding rationales will provide strong theoretical development of the tacit IC field.

This chapter's contributions have practical consequences for advancing tacit IC research gap-spotting, the tacit IC literature review process, tacit IC research coding processes and data analysis, and our overall understanding of tacit IC. We believe that such research development will reveal and clarify several practical implications:

(a) The identification of emerging types of tacit IC components pertinent to organizations working in digital and remote environments.
(b) The discovery of appropriate performance measures for tacit IC that take into account organizational, ethical, and sustainable options.
(c) The detection of adequate strategies and practices to retain tacit IC in organizations, by turning individual forms of tacit knowledge into collective forms of tacit knowledge in an industry context.

5 Future Tacit IC Research and Practice

We propose that future IC research engage in mixed methods GT in tacit IC by developing useful measures of tacit IC and testing qualitative and quantitative models (Fig. 6). Such work may (a) provide new definitions of tacit IC suitable for upcoming organizational challenges; (b) characterize the intangible essence of tacit IC; (c) identify the quality, quantity, and context shaping tacit IC; (d) uncover the role of tacit IC in defining human and IC; (e) reveal the social complexity and social networks that tacit IC involves; and (f) offer new models for better understanding tacit IC reporting.

Forthcoming tacit IC practices will offer new support for sustainable competitive advantages. Tacit IC governance development in organizations will increase after the identification of emerging types of tacit IC components. Challenges pertaining to digital and remote environments for tacit IC management can be more suitably addressed. Tacit IC auditing will flourish when appropriate performance measures are used. Additionally, we expect that various organizational, ethical, and sustainable options will motivate the creation of distinct measures. Lastly, tacit IC retention will result from the discovery of adequate strategies and practices to turn individual forms of tacit knowledge into collective forms of tacit knowledge. Particular attention should be paid to industrial contexts when designing strategic actions and management procedures to capture, retain, and develop tacit IC to its fullest extent.

Acknowledgments The authors gratefully thank the Fundação para a Ciência e a Tecnologia (FCT), under the project UIDB/04521/2020, for making this work possible.

References

Abeysekera, I. (2006). The project of intellectual capital disclosure: Researching the research. *Journal of Intellectual Capital, 7*(1), 61–77. https://doi.org/10.1108/14691930610639778

Abhayawansa, S., Aleksanyan, M., & Cuganesan, S. (2018). Conceptualisation of intellectual capital in analysts' narratives: A performative view. *Accounting, Auditing & Accountability Journal, 31*(3), 950–969. https://doi.org/10.1108/aaaj-03-2017-2873

Alammar, F., Intezari, A., Cardow, A., & Pauleen, D. J. (2019). Grounded theory in practice: Novice researchers' choice between Straussian and Glaserian. *Journal of Management Inquiry, 28*(2), 228–245. https://doi.org/10.1177/1056492618770743

Amoozesh, N., Mohseni, A., & Ghasemi, M. (2024). Modeling the determinants of spiritual capital in companies based on the grounded theory and structural equation modeling (SEM). *International Journal of Nonlinear Analysis and Applications, 15*, 131–141. https://doi.org/10.22075/IJNAA.2023.29793.4262

Attaran, M. (2022). Blockchain technology in healthcare: Challenges and opportunities. *International Journal of Healthcare Management, 15*(1), 1–14. https://doi.org/10.1080/20479700.2020.1843887

Bamel, U., Pereira, V., Del Giudice, M., & Temouri, Y. (2022). The extent and impact of intellectual capital research: A two decade analysis. *Journal of Intellectual Capital, 23*(2), 375–400. https://doi.org/10.1108/jic-05-2020-0142

Beattie, V., & Thomson, S. J. (2007). Lifting the lid on the use of content analysis to investigate intellectual capital disclosures. *Accounting Forum, 31*(2), 129–163. https://doi.org/10.1016/j.accfor.2007.02.001

Birks, M., & Mills, J. (2015). *Grounded theory: A practical guide*. Sage.

Bryman, A., & Bell, E. (2003). *Business research methods*. Oxford University Press.

Buenechea-Elberdin, M., Sáenz, J., & Kianto, A. (2017). Exploring the role of human capital, renewal capital and entrepreneurial capital in innovation performance in high-tech and low-tech firms. *Knowledge Management Research & Practice, 15*(3), 369–379. https://doi.org/10.1057/s41275-017-0069-3

Buenechea-Elberdin, M., Sáenz, J., & Kianto, A. (2018). Knowledge management strategies, intellectual capital, and innovation performance: A comparison between high- and low-tech firms. *Journal of Knowledge Management, 22*(8), 1757–1781. https://doi.org/10.1108/jkm-04-2017-0150

Cabrilo, S., Kianto, A., & Milic, B. (2018). The effect of IC components on innovation performance in Serbian companies. *VINE Journal of Information and Knowledge Management Systems, 48*(3), 448–466. https://doi.org/10.1108/vjikms-06-2016-0033

Charmaz, K. (2006). *Constructing grounded theory: A practical guide through qualitative analysis*. Sage.

Charmaz, K. (2008). Reconstructing grounded theory. *The SAGE Handbook of Social Research Methods*, 461–478.

Charmaz, K. (2014). *Constructing grounded theory* (2nd ed.). Sage.

Charmaz, K., & Thornberg, R. (2021). The pursuit of quality in grounded theory. *Qualitative Research in Psychology, 18*(3), 1–23. https://doi.org/10.1080/14780887.2020.1780357

Chen, L. (2012). *A mixed methods study investigating intangibles in the banking sector* (Doctoral dissertation, University of Glasgow).

Chen, Y., Zhou, L., & Wang, Y. (2023). The role and evolution of knowledge network-based intellectual capital in the corporate university. *Journal of Intellectual Capital, 24*(6), 1604–1631. https://doi.org/10.1108/jic-12-2022-0238

Clark, S. M., Gioia, D. A., Ketchen, D. J., & Thomas, B. (2010). Transitional identity as a facilitator of organizational identity change during a merger. *Administrative Science Quarterly, 55*, 397–438. https://doi.org/10.2189/asqu.2010.55.3.397

Corbin, J., & Strauss, A. (1990). Grounded theory research: Procedures, canons and evaluative criteria. *Zeitschrift für Soziologie, 19*(6). https://doi.org/10.1515/zfsoz-1990-0602

Corbin, J., & Strauss, A. (1998). *Basics of qualitative research: Techniques and procedures for developing grounded theory*. Sage.

Cosa, M., Pedro, E., & Urban, B. (2023). How to assess the intellectual capital of firms in uncertain times: A systematic literature review and a proposed model for practical adoption. *Journal of Intellectual Capital, 25*(7), 1–22. https://doi.org/10.1108/jic-05-2023-0096

Creswell, J. W. (2015). *Educational research: Planning, conducting, and evaluating quantitative and qualitative research* (5th ed.). Pearson.

Creswell, J. W., & Creswell, J. D. (2018). *Research design: Qualitative, quantitative & mixed methods approaches*. Sage.

Creswell, J. W., & Plano Clark, V. L. (2018). *Designing and conducting mixed methods research* (3rd ed.). Sage.

Cuozzo, B., Dumay, J., Palmaccio, M., & Lombardi, R. (2017). Intellectual capital disclosure: A structured literature review. *Journal of Intellectual Capital, 18*(1), 9–28. https://doi.org/10.1108/jic-10-2016-0104

Curado, C., Henriques, L., & Bontis, N. (2011). Intellectual capital disclosure payback. *Management Decision, 49*(7), 1080–1098. https://doi.org/10.1108/00251741111151154

Dabić, M., Vlačić, B., Scuotto, V., & Warkentin, M. (2021). Two decades of the Journal of Intellectual Capital: A bibliometric overview and an agenda for future research. *Journal of Intellectual Capital, 22*(3), 458–477. https://doi.org/10.1108/jic-02-2020-0052

Dahiyat, S. E., Khasawneh, S. M., Bontis, N., & Al-Dahiyat, M. (2023). Intellectual capital stocks and flows: Examining the mediating roles of social capital and knowledge transfer.

VINE Journal of Information and Knowledge Management Systems, 53(1), 11–42. https://doi.org/10.1108/vjikms-06-2020-0110

Dumay, J. C. (2009). Intellectual capital measurement: A critical approach. *Journal of Intellectual Capital, 10*(2), 190–210.

Dumay, J., & Cai, L. (2015). Using content analysis as a research methodology for investigating intellectual capital disclosure. *Journal of Intellectual Capital, 16*(1), 121–155. https://doi.org/10.1108/jic-04-2014-0043

Dumay, J., & Cuganesan, S. (2011). Making sense of intellectual capital complexity: Measuring through narrative. *Journal of Human Resource Costing & Accounting, 15*(1), 24–49. https://doi.org/10.1108/14013381111125305

Dumay, J., & Guthrie, J. (2017). Involuntary disclosure of intellectual capital: Is it relevant? *Journal of Intellectual Capital, 18*(1), 29–44. https://doi.org/10.1108/jic-10-2016-0102

Dumay, J., & Roslender, R. (2013). Utilising narrative to improve the relevance of intellectual capital. *Journal of Accounting & Organizational Change, 9*(3), 248–279. https://doi.org/10.1108/jaoc-07-2011-0034

Dunne, C. (2011). The place of the literature review in grounded theory research. *International Journal of Social Research Methodology, 14*(2), 111–124. https://doi.org/10.1080/13645579.2010.494930

Fendt, J., & Sachs, W. (2008). Grounded theory method in management research. *Organizational Research Methods, 11*(3), 430–455. https://doi.org/10.1177/1094428106297812

Fetters, M. D., Curry, L. A., & Creswell, J. W. (2013). Achieving integration in mixed methods designs: Principles and practices. *Health Services Research, 48*, 2134–2156. https://doi.org/10.1111/1475-6773.12117

Ganguly, A., Talukdar, A., & Chatterjee, D. (2019). Evaluating the role of social capital, tacit knowledge sharing, knowledge quality and reciprocity in determining innovation capability of an organization. *Journal of Knowledge Management, 23*(6), 1105–1135. https://doi.org/10.1108/jkm-03-2018-0190

Gioia, D. A., Corley, K., & Hamilton, A. (2012). Seeking qualitative rigor in inductive research: Notes on Gioia methodology. *Organizational Research Methods, 16*, 15–31. https://doi.org/10.1177/1094428112452151

Gioia, D. A., Price, I. N., Hamilton, A. L., & Thomas, J. B. (2010). Forging an identity: An insider-outsider study of processes involved in the formation of organizational identity. *Administrative Science Quarterly, 55*, 1–46. https://doi.org/10.2189/asqu.2010.55.1.1

Glaser, B. G. (1992). *Emergence vs forcing: Basics of grounded theory analysis*. Sociology Press.

Glaser, B. G. (2005). *The grounded theory perspective III: Theoretical coding*. Sociology Press.

Glaser, B. G., & Strauss, A. L. (1967). *The discovery of grounded theory: Strategies for qualitative research*. Aldine Publishing.

Gonçalves, T. (2022). Knowledge hiding and knowledge hoarding: Using grounded theory for conceptual development. *Online Journal of Applied Knowledge Management, 10*(3), 26–46. https://doi.org/10.36965/ojakm.2022.10(3)6-26

Goswami, A. K., & Agrawal, R. K. (2018). A reflection on knowledge sharing research: Patterns and trends. *VINE Journal of Information and Knowledge Management Systems, 48*(3), 352–372. https://doi.org/10.1108/VJIKMS-08-2017-0049

Guba, E., & Lincoln, Y. (2005). Paradigmatic controversies, contradictions and emerging confluences. In E. Guba & Y. Lincoln (Eds.), *The Sage handbook of qualitative research* (pp. 191–215). Sage.

Guetterman, T. C., Babchuk, W. A., Howell Smith, M. C., & Stevens, J. (2017). Contemporary approaches to mixed methods–grounded theory research: A field-based analysis. *Journal of Mixed Methods Research, 13*(2), 179–195. https://doi.org/10.1177/1558689817710877

Hakanson, L. (2007). Creating knowledge: The power and logic of articulation. *Industrial and Corporate Change, 16*(1), 51–88. https://doi.org/10.1093/icc/dtl033

Hennink, M., & Kaiser, B. N. (2022). Sample sizes for saturation in qualitative research: A systematic review of empirical tests. *Social Science & Medicine, 292*(1), 1–10. https://doi.org/10.1016/j.socscimed.2021.114523

Holland, J. (2017). Rethinking models of banks and financial institutions using empirical research and ideas about intellectual capital. In *The Routledge companion to intellectual capital* (pp. 113–129). Routledge.

Holton, J. (2010). The coding process and its challenges. *The Grounded Theory Review, 9*(1), 21–40.

Holton, J. A., & Walsh, I. (2017). *Classic grounded theory: Applications with qualitative and quantitative data*. Sage.

Howell Smith, M. C., Babchuk, W. A., Stevens, J., Garrett, A. L., Wang, S. C., & Guetterman, T. C. (2020). Modeling the use of mixed methods–grounded theory: Developing scales for a new measurement model. *Journal of Mixed Methods Research, 14*(2), 184–206. https://doi.org/10.1177/1558689819872599

Inkinen, H., Kianto, A., Vanhala, M., & Ritala, P. (2017). Structure of intellectual capital–An international comparison. *Accounting, Auditing & Accountability Journal, 30*(5), 1160–1183. https://doi.org/10.1108/AAAJ-11-2015-2291

Johnson, R. B., McGowan, M. W., & Turner, L. A. (2010). Grounded theory in practice: Is it inherently a mixed method? *Research in the Schools, 17*(2), 65–78.

Johnson, R. B., & Onwuegbuzic, A. J. (2004). Mixed methods research: A research paradigm whose time has come. *Educational Researcher, 33*(7), 14–26. https://doi.org/10.3102/0013189X033007014

Johnson, R. B., & Walsh, I. (2019). Mixed grounded theory: Merging grounded theory with mixed methods and multimethod research. In A. Bryant & K. Charmaz (Eds.), *The Sage handbook of current developments in grounded theory* (pp. 517–531). Sage.

Karimi, S., Pakmaram, A., Sales, J. B., & Kangarloi, S. J. (2023). Developing the concept of sustainability accounting based on the tacit knowledge of managers in Iran. *International Journal of Finance and Managerial Accounting, 8*(28), 159–172. https://doi.org/10.30495/ijfma.2022.64750.1768

Kenny, M., & Fourie, R. (2014). Tracing the history of grounded theory methodology: From formation to fragmentation. *The Qualitative Report*. https://link.gale.com/apps/doc/A397135420/AONE?u=anon~2fd0263e&sid=googleScholar&xid=3e9d42a3.

Kianto, A., Cabrilo, S., & Hussinki, H. (2023). Futurizing intellectual capital theory to uncover pertinent and unexplored horizons. In C. Bratianu, M. Handzic, & E. Bolisani (Eds.), *The future of knowledge management. Knowledge management and organizational learning* (Vol. 12, pp. 67–90). Springer. https://doi.org/10.1007/978-3-031-38696-1_4

Kianto, A., Hurmelinna-Laukkanen, P., & Ritala, P. (2010). Intellectual capital in service- and product-oriented companies. *Journal of Intellectual Capital, 11*(3), 305–325. https://doi.org/10.1108/14691931011064563

Krippendorff, K. (1990). *Metodologia de análisis de contenido: teoria e práctica. Ediciones* Barcelona: Paidós.

Kucharska, W. (2022). Tacit knowledge influence on intellectual capital and innovativeness in the healthcare sector: A cross-country study of Poland and the US. *Journal of Business Research, 149*, 869–883. https://doi.org/10.1016/j.jbusres.2022.05.059

Kucharska, W., & Rebelo, T. (2022). Knowledge sharing and knowledge hiding in light of the mistakes acceptance component of learning culture – knowledge culture and human capital implications. *The Learning Organization, 11*(3), 649–669. https://doi.org/10.1108/tlo-03-2022-0032

Makri, C., & Neely, A. (2021). Grounded theory: A guide for exploratory studies in management research. *International Journal of Qualitative Methods, 20*(1), 1–14. Sagepub. https://doi.org/10.1177/16094069211013654

McGill, T. P. (2006). *Harnessing intellectual capital: A study of organizational knowledge transfer* (Doctoral dissertation, Touro University International).

Moghadam, A. K., & Makvandi, R. (2019). Investigating the relationship between spiritual capital and job performance with organizational citizenship behaviors in employees (Evidence from Iran). *Cogent Business & Management, 6*(1), 1692484. https://doi.org/10.1080/23311975.2019.1692484

Mouritsen, J., & Larsen, H. T. (2005). The 2nd wave of knowledge management: The management control of knowledge resources through intellectual capital information. *Management Accounting Research, 16*(3), 371–394. https://doi.org/10.1016/j.mar.2005.06.006

Nag, R., Corley, K. G., & Gioia, D. A. (2007). The intersection of organizational identity, knowledge, and practice: Attempting strategic change via knowledge grafting. *Academy of Management Journal, 50*, 821–847. https://doi.org/10.5465/amj.2007.26279173

Nahapiet, J., & Ghoshal, S. (1998). Social capital, intellectual capital, and the organizational advantage. *Academy of Management Review, 23*(2), 242–266.

Ngulube, P. (2020). Mixed methods research in knowledge management studies (2009–2014): A content analysis of journal articles. *Journal of Information & Knowledge Management, 19*(03), 2050016. https://doi.org/10.1142/S0219649220500161

Nonaka, I. (2007). The knowledge-creating company. *Harvard Business Review, 26*(August), 598–600.

O'Donnell, D., Bo Henriksen, L., & Voelpel, S. C. (2006). Guest editorial: Becoming critical on intellectual capital. *Journal of Intellectual Capital, 7*(1), 5–11. https://doi.org/10.1108/14691930610639732

Oliveira, M., Curado, C., Balle, A. R., & Kianto, A. (2020). Knowledge sharing, intellectual capital and organizational results in SMES: Are they related? *Journal of Intellectual Capital, 21*(6), 893–911. https://doi.org/10.1108/jic-04-2019-0077

Paoloni, P., Modaffari, G., Ricci, F., & Della Corte, G. (2023). Intellectual capital between measurement and reporting: A structured literature review. *Journal of Intellectual Capital, 24*(1), 115–176. https://doi.org/10.1108/jic-07-2021-0195

Pinnington, B. D., Meehan, J., & Scanlon, T. (2016). A grounded theory of value dissonance in strategic relationships. *Journal of Purchasing and Supply Management, 22*(4), 278–288. https://doi.org/10.1016/j.pursup.2016.04.005

Peet, M. (2012). Leadership transitions, tacit knowledge sharing and organizational generativity. *Journal of Knowledge Management, 16*(1), 45–60. https://doi.org/10.1108/13673271211198936

Polanyi, M. (1966). *The tacit dimension*. Routledge and Kegan Paul.

Qureshi, H. A., & Ünlü, Z. (2020). Beyond the paradigm conflicts: A four-step coding instrument for grounded theory. *International Journal of Qualitative Methods, 19*. https://doi.org/10.1177/1609406920928188

Ritala, P., Kianto, A., Vanhala, M., & Hussinki, H. (2023). To protect or not to protect? Renewal capital, knowledge protection and innovation performance. *Journal of Knowledge Management, 27*(11), 1–24. https://doi.org/10.1108/jkm-11-2021-0866

Roos, G. (2017). Knowledge management, intellectual capital, structural holes, economic complexity and national prosperity. *Journal of Intellectual Capital, 18*(4), 745–770. https://doi.org/10.1108/jic-07-2016-0072

Sadangharn, P., & Joungtrakul, J. (2018). Retention of old-aged human capital in the Thai automotive industry. *International Journal of Learning and Intellectual Capital, 15*(1), 65–82.

Saint-Onge, H. (1996). Tacit knowledge the key to the strategic alignment of intellectual capital. *Planning Review, 24*(2), 10–16. https://doi.org/10.1108/eb054547

Sandberg, J., & Alvesson, M. (2011). Ways of constructing research questions: Gap-spotting or problematization? *Organization, 18*(1), 23–44. https://doi.org/10.1177/1350508410372151

Sebastian, K. (2019). Distinguishing between the strains grounded theory: Classical, interpretive and constructivist. *Journal for Social Thought, 3*(1), 1–9.

Shafiee, M. (2022). Competitive advantage via intellectual capital: A moderated mediation analysis. *Journal of Intellectual Capital, 23*(5), 957–997. https://doi.org/10.1108/jic-05-2020-0152

Shim, M., Johnson, B., Bradt, J., & Gasson, S. (2021). A mixed methods–grounded theory design for producing more refined theoretical models. *Journal of Mixed Methods Research, 15*(1), 61–86. https://doi.org/10.1177/1558689820932311

Sikombe, S., & Maxwell, A. P. (2019). Exploring tacit knowledge transfer and innovation capabilities within the buyer–supplier collaboration: A literature review. *Cogent Business & Management, 6*(1), 1683130. https://doi.org/10.1080/23311975.2019.1683130

Spender, J. C. (2006). Method, philosophy and empirics in KM and IC. *Journal of Intellectual Capital, 7*(1), 12–28. https://doi.org/10.1108/14691930610639741

Stern, P. N. (2007). On solid ground: Essential properties for growing grounded theory. In A. Bryant & K. Charmaz (Eds.), *The Sage handbook of grounded theory* (pp. 114–126). Sage.

Thornberg, R., & Dunne, C. (2019). Literature review in grounded theory. In A. Bryant & K. Charmaz (Eds.), *The Sage handbook of current developments in grounded theory* (pp. 206–221). Sage.

Tie, Y. C., Birks, M., & Francis, K. (2019). Grounded theory research: A design framework for novice researchers. *SAGE Open Medicine, 7*(1), 1–8. NCBI. https://doi.org/10.1177/2050312118822927

Tranfield, D., Denyer, D., & Smart, P. (2003). Towards a methodology for developing evidence-informed management knowledge by means of systematic review. *British Journal of Management, 14*(3), 207–222. https://doi.org/10.1111/1467-8551.00375

Vasileiou, K., Barnett, J., Thorpe, S., & Young, T. (2018). Characterising and justifying sample size sufficiency in interview-based studies: Systematic analysis of qualitative health research over a 15-year period. *BMC Medical Research Methodology, 18*(1), 1–18. https://doi.org/10.1186/s12874-018-0594-7

Venkitachalam, K., & Busch, P. (2012). Tacit knowledge: Review and possible research directions. *Journal of Knowledge Management, 16*(2), 357–372. https://doi.org/10.1108/13673271211218915

Vollstedt, M., & Rezat, S. (2019). An introduction to grounded theory with a special focus on axial coding and the coding paradigm. In G. Kaiser & N. Presmeg (Eds.), *Compendium for early career researchers in mathematics education* (pp. 81–100). Springer Open.

Wang, Z., Wang, N., & Liang, H. (2014). Knowledge sharing, intellectual capital and firm performance. *Management Decision, 52*(2), 230–258. https://doi.org/10.1108/md-02-2013-0064

Walsh, I. (2015). Using quantitative data in mixed-design grounded theory studies: An enhanced path to formal grounded theory in information systems. *European Journal of Information Systems, 24*(5), 531–557. https://doi.org/10.1177/1094428114565028

Carla Curado, Ph.D., is an Associate Professor in Human Resources Management and Organizational Behavior at ISEG, University of Lisbon, Portugal, where she has been teaching at Master's and Doctoral Programs. Her research interests are primarily related to knowledge management, human resource management, and organizational behavior. Professor Curado has held several high-profile leadership positions, including over a decade as the Academic Director of the Master's Program in HRM and the Master's Program in Corporate Sciences at ISEG. She is a founder-board member of the ADVANCE Research Center in Management, where she has been serving since 2008. She received several university and international awards for research achievements and knowledge dissemination. She regularly presents her work in leading international conferences and her research appears in numerous international influential journals. Carla Curado serves in various international conferences and scientific committees and on the editorial review board for several international peer-reviewed journals, regularly guest editing special issues. She is an Associate Editor of the Journal of Organizational Effectiveness: People and Performance. She represents the University of Lisbon at the International Organization for Standardization. She is part of Stanford's List of World's Top 2% Scientists in 2021, 2022, and 2023.

Tiago Gonçalves, Ph.D., is an Invited Assistant Professor and Ph.D. in Management at ISEG—Lisbon School of Economics and Management, Universidade de Lisboa, Portugal—and an integrated researcher of the ADVANCE Research Center in Management. His teaching experience includes diverse levels of higher education, in particular Bachelor's and Master's Programs. His research interests include knowledge management, human resource management, and organizational psychology and behavior. His recent research includes the study of knowledge management characteristics and related phenomena in healthcare organizations, with a focus on counterproductive forms of knowledge behavior. His research is published in leading international journals (e.g., the Journal of Business Research and the International Journal of Information Management) and presented at both national and international leading conferences.

Part II

Smart Societal Growth: Intellectual Capital in Sustainable Ecosystems

IC as Intellectual Companionship

Günther M. Szogs

Abstract

When former president of EU-Commission Jacques Delors died in December 2023, European heads of states gathered in commemoration of his great deeds for the Union. Another achievement meant just as much to him: The *agenda for education in the twenty-first century*, composed by the UNESCO commission under his chairmanship, advised by politicians, artists, business people and researchers—poetically named: *Learning: the treasure within*, a holistic approach of tremendous *relevance*—that was hardly commemorated.

Outstanding IC (intellectual capital) accomplishments like IC reporting or the future-centre endeavour, once developed as *two sides of a coin* in the pursuit of bonding, knowing, feeling, and acting share a similar fate. Approaches are fragmented and each specialisation is commercialised. Much of the *transformative energy* and sense of *societal relevance* faded.

Now actors in other not strictly academic fields like "the arts" are inviting academic disciplines to co-create; also Frankfurt International Book Fair debates sources of critical thinking; and Global Assembly, a kind of modern agora, is the place to go, all *without labelling* themselves IC.

This chapter compares this paradoxical fulfilment of IC goals rather outside than inside the IC communities and thus reveals *intellectual companionship* as a valuable essential to re-paradigm IC tools and approaches. *Transformative societal innovation* needs to leverage *IC's own "treasures within"*—best in *companionship with the unlabelled* in the regained sense of *relevance*.

G. M. Szogs (✉)
The New Club of Paris, Vienna, Austria

A. Kianto et al. (eds.), *Futurizing Intellectual Capital*, Knowledge Management and Organizational Learning 15, https://doi.org/10.1007/978-3-031-80197-6_7

1 Prelude: Wolf

A strange sound, macro view on a string from a violin, next: focus on the bow. Cut: distant view from a forest in the dark to a concert hall. Chatting people. Peter and the Wolf by Sergei Prokofiev is being performed. End of the film: list of numerous contributing institutions of natural science, communities and transnational experts of nature preservation. Film-director: Cees van Kempen. The title is "Wolf–Wanderer Without Borders." Script: the Wolf.

This film broadcasted by ARTE on 11 February 2024 is a project that addresses the challenge caused by wolves being helped to re-enter their original habitat in Western Europe. If monitored by an intellectual capital report, you would have an illustrious list of talented people as *human capital*: musicians, filmmakers, advisors, etc.; enormous *structural capital* has to be in place to cover tools and equipment for accompanying the wandering wolf across the Western European countries on his journey, and the *relational capital,* involving financing, permissions, sales and distribution, makes it a very complex endeavour. Purpose: promotion of knowledge about wolves and their behaviour in order to deal with changing circumstances in a respectful understanding manner.

Human capital is extended to *nature capital*. To better understand the wolf, he is *accompanied*, seen as a *companion*, as the one writing the script, not "just" being an object to be observed. An impressive way of extending the mindset whilst navigating knowledge-based value creation. Are we fully aware of it?

2 Hype, Hubris, Nemesis, and Regress: Some IC Metamorphoses

The editors of this book hope for fresh perspectives and the impact of IC, not just for firms but also societies; they address both scholars and practitioners in the field and most importantly hope that the authors "offer ways forward with a revised understanding of IC and its role in organisational viability and global sustainability". A revised understanding requires a revision. If we observe that IC in some ways is more and more "detached from reality", it might be worthwhile to examine some reasons for it in a recapture of some milestones of its development. Having been an analytical practitioner in the field with close connections to universities and international networks but based in Frankfurt, the scope of observations naturally is glocal (whilst rooted locally, try to think and act globally and locally).

The German IC narrative overlaps with developments in other pioneering countries but has noteworthy differences and specialties. Surprisingly for some in the international community may be that *language* is an essential component that caused a gap between innovative developments in German-speaking countries and the more English-affine international cooperations. To give a striking example: The late Prof. Ursula Schneider was cofounder of the Austrian *Wissensbilanz* (intellectual capital report), which in Austria is mandatory to use in universities. Up till today, her groundbreaking contribution to the analysis of the ambiguity of knowledge and the way we deal with it "Das Management der Ignoranz—Nichtwissen als Erfolgsfaktor" (The management of ignorance—not knowing as a success factor) (Schneider, 2006) has not even been translated to English. It was published in 2006 following a series of other publications in the 1990s and has addressed many of IC issues from its inner logic. They were being discussed in a rather superficial manner in the IC community many years later.

The rather brief review of some national and international stages in IC developments serves as framing for the question of public recognition, which is necessary for impact (an elaborated analysis of the academic development in Peter Pawlowsky and Leif Edvinsson "Intellektuelles Kapital und Wettbewerbsfähigkeit" (intellectual capital and competitiveness) (Pawlowsky & Edvinsson, 2012)). In our context, we look (a) at the initial *hype* due to societal relevance; (b) at a *hubris* caused by inadequate commercialisation, which cost it the rooting; and (c) at a resulting *nemesis* with a tremendous loss of public interest and recognition.

2.1 IC Hype

In Germany, the IC Hype has had diverse sources. After its postwar economic success (*Wirtschaftswunder,* economic wonder) and its technological advancements, the need for a much more flexible and broader educational system to cope with new needs was diagnosed (Georg Picht: Die Deutsche Bildungskatastrophe (Picht, 1964)). Alongside a societal evolution with a new government led by German Social Democrats and the promise to "dare more democracy" (Willy Brandt), reforms took place in universities and schools. Educational science became a new course of study but in the beginning, the graduates found it hard to get employment in companies. Corporate learning stuck to classical trainings organised by their human resources professionals. Nevertheless, with the rise of digitisation, pressure occurred for the firms to adjust. Whilst they were accustomed to teaching according to rather stable curricula, suddenly new skills were indispensable due to a tremendous drop of a half-value period of applicable knowledge. Interoperability of departments, especially with the new IT specialists, became indispensable. Whilst public educational systems and their slow bureaucratic procedures did provide little professional preparation, companies which had to compete internationally had no time to lose. Besides the fast-changing special skills in which they had to train their staff, they had to *rethink* and *redesign* the *interoperability as such.*

This was mirrored in the big knowledge and learning business fairs nurtured from three poles. The trade fair Didacta focused on new methods in classical learning, and the trade fair LearnTec, founded by Professors Winfried Sommer and Uwe Beck, made educational technologies with their learning and knowledge implications their core issue. The Industry Association of Information Technology BITCOM organised the annual event KnowTech under the guidance of the late Dr. Mathias Weber. Explicitly, IC strategies were presented and debated to cope with complex demands and the need to find standards for competition as well as for sharing. The internationally best-known trade fairs CeBIT in Hannover (put on hold in 2018) and

Frankfurter Buchmesse (Frankfurt International Bookfair) backed this industry approach in associated sessions. Since most companies could not get specialists in time to command these new ecosystems of interdependent skills, they heavily relied on expensive consultancies who in turn were dependent on input from internals. Often, that resulted in redundancies of competencies not always well orchestrated to shape high-performance teams.

Daily business management of learning and knowledge, which everyone has to perform within the scope of a special skill, needed to be complemented by the meta-skill of management of the intertwined components of IC. Inconsistencies between corporate and public educational and knowledge systems (OECD certified in PISA evaluation that Germany was lacking behind) in addition inspired ideas to professionalise knowledge management and—just one example—implement an executive master course of studies at the intersection of university and the corporate world. Professor Peter Pawlowsky from University of Technology Chemnitz, Germany, involved leading minds of German speaking IC scholars and pioneered with innovative companies and public institutions this well-designed course (Szogs, 2006).

Media engaged in this hype. German Commerzbank, together with Financial Times Germany and the manager trade journal Impulse, initiated the "Knowledge Manager of the Year Award" high-level festive event in Berlin. Handelsblatt, another prominent German business newspaper, organised conferences on IC and invited famous international innovators, like Prof. Ursula Schneider, Prof. Georg von Krogh and Prof. Leif Edvinsson (Wissensmanager, n.d.). Those conferences, fairs, award ceremonies and university courses were used for mutual inspiration and straightforward cooperation in a spirit of *companionship*. Results were internationally presented, and new forms of cooperation were tested in international innovation camps, like ACSI (Aalto Camp for Societal Innovation) in Finland; IC conferences in Paris; Prism, a follow-up of EU IC initiatives in London; and Future Center Summits in Stockholm, Utrecht and Tokyo. Political shortcomings were addressed in cooperation with UNESCO and OECD, for example, at LearnTec, as early as 2001, involving experts of almost all continents (LEARNTEC, 2001). Industry-specific knowledge and learning associations were initiated as well, in Germany with IBM-friendly Guide-Share Europe or the independent German Gesellschaft für Wissensmanagement GfWM (association for knowledge management).

All this led to *spirals of engagements*. In my case, I was head of knowledge management and skill resources in the financial industry; experimented with international colleague's versions of IC reporting ("Grübel, North und Szogs haben.. aktuelle Modelle des Intellectual Capital auf ein konkretes Praxisbeispiel angewendet..". North and Gruebel, p 109, 2005, Gruebel et al., 2004), among them "Wissensbilanz Made in Germany" (Wissensbilanz, 2008); helped the bank to run the Knowledge Manager of the Year Award in Berlin; presented the laureates and my international colleagues on stage at LearnTec and KnowTech; and tested with own staff the Executive Master of Knowledge Management.

2.2 IC Hubris

Paradoxically, the surge of Knowledge Management and IC and its success became a problem. "Knowledge" was the buzzword. Germany had a wave of admirable initiatives, which were awarded and annually documented in a yearbook of "Land der Ideen" (country of ideas) (Dumont Reiseführer, 2006). Negative comparisons to other countries in the context of OECD's PISA, for example, were pushed aside by proudly announcing the "Bildungsrepublik Deutschland" (Nationaler Bildungsbericht, 2008), playing with words by exchanging the federal (Bundes-) republic by "knowledge-based" (Bildung-) republic of Germany. The aspiration was to become world champion in this discipline within a few years. Confidence was taken by Germany's strong economy and the positive role of the dual practical/theoretical vocational training system providing quite a formidable skilled workforce. New professions were created, especially in the IT sector. Since Germany is poor in terms of natural resources, it was popular to point to the intellectual resources the country's wealth relied upon. The opportunity to use sceptical international data to overcome the fractionalised German education system, which in its authority is split among the 16 federal states, was not taken. Exiting experimental endeavours are run in parallel to a school system that is still struggling with the basic necessities of digitisation and holistic concepts, now even for decades.

The need to redesign interoperability was seen in leading firms. They established departments with specific roles in IC. In general, most emphasis was put on specialisation. With "knowledge management" becoming a special skill, even a profession, it was necessary to embed it adequately within an organisation or a company. For those who relied on it for their living, they had to find a job in an institution or a company or make it a business case as consultants. Thus, parallel to all the hundreds of professions in which people had to handle their special skills and apply their knowledge, there were these specialists in "knowledge" as such. This resulted in sometimes hollow self-marketing.

When listening to a panel of IC experts on a podium near the Springers Research publishing booth at Frankfurter Buchmesse, scientists strolling around as visitors were amused: the panelists seemed to lecture them in regard of what knowledge actually is, how to manage it and what kind of consultants were needed to get the job done (Deutsche Fach, 2013). Bizarre. Since all humans are both intellectuals and social beings, they always have to somehow manage their intellectual judgements and outcomes regardless of which terminology is being used for those processes.

Whilst important sources of IC—education, learning and managing knowledge and their resources—strongly emphasised holistic approaches, those were eroded by their subordination under the shortsighted profit regime. Jacques Delors, in his acceptance speech for the "Leonardo European Corporate Learning Award," praised how prominent artists, politicians, educationalists, public servants and philosophers jointly proclaimed the common purpose for society and for individuals' education in the twenty-first century. A purpose that included "learning to know, learning to do, learning to live together, learning to be" as the "treasures within", which should be pursued according to UNESCO recommendations he chaired (Delors, 2010). To help leverage all this talent in a coherent, balanced way and thus benefit an individual, an organisation or even a society—that was the claim of the diverse intellectual capital navigation and monitoring systems. Those inner bonds were weakened when cost-cutting specialisation and outsourcing became predominant. Many firms even made "values" a specialty and "outsourced" to external consultants offering workshops to employees.

2.3 IC Nemesis

As pointed out in many articles right from the start, many pioneers warned us to not misinterpret them. "You can't manage knowledge, you can just enable it" reminded us Nonaka et al.; the same was proclaimed in variations. By Leif Edvinsson: "Intellectual capital really is fundamental to all companies, communities and, even, societies. It is not a management technique like reengineering which you can choose to apply or not as the case may be. It is more fundamental than that (Edvinsson, 2002) or by Ursula Schneider: "Im direkten Sinne kann man Nichtwissen genauso wenig managen wie Wissen" ("In a direct sense you cannot manage ignorance just as you cannot manage knowledge") (p. 129, Schneider, 2006) (Nonaka et al., 2000). To frame the same thought dialectically from the perspective of the "objects" of many IC projects: "Everybody is a knowledge manager" (Szogs, 2002). It was an attempt to caution against what might be seen as a "false abstraction" following the hype and hubris of "knowledge management".

This warning was not meant to stop the efforts to do whatever possible to enhance a more meaningful dealing with knowledge and to make transparent the impact that different intellectual approaches have on designing diverse organisational systems. Pioneers were convinced that their analysis of how knowledge was dealt with in conventional corporates meant that essential perspectives were excluded. They urged for a fundamental paradigm shift; developed tools to make both the loss and the gain of human, structural and relational intellectual potential visible, and advised how they might be better balanced. Redirecting the corporates navigation was the new good idea.

They did not accuse anybody of not acting "knowledge-based", and therefore, they did not propagate a "knowledge-based" society or economy. They questioned judgements that were being made, showed that classical balance sheets often served a shortsighted purpose and argued for new more sustainable systems of evaluation. They were aware of the content-dependency of their endeavour. That's why it made quite a difference whether IC projects concerned the academic or the corporate world, whether IC developments of countries were analysed in their comparison (Lin et al., 2019) or debated in context with sociopolitical issues like the five steps for Finland's future. Artificial intelligence was assessed using international platforms like NCP (New Club of Paris)—UNESCO conferences (The World Conference on Intellectual Capital for Communities, 2019).

Whenever IC projects reduce their spectrum basically to corporate consultancy, they lose this public visibility. It is difficult to understand the unique selling point in comparison to the multitude of business tools to make a firm more efficient. Most pioneers, both in the learning and knowledge revolution, challenged the *pattern of thinking* of a company or even of a society, and the proposed *mind shift* was accompanied by debates not just with IC departments who anyhow were converted but with decision-makers in business, politics and society. When congresses, public events and fairs focus just on business cases for technological tools and didactical methods, they might be quite successful but lose their innovative transformative societal dimension. IC communities mutate to self-reference, events are judged by "… is there an opportunity in place for me?" and they are hijacked as a stage for profiling. The associations reduce their activities to undoubtedly important mutual support in operational IC-related responsibilities for their respective firms but hardly have any ambitions to address societal or even corporates fundamental IC incoherences.

What followed was a *massive sobering loss of IC specific platforms* for national and international debate, because there was little "specific" seen in it. Bitcom stopped their prestigious KnowTech event, and the humble, modest and impressive head of its organisation, the late Dr. Mathias Weber, got little acknowledgement, same is sadly true for Professors Winfried Sommer and Uwe Beck who, as mentioned, initiated LearnTec, Europe's biggest fair for educational technologies, and who attached high-level congresses and excellently published the results annually (Every year, n.d.). In 2023, the 30th anniversary of LearnTec was celebrated as a purely business-success event; the names of the founders were not even mentioned. *Wissensmanager des Jahres* (knowledge manager of the year), the annual event with Germany's government participation, celebrated at Commerzbank's exclusive location next to Berlin Gates, was stopped; the *Executive Master of Knowledge Management* course of studies didn't get enough support; and its intended internationalisation never got on its way. The *Leonardo European Corporate Learning Award* with Jacques Delors, being the first laureate, had to be halted. From an international perspective, the laureates couldn't have been from higher esteem. Prof. Hans Rosling, together with son Ola and daughter-in-law Anna, Otto Scharmer and Kiron University for refugees were awarded at the last event in 2016 (Transfer Meeting, 2016). The book "Factfulness" by the Roslings had already 17 editions within a few years after the death of Hans. In German public media, they were not regarded worth mentioning at the time of winning the Leonardo.

Some educational magazines reported about the last Leonardo event. One of the most relevant, Wirtschaft und Weiterbildung from Haufe publishers, made Otto Scharmer and the U-Theory their title story. But, there was no interview, neither with him nor with representatives of the award, nor the international Leonardo Ambassadors, just a long critique of U-theory written by a professor who had not even been present at the event (Wirtschaft & Weiterbildung, 2016).

The list of decay is much longer; in this context, we stick to previously mentioned events to illustrate the *fate* they had in common, although they themselves did not cause it.

Let me conclude this stage of downwards spirals with an example that illustrates more generally the tremendous gap between dramatic societal challenges for which IC assets would be most valuable and inadequate responses not just in economic-political but in intellectual terms. The financial crisis of 2008–2009 didn't result in systemic rethinking but rather in perfection of the old metrics that caused the disaster.

The *subprime crisis* was named this way due to the absurdity that it was a speculation on *high-risk loans* (subprime), which nevertheless got top ratings by first-class skilled rating agencies. This was consistent with their short-term cynical framing. High risk meant high-profit margins and quick returns. After the collapse, the excuse of Germany's head of Goldman Sachs was that they drew out of the game too late. In other words: speculation on the ruin of people is ok as long as you pull out your own investment in time—to avoid the *inbuilt inevitable catastrophe* after having leveraged the risk as profit. (Szogs, 2008).

In analogy to the subprime crisis, we, in articles and presentations, coined (sic) this pattern of thinking and the obscene use of expertise as *subprime knowledge*. Of course, we were not megalomaniacs to hope to cause a mind shift in public commentary and understanding. We saw it from the NCP perspective as a contribution to re-paradigm IC understanding just as the Club of Rome continuously pointed to the need to redirect navigation concerning the preservation of nature. But even *Occupy Wall Street* as an emancipative movement, which got support from scholars like Nobel laureate Prof. Paul Krugman, in the end, had little impact on the way *we* as modern societies "think" in regard to our political-social-economic order. *Interesting opinions* at best is how public is judging those critiques.

2.4 IC Regress

We observed that "being detached from reality" for some developments in IC meant paradoxically "to be too intensively intertwined with reality" so that critical distance might lack and the differentia specifica hardly can be detected. There is danger to mutate to just variations of efficient business management with little transformative impetus. Let's have a look at a debate the GfWM editors team Stefan Zillich and Andreas Matern quite bold kicked off in a series of volumes they named *Das Kuratierte Dossier* (the curated dossier). In addition to the individual issues, they have recently published a knowledge map of all the contributions and authors, inviting readers to explore connections and developments in the ideas published (Das Kuratierte Dossier, 2024). Not always do discussions take the intended transformative turn. To illustrate it we start backwards with the second last Volume 5 of the series, first. Its title *Knowledge Management Essentials* evokes curiosity. The introductory overview is given by Prof. Peter Heisig (University of Applied Sciences, Potsdam, Germany) about *knowledge management today,* "Wo stehen wir und wohin sollten wir gehen?" (*Where are we now, where should we go?*) (Heisig, 2024). He underscores that his "GPO-WM-Modell" *Geschäftsprozessorientiertes Wissensmanagement-Modell* (business process-oriented knowledge management model) is distilled from 160 KM frameworks, and he basically gives an inventory of IC process components. Who is involved, what tasks have to be fulfilled and how creating and using knowledge is intertwined, he mentions as key to the analytical stages of knowledge activities, like create, store, share, use and add the success factors culture, strategy and leadership, skills and motivation, information technology, governance and controlling. He declares it essential that IC people should be informed about diverse methodologies, like communities of practice, Yellow pages, storytelling, etc. The second last on the list is *Wissensbilanz* (Skandia-Navigator, IC-Monitor). He misses adequate academic courses of studies on the "master" level.

Remarkable is that hardly any arguments are given about *why* components are missing or what the specific added value is about. If he misses a "master course", why does he make no reference to the enormous efforts made in that direction by the "Executive Master of Knowledge Management" we talked about before? Why is it a rather technocratic compilation of IC ingredients with little indication of their transformative power, if used for the proper cooking of an IC meal, answering his initial question: where should we go? His former colleagues from Fraunhofer Institute for Production Systems and Design Technology, Berlin (Fraunhofer IPK), complement more operational details in a contribution in the same publication (Will et al., 2023). They offer a case study in the Brazilian Senai Innovation Institute, explaining how they adapted the stages of strategy, business-process orientation and change management compatible with ISO 30401 regulations. Documentation is central, results must be useful for independent audits, etc. Nothing wrong with such. Surely, it is useful for the companies who engage in them.

Disappointing, it is from the perspective of IC contextualisation and a culture of transformative IC companionship. The issue to which they contributed their "Essentials" was the last in a series of *Das Kuratiertes Dossier* titled *Wissensmanagement quo vadis? Teil 1*, *Wissensmanagement Quo Vadis? Teil 2*, *Wissensmanagement New Normal* and, finally the one with their articles, *Wissensmanagement Essentials*. In the prior three volumes, there was a vivid debate on what were regarded urgent challenges for IC given the structural and political incoherences resulting in dilemma in many spheres: mobility, health, nutrition, climate and education. The specific challenge by the SDGs (Sustainable Development Goals) were connotated with the question how IC in a duality of future literacy approaches and monitoring by Wissensbilanz might be well equipped to offer help to better understand and navigate the interdependencies f.e. of the 16 SDGs (Edvinsson et al., n.d.-a). This diagnosis provoked in good IC companionship and depth an alternative recapture of IC developments and essentials *Wissensmanagement Quo Vadis* part 2 by Prof. Peter Pawlowsky (Pawlowsky, n.d.). In the "New Normal" edition, this dialogue was even taken further. In the coauthored article "UnCredited—Ambivalence of Intellectual Currencies" (L. Edvinsson, A. Szogs, G.M. Szogs), it was asked visually and explicitly "Unlock Wissensbilanz! Why not make it a common mindset for societal IC?" (Edvinsson et al., n.d.-b). We referred to the first meeting of the international advisory board of "Wissensbilanz Made in Germany" (in which Frauenhofer IPK was the coordinating institution) that kicked off an amazing wave of awareness by a regime of road shows supported by Arbeitsgemeinschaft Wirtschaft und Verwaltung, AWV (Working Group for Economic Administration) and the German Federal Ministry for Economic Affairs with numerous events in Germany. If in the Dossier issue *Essentials*, which is building on the former ones none of the controversies, are taken notice of and hardly any transformative answers are given, we are not advancing to *essentials* but regressing to *basics*.

3 Artful Companionship

3.1 Exhibition Partnership

Peter Heisig and the team from Fraunhofer IPK are highly knowledgeable, very good experts and, of course, trusted colleagues. And solid business consultancy is a simple necessity in any profession. But in the context of an IC community positioning itself in various issues of the Dossiers series regarding their assets towards current elementary societal challenges, the scope of one's own current projects and obligations should be transcended. That's why it is important to raise the question: Why do *they* and why do *we* as an IC community lack the boldness of the Dossier editors to take up those challenges beyond the boxes of our daily business? This discussed case serves just as an example because we shared the journey of "Wissensbilanz Made in Germany" and I profited from above mentioned colleagues. Those divergent arguments need constructive continuity from all of us. How might transcending approaches look like?

Another Frauenhofer institution and its partners might illustrate a transformative IC companionship. *Bending the Curve* is an impressive exhibition in art and exhibition space *Frankfurter Kunstverein* in Frankfurt. Among the scientific research institutions invited to present their findings in Frankfurt are the *Fraunhofer Institute for Applied Polymer Research IAP*, the *Max Planck Institute of Animal Behavior* and the *Karlsruhe Institute of Technology* (Faculty of Architecture).

Their explanation for companionship: "Without biodiversity, human existence on planet Earth would not be possible. However, this biodiversity has been declining for far too long, and at an alarming rate. This realisation unites the curatorial team of the Frankfurter Kunstverein, which has invited the Senckenberg Biodiversity and Climate Research Centre and Frankfurt Zoo to collaborate in the form of an interdisciplinary partnership. The result is the new exhibition titled 'Bending the Curve—Knowing, Acting, Caring for Biodiversity,' which alludes to the concept of 'Bending the Curve of Biodiversity Loss'" (Bending the curve, 2024).

Without labelling it IC or "Knowledge Management", the arts actively go ahead in re-paradigming societal innovation. "Both the artistic and scientific exhibits go beyond symbolic references. Instead, *Bending the Curve* showcases artists, research projects and initiatives whose work focuses on active transformation. What they present in the exhibition is born from the idea of co-creation, representing a shared interdisciplinary creative process that encompasses creatures both human and non-human" (Bending the curve, 2024). It is not a one-time lighthouse project but, by now, is well established not just in a series of exhibitions but also with public debates and other prominent research institutions. The famous Frankfurter Institut für Sozialforschung (University of Frankfurt Institute for Social Research) is cooperating. "Law and Time" was one of the university lectures by excellent law professors on 20 February 2024 with a former judge of Germany's constitutional court. The German government for the first time was charged to comply to needs of future generations in their regulations regarding fighting climate change. In the museum, the characteristics of this "inter-temporal law" were debated with participants from art and diverse other sciences (Forschungszentrum, 2024).

It reminds us of the 13. version of dOCUMENTA, the art exhibition in Kassel that takes place in a 5-year sequence, where they researched the central means of art to assist in better understanding the world. They coined their approach "Maybe Education" and cooperated with the Nobel Prize Winner 2023, the Quantum-Physicist, Anton Zeilinger in an artful installation. We discussed learnings from it for IC's relation to art and titled the articles for GfWM publications "Maybe Knowing I" and "Maybe Knowing II" (Szogs, 2012, 2013b) (dOCUMENTA, 2012).

At dOCUMENTA 13, this position was quite radically addressed in the dedication of the exhibition (which was further internationalised by simultaneously having locations in Kabul, Alexandria-Kairo and Banff), given by its art director Carolyn Christov-Bakargiev. Her arguments can't be directly transferred in the academic world but are a tremendous provocative stimulus for thought. "dOCUMENTA 13 is dedicated to artistic research and forms of imagination that explore commitment, matter, things, embodiment, and active living in connection with, yet not subordinated to, theories. dOCUMENTA 13 is driven by a holistic and non-local centric vision that is sceptical of the persisting believe in economic growth". And—for many of us may be hard to swallow—a bit in the spirit of the "Wolf"in our introductory: "this vision is shared with, and recognises, the shapes and practices of knowing of all the animate and inanimate makers of the world, including people" (dOCUMENTA 13, 2012).

3.2 Coauthoring: Ljubljana Reading Manifesto

The quite famous *Stairs of Knowledge* (Wissenstreppe) from Prof. Klaus North, by which signs plus syntax constitute data, plus meaning: information, plus connections: knowledge, plus application ability: skills, plus willingness: acting, these stairs are stepped down rather than up by many of today's readers, who prefer *going back* to simple superficial information. That at least is the diagnosis of international research that resulted in the *Ljubljana Reading Manifesto*. It was presented in a prominent setting with the ministers of culture present of Germany and the honorary guest country Slovenia at the international Frankfurter Buchmesse. "The digital realm may foster more reading than ever in history, but it also offers many temptations to read in a superficial and scattered manner—or even not to read at all" (The Ljubljana Reading Manifesto, n.d.). This is seen as a danger for the most elementary cornerstone of IC: *critical thinking*. That's why the manifesto underscores the importance of *higher-level reading*. "Higher-level reading is our most powerful tool for analytic and critical thinking. It exercises metacognition and cognitive patience, expands our conceptual capacities, trains cognitive empathy and perspective-taking social skills which are indispensable for informed citizens in a democratic society". Amazing that the Higher Reading Manifesto has been the central message by the guest of honour at the fair's 75th edition with its formula *interest follows relevance*. AI and TikTok stage had been included; the event welcomed 215.000 visitors, over

4000 exhibitors from 95 countries and 7000 media representatives; and the guest of honour pavilion had been a *crowd pleaser* (#fbm23, n.d.). The Manifesto was explicitly and officially supported by International Publishers Association (IPA), Deutsche Akademie für Sprache und Dichtung (German Academy for Language and Literature), Federation of European Publishers EU-READ, Consortium of European reading promotion organisations, PEN International, International Federation of Library Associations and Institutions (IFLA) and the International Board on Books for Young People (IBBY). This overwhelming support shows that current research and surveys caused extreme concern about the obvious decay of the very basis of analytical abilities and as such of societal IC. What have "higher reading" *capabilities* to do with *IC companionship*?

4 IC Companionships Constituents

4.1 Boëtheia and Scholê

To present the manifesto Director of Regensburg University Library, Dr. André Schüller-Zwierlein was chosen a key author of the joint manifesto, who, for an explanation, refers to his book "Die Fragilität des Zugangs" (Fragility of Access) (Schüller-Zwierlein, 2023). In this remarkable study, he recaptures the way essentials in modern analytical thinking are shaped by Platon. In our context, we focus on two elements important to enable us to understand IC companionship better. In the dialogue "Phaidros", Platon makes Socrates explore the interaction of written and spoken word, the word that requires presence and is synchronous whilst the other one is asynchronous and comes consecutively. Both in a way are orphans, speech and script can't stand for themselves, and they need to be questioned by people one trusts. They are always incomplete, need to be challenged by other perspectives, tested and valued in every possible way, at least if the search for the truth and wisdom, i.e. *philo-sophy*, is core. In this state of imperfection, they need help, assistance, in classical Greek *boëtheia (*Ebd. P. 14,15, n.d.*)*. If one reads something one does not understand, one might ask—if still available—even the writer or the father/mother of the thought, what he/she actually means. But the speaker/writer also can take possible objections into account and help/assist him/herself, giving *boëtheia* to refine one's thought.

To practice this companionship among each other and even with oneself both in discourse with written and with actual speech, a time during which one is not pressured is indispensable. This kind of leisure interestingly in classical Greek is named *scholê (*Ebd. P. 23, n.d.*)*. The modern word *school* is derived from it and often one would not expect a kind of "un-pressured time". Many might associate "school" with the time in which you have to perform and during which you have to deliver and produce results in exams quite regularly supervised by a stopwatch. For Socrates, that would be almost a horror scenario. In "Theaitetos", another Platon dialogue, Socrates explains why those who strive for analytical thinking would be quite untalented speakers (rhetorics) in court and at contests. While searching for knowledge is done in peace and with adequate time, the speakers who are contesting in contrast are always in a hurry and timed by the *klepsydra,* a *water clock* comparable to a sand clock. (Ebd. P. 24, n.d.) Those speakers are unilateral, and they lag the multilateral dimension of the companionship, someone willing to *share time to help* in understanding and search for knowing.

André Schüller-Zwierlein walks us through the philosophical cultural history debates by those who gratefully turned to Platon and discussed the obstacles and complications, the attacks on cultural memory, the totalitarian perversions of thought and the ethical dimensions of the challenges this kind of human companionship in the quest of a life in dignity holds for us.

We just take two representations he quotes at the beginning of this study. (Ebd. P. VII, n.d.)

Hannah Arendt in "Socrates", 1954: *niemand, der nicht fähig ist, mit sich selbst einen Dialog zu führen, kann sein Gewissen bewahren* (no one, who is unable, to have a dialogue with himself, can keep his conscience).

Amartya Sen in "Identity and Violence", 2006: *the hope of harmony in the contemporary world lies to a great extent in a clearer understanding of the pluralities of human identity.*

4.2 Transformative Power in the Roots

Many currently turn to those roots of our civilisation's cultural history of thought as important sources. It helps to reestablish a prerequisite for progressive transformation. It is this innate attitude of sincerity, honesty, mutual respect and humbleness which does not need to be proclaimed and is rather a livestock. At a conference of the project IMO (International Monitoring) organised by the chair for information management in the RWTH Aachen University, Karl Erik Sveiby, the Swedish IC pioneer, was present (In Context, n.d.). Interestingly, he stopped his IC studies in Western companies and continued research in Australia with Indigenous people. He reported that they have *no word for "knowledge"* because they are dwelling in it. It is a kind of simply living the attitude we described. They have no idea of the artificial exclusion that constitute intellectual property rights. Those neglect that all our ideas have an endless list of contributors who make them come to existence. Who could name all the true co-owners? For these indigenous people, knowledge therefore is a natural common good. Further expertise was given in the two versions (English/German) of the book "Enabling Innovation - Innovative Capability - German and International Views" edited by the RWTH team Sabina Jeschke & all 2011. I contributed the chapter on "Future Center - An Unconventional Approach to promote Intellectual Potential" (p. 393 ff.) kindly put in a broader context in a commentary by the cofounder of the Future Center Alliance Hank Kune "Facilitating the Future" (p. 407ff).

In the February 2024 newsletter of the GfWM, Prof. North, in an interview, reported on his current activities. He focuses now personally in his courses on knowledge management in Donau-Universität in Krems and at Universidad Federal de Santa Catarina in Brasilia on the *key competence of critical thinking*. For him, it is essential in an open society, where we live in respect and regardful with each other. He introduced practical training in critical thinking using *Socratic questioning* (gfwm newsletter, 2024).

The "Global Assembly" is an international activist-congregation created in context with the 175. anniversary of the 1848 Frankfurt St. Paul's Church assembly, in which the first proposal for a German democratic constitution was debated. In preparation for their next event, they invited Prof. Eva von Redecker, author of "Bleibefreiheit" (Freedom to Stay). With her, we encounter from another angle the same revival of the Socratic dialogues. She puts them in the context of basic human questions. In a capitalist economy, individual freedom is antagonistic and the individual "owns" itself, so if it has no means of production, its freedom is to compete with its ownership of its "self" by selling itself. Freedom thus is constantly limited by all the others. Redecker reminds us of conceptions by which in contrast freedom is achieved if our fellowmen are actually the constituents of our freedom (Hegel/Marx) (von Redecker, 2023)—the Socratic concept of trustful sharing *help* and *time*.

The psychologist Rainer Mausfeld, a prof. Emeritus who according to Neue Züricher Zeitung illuminates us in the thought tradition of Humboldt, Deweys and Chomsky, has written an analysis of de-civilisation, in which he elaborates "nemesis" (Mausfeld, 2023). He puts the great impact of ancient Athens in a context that bridges to the associated *futurizing facets* of our argument for IC companionship. Compared to other civilisations, the societal atmosphere had quite a high level of openness and tolerance, political debate was enjoyed and a curiosity and playful discovery of intellectual worlds and questioning of what was publicly regarded as self-understood was quite common. Thus they discussed different versions of how one might see the world which incited them to creatively think things through and try out different societal arrangements (page 464): the *transformative power* of the *multi-plurality of perspectives*.

5 IC Companionship: A Re-Paradigming Mindshift

It is this *mindset of playfulness* that in *trustful companionship* is testing out the intellectual and physical and the intangible and tangible resources to find out what works best within the limits of a given societal situation. It combines academic discipline and analytical vigour with holistic artful learning approaches that use all senses to stimulate meaningful ways of acting together. That's why this *combination* was and still is at the core of the specific contribution intellectual capital management has offered society and by which it still can make the difference in both the micro-organisational context of a company, a public institution or a broader context of developments of cities, regions and nations. The concept of *Ba*, the inspirational space, goes hand in hand with the Japanese driver's seat position in modern knowledge management's theoretical advancements. Skandia has had its famous "navigator" being an intellectual blueprint for many scholars in the field of ICM, and in parallel, the concept of the future centre was put into reality. The "Executive Master of Knowledge Management" we talked about had events in which the Circus

Roncalli director involved students and their accompanying corporate affiliates in creative experiments. The LearnTec platform was used to get the leading minds of IC to interact with excellent musicians or world-class sportspeople. The NCP co-organised Aalto Camp for Societal Innovation and used the Aalto University campus as a meeting place for stakeholders of challenges in communities and cities. They invited international experts who took part not as highly paid business consultants but as internationals paid by the currency of mutual sharing of knowledge and experience. Results were presented to each other in an ACSI-bition (Szogs, n.d.). The co-founder of the future center alliance Hank Kune confirms this observation: "As Guenther Szogs points out….there are many ways to enable innovation and facilitate the future...ACSI …facilitates a mind shift…at different levels. It is all about how people reframe their problems and how organisations and regions think about the future" (Kune, 2011, p 410). Progressive mutual inspirations with the Frankfurt Kulturcampus initiative were documented in the collection of expertises of the IMO Action-field "Transfer" (Szogs 2013c). All these efforts had one thing in common: IC-decay—if caused by societal stagnation of thinking outside the box—needs to be overcome by a *co-creative artful experimental companionship*.

These patterns, which once were IC essentials, are nowadays quite well-established in many progressive platforms (Szogs, 2013a). It's not about revival; it's about adaptation and cooperation in the spirit of openness that others already are practicing. IC is *measured* by living that essence, *not by the label* we put on it.

"Future Skills Knowledge Management" is the title of GfWM's latest volume of their series "Das Kuratierte Dossier". In the article "Skill Is an Entity That Contains a Cosmos" (Edvinsson et al., 2024), learning journeys with this mindset are presented. The result of an ACSI co-creation workshop shared in Finland is a mosaic stone for the C*lassroom of the Future* orchestrated by Roland Burger with the guest of honour Indonesia on the International Frankfurter Buchmesse. School classes from the region are invited as food explorers to experience Indonesian cuisine alongside cooks with a high reputation. Curiosity and awareness are stimulated to learn about tangible and intangible cultural ingredients of a dish and of all the skills needed in the production and supply chain. As the New York Times in their review of the film *The Taste of Things* puts it: "…there are the true artists, the chef and the cook. For them, the culinary arts are the highest expression of humanity because they are a product of everything that makes us human: time and attention, every sense, every sensation and, in the end, it's entirely fleeting" (NYT, 08.02.2024).

Eunice Mercier-Laurent and Leif Edvinsson use this IC philosophy provoking with the title of their book: "World Class Cooking for Solving Global Challenges: Reparadigming Societal Innovation". For them, it is more than a metaphor; they take up the great tradition of the French training system *compagnonnage* (companionship), detailing "Cooking Future Society" by clarifying that the recipe to leverage companionship includes, among others, caring for a pleasing atmosphere (Mercier-Laurent & Edvinsson, 2021). In the preface, Jean-Eric Aubert, former innovation policy adviser at OECD and World Bank, now president of the Société Francaise de Prospective, binds together the challenges, the ingredients and the companionship: "in times of climate change, digital revolution, global pandemics … we need to cook new societies, new ways of life, new forms of business… the ingredients are there: technologies, motivations, ideas, etc. As well as the actors: peoples, groups, individuals, you and me!" In other words: *IC as Intellectual Companionship* is this imaginative visionary design of coherent societal renewal in a spirit of generously sharing all relevant available physical and mental resources.

References

#fbm23: the meeting place of the International publishing industry proves its unique position and is defined by committed political discourse, www.buchmesse.de/en/press/press-releases, downloaded 5.11.23.

Bending the curve, knowing, acting, caring for biodiversity, in collaboration with the Senckenberg Biodiversity and Climate Research Centre and Frankfurt Zoo, Frankfurter Kunstverein, on view 13.10.2023–17.03.2024.

Access to all volumes of "Das Kuratierte Dossier" (2024). https://www.gfwm.de/das-kuratierte-dossier/english. The overview as knowledge map is accessible by https://www.gfwm.de/wp-content/uploads/2024/04/Das-Kuratierte-Dossier-Knowledge-Map-2024-04-.pdf

Jacques Delors, Acceptance Speech, Leonardo European Corporate Learning Award, www.leonardo-award.eu, 2010 and Learning: The Treasure Within, UNESCO Publishing, second edition 2010.

Deutsche Fach Presse, Buchmesse Fachpresse Panel, 10. Oktober 2013.

dOCUMENTA 13, The Guidebook, Hatje Cantz, 2012, p. 134, p. 449.

dOCUMENTA 13, The Guidebook, Hatje Cantz, 2012, p. 2.

Dumont Reiseführer in cooperation with Deutsche Bank, Land der Ideen – Der Reiseführer, 365 Orte und Veranstaltungen, 2006.

Ebd. P. 14,15.

Ebd. P. 23.

Ebd. P. 24.

Ebd. P. VII.

Leif Edvinsson. (2002). Corporate Longitude – Navigating the Knowledge Economy, p. 26.

Leif Edvinsson, Astrid Szogs, & Günther M. Szogs: Skill Is An Entity That Contains A Cosmos: Das Kuratierte Dossier Vol. 6 "Future Skills Knowledge Management" March 2024, ISSN (print) 2940 1372 (print + online PDF).

L. Edvinsson, A. Szogs, & G. Szogs (n.d.-a) ICM for future knowledge navigation, supreme versus sub-prime knowledge, Kuratiertes Dossier Bd. 2, p 5–9.

L. Edvinsson, A. Szogs, & G. Szogs (n.d.-b) Uncredited – ambivalence of intellectual currencies, Kuratiertes Dossier Bd. 4, page 18–23.

Every year volumes with all branches. Published like 6.

Forschungszentrum Normative Ordnungen der Goethe Universität Frankfurt, Professor Rainer Forst, Direktor Forschungszentrum Normative Ordnungen, Professor Klaus Günther, Professor Gabriele Britz, Professor Christoph Borchardt in Cooperation with Frankfurter Kunstverein, title: Strafrecht und Zeit in der Klimakrise, 20.2.2024.

gfwm newsletter, Februar 2024, Nr. 111, www.gfwm.de, downloaded 26.02.2024.

Daniela Gruebel, Klaus North, & Günther Szogs, Intellectual Capital Reporting – ein Vergleich von vier Ansätzen, ZFO wissen 1/2004, 19–27.

Peter Heisig, Wissensmanagement heute, wo stehen wir und wohin sollten wir gehen? In: Knowledge Management Essentials, Das Kuratierte Dossier, Bd. 5, 2024, p 8–13, Overview: (Das-Kuratierte-Dossier-Knowledge-Map-2024-04-).

In Context "Innovationsfähigkeit und neue Wege des Wissenstransfer, Expertisen aus dem IMO – Aktionsfeld Transfer", RWTH Aachen University, Volume 8 (n.d.)

Commentary by Hank Kune "Facilitating the Future". In "Enabling Innovation – Innovative Capability – German and International Views", Springer, 2011.

LEARNTEC 9th European Congress and Trade Fair for Educational and Informational Technology 2001, Proceedings, UNESCO, editors Uwe Beck, Winfried Sommer.
Lin, C., Edvinsson, L., & Consunji, M. A. (2019). *National intellectual capital year book*. Taiwan Intellectual Capital Research Center.
Rainer Mausfeld, Hybris und Nemesis, Wie uns die Entzivilisierung von Macht in den Abgrund führt – Einsichten aus 5000 Jahren, Westend 2023.
Eunice Mercier-Laurent, & Leif Edvinsson, "World Class Cooking for Solving Global Challenges – Reparadigming Societal Innovation", p 63, p 77, emerald publishing 2021.
Nationaler Bildungsbericht: Merkel ruft Bildungsrepublik aus, 12.6.2008 FAZ.NET.
Ikujiro Nonaka, Kazoo Ichijo, & Georg von Krogh, Enabling Knowledge Creation, 2000, Chapter 1.
Klaus North, & Daniela Gruebel, von der Intervention zur Wirkung: das mehrstufige Indikatoren Modell, in Wissensbilanzen, Intellektuelles Kapital erfolgreich nutzen und entwickeln, Springer 2005, editors Kai Mertins, Kay Alwert, , 109–119.
Peter Pawlowsky (n.d.) Intellectual capital management – unde venis – quo vadis? Kuratiertes Dossier Bd. 3, 16–25.
Pawlowsky, P., & Edvinsson, L. (2012). *Intellektuelles Kapital und Wettbewerbsfähigkeit*. Springer.
Picht, G. (1964). *Die deutsche Bildungskatastrophe: Analyse und Dokumentation*. DTV.
Ursula Schneider, Das Management der Ignoranz, Nichtwissen als Erfolgsfaktor, Deutscher Universitätsverlag Mai 2006.
André Schüller-Zwierlein, Die Fragilität des Zugangs, eine Kritik der Informationsgesellschaft, de GRUYTER Saur, 2023.
Szogs, G. Jeder Mitarbeiter ist ein Wissensmanager, in: Wissensmanagement – das Magazin für Führungskräfte. 5/2002 Abrufbar unter: https://www.wissensmanagement.net/print/archiv/2002/wissensmana
Günther M. Szogs, Knowledge Management, Intellectual Capital and the Rating Exercise – An Unconventional Approach, Chapter 6 in Capital immatériel. connaissance et performance, sous la direction d' Ahmed Bounfour, L' Harmattan 2006, effects of "Executive Master of Knowledge management".
Günther M. Szogs, Professor Leif Edvinsson, Subprime Knowledge, BITKOM KnowTech, Wissen – Macht – Finanzen: Dialog für die Wissensgesellschaft, 9.10.2008 in Frankfurt (Forum 8), Kongressband.
Günther M. Szogs. "Maybe Knowing" – an impulse regarding cross-fertilization of knowledge and art in: gfwm THEMEN 3/Sep 2012 PDF Download http://www.gfwm.de/wp-content/uploads/2014/12/gfwmTHEMEN3-September2012.pdf
Günther M. Szogs, "Beyond Planning – a few observations on Metropolitan Region Frankfurt" in Skanör Conversation June 4–5, 2013a, co-organised by Skåne and the New Club of Paris, p 16–18.
Günther M. Szogs. "Maybe Knowing II" – some further aspects on cross-fertilization of knowledge and art In: gfwm THEMEN 4/January 2013b PDF Download http://www.gfwm.de/wp-content/uploads/2014/12/gfwmTHEMEN4-Januar2013.pdf
Günther M. Szogs, Das finnische ACSI und der Kultur Campus Frankfurt – international vergleichende 'mediale Exploration' zur Co-Creation von Wirtschaft, Wissenschaft, Kultur und Politik. Expertise für das Internationale Monitoring (IMO) Aktionsfeld Transfer, RWTH Aachen University, 2013c.
Günther M. Szogs (n.d.) "Future Center – an unconventional approach to promote intellectual capital potential. An overview over international development and the perspective of national adaptation".
The Ljubljana Reading Manifesto: Why higher-level reading is important, https://readingmanifesto.org/#, p. 1 downloaded 9.11.23.
The World Conference on Intellectual Capital for Communities, 15th edition, organised by the European Chair on Intellectual Capital and Unesco Intergovernmental Information for all Programs, partnership EU, OECD, New Club of Paris: Artificial intelligence and the next generation of competencies, July 11&12, 2019.

Transfer Meeting and 7. Festive Ceremony of the European Corporate Learning Award, September 19, 2016, Hotel Kameha Grand Bonn, Germany.
Eva von Redecker, "Bleibefreihei", S. Fischer 2023, p 42.
Markus Will, Ronald Ort, Felix Budde (Fraunhofer IPK Berlin), Wieviel Essentials stecken in den neuen Wissensmanagement Standards? Ein Erfahrungsbericht, Kuriertes Dossier Bd. 5, 2023 p 26–37.
Wirtschaft & Weiterbildung: Das Magazin für Führung, Personalentwicklung und e – Learning, Okt. 2016, Pro & Kontra "Theorie U", die blinden Flecken des Claus Otto Scharmer.
Wissensbilanz – Made In Germany, Leitfaden 2.0 zur Erstellung einer Wissensbilanz, www.bmwi.de, 2008, Projektleitung Prof. Mertins, Frauenhofer IPK, Team: Alwert, Bornemann, Ebner, Heisig, Kivikas, Nagel, Orth, Pfeifer, Reinhardt, Will, Wuscher. Internationale Expertengruppe: Andriessen, Edvinsson, Fischer, Leitner, North, Szogs.
"Wissensmanager" in Wikipedia, accessed 28.02.24.

Günther M. Szogs is educationalist and system analyst. In the metropolitan region, Frankfurt Rhein-Main he was part of the think tank to develop the Knowledge Region. In his long career as head of skill and knowledge management at Commerzbank, he acted in different roles (initiator, advisor, speaker) in pioneering platforms for national and international cross-sectional discourse in the field of intellectual capital and societal innovation.

He was a member of the international expert team that advised "Wissensbilanzen Made in Germany" and of IMO (International Monitoring), a project of RWTH Aachen University for the German Federal Ministry of Education and Research. On the advisory board of the Executive Master of Knowledge Management of TU Chemnitz, of LearnTec and of BITCOM's KnowTech and as cofounder of BIGA, an educational association of Germany's major financial institutions, he advocated a more integral cooperation of the academic sphere, the corporate world and civil society. Challenges in all mentioned fields he presented at national and international conferences. He has been the secretary of the Leonardo European Corporate Learning Award and is a founding member of the New Club of Paris

Sustainable National Intellectual Capital (SNIC) and Its Applications

Carol Y. Y. Lin

Abstract

Sustainability has become the latest global buzzword. Intangibles are key elements in supporting sustainability, such as intellectual capital (IC), including knowledge, technology, and human talents. Over the past few decades, intellectual capital research has proliferated to maturity. Introducing how organizations and governments can utilize IC research results to become more sustainable and proposing the next stage of IC research are the main purposes of this study.

This chapter first briefly describes the evolution of IC research. Afterward, a sustainable national intellectual capital (SNIC) model with a special focus on health, connectivity, and sustainability is introduced. Furthermore, country comparisons reveal that 12 out of the top 15 countries of SNIC overlap with those of IMD World Competitiveness. Particularly, four small countries, Denmark, Switzerland, Netherlands, and Singapore, are in the top five in both SNIC and IMD ranking, indicating good targets for future IC research. The public structure has the greatest explaining power for GDP. Graphs and trajectories are mapped based on SNIC vs. GDP. This chapter contributes to the futurizing of IC theory with IC ecosystems and futurizing IC practices through the SNIC model. They provide guidelines for utilizing SNIC data for the purposes of enhancing national intangible assets and proposing a more comprehensive IC field of research.

C. Y. Y. Lin (✉)
National Chengchi University, Taipei, Taiwan
e-mail: yehyunln@nccu.edu.tw

A. Kianto et al. (eds.), *Futurizing Intellectual Capital*, Knowledge Management and Organizational Learning 15, https://doi.org/10.1007/978-3-031-80197-6_8

1 Introduction

The value of intellectual capital has caught the attention of academia, business consultants, institutional researchers, and policymakers for more than 20 years. This stream of research has evolved from concept promotion, reporting and disclosure, measurement and management to ecosystems, linked with firm strategy, performance, knowledge management, human resource practices, etc. (Lin & Edvinsson, 2021). Over the past two decades, relevant journals, particularly the Journal of Intellectual Capital (JIC), have published numerous papers reporting on this field's development, transformation, and contributions regarding the importance of intangibles.

Furthermore, in the current sharing economy, both tangibles (cars, Uber; houses, Airbnb) and intangibles (knowledge) can be shared. Sharing intangibles does not entail the depletion of resources over time; rather, they may be enhanced by the exchange of knowledge. Especially intangibles, such as service, innovation, and renewal capability, are becoming more and more important in the era marked by the transformation from the industrial economy to the service economy.

The focus of this field of research is mainly at the organizational level, with only a small percentage of papers investigating city, national, or regional levels, very likely due to the difficulty of obtaining quality data for comparative purposes (Lin & Edvinsson, 2021). However, due to the increasing number of international interactions in the borderless global economy enhanced by AI technology and the shared economy, organizational operations will definitely be influenced by the national macro environment, which is an indication of the growing importance of national intellectual capital (NIC). Hopefully, this research can contribute to the enhancement of futurizing IC theory and futurizing IC practices to accumulate national intangibles for the well-being of organizations, societies and nations alike.

This chapter first describes the development of intellectual capital and its extant applications. Second, a sustainable national intellectual capital (SNIC) model is introduced, with the SNIC ranking of the studied 59 major countries. Third, the SNIC country ranking is compared with the country ranking of IMD World Competitiveness. Fourth, the relationships between SNIC and GDP per capita (ppp) (hereinafter GDP for brevity's sake) are presented. Fifth, suggested ways of utilizing SNIC data are introduced. Finally, a proposed intellectual capital ecosystem is shared.

2 Intellectual Capital Research Background

In the industrial age, win-lose was the dominant logic as companies competed for limited resources. Over the past few decades, organizations have employed various methods to win over competitors and to strive for profit maximization and market share. However, the transformation from an industrial economy to a service economy has changed the rules of the game. A service economy generates values mainly on intangibles, such as service experiences, innovation, and renewal rather than on hard assets (Nahapiet & Ghoshal, 1998; Lev, 2001; Edvinsson, 2013; Stahle et al., 2015). The variation of stock prices in the same industry also indicates that intangibles explained the price differences, which facilitated the introduction of the intellectual capital Skandia model (Edvinsson & Malone, 1997). Furthermore, the development of information technology (IT) and robot technology has increased the probability that the routines of everyday life will be increasingly replaced or controlled by computerized systems. What remains distinctively human are the intangibles, such as tacit knowledge, emotions, feelings, etc.

3 How Intellectual Capital Research Was Developed

In a study reflecting the 20-year history of the Journal of Intellectual Capital (JIC), Lin and Edvinsson (2021) reported on the four stages of intellectual capital research development. In the first stage, the definition/characterization and awareness of IC are the focus; in the second stage, reporting and disclosure are prevalent; in the third stage, measurement and management assume the center of attention, with an emphasis on performance-creating strategies; the fourth stage entails investigating IC ecosystems by integrating the IC of firms, cities, and/or nations (Lin & Edvinsson, 2021). Such integration enables the building of strong economic, social, and environmental ecosystems, where healthy organizations can flourish (Dumay, 2013).

Compared with general management research, intellectual capital research is relatively new. Yet, its history of more than 20 years enables us to see the birth of a new stream of research and the manner in which it has matured. The theories of "social construction of knowledge" and "knowledge diffusion and inheritance" can accurately explain the "forming and norming" of this field of study. During the first stage of IC reports which were characterized by definition and concept promotion, a number of scholars devised the concept of IC and shared their viewpoints in various journals and publications. Interested scholars joined the conversation to provide additional views and to help create a more comprehensive picture of what IC is and why it is important. The formation of IC knowledge takes place through social construction involving a community of scholars.

The norming stage is manifested by the diffusion and inheritance of IC knowledge. The diffusion of knowledge takes place between individuals, groups, and organizations by communicating research outcomes and innovations (Carter et al., 2007; Kumar, 2018). The diffusion and inheritance of IC knowledge explain the second and third stages of creating IC guidelines and standards (reporting and disclosure), identification, and measurement while continuously promoting the first stage of IC knowledge. The inheritance of IC knowledge is manifested by the increasing number of JIC publications authored by scholars from all over the world. The contextualizing of IC to local contexts enriches the original knowledge (Agarwal et al., 2004; Rodríguez-Muñiz, 2015), making it possible for a specific discipline to become mature.

4 National Intellectual Capital

Traditionally, economists utilized metrics such as GDP per capita and other similar economic indicators as a measure of a country's growth and progress. In recent years, there has been a shift away from models of productivity that focus on tangible assets—capital, machinery, land, and raw materials—to intangible assets such as knowledge, skills, information, and innovation. National as well as corporate competitiveness relies more and more on intangibles, reflected as the possession of talented manpower, national/corporate image, government efficiency, and networking for sustainability. Particularly in the post-financial crisis era, it has become clear that countries with a high level of national intangibles weathered the crisis better and rebounded more robustly than those with a lower level of intangibles (Lin et al., 2014). The 2008 financial crisis also exhibited the inability of traditional monitoring tools to prevent crises. As a result, there is a growing need to monitor and analyze trends of national intangibles (Stahle et al., 2015).

A large-scale NIC comparison was undertaken by Lin and Edvinsson (2011), consisting of human capital, market capital, process capital, and renewal capital. Based on the 700 JIC paper titles reviewed, only 14 of them were national-level IC studies (Lin & Edvinsson, 2021). Since organizations, including MNCs (multinational corporations), function in a particular national context, the quality of manpower supply (human capital), corporate tax encouragement (market capital), government efficiency (process capital), and IP rights protection (renewal capital) affect the value creation of those organizations. As a result, incorporating national intangibles such as NIC into international expansion may ensure smoother overseas operations.

5 Extant Applications of Intellectual Capital Research

5.1 Organizational IC Applications

Initially, intellectual capital research was regarded as accounting-oriented. With an ever-increasing number of IC papers being published, topics devoted to knowledge management, performance, human resources, and strategy are on the rise (Lin & Edvinsson, 2021). Research on the private sector includes fashion, banking, accounting, information technology, biotechnology, hospitality, insurance, and construction while public-sector research covers topics related to government and universities (Lin, 2020a; Lin & Edvinsson, 2021). Having reviewed the IC research of 127 journal papers and 43 PhD dissertations in Taiwan over the past 20 years, this author found positive relationships between intellectual capital and organizational performance, market/organizational value, profit, competitiveness, productivity, organizational commitment, governance, and knowledge management (Lin, 2020a).

5.2 Connecting National IC with Organizational IC

Connecting national-level IC with organizational IC will benefit companies as well as societies as evidenced by the following researches. Utilizing the data analysis of 125 industries investing in 44 different countries with 29,396 overseas investment observations, Chang and Lin (2015) combined organizational and national IC data and found that overseas success is related to host country NIC after control for national distance. The study clearly shows that connecting organizational IC with NIC helps companies make better decisions in terms of international opportunity identification, risk control, site selection, and market segmentation. In other words, NIC provides additional information for organizations to make better foreign investment decisions.

In a working paper investigating the role intellectual capital played in pandemic prevention, Peng et al. (2023) reported a closely connected national IC (NIC) and organizational IC system that successfully controlled the spread of COVID-19 in Taiwan. As a result, the healthcare system in Taiwan did not suffer a breakdown during the 3-year pandemic (Hwang et al., 2020). The effective and efficient deployment of both national IC and organizational IC greatly mitigated the severity of the pandemic's impact in Taiwan compared to the experience of other countries.

Multiple-level studies prompt businesses to become context-conscious in the increasingly globalized economy. As a result, an organizational study that did not consider NIC might fail to include a major source of critical information when expanding to other countries.

6 Sustainable National Intellectual Capital (SNIC) Model

The first NIC 1.0 model contained 28 indicators (Lin & Edvinsson, 2008, 2011). NIC 2.0 was enriched to 48 indicators (Stahle et al., 2015). Although the two NIC models are still valid, in responding to the rising concerns of health, environment, and information technology, a sustainable intellectual capital (SNIC) model was developed as NIC 3.0 (Lin, 2020b).

Still based on the NIC 1.0 and 2.0 models of human capital, market capital, process capital, and renewal capital, SNIC was modified to include five dimensions, namely, health, public structure, education, renewal, and CNC (connectivity and contactivity). The public structure is somewhat similar to process capital, education to human capital, and renewal capital remains the same. Two new dimensions, "health" and "CNC" have been added. Since SNIC depicts sustainability, we adopted futuristic thinking and replaced market capital with the dimensions of health and CNC, envisioning the issues aroused by rapidly aging societies and an increasingly connected world. Also, we adopted the rationale that when the public structure is sound and connectivity is strong, market capital should naturally follow. We drew four interlocking circles (health, public structure, education, and renewal) with a ring of CNC superimposed upon them to reinforce the linkage of the four circles and to forge their relationships, as shown in Fig. 1.

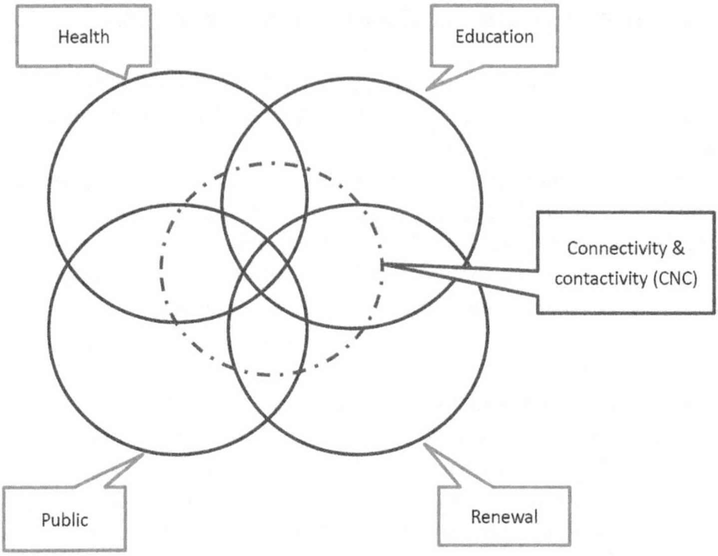

Fig. 1 The SNIC model

The data source of the SNIC model is, as was the case for NIC 1.0 and 2.0, from the widely accepted International Institute for Management Development (IMD) database. The institution has published the World Competitiveness Yearbook for over 30 years. The IMD database provides valid and quality data, enabling the updating of annual data, and covers both qualitative and quantitative indicators suitable for the calculation of intangible assets, as intangibles cannot be fully represented by simply adding up various objective indicators.

Since the SNIC is positioned to be a supplement of the NIC model, we used different indicators to achieve synergy and confirm the effect of the NIC 2.0 model. During the validation process, around 60 indicators out of IMD's 300-plus indicators were selected. SEM (structural equation modelling) analyses retained 44 indicators in five dimensions with good reliability ranging from 0.81 to 0.88 and good explaining power of each indicator against each dimension. Readers can refer to Appendix 1 for the selected indicators of the SNIC model, which cover SDG 3 (health and well-being), SDG 4 (quality education), SDG 7 (affordable and clean energy), SDG 9 (innovation and infrastructure), and SDG 17 (partnership for goals). Data analysis found a very high correlation of around 0.95 between SNIC and NIC for the comparison of both scores and rankings. With different sets of indicators, the high correlation between the two models indicates that SNIC can provide valuable information for examining another set of national intangible assets, with special focuses on health, sustainability, and connectivity.

The most current 2023 SNIC country ranking (based on 2022 data) is shown in Table 1. For the purpose of comparison, the second column of the ranking shows the 2023 vs. the 2020 ranking (Lin, 2020b). For the 2023 ranking, the top ten SNIC

Table 1 The most current 2023 SNIC ranking of 59 countries

Country	2023 (2020) ranking	Overall SNIC	#	Health	#	Public	#	Education	#	Renewal	#	CNC
Denmark	1(1)	36.55	3	7.48	4	7.19	4	7.62	1	7.52	1	6.73
Switzerland	2(2)	36.07	2	7.50	5	7.16	1	7.92	3	7.31	6	6.18
Netherlands	3(4)	35.43	4	7.39	8	6.89	2	7.71	7	7.05	3	6.39
Singapore	4(5)	35.19	12	6.82	3	7.47	3	7.71	9	6.99	5	6.20
Finland	5(6)	34.97	6	7.25	6	7.10	6	7.53	10	6.96	8	6.13
Iceland	6(11)	34.84	5	7.27	9	6.88	7	7.44	6	7.10	7	6.16
Sweden	7(7)	34.24	7	7.14	18	6.37	9	7.33	2	7.38	9	6.01
Norway	8(3)	33.74	8	7.06	11	6.72	8	7.43	11	6.69	10	5.83
UAE	9(10)	33.55	14	6.70	**1**	**7.82**	12	7.01	18	6.31	14	5.70
Qatar	**10(17)**	33.40	**1**	**7.70**	2	7.66	26	6.51	21	6.13	27	5.40
Canada	11(9)	32.95	13	6.77	12	6.56	5	7.53	12	6.64	24	5.45
Taiwan	**12(20)**	32.44	26	6.30	13	6.52	11	7.07	8	7.05	22	5.50
Austria	13(13)	32.30	10	7.03	10	6.72	25	6.54	16	6.31	12	5.70
Luxembourg	14(8)	32.18	20	6.48	16	6.44	18	6.84	25	5.86	2	6.56
USA	15(16)	32.18	15	6.70	19	6.33	13	6.99	5	7.15	39	5.01
Hong Kong	16(14)	32.10	34	5.82	7	6.89	15	6.92	20	6.19	4	6.29
Belgium	17(15)	32.02	16	6.63	24	6.06	10	7.26	14	6.35	11	5.72
Germany	18(18)	31.75	9	7.04	15	6.46	24	6.61	17	6.31	29	5.33
Israel	*19(12)*	31.72	17	6.61	25	6.05	14	6.94	4	7.26	40	4.87
China	**20(33)**	31.40	24	6.32	17	6.42	23	6.63	13	6.61	26	5.41
Australia	21(21)	30.64	11	6.87	20	6.27	19	6.83	38	5.26	25	5.41
Ireland	22(19)	30.40	35	5.82	21	6.19	17	6.85	24	5.87	15	5.68

(continued)

Table 1 (continued)

Country	2023 (2020) ranking	Overall SNIC	#	Health	#	Public	#	Education	#	Renewal	#	CNC
S. Korea	23(29)	30.24	22	6.38	29	5.98	27	6.46	15	6.34	36	5.08
France	24(23)	30.15	18	6.56	28	6.00	29	6.32	19	6.23	38	5.04
Czech Rep.	25(32)	29.97	25	6.32	14	6.46	30	6.31	35	5.33	18	5.56
Slovenia	26(31)	29.93	28	6.11	30	5.95	20	6.74	32	5.44	13	5.70
United Kingdom	27(22)	29.93	27	6.24	22	6.11	21	6.72	22	6.09	46	4.77
Portugal	28(24)	29.70	29	6.09	37	5.64	16	6.88	29	5.63	23	5.46
Estonia	29(28)	29.64	32	5.87	27	6.00	22	6.66	30	5.58	20	5.52
Lithuania	30(39)	29.63	36	5.78	23	6.09	32	6.21	23	5.92	16	5.63
Spain	31(34)	28.76	21	6.42	40	5.32	34	6.19	28	5.70	34	5.13
Thailand	32(38)	28.65	38	5.77	26	6.04	45	5.48	26	5.83	19	5.54
Japan	*33(25)*	28.62	23	6.35	36	5.69	38	6.00	27	5.76	42	4.82
New Zealand	*34(27)*	28.52	30	5.99	32	5.84	31	6.22	36	5.32	33	5.14
Jordan	35(35)	28.08	31	5.94	41	5.26	33	6.19	34	5.34	28	5.34
Italy	36(37)	28.07	19	6.48	43	5.00	35	6.06	39	5.26	30	5.27
Malaysia	*37(26)*	28.00	39	5.64	31	5.93	37	6.05	31	5.56	43	4.82
India	38(41)	27.44	41	5.30	34	5.76	40	5.87	37	5.28	31	5.23
Chile	39(39)	27.29	33	5.83	35	5.72	43	5.57	33	5.37	44	4.80
Kazakhstan	40(36)	26.94	42	5.30	38	5.54	28	6.43	41	4.93	47	4.74
Greece	41(44)	26.59	37	5.77	49	4.64	36	6.05	44	4.64	21	5.50
Hungary	42(43)	26.30	43	5.26	33	5.82	48	5.25	40	5.14	41	4.83
Indonesia	43(47)	25.90	49	4.98	39	5.48	50	5.17	43	4.70	17	5.58
Croatia	**44(55)**	25.27	40	5.46	42	5.10	46	5.41	55	4.15	32	5.15
Slovak Rep.	45(49)	24.99	45	5.16	44	4.97	49	5.19	45	4.57	35	5.10

Country	2023 (2020) ranking	Overall SNIC	#	Health	#	Public	#	Education	#	Renewal	#	CNC
Ukraine	46(56)	23.76	57	4.32	54	4.16	41	5.85	50	4.37	37	5.07
Turkey	47(43)	23.73	44	5.26	45	4.80	52	5.02	49	4.41	54	4.25
Poland	*48(40)*	23.65	56	4.67	52	4.57	42	5.75	48	4.41	55	4.24
Russia	49(45)	23.60	55	4.69	48	4.65	39	5.99	53	4.26	57	4.02
Romania	50(48)	23.42	54	4.71	50	4.58	56	4.78	42	4.89	51	4.46
Philippines	51(46)	23.34	58	3.78	46	4.79	44	5.49	46	4.52	45	4.77
Bulgaria	52(50)	23.29	51	4.88	47	4.75	58	4.68	47	4.50	50	4.48
Colombia	53(57)	23.15	50	4.94	51	4.57	57	4.74	51	4.33	48	4.56
Peru	54(53)	23.11	48	5.00	53	4.53	53	5.01	57	4.04	49	4.53
Mexico	55(54)	22.22	53	4.74	55	4.10	55	4.84	56	4.14	52	4.41
South Africa	56(51)	21.89	47	5.02	58	3.07	47	5.26	54	4.24	53	4.31
Brazil	57(58)	21.56	46	5.04	56	3.88	59	4.26	52	4.28	56	4.10
Argentina	58(52)	20.56	52	4.82	57	3.13	51	5.09	58	4.02	58	3.49
Venezuela	59(59)	16.63	59	3.44	59	2.28	54	4.88	59	3.06	59	2.96

countries by rank are Denmark, Switzerland, Netherlands, Singapore, Finland, Iceland, Sweden, Norway, UAE, and Qatar. Nordic countries are the forerunners in terms of sustainable intangibles. Three small countries, Switzerland, Netherlands, and Singapore, are another set of outstanding performers. UAE and Qatar are surprisingly among the top 10, with the UAE ranked number one in public structure and Qatar ranked number one in health. Both dimensions are highly related to money investment. Another important piece of information shows that China has advanced from its previous number 33 ranking (Lin, 2020b) to number 20 in just 3 years. Some cells in Table 1 are highlighted in boldface (advancement) and in italics (regression), respectively, to indicate that a change in ranking exceeds seven places.

In just 3 years, 2023 vs. 2020 SNIC rankings of Qatar (10 vs. 17), Taiwan (12 vs. 20), China (20 vs. 33), and Croatia (44 vs. 55) were greatly enhanced, with China undergoing the greatest improvement (20 vs. 33). Ukraine (46 vs. 56) also advanced its SNIC ranking by 10 ranks in 3 years. However, a trajectory check found that its 2022 data were similar to what was recorded in 2001; this is unlike the other four countries that have demonstrated SNIC advancement over the years. As a result, Ukraine is not included in Fig. 8. On the other hand, the rankings of Israel (19 vs. 12), Japan (33 vs. 25), New Zealand (34 vs. 27), Malaysia (37 vs. 26), and Poland (48 vs. 40) all regressed.

7 SNIC Country Rankings vs. IMD World Competitiveness Rankings

In addition to the comparison of the rankings for the 2023 SNIC vs. 2020 SNIC and the high correlation between SNIC and NIC of 0.95, comparing the rankings of the 2023 SNIC with those of the 2023 IMD World Competitiveness can further confirm the value of the SNIC model. For brevity's sake, only the top 15 countries of each model are compared. Table 2 shows that 12 out of the top 15 countries overlap (bold-faced); the top 5 countries, in particular, are highly similar. Denmark ranked number one in both the SNIC and the IMD World Competitiveness models; Switzerland ranked number two in SNIC and number three in IMD; Netherlands ranked number three in SNIC and number five in IMD, and Singapore ranked number four in both models.

IMD World Competitiveness covers four dimensions, namely, national economic performance, government efficiency, business efficiency, and infrastructure, with over 300 indicators. This very comprehensive model reports the four major areas in which each nation either excels or needs to improve its performance. However, it requires a fleet of researchers with abundant resources to complete the yearbook each and every year. The SNIC model consists of only 44 indicators, which is within the capability of just a few researchers with very limited resources. Although much smaller in scale, the SNIC model provides relatively reliable and valuable information that is easily updated and has a particular focus on health, information technology, and renewal for national sustainability.

Table 2 Ranking comparison of the top 15 SNIC and IMD World Competitiveness countries

Country	SNIC 2023 ranking	Country	IMD, 2023 ranking
Denmark	1	**Denmark**	1
Switzerland	2	Ireland	2
Netherlands	3	**Switzerland**	3
Singapore	4	**Singapore**	4
Finland	5	**Netherlands**	5
Iceland	6	**Taiwan**	6
Sweden	7	Hong Kong	7
Norway	8	**Sweden**	8
UAE	9	**USA**	9
Qatar	10	**UAE**	10
Canada	11	**Finland**	11
Taiwan	12	**Qatar**	12
Austria	13	Belgium	13
Luxembourg	14	**Norway**	14
USA	15	**Canada**	15

Source: this study and IMD (2023) World Competitiveness Yearbook

Table 2 reveals a noteworthy fact. Finland and Norway ranked 5 and 8 in SNIC but ranked 11 and 14 in IMD competitiveness, respectively. Taiwan and USA ranked 12 and 15 in SNIC but ranked 6 and 9 in IMD competitiveness, respectively. That is, countries that excel in sustainability may not be equally competitive in terms of economic performance and vice versa. Resources are always limited; each country has its own value system to decide how to strategically allocate its resources to achieve national goals. There is no good or bad result. Such comparisons only serve to provide a reference for policymakers to reflect on their national policies for better allocation of strategic resources in adhering to national aims of prioritizing economic performance or sustainability.

The misconception that large rich countries have greater resources and more potential to develop SNIC may exist; nevertheless, four small countries, Denmark, Switzerland, Netherlands, and Singapore, are outstanding performers in SNIC. With limited land and natural resources, they have remained atop the rankings over the years. Their national policy in building intangible assets to excel while retaining economic might shed some light on other countries and are good topics for future IC research.

8 SNIC and GDP

To show the full picture of the sustainable intangibles of the investigated 59 countries, Figs. 2, 3, 4, 5, 6, 7 map the relationships of SNIC and its components with GDP. Each bubble represents a specific country, and each figure shows four dimensions, with the *Y*-axis being the GDP; the *X*-axis, SNIC or its components; color, renewal capital; and bubble size, population. The color orange represents high

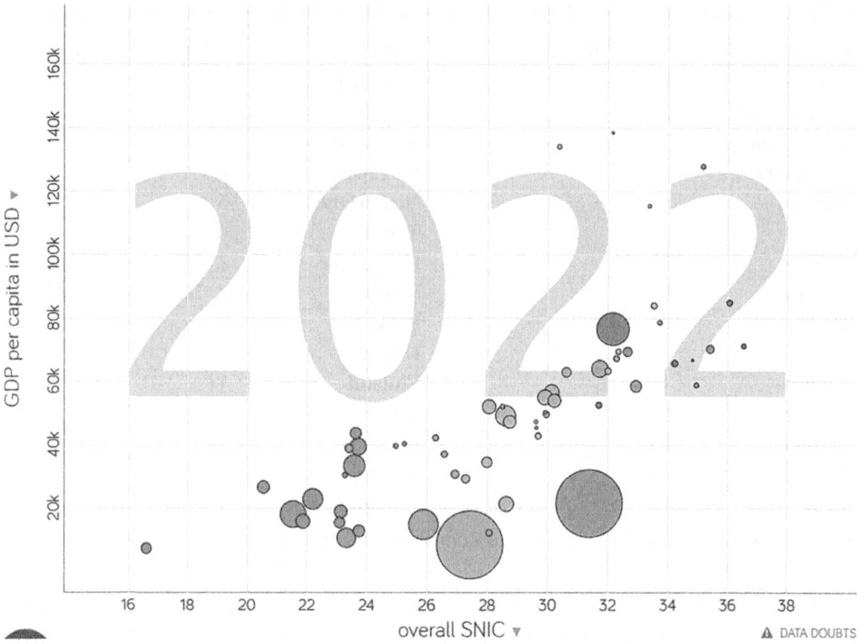

Fig. 2 Relationship between GDP and overall SNIC

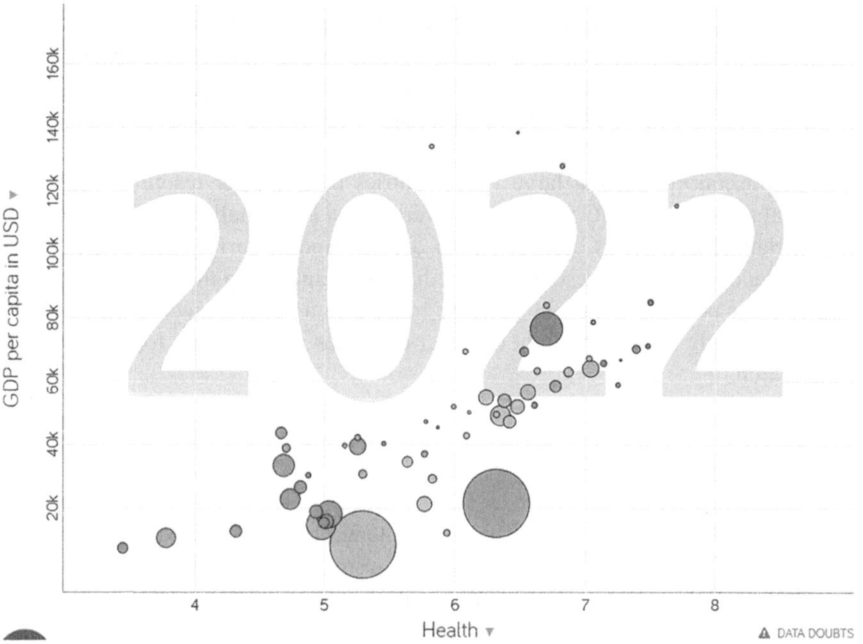

Fig. 3 Relationship between GDP and health

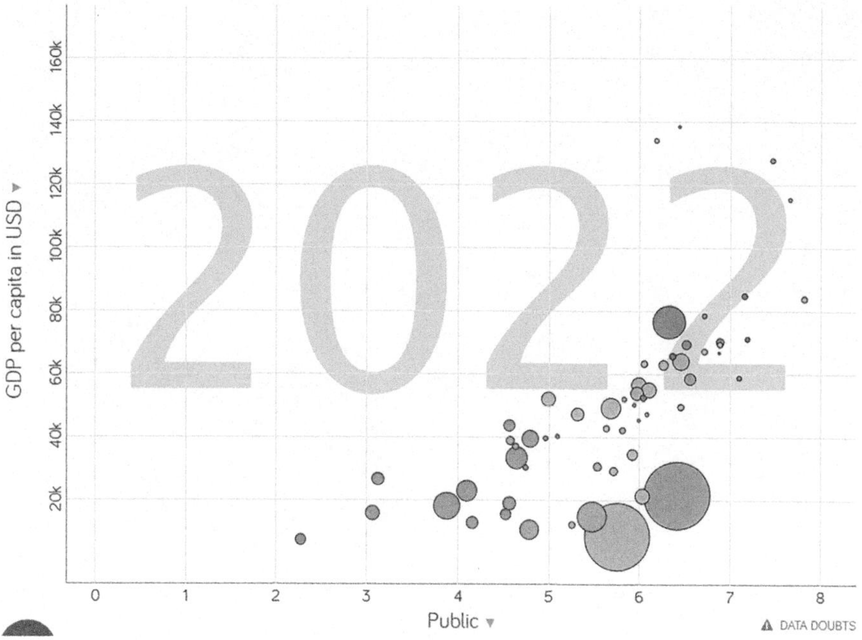

Fig. 4 Relationship between GDP and public structure

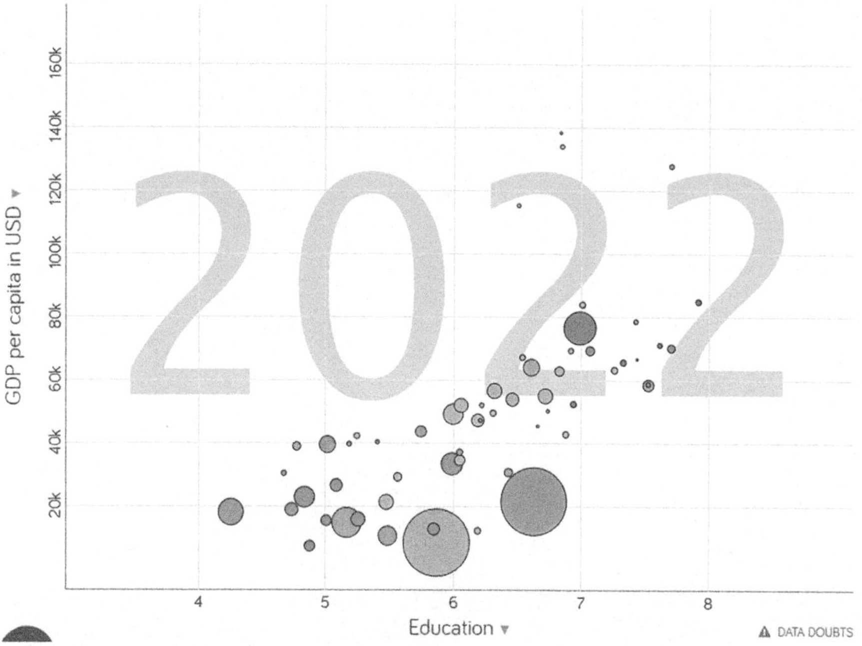

Fig. 5 Relationship between GDP and education

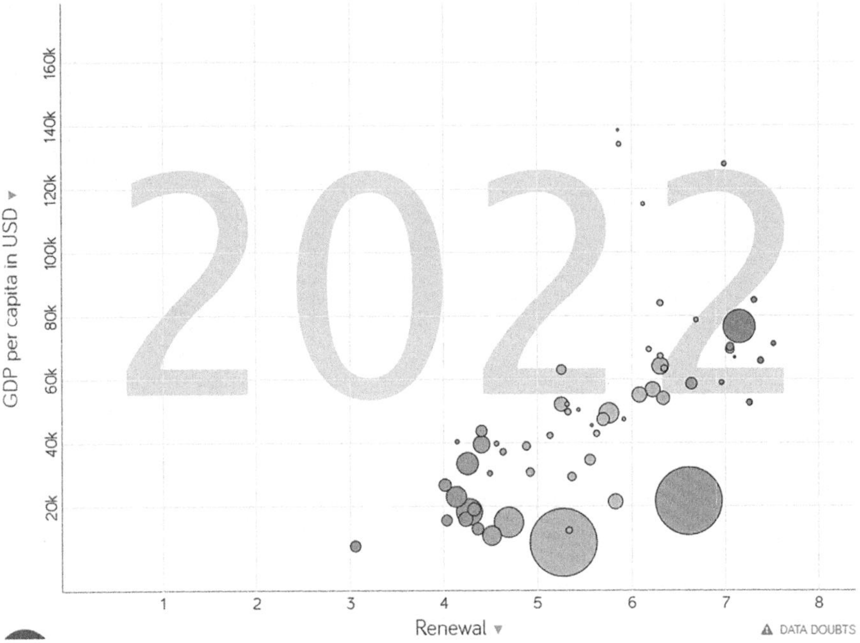

Fig. 6 Relationship between GDP and renewal

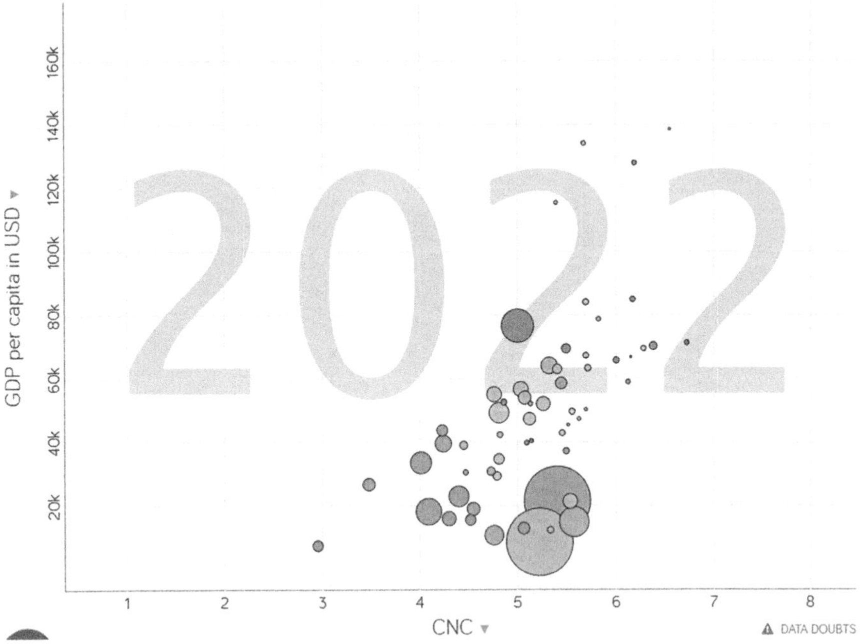

Fig. 7 Relationship between GDP and CNC

renewal capital, and green represents low renewal capital. Readers can pay special attention to the positional change of the orange middle-sized bubble (USA), the light brown big bubble (China), and the light green big bubble (India). Figures 2, 3, 5, and 6 show similar relative positions of the three countries. Figure 4 clearly shows that China and India are catching up with the USA in terms of public structure. Figure 7 indicates that China has surpassed the USA in CNC and India is on par with the USA in that category. These figures indicate that some developing countries investing in building a stronger infrastructure and connectivity/contactivity are outcompeting some advanced countries in sustainable intangibles.

Figures 2, 3, 4, 5, 6, 7 also show the most current year's positive correlations of SNIC and its components with GDP, indicating that investing in enhancing SNIC brings about improved economic performance for developed and developing countries alike.

Based on the SNIC rankings of 2023 vs. 2020 displayed in Table 1, Fig. 8 shows the trajectories of how the four SNIC advancing countries—China, Croatia, Qatar, and Taiwan—have progressed over the years. Qatar has made the greatest improvement in SNIC over the past 22 years (2001–2022). Over the years, China has made relatively large and steady progress, while Croatia and Taiwan have progressed as well as regressed; both, however, have made progress when compared to their 2001 SNIC scores. The five regressing countries are mapped into two graphs to avoid overlapping bubbles. Figure 9 shows the regression for both Israel and Japan over the past 22 years, with Israel having regressed more with respect to SNIC than Japan. Figure 10 exhibits the SNIC regression in rank for New Zealand, Malaysia, and Poland. New Zealand's 2023 SNIC regression was larger compared to its performance in both 2020 and 2001. Malaysia's 2023 SNIC regressed from its 2020

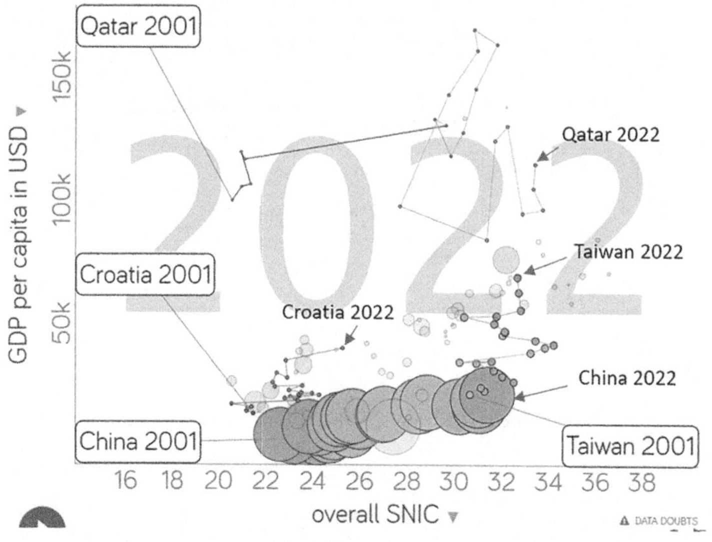

Fig. 8 Trajectory of the four 2023 vs. 2020 SNIC advancing countries—China, Croatia, Qatar, and Taiwan

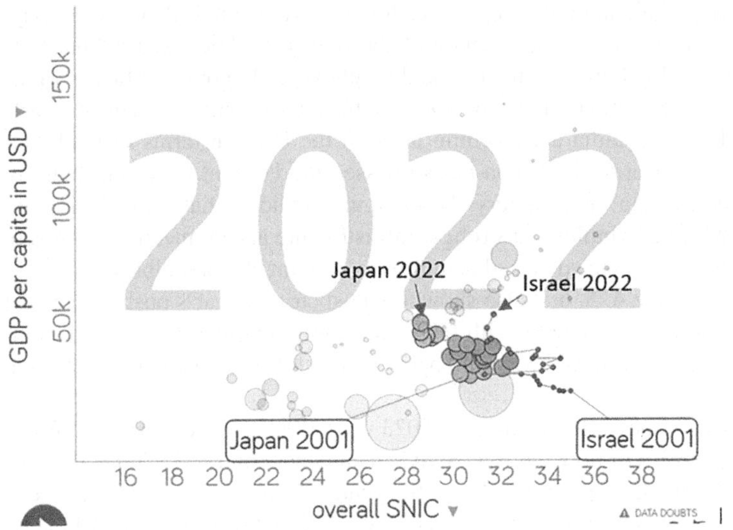

Fig. 9 Trajectory of the two 2023 vs. 2020 SNIC regressing countries—Japan and Israel

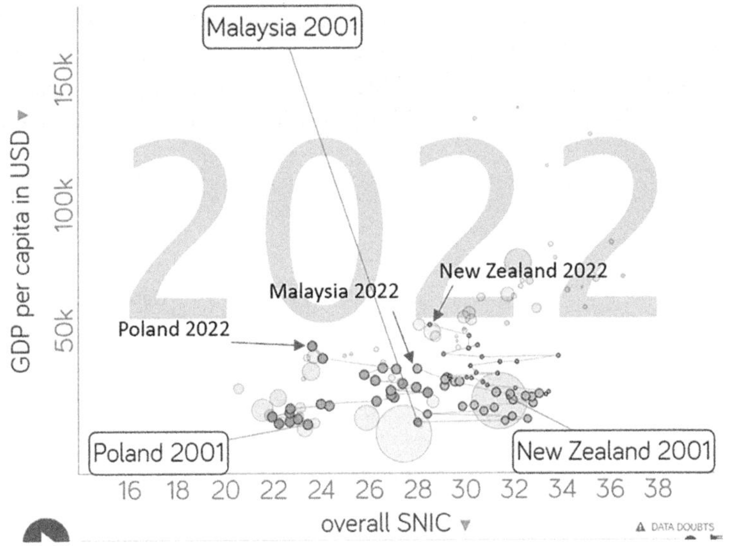

Fig. 10 Trajectory of the three 2023 vs. 2020 SNIC regressing countries—New Zealand, Malaysia, and Poland

score yet is similar to its 2001 score. Poland's 2023 SNIC is down from its 2020 score; it has made little progress compared to its 2001 score.

To further check the effect of SNIC components and each indicator on GDP, seven stepwise regression models were conducted with all the models significant at 0.001 level, as exhibited in Table 3. Adopting a stepwise regression model allows one to see which component or which indicator enters into the model and better explains GDP. To facilitate reading, only the beta in boldface and italic underlined is explained hereunder.

Model 2 shows that, among the five SNIC components, public structure has the greatest explaining power of 0.589 for GDP. Model 3 shows that among the six indicators of health, perceived quality of life has the greatest influence of 0.723, followed by health expenditure of -0.297 and medical assistance of 0.203. Model 4 shows that among the six indicators of public structure, "personal security and personal property protection" has the greatest influence of 0.357, followed by a dependency ratio of 0.254. Model 5 shows that among the seven indicators of education, the Human Development Index of 0.472 has the highest beta, followed by the educational system at 0.221. Model 6 shows that among the five indicators of renewal capital, knowledge transfer has the highest beta of 0.464, followed by internet speed at 0.271. Model 7 shows that among the eight indicators of CNC, social cohesion has the highest beta of 0.329, followed by worker motivation at 0.209.

Table 3 reveals some important information that deserves further consideration. For example, the negative beta of population means smaller countries have better GDP performance, the -0.297 of health expense may indicate more effective utilization (not necessarily larger amount) of health expense is better for GDP growth. Among the SNIC components, sound public structure explains GDP growth the best. For the individual indicators of each component, it is apparent that perceived quality of life, perceived personal security and personal property protection, perceived sound educational system, perceived knowledge transfer, and perceived social cohesion have a higher beta than the hard data of medical support, dependent ratio, internet speed, and trade to GDP. That means, national intangibles, and especially citizens' perceptions, can also influence GDP growth. Of course, such perception comes from enhancing public structure, leading to, for example, clean air, a good quality food supply, convenient transportation, cultural activities for a good quality of life, etc. Such factors comprise the infrastructure that each city and nation is building. However, how they function varies. Are they minimally functional or are they highly rated by citizens? Intangibles have become increasingly important over the years, such that governments cannot ignore them. Table 3 provides good references for relevant parties to work on improving citizens' perceptions.

Table 3 Stepwise regression analysis with GDP as the criterion variable

Variable	M1 Beta	Variables SNIC	M2 Beta	Variables Health	M3 Beta	Variables Public structure	M4 Beta	Variables Education	M5 Beta	Variables Renewal	M6 Beta	Variables CNC	M7 Beta
Population	−0.234	Public structure	**0.589**	Q of life	**0.723**	P. security & P. property	**0.357**	Edu. system	**0.221**	Knowledge transfer	**0.464**	Soc. cohesion	**0.329**
		Population	−0.177	*Health expense*	*−0.297*	Dependency	**0.254**	Human dev. Ind	**0.472**	Internet speed	**0.271**	Trade GDP	**0.207**
		CNC	−0.143	Medical	**0.203**	Population	−0.163	*Education expense*	*−0.205*	Population	−0.199	Population	−0.203
		Education	0.113	H. life exp	0.194	Youth unemp	0.124	Language	0.161	R&D expen	−0.099	Communication	0.134
				Population	−0.102	Cyber security	0.161	PISA	−0.184	Tech. cooper	0.107	Worker motivation	**0.209**
				Health problem	−0.150	Energy infrastructure	0.097	Skilled labor	−0.151			F. investors	−0.113
								Science in sch.	0.219			Study mobility	0.092
												Flexibility	−0.076
R^2	0.055		0.396		0.546		0.523		0.545		0.517		0.458
Adjusted R^2	0.054		0.395		0.542		0.518		0.541		0.514		0.450

9 Suggested Ways of Utilizing SNIC Data

We live in a global village with close international connections. Intangibles are becoming more and more important for all entities, from individuals, teams, organizations, and industries, to cities, nations, and regions. Although regional economies have been on the rise in the years after the COVID-19 pandemic, the global supply chain is disrupted. Yet, in light of proprietary high technology development, some companies are being requested to set up factories in particular regions and countries, as is the case with TSMC (Taiwan Semiconductor Manufacturing Company), which is expanding its manufacturing facilities to Germany, Japan, and the USA. With such a trend, national indicators, such as human capital, tax incentives, government efficiency, intellectual property protection, and cyber security, are crucial references in selecting a particular country for international operations.

Country environment as a combination of factors definitely shapes firms' capabilities to accumulate firm-level resources and extract value from them. Empirical evidence discloses that the differences in country environments have an enduring impact on the relationship between firm-level intellectual capital and innovation performance (Wan & Hoskisson, 2003). Andreeva et al.'s (2021) study also shows that country-level factors moderate the performance effects of firm-level intellectual capital. Petty and Guthrie (2000) suggested that scholars conduct more research on how to use IC data to enhance decision-making. In other words, IC research should explore hidden values and future impacts, which in turn could create business value and make a significant contribution to companies and to societies (Ståhle & Bounfour, 2008; Ståhle & Ståhle, 2012).

The following steps are proposed to facilitate the use of SNIC in policy and international business decision-making. Since IMD data are easily accessible, obtaining SNIC data should not be difficult.

For policymakers: As public structure best explains GDP, policymakers can benchmark UAE (#1 in public structure) and find the relative position of their own country. They should pay special attention to its high beta indicators (Table 3), personal security and private property rights and dependency ratio, and enhance citizen's personal security and property rights. Since the dependency ratio takes time to adjust, cyber security and youth unemployment can be more efficiently dealt with. In addition, policymakers can look into why four small countries, Denmark, Netherlands, Singapore, and Switzerland, are strong in both intangibly sustainable (SNIC ranking) and economically performing (IMD ranking).

For international business: Before a foreign investment site selection decision is made, it is wise to check the macro indicators of the targeted country. Special attention should be paid to those relatively high beta indicators, such as knowledge transfer, social cohesion, internet speed, educational system, and worker motivation.

For expatriates: Quality of life, health infrastructure, accessibility of quality medical assistance, and the educational system of the host countries are crucial. International businesses should also look into the factors that concern expatriates the most in order to attract and deploy qualified expatriates.

With resource constraints, the indicators of the SNIC model provide valuable information for making more informed government and foreign investment decisions. Even though the above indicators are described individually, actually they are and should be integrated for a synergetic effect, as the CNC circle superimposed on the four dimensions indicates. For example, Internet speed facilitates knowledge transfer, sound health infrastructure, educational system, and the building of renewal capital.

Linking organizational-level IC with national-level NIC has been proved to be valuable as described in previous studies (Chang & Lin, 2015; Peng et al., 2023). The indicators and country ranking of SNIC (Table 1) can provide valuable references for governments, organizations, and relevant parties to strategically allocate limited resources and make better decisions.

10 Proposed Intellectual Capital Ecosystem for Future Research

In times of VUCA (volatility, uncertainty, complexity, and ambiguity), a single-dimension solution can no longer effectively resolve complex problems for organizational, social, and national well-being. Consequently, an ecosystem approach needs to be adopted to achieve better results.

The concept of an ecosystem has been constantly discussed in the field of strategy, mainly for the reason that researchers are paying attention to the interdependent elements in the dynamic network of people, organizations, and environments (Smorodinskaya et al., 2017; Wu & Lin, 2019). While many scholars have defined ecosystem from a variety of perspectives, Adner's (2017) twofold definition of ecosystem as an affiliation and as a structure is an appropriate fit for this study. Ecosystem-as-affiliation sees the system as a community of associated actors (IC scholars) defined by their networks and platform affiliations (journals, media). Ecosystem-as-structure defines the system as "the alignment structure of the multilateral set of partners (IC scholars study the firm, city, and national levels of IC) that need to interact in order for a focal value proposition to materialize" (Adner, 2017; Wu & Lin, 2019).

Although the above definitions of ecosystem somehow encompass the development of the IC community, they are still confined to a small group of IC scholars. A full flange of the IC ecosystem is dependent on the development of the fourth stage of IC, described in the work of Lin and Edvinsson (2021). This stage extends to the city and national levels, taking into consideration the external environment, such as the Sustainable Development Goals (SDGs). It also incorporates scholars from other disciplines including the natural sciences.

In 2013, Edvinsson (2013) advocated that:

> In the modern knowledge economy, we have to keep looking for those invisible opportunity spaces…. We should take an outside-in view! … to think in terms of cross-disciplinary systematized perspectives.

Dumay (2014) suggested including other disciplines, such as psychology, information technology, sociology, and other science-based disciplines (e.g., engineering).

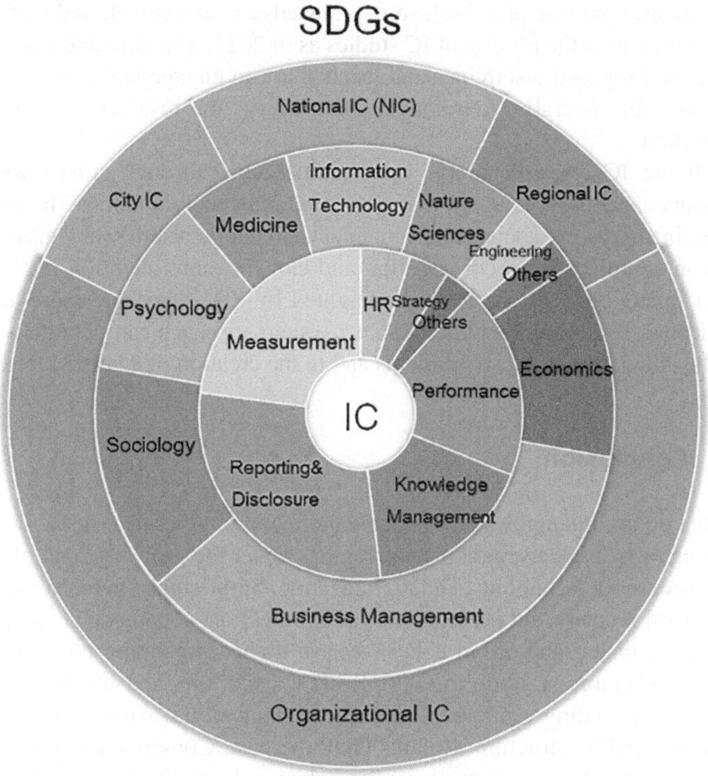

Fig. 11 Ecosystem of intellectual capital. Source: Lin and Edvinsson (2021)

Zambon (2016) also proposed multi- and interdisciplinary academic research on intangibles to "capture" new dimensions from various disciplines, as nowadays many top managers, professionals, academics, consultants, and policymakers recognize the role of intangibles at every level of the economy as a whole and not only within companies. As a result, IC research needs to shift from organizations to ecosystems by examining why, what, who, and how (Lin & Edvinsson, 2021).

Although the above suggestions for future direction are still valid today, they were mainly promoted in business-related publications. With the rapidly changing global economy, we need to take into account the economic and social environment and the latest stage of technological development that has occurred since then. Key factors affecting global economic and social development can largely be represented by the 17 SDGs. There is also a global trend of reporting ESG (environment, social, governance) results in corporate annual reports. Embedding the world-recognized SDGs and ESG elements into IC research can trigger a dialogue with scholars from other disciplines for engaging in interdisciplinary research. Particularly, the engineering of environment management is a new area worth exploring.

Envisioning the advancement of future IC research, Lin and Edvinsson (2021) proposed an IC ecosystem as exhibited in Fig. 11. In the figure, the second circle of measurement, reporting and disclosure, knowledge management, and performance largely represented the portion of IC studies as of 2021. The third and fourth circles describe the proposed disciplines and levels that can engage in IC research. SDGs encompass the overall environment that every IC research can take into consideration.

For future IC research, ample opportunities exist through cross-level, cross-disciplinary, and cross-country combinations and recombinations. In particular, those aiming to resolve social, environmental, and public health problems to achieve SDGs can stimulate more conversation and call for more attention regarding the value of intangibles. As the goals highlighted by SDGs become more and more sophisticated, IC researchers taking an ecosystem approach can definitely contribute to the alleviation of those problems and to the creation of a better future world.

11 Conclusion

Without a doubt, intangibles will become more and more critical in facilitating the well-being of individuals, nations, and regions under the growing trend of artificial intelligence, robot technology, and digitalization. Surprisingly, perceived quality of life, personal security and personal property protection, sound educational system, knowledge transfer, and social cohesion have higher explaining power than such hard data indicators as trade to GDP, R&D expenditure, and number of foreign investors. This finding reinforces the value of intangibles. Among the five SNIC components, public structure explains GDP the best. Consequently, policymakers and government officers are suggested to enhance the positive perceptions of citizens by building a stronger public structure with the support of CNC. The linking effects of CNC should be prioritized. Even though digital technology is very important, it needs to be integrated with other operations, such as education and renewal, and then needs to be transformed into other types of intangible assets in order to maximize its benefits.

This study contributes to the futurizing of IC theory by presenting an IC ecosystem for a more comprehensive IC field of research to tackle problems in an increasingly sophisticated world. As for futurizing IC practices, the SNIC model provides a guideline for utilizing SNIC data to enhance national intangible assets and to prioritize government investment, as well as assisting international businesses to make better international expansion decisions.

A limitation of this study is that the proposed IC ecosystem does not include individual-level IC, due to the fact that the concept of IC originated at the organizational level; in addition, individual-level IC may fall into the realm of organizational behavior (OB) study. Since the discipline of psychology is included in the third circle of the IC ecosystem, IC research at the individual level yet distinguished from OB study can be justified in the future.

To extend its boundaries, IC research should focus more on a looking-ahead rather than a looking-back type of interdisciplinary and transdisciplinary approach by adopting an ecosystem perspective (Lin & Edvinsson, 2021). Keeping in mind

SDGs and ESG will enhance the contributions of this field of research for mitigating complex social and environmental threats to organizations and societies. Issues such as "what percentage of poverty reduction (SDG 1) can be achieved by increasing 0.5% of educational investment? How can private organizations contribute to such poverty reduction?" can be on the future agendas of IC researchers for expanding the contributions of IC research.

Appendix

Appendix 1 Indicators of sustainable national intellectual capital (SNIC) model

Cronbach's alpha	Indicator	Subjective indicator
0.84	Healthy life expectancy	
Health	Quality of life	S
SDG 3	Total health expenditure (%)	
(Good health & Well-being)	Health infrastructure	S
	Medical assistance (per physician & per nurse)	
	Health problems[a]	S
	Pension funding	S
0.872	Energy infrastructure	S
Public structure	Future energy supply[b]	S
SDG 7	Dependency ratio (age −15 & 64+/active population)	
(Affordable & clean energy)	Credit (credit is easily available for business)	S
	Legal and regulatory framework	S
SDG 9	Adaptability of government policy	S
(Infrastructure)	Cyber security	S
	Youth unemployment	
	Personal security and private property rights	S
	Gini index	
0.881	Human development index	
Education	Total public expenditure on education (%)	
SDG 4	Higher education achievement (%) (WCY)	
(Quality education)	Educational assessment—PISA	
	Educational system	S
	Science in schools	S
	Management education	S
	Language skills	S
	Skilled labor	S
0.874	Internet bandwidth speed	
Renewal	Information technology skills	S
SDG 9	Technological cooperation	S
(Innovation)	Knowledge transfer	S

(continued)

Appendix 1 (continued)

Cronbach's alpha	Indicator	Subjective indicator
	Innovative capacity	S
	Total expenditure on R&D (%)	
	Entrepreneurship	S
	Sustainable development	S
	Public and private partnership	S
0.81	Connectivity[c]	S
CNC	Worker motivation	S
(Connectivity & contactivity)	Flexibility and adaptability	S
SDG 17	Social responsibility	S
(Partnership for the goals)	Foreign investors	S
	Social cohesion	S
	Trade to GDP ratio	
	Student mobility outbound	
	Communications technology	S

Remarks: "S" represents the expert's subjective rating. Due to IMD data discontinuity, some indications were changed.

[a]Health problem was substituted by exposure to particle pollution since 2017

[b]Future energy supply was substituted by distribution infrastructure since 2017

[c]Connectivity was substituted by investment in telecommunication since 2017

References

Adner, R. (2017). Ecosystem as structure: An actionable construct for strategy. *Journal of Management, 43*(1), 39–58.

Agarwal, R., Echambadi, R., Franco, A. M., & Sarkar, M. (2004). Knowledge transfer through inheritance: Spin-out generation, development, and survival. *Academy of Management Journal, 47*(4), 501–522.

Andreeva, T., Garanina, T., Sáenz, J., Aramburu, N., & Kianto, A. (2021). Does country environment matter in the relationship between intellectual capital and innovation performance? *Journal of Business Research, 136*, 263–273.

Carter, C. R., Leuschner, R., & Rogers, D. S. (2007). A social network analysis of the journal of supply chain management: Knowledge generation, knowledge diffusion and thought leadership. *Journal of Supply Chain Management, 43*(2), 15–28.

Chang, C. C., & Lin, C. Y. Y. (2015). Host country intellectual capital, inter-country distances and international market selection. *Innovative ecosystems, joint intangibles and territories: The World Conference on Intellectual Capital for Communities 11th edition*, Paris, May 28–29, 2015.

Dumay, J. (2013). The third stage of IC: Towards a new IC future and beyond. *Journal of Intellectual Capital, 14*(1), 5–9.

Dumay, J. (2014). 15 years of the Journal of Intellectual Capital and counting: A manifesto for transformational IC research. *Journal of Intellectual Capital, 15*(1), 2–37.

Edvinsson, L. (2013). IC 21: Reflections from 21 years of IC practice and theory. *Journal of Intellectual Capital, 14*(1), 163–172.

Edvinsson, L., & Malone, M. S. (1997). *Intellectual capital: Realizing your company's true value by defining its hidden brainpower*. Harper Business.

Hwang, T. J., Lin, Y. T., Shen, L. J., Tang, L., & Lapid, M. I. (2020). How Taiwan prevented the outbreak of Covid-19: A focus on psychological strategies and measures. *International Psychogeriatrics, 32*(10), 1121–1124. https://doi.org/10.1017/S1041610220001568

IMD. (2023). *World competitiveness ranking 2023 – IMD business school for management and leadership courses*. https://www.imd.org/centers/wcc/world-competitiveness-center/rankings/world-competitiveness-ranking/

Kumar, A. (2018). *Global knowledge diffusion vocational education and training*. Retrieved from http://hdl.handle.net/10603/214059

Lev, B. (2001). *Intangibles: Management, measurement, and reporting*. The Brookings Institution Press.

Lin, C. Y. Y. (2020a). Chapter 11 Sustainable national intellectual capital in digital age: A global outlook. In P. de Pablos & L. Edvinsson (Eds.), *Intellectual capital in the digital economy*. Routledge, Taylors & Francis Group. ISBN: Hardback: 978-0-367-25067-6, eBook: 978-0-429-28588-2.

Lin, C. Y. Y. (2020b). Application of intellectual capital research. *Industry and Management Forum, 22*(4), 4–29. (in Chinese).

Lin, Y. Y., & Edvinsson, L. (2008). National intellectual capital: Comparison of the Nordic Countries. *Journal of Intellectual Capital, 9*(4), 525–545.

Lin, C. Y. Y., & Edvinsson, L. (2011). *National intellectual capital: A comparison of 40 countries*. Springer. ISBN: 978-1-4419-7376-45.

Lin, C. Y. Y., & Edvinsson, L. (2021). Reflections on JIC's twenty-year history and suggestions for future IC research. *Journal of Intellectual Capital, 22*(3) ISSN: 1469-1930, (2018 IF: 3.744).

Lin, C. Y. Y., Edvinsson, L., Chen, J., & Beding, T. (2014). *Navigating intellectual capital after the financial crisis*. Springer Publishing. ISBN 978-1-4939-1294-0.

Nahapiet, J., & Ghoshal, S. (1998). Social capital, intellectual capital, and the organizational advantage. *Academy of Management Review, 23*(2), 242–266.

Peng, C. Z., Huang, T. C, Lin, C. Y. Y., & Cheng, T. C. (2023). *What role did intellectual capital play during COVID-19 pandemic quarantine?* Coping measures of Taiwan, working paper.

Petty, R., & Guthrie, J. (2000). Intellectual capital literature review measurement, reporting and management. *Journal of Intellectual Capital, 1*(2), 155–176. https://doi.org/10.1108/14691930010348731

Rodríguez-Muñiz, M. (2015). Intellectual inheritances: cultural diagnostics and the state of poverty knowledge. *American Journal of Cultural Sociology, 3*, 89–122. https://doi.org/10.1057/ajcs.2014.16

Smorodinskaya, N., Russell, M. G., Katukov, D., & Still, K. (2017). Innovation Ecosystem vs. innovation systems in terms of collaboration and co-creation of value. *Proceeding of the 50th Hawaii international conference on system science*, pp. 5245–5254.

Ståhle, P., & Bounfour, A. (2008). Understanding dynamics of intellectual capital. *Journal of Intellectual Capital, special issue of Intellectual Capital of Communities: The Next Step, 9*(2), 164–177.

Ståhle, S., & Ståhle, P. (2012). Towards measures of national intellectual capital: A critical analysis of the CHS model. *Journal of Intellectual Capital, 13*(2), 164–177.

Stahle, P., Stahle, S., & Lin, C. Y. Y. (2015). Intangibles and national economic wealth: A new perspective on how they are linked. *Journal of Intellectual Capital, 16*(1), 20–57.

Wan, W. P., & Hoskisson, R. E. (2003). Home country environments, corporate diversification strategies, and firm performance. *Academy of Management Journal, 46*(1), 27–45. https://doi.org/10.5465/30040674

Wu, S. H., & Lin, Y. Y. (2019). *Innovation and entrepreneurship in an educational ecosystem: Cases from Taiwan*. Springer. ISBN 978-981-32-9444-8.

Zambon, S. (2016). Ten years after: The past, the present and the future of scholarly investigation on intangibles and intellectual capital (IC). *Journal of Intellectual Capital, 17*(1). https://doi.org/10.1108/JIC-11-2015-0093

Dr. Carol Yeh-Yun Lin is Distinguished Professor of the Department of Business Administration at National Chengchi University (NCCU). Dr. Lin has served in several first-level management positions at NCCU, including the Dean of Office of International Cooperation, Dean of Students Affairs, and the Founding Director of International MBA program at NCCU. Dr. Lin has also obtained Outstanding Research Award conferred by the Taiwan Ministry of Science and Technology (MOST), multiple times of Special Talent Award by MOST, Outstanding Public Servant Award by the Taiwan Ministry of Education, and Outstanding Service Award, Special Teaching Award, and multiple times of Special Research Award by NCCU. Dr. Lin's research areas include social innovation, intellectual capital, strategic human resource management, and SME management. Other than publishing more than 170 academic papers, Dr. Lin also published 16 books in English by Springer. For international service, Dr. Lin was the Treasurer and Board Member of the New Club of Paris in France and Overseas Advisor for SAIKA (Intellectual Capital as a Driver of National Economy in Finland). In Taiwan, Dr. Lin has served as a Board Member and a Supervisor of ICDF (International Cooperation Development Fund), an affiliation of the Taiwan Ministry of Foreign Affairs.

Relevance and the Future of Intellectual Capital Management in the Public Sector

Harri Laihonen and Paula Pusenius

Abstract

The public sector is among the least addressed areas in intellectual capital (IC) research, and in this chapter, our aim is to better understand the specific needs of the public sector context regarding IC management. We argue that by better understanding these contextual characteristics, it is possible to develop both the theory and practice of IC. Our analysis shows that most IC research does not justify its choice of the public sector as its context. The reasons evinced in those studies choosing the public sector were mainly related to the use of public funding to create public value, a strong claim for transparency, the complexity of objectives, and, more recently, the ecosystemic role of the public sector and its obligation to support sustainable development. The central argument of the chapter is the need to better understand the special characteristics of public value creation when applying IC theory in the public sector to support the management of public organizations and in managing public services.

1 Introduction

Intellectual capital (IC) theory stems from efforts to prove and explain the higher valuation of companies' equity value in the market (e.g., Edvinsson & Malone, 1997; Roos et al., 1997; Sveiby, 1997). Various measurement methods have been developed, but their ability to capture the intangible capital of firms has proven inadequate and their validity questionable (Kujansivu & Lönnqvist, 2007). Also, managers seem to struggle with the problems of applying theoretical IC models in

H. Laihonen (✉) · P. Pusenius
University of Eastern Finland, Kuopio, Finland
e-mail: harri.laihonen@uef.fi; paula.pusenius@uef.fi

A. Kianto et al. (eds.), *Futurizing Intellectual Capital*, Knowledge Management and Organizational Learning 15, https://doi.org/10.1007/978-3-031-80197-6_9

the real world (Kujansivu, 2009). Recently, Kianto et al. (2023) argued that normative approaches to conceptualizing IC and its performance relevance would benefit from updating due to large-scale changes in companies' operating environments and working life.

In this chapter, we focus on public sector management and highlight the specific needs of IC management that have not been thoroughly discussed and dealt with in earlier literature. The chapter presents an overview of the public sector IC literature and, based on this review, discusses the relevance and future needs of IC management research in the public sector context, the area where the least research on IC has been conducted (Dumay et al., 2015; Guthrie et al., 2012). Nevertheless, due to its significant societal role, the public sector provides an intriguing context for exploring the relevance of IC theory and the possible contextual implications for theory development.

Many governments have recently emphasized the potential of various data-driven approaches and pursued evidence-based decision-making (cf. Laihonen et al., 2023; Federal Data Strategy, 2022; Government of the United Kingdom, 2022), but the intangible value drivers and the capabilities needed to tackle wicked societal problems have been less discussed recently. In the IC management literature, the evidence-based trend is illustrated by the strong focus on IC accounting, IC indicators, and IC disclosure instruments (see Hussinki et al. (2024) for a review). This raises the important and profound question of whether IC management and other knowledge-based management approaches are perceived more as a managerial toolbox than as a strategic approach to organizational value creation. Answering this question is critical when considering the future of IC research and the development of IC theory.

In this chapter, we consider IC management more as a theoretical lens for analyzing what (public) organizations do and what justifies their existence. According to the public management literature, public managers must balance competing values and expectations (Christensen & Lægreid, 2011; Torfing & Triantafillou, 2013) and the classic dilemma between efficiency and effectiveness (Lipsky, 1980). The aim of this chapter is to ascertain what kind of an empirical context public management sets for IC management and discuss the specific needs of the public sector context regarding IC management.

The chapter is organized as follows: Section 2 provides an overview of the IC literature in the public sector. In Sect. 3, we discuss some of the public sector's critical contextual characteristics for IC management. In Sect. 4, we discuss the relevance and future of IC management research in the public sector and propose some avenues to enhance the relevance of IC research in the public sector.

2 An Overview of the Intellectual Capital Literature on the Public Sector

To understand the status of IC research in the public sector, we conducted a systematic search to survey the literature on IC within the public sector and in public administration. Our focus was on peer-reviewed empirical research papers, aiming to elucidate the practical implications of IC in the public sector and how the specificities of the public sector are presented. The search yielded 125 results, of which 18 were retained for further analysis, with a focus on IC and clear justification for public sector research (see Table 1).

Seven articles were published in *the Journal of Intellectual Capital* (*JIC*) and two in *the Journal of Management and Governance*. The remaining articles were published in various other scientific publications. While earlier reviews by Dumay et al. (2015) and Guthrie et al. (2012) emphasized aspects of IC and how these have been studied in the public sector context, with a marked emphasis on accounting, our research focuses more on the peculiar nature of the public sector as the context of IC management, that is, why it is interesting and essential to study IC in the public sector in the first place.

Turning our attention to the geographical distribution of the studies, the majority were authored by researchers from Italy (6 studies), Australia (4 studies), or Spain (3 studies). A total of 11 studies were from Europe, four from Australia, and three from developing countries, totaling seven different nations. We further classified the literature into seven groups to describe the public context according to Wall's previous classification (2005). The context for most of the publications was "government department" (four studies), followed by "local authority" (four studies), "education" (three studies), "executive agency and nondepartmental public body" (two studies), "health" (one study), and "other" consisting of four studies with several groups of contexts and one study which examined the national intellectual capital in European countries. Surprisingly, our results did not show as strong an emphasis on universities and the education field as the earlier review by Bellucci et al. (2021).

The study of IC has undergone several stages, concurrently rather than successively (Petty & Guthrie, 2000). Previous reviews have pointed out that public sector IC research has bypassed stages of *raising awareness* and *legitimizing IC research* and jumped straight to the *performative* stage (Guthrie et al., 2012; Guthrie & Dumay, 2015) examining how IC works in organizations (e.g., Veltri & Silvestri, 2015; Massingham & Tam, 2015). Our results corroborate these findings. In our review, only a few recent studies reached the fourth stage by considering *IC ecosystems* (cf. Guthrie & Dumay, 2015), while most emphasis has been on case study research investigating how IC works in organizations.

From the viewpoint of this chapter, the most interesting observation is that in most studies no explicit reasons were provided for selecting the public sector as a research context. In some studies, the selection was solely justified by referring to existing literature reviews recognizing the public sector as the most neglected area of IC research. Several articles also noted that the public sector had been transformed by the New Public Management (NPM) reform in a private-sector direction

Table 1 IC theory and public sector research

Author	Justification for public sector research
Iacuzzi and Pauluzzo (2023)	Economic and social value creation for the public sector, ecosystem view, role as a promoter of value co-creation with multiple stakeholders
Ramírez et al. (2022)	Need for participation and transparency
Melo and De la Gala Velásquez (2022)	Complex and dynamic environment, need for transparency, criticism of public administration, accountability, major national problems in developing countries, sustainable development
Belmonte da Silva et al. (2021)	Value for society, bureaucratic environment
Veltri and Puntillo (2020)	International recommendations and national legislative requirements
Iacuzzi et al. (2020)	Stewardship responsibility, participation of citizens, value co-creation at ecosystem level, stakeholder engagement, promotion of values
Matos et al. (2018)	Need for transparency, innovativeness, effectiveness, and efficiency; scarce resources; complex political, economic, and social context; need for trust
Martin-Sardesai and Guthrie (2018)	Public funding and the need to create public good
Cavicchi (2017)	Responsibility to support sustainable development at the societal level
Manes Rossi et al. (2016)	Social reporting, public values, open data policy
Massingham and Tam (2015)	Limited opportunities to reward, attract, and retain staff, due to salary regulations in the public sector
Veltri and Silvestri (2015)	Demand for transparency to satisfy stakeholders' needs, opportunity to differentiate from others by integrated reporting, obligation to report nonfinancial information
Joia (2008)	Societies' increasing call for more accountable public administration for economic reasons, need to measure performance with other than market value
Cuganesan et al. (2007)	Value creation for stakeholders and public, communication of value creation
O'Connor et al. (2007)	Multiple stakeholders, corporate control, different perspectives in value relationships, cultural aspects
Bueno Campos et al. (2006)	The legitimacy of public entities; economic, social, political-institutional, and cultural context
Wall (2005)	Need for external reporting, multiplicity of goals, intangible outcomes of public services
Serrano Cinca et al. (2003)	Distinctive features of intangible assets in the public sector, the difference in IC models, the difference between IC components

and considered organizations as if they were enterprises. These studies apply private sector solutions directly, mostly ignoring the fact that the public sector undeniably differs from the private sector. We found only 18 studies including a clearly articulated reason for choosing the public sector as the context of the study. These studies and their justifications for public sector research are summarized in Table 1.

As shown in Table 1, the public sector as the research context has been justified through the use of public funding to create public value (Cuganesan et al., 2007;

Bueno Campos et al., 2006), with a strong claim for transparency (Veltri & Silvestri, 2015; Matos et al., 2018; Ramírez et al., 2022), which further implies external reporting (Wall, 2005; Veltri & Silvestri, 2015). It has been noted that external reporting in the public sector must consider both economic and more complex objectives in contrast to the private sector (Manes Rossi et al., 2016). A few studies also mentioned the role of regulatory factors and international recommendations (e.g., at the EU level) as a juridical discourse (Manes Rossi et al., 2016; Veltri & Puntillo, 2020). Researchers from developing countries highlighted the complexity of the public context and the multiple pressures on the public sector caused by societal changes (Matos et al., 2018; Melo & De la Gala Velásquez, 2022).

The public sector's obligation to support sustainable development is an emerging theme in IC research (e.g., Cavicchi, 2017). Otherwise, there was surprisingly little discussion on values, despite the political nature of the public sector and the growing need for a debate on values in the light of recent societal changes acknowledged in the recent public sector accounting literature (Bracci et al., 2021). The literature also noted the limited opportunities for public sector organizations to reward, attract, and retain staff due to regulations in the public sector (Massingham & Tam, 2015). This is a concrete example of the impact of the bureaucratic and rigid nature of the public sector affecting the practice of IC management. Recent studies (Iacuzzi et al., 2020; Iacuzzi & Pauluzzo, 2023) highlight the ecosystemic role of the public sector and the co-creation of value with stakeholders.

Overall, the literature review shows that the literature focusing on IC in the public sector is evolving but still fragmented in terms of journals, authors, and subject areas, as well as of the justifications for studying IC in the public sector. Next, we will analyze the specific requirements that the public sector imposes for IC management.

3 The Public Sector as the Context of IC Management

As shown in the previous section, the focus of public sector IC research has been predominantly on how public organizations do accounting and reporting, and thus, many of the special characteristics of public management have not been thoroughly discussed in relation to IC management. These characteristics relate to fundamental questions of how the public sector is defined and what the level and unit of analysis are.

The purpose of this chapter is not to define the public sector or public administration but to illustrate some of the special characteristics that should be considered by IC scholars and developers when applying IC theory in the public sector. Most importantly, it is crucial to understand and clearly articulate what makes the public sector public and what the task of public administration is in the given context.

One distinctive characteristic of the public sector relates to the perception of value and value creation processes. Moore (1995) states that the aim of public managers is to create public value, meaning the value that an organization or activity contributes to society. Moore's well-known strategic triangle connects the authorizing environment, operational capability, and delivering public value at a reasonable cost. Later, Moore relates his public value theory to democratic values, institutions, and processes (Moore, 2014). Public administration as an academic discipline has a long history of studying "how the public sector serves the public good through developing and implementing public policies and what is needed to conduct this business in an efficient, effective, legitimate and rational way, in order to optimize serving the public good" (de Vries 2016, 6).

From the aim of creating public value and serving the public good, there arises the question that should be posed for IC theory and management: how can IC theory and management contribute to the understanding and generation of public value? This question conceals an intriguing corollary: how does IC management in the public sector differ from that in the private sector? If there is indeed a difference, as this chapter argues, what are the distinguishing features? Next, we approach these questions from three perspectives critical for IC theory and management to consider: (1) multilevel governance and policymaking, (2) complexity of institutional framework, and (3) management of public services.

Multilevel governance and policymaking are present at different administrative levels (national, regional, and local), all of which have interested IC scholars in recent decades. However, IC studies have mostly left the political-administrative interface without further investigation. IC management at the national level deals with the national competitiveness and recognition of national IC resources (e.g., Ståhle & Bounfour, 2008; Käpylä et al., 2012). The management of society's intellectual capital aims to improve the effectiveness of decision-making and situation handling (Wiig, 2002). Wiig (2002) notes that at the national level, the participation of the public and the building of societal IC capabilities and a competitive workforce are essential tasks of public administration. However, policymakers are not always familiar with the concept of national IC even though the elements of national IC are identified and highly valued and IC measurement models are considered to produce potentially valuable information for policymaking (Salonius & Lönnqvist, 2012). In our search, only Matos et al. (2018) concentrated on a national level, found evidence of a relationship between national intellectual capital (NIC) and trust perception, and concluded that NIC scores can be used in strategic planning and in the formulation of national policies.

The levels of regional (Lerro & Carlucci, 2007; Lönnqvist et al., 2014) and local government (e.g., Yigitcanlar & Lönnqvist, 2013; Manes Rossi et al., 2016) have also interested IC scholars. The earlier literature highlights the idiosyncratic nature of regional and local knowledge assets (e.g., Lönnqvist et al., 2014); regions must not only adjust their local economies but also invest in their society, environment, and institutions to maintain competitiveness (e.g., Yigitcanlar & Lönnqvist, 2013). There is a call for further research to explore how IC could influence strategic planning to support innovation managerialism among local authorities (Manes Rossi et al., 2016). Moreover, managing regional knowledge assets involves accessing national and international assets in addition to developing a region's internal knowledge assets (Lönnqvist et al., 2014).

Multilevel governance and policymaking are phenomena conspicuous by their absence from the current research agenda of IC despite the recent and significant changes in public organizations' external and internal environments. Notably, the viewpoints of democratic decision-making and public value(s) have not aroused interest among IC scholars, even though they significantly affect national policy planning and implementation, as well as regional and local policies and strategies, resource allocation, and, further, IC management. Thus, a more profound understanding of the collective knowledge formation underlying public sector decision-making is needed (cf. Laihonen et al., 2023). Public sector IC research has so far paid very limited attention to the need for and implications of participation and transparency in managing IC (e.g., Ramírez et al., 2022). Moreover, the literature shows how the value for society aspect is essential in managing public services and that investments in structural capital (processes, structures, organizational philosophy) in the bureaucratic public environment may go far to meet the social demands of the local communities (Belmonte da Silva et al., 2021).

Together with multilevel governance and policymaking, the *complexity of the institutional framework* affects IC management in many ways. This often goes unaddressed in IC literature, and only a few studies have connected knowledge-based management and institutional complexity (e.g., Currie & Suhomlinova, 2006; Laihonen & Kokko, 2020). As noted above, societal values, democratic decision-making, and public policies define the objectives of public administration, which determine the overall starting point for IC management in public organizations. Based on these, limited public resources are allocated to various administrative sectors (e.g., education, health, or infrastructure). These allocative decisions and the underlying preparatory work are critical elements in the building of societal IC and managing public sector IC because these determine what knowledge resources are considered the most valuable for the well-being of present-day citizens and future generations.

According to recent global policy agendas, values, like social, financial, and ecological sustainability, are to be considered when allocating public resources. These policy objectives call for long-range planning in terms of IC, which differs from the rules of the quartile economy followed by private companies. In IC literature, Kianto et al. (2023) have acknowledged this by describing organizational performance consisting of environmental, economic, and social sustainability aspects. Whereas private managers are committed to creating value for shareholders, public managers should be driven by the aim of producing public value for the citizens of today and tomorrow (cf. Moore, 2014). This is also evident in the recent IC literature, where sustainable development is raised as one justification for public sector research (e.g., Melo & De la Gala Velásquez, 2022; Cavicchi, 2017).

As mentioned earlier, the literature shows that the interest of IC scholars in public organizations has at least partly followed the ideology of NPM that introduced management ideas, such as customer orientation and managing by results, from the private sector into the public sector (e.g., Martin-Sardesai & Guthrie, 2018; Cuganesan et al., 2007). The recent literature on public administration paints a more ambiguous picture of public governance, which may open up very different views on the management of IC. Digital era governance, public value management, and new public governance are only some examples and conceptualizations of the public governance paradigms that have followed NPM (cf. Torfing et al., 2020), and there would be a need to also analyze the implications of these management paradigms for IC management.

Modern public governance models challenge the organization-specific management models in many ways. In networked and hybrid organizational structures knowledge assets are scattered among government organizations, private businesses, civil society, and service users, which entails new requirements for IC management (Laihonen & Huhtamäki, 2020). IC management is then challenged by different expectations and objectives, multiple and sometimes conflicting objectives, mixed accountabilities, and the difficulty in composing the evidence base for evaluating the success of public policies and strategies (Laihonen & Kokko, 2020; Rajala et al., 2024). Our review highlighted the public sector's responsibility to engage different stakeholders in value co-creation at the ecosystem level (Iacuzzi et al., 2020; Iacuzzi & Pauluzzo, 2023). Also, Kianto et al. (2023) recognize the growing role of ecosystems as a part of relational capital reflecting the large-scale changes in the operating environment. All these perspectives highlight the need for clearly defined roles in IC management as the traditional institutional boundaries are changing, and, for example, legitimacy and accountability for managing IC become confused.

Finally, the *management of public services* needs to be capable of harnessing the potential of IC and turning it into something of value for service users and the public workforce. This is the most familiar arena for many IC scholars. However, some characteristics distinguish public organizations and services from their private counterparts. For example, Serrano Cinca et al. (2003) list distinctive features of intangible assets in the public sector: lower motivation for the adoption of new management practices, multiple nonfinancial objectives, social responsibility and concern for the environment, managers facing more constraints and limitations, and having less room to maneuver and less urgency to quantify the intangible assets. Wall (2005) highlights that private sector organizations only measure performance that reflects their improvement priorities, whereas in the public sector, performance is measured to report externally to satisfy the information requests of several stakeholders. Further, suboptimization is a common phenomenon in today's public environments and may result from the lack of congruence between multiple and partly contradictory public interests (e.g., Vakkuri & Meklin, 2006).

IC theory can help public managers to better understand the intangible and specific nature of value creation in public services. Intangibility is a key characteristic of public services, and therefore, IC theory can enhance the understanding of the value creation processes where the service provider's and customer's intangible resources are combined and transformed into services and customer value (e.g., Laihonen & Lönnqvist, 2010; Serrano Cinca et al., 2003). Public service organizations co-create value in interaction with service users through dynamic relationships (Osborne, 2021). Osborne (2018) illustrates the distinctive context and nature of public service management with four examples. First, customer retention is more likely to be a sign of service failure rather than of success. Second, coerced customers contradict the notion of voluntary agency and participation in value creation. Third, public services may have multiple end users and stakeholders with different and conflicting definitions of a successful outcome of a service. Fourth, public service users are both the users of public services and citizens who may have a broader societal interest in the outcomes of public services. Still, according to Grönroos (2019), there are no inbuilt barriers to service-oriented and user-friendly operations in a public service organization; it is about effective service management.

To conclude, when considering the future of IC management in the public sector, it is important to briefly consider the future of the most important resource of public services, that is, the public workforce. Well-trained and motivated staff contribute to better service delivery and societal outcomes. It has been argued that the future public workforce will be smaller and focused on policy, not service delivery (Dickinson & Sullivan, 2014), which may significantly change capability and competence requirements in the public sector. Also, the shifting boundaries of public services are affecting ethics and values, which raises concern as to whether the public sector ethos—an intrinsic motivation to serve the public—can survive in the context of increased outsourcing (Dickinson & Sullivan, 2014). These issues are also imperative for IC theory and management to gain a more profound understanding of the multifaceted capabilities and incentives that drive individuals to serve the public.

4 Futurizing IC Management in the Public Sector

The central message of this chapter is that IC theory offers valuable tools and perspectives for public sector leaders and managers to optimize their intellectual assets, drive innovation, and create meaningful impact for citizens and communities. However, harnessing this potential entails considering certain distinguishing characteristics of the public sector when applying IC models developed in other contexts. So far, it seems that IC scholars have not very thoroughly considered these characteristics, which may partly explain the modest application of IC models in this context. In Table 2, we name three themes and several possible research questions for futurizing IC management in the public sector.

As summarized in Table 2, this chapter highlighted three viewpoints to consider when studying or managing IC in the public sector. These connect to the fundamental question of what makes the public sector public and to acknowledging the increasing institutional complexity creating new demands for managers, personnel, and also for citizens. These viewpoints are conducive to the further development of IC management in the public sector to support co-creation of public value, citizen participation, and strategic workforce planning to ensure the essential role of public service for the future well-being and functioning of society.

First, we raised the need for connecting IC theory to discussions on public value (and public values) which is considered to be the purpose of public managers (cf. Moore, 1995). This is where IC management needs to take a wider perspective than

Table 2 Futurizing IC management in the public sector—themes and possible research questions

Theme	Possible research questions
1. IC management to support pluralistic dialogue on public value(s)	– What will the future relationships be between societal values and IC management in the public sector? – How do IC theory and management take account of the growing pluralism and diversity of society? – How to manage IC for sustainable development considering economic, environmental, and social perspectives?
2. IC management to enable hybrid governance and systemic renewal	– How can IC theory and management support systemic renewal, new ways of thinking, and social innovations? – How does IC management enable and support dialogue reconciling disparate values and institutional logics in hybrid governance of multi-stakeholder networks? – What are the effects of new organizational models and new forms of work on IC management, or vice versa?
3. IC management as an administrative capability	– What administrative capability is needed to harness the potential of IC (human, structural, or relational capital)? – What organizational and technical solutions can be used to avoid siloing and suboptimization of IC or, conversely, to promote interorganizational and cross-disciplinary cooperation? – What are the competencies and motivational factors driving the public workforce to serve the public good?

in the business world. In the public sector, IC management cannot only consider the organizational goals of efficiency, cost minimization, or profit maximization; it must also consider aspects such as fairness, accessibility, and benefits to society. Without understanding the plurality of values in societies and the ambiguity of public value creation, it is almost impossible to develop managerial approaches and tools to serve the needs of public managers. The COVID-19 pandemic further highlighted the diversity within our societies and the trade-offs between values; the expansion of digital platforms, particularly social media, further amplifies these differences by allowing diverse expressions of interests and values (Bracci et al., 2021). Therefore, the first task for IC management in the public sector is to identify the societal values that drive the development of the public sector. Only then is it possible to define and develop IC—human, structural, and relational capital—to enable the creation of public value and the pluralistic dialogue required to tackle wicked problems such as sustainability (cf. Sinervo & Laihonen, 2024).

Second, the complexity of the institutional framework requires that the unit of analysis, also in public sector IC management, needs to change from individual organizations and the mapping of their IC to hybrid value creation (cf. Vakkuri & Johanson, 2020) combining the IC of public (government), private (business), and the third (civil society) and fourth sectors (combining elements of the public, private, and nonprofit sectors with social and environmental aims). Therefore, IC management in the public sector must look at IC as well as the processes of its development and utilization across organizational boundaries at the ecosystem level (cf. Laihonen, 2012; Guthrie & Dumay, 2015; Kianto et al., 2023). In the public sector, the choices of individual organizations are subordinate to the political will and the objectives set in the political decision-making processes. In practice, IC management in the public sector may confront obstacles that relate to the power structures, legitimacy, and accountability issues recently discussed in the hybrid governance and value creation literature (cf. Vakkuri & Johanson, 2020; Rajala et al., 2024). It is not always clear whose values and objectives should drive the development and management of IC.

Third, highlighted by the changes in both the expectations toward public services and the ways of organizing such services, we perceive an urgent need to gain new insights into public sector IC management. In our view, a more profound understanding of administrative capabilities enabling the utilization of IC is needed. Interorganizational and cross-disciplinary collaboration in public sector IC management must acknowledge the processes of integrating, reconfiguring, gaining, and releasing knowledge resources (cf. Teece et al., 1997; Eisenhardt & Martin, 2000). Also, publicly funded services are being increasingly called upon to justify their existence and the IC literature provides frameworks and practices for measuring and reporting intangible assets (e.g., Hussinki et al., 2024). By systematically assessing their IC, public organizations can gain insights into their knowledge-related strengths and weaknesses, and transparent reporting enhances accountability and informs effective decision-making, thereby contributing to organizational learning and public value. In addition to organizational capabilities, that is, structural and relational capital, it is essential also to manage human capital and attract and retain competent employees having shared and clear objectives.

What seems inevitable is that IC management in the public sector calls for multidisciplinarity. This is not to say that in the private sector, the challenges of IC management could or should be resolved within a certain discipline but to underscore that, especially in the public context, IC management is more than a matter of accounting or reporting. More importantly, it is a question of value judgment—what does society consider valuable? These value judgments are made in the democratic decision-making processes necessitating collective knowledge formation (Laihonen et al., 2023). Thus, knowledge-based management becomes a dialogue where participants make sense of different types of information, interpret, and attach meanings to each other's viewpoints (Laihonen & Mäntylä, 2018). These processes are always value-driven and represent a timely policy environment. Therefore, to be relevant to public managers, IC theory must recognize and appreciate these contingencies defining the public sector.

Finally, we want to close the discussion by acknowledging the potential that we perceive in applying IC theory in the public sector. The IC literature provides public managers with many simple and easy-to-apply managerial frameworks, practices, and tools, like Intellectual Capital Statements (Mouritsen et al., 2003) or the Meritum Guidelines (Meritum, 2001), to guide them in the application and development of their organization's knowledge resources. By systematically managing IC and leveraging intangible resources effectively, public organizations can enhance their capacity to address societal challenges and deliver valuable services. IC theory encourages innovation and creativity that are indispensable for public organizations when harnessing their IC to develop novel solutions, improve processes, and create value for citizens. Further, IC theory underscores the importance of collaboration and partnerships and thus relational capital, critical for addressing complex issues collectively. Public organizations can serve as platforms or ecosystems and pool national, regional, and local IC to enhance collaboration and create public value. Also, IC theory calls for continuous learning and capacity building that results in a capability perspective, which provides an interesting avenue for approaching IC in the public sector.

References

Bellucci, M., Marzi, G., Orlando, B., & Ciampi, F. (2021). Journal of Intellectual Capital: A review of emerging themes and future trends. *Journal of Intellectual Capital, 22*(4), 744–767. https://doi.org/10.1108/JIC-10-2019-0239

Belmonte da Silva, R., Fernández Jardón, C. M., & Veiga Avila, L. (2021). Effects of structural intellectual capital on the innovation capacity of public administration. *Journal of Technology Management & Innovation, 16*(3), 66–78. https://doi.org/10.4067/S0718-27242021000300066

Bracci, E., Saliterer, I., Sicilia, M., & Steccolini, I. (2021). Accounting for (public) value(s): Reconsidering publicness in accounting research and practice. *Accounting, Auditing & Accountability Journal, 34*(7), 1513–1526. https://doi.org/10.1108/AAAJ-06-2021-5318

Bueno Campos, E., Salmador, M. P., & Merino, C. (2006). Towards a model of intellectual capital in public administrations. *International Journal of Learning and Intellectual Capital, 3*(3), 214–232. https://doi.org/10.1504/IJLIC.2006.011311

Cavicchi, C. (2017). Healthcare sustainability and the role of intellectual capital: Evidence from an Italian Regional Health Service. *Journal of Intellectual Capital, 18*(3), 544–563. https://doi.org/10.1108/JIC-12-2016-0128

Christensen, T., & Lægreid, P. (2011). Complexity and hybrid public administration—Theoretical and empirical challenges. *Public Organization Review, 11*, 407–423. https://doi.org/10.1007/s11115-010-0141-4

Cuganesan, S., Boedker, C., & Guthrie, J. (2007). Enrolling discourse consumers to affect material intellectual capital practice. *Accounting, Auditing & Accountability Journal, 20*(6), 883–911. https://doi.org/10.1108/09513570710830281

Currie, C., & Suhomlinova, O. (2006). The impact of institutional forces upon knowledge sharing the UK NHS: The triumph on professional power and the inconsistency of policy. *Public Administration, 84*(1), 1–30. https://doi.org/10.1111/j.0033-3298.2006.00491.x

De Vries, M. S. (2016). *Understanding public administration*. Palgrave Macmillan.

Dickinson, H., & Sullivan, H. (2014). *Imagining the 21st century public service workforce*. Melbourne School of Government, Melbourne, Australia.

Dumay, J., Guthrie, J., & Puntillo, P. (2015). IC and public sector: A structured literature review. *Journal of Intellectual Capital, 16*(2), 267–284. https://doi.org/10.1108/JIC-02-2015-0014

Edvinsson, L., & Malone, M. S. (1997). *Intellectual capital: Realizing your company's true value by finding its hidden brainpower*. Harper Business.

Eisenhardt, K. M., & Martin, J. A. (2000). Dynamic capabilities: What are they? *Strategic Management Journal, 21*(10–11), 1105–1121. https://doi.org/10.1002/1097-0266(200010/11)21:10/11<1105::AID-SMJ133>3.0.CO;2-E

Federal Data Strategy. (2022). *FDS framework mission, principles, practices, and actions*. Available from https://strategy.data.gov/assets/docs/2020-federal-data-strategy-framework.pdf (Accessed May 10, 2024).

Government of the United Kingdom. (2022). *Data saves lives: Reshaping health and social care with data*. Available from https://www.gov.uk/government/publications/data-saves-lives-reshaping-health-and-social-care-with-data/data-saves-lives-reshaping-health-and-social-care-with-data (Accessed May 10, 2024).

Grönroos, C. (2019). Reforming public services: Does service logic have anything to offer? *Public Management Review, 21*(5), 775–788. https://doi.org/10.1080/14719037.2018.1529879

Guthrie, J., & Dumay, J. (2015). New frontiers in the use of intellectual capital in the public sector. *Journal of Intellectual Capital, 16*(2), 258–266. https://doi.org/10.1108/JIC-02-2015-0017

Guthrie, J., Ricceri, F., & Dumay, J. (2012). Reflections and projections: A decade of intellectual capital accounting research. *The British Accounting Review, 44*(2), 68–92. https://doi.org/10.1016/j.bar.2012.03.004

Hussinki, H., King, T., Dumay, J., & Steinhöfel, E. (2024). Accounting for intangibles: A critical review. *Journal of Accounting Literature*, Vol. ahead-of-print No. ahead-of-print. https://doi.org/10.1108/JAL-05-2022-0060.

Iacuzzi, S., Massaro, M., & Garlatti, A. (2020). Value creation through collective intelligence: Managing intellectual capital. *The Electronic Journal of Knowledge Management, 18*(1), 68–79.

Iacuzzi, S., & Pauluzzo, R. (2023). Looking for missing outcomes: Accounting for intellectual capital and value creation in ecosystems. *Journal of Management and Governance*. https://doi.org/10.1007/s10997-023-09688-3

Joia, L. A. (2008). The impact of government-to-government endeavors on the intellectual capital of public organizations. *Government Information Quarterly, 25*(2), 256–277. https://doi.org/10.1016/j.giq.2007.06.004

Käpylä, J., Kujansivu, P., & Lönnqvist, A. (2012). National intellectual capital performance: A strategic approach. *Journal of Intellectual Capital, 13*(3), 343–362. https://doi.org/10.1108/14691931211248909

Kianto, A., Cabrilo, S., & Hussinki, H. (2023). Futurizing intellectual capital theory to uncover pertinent and unexplored horizons. In C. Bratianu, M. Handzic, & E. Bolisani (Eds.), *The future of knowledge management* (pp. 67–90). Springer. https://doi.org/10.1007/978-3-031-38696-1_4

Kujansivu, P. (2009). Is there something wrong with intellectual capital management models? *Knowledge Management Research & Practice, 7*, 300–307. https://doi.org/10.1057/kmrp.2009.23

Kujansivu, P., & Lönnqvist, A. (2007). Investigating the value and efficiency of intellectual capital. *Journal of Intellectual Capital, 8*(2), 272–287. https://doi.org/10.1108/14691930710742844

Laihonen, H. (2012). Knowledge structures of a health ecosystem. *Journal of Health Organization and Management, 26*(4), 542–558. https://doi.org/10.1108/14777261211251571

Laihonen, H., & Huhtamäki, J. (2020). Organizational hybridity and fluidity: Deriving new strategies for dynamic knowledge management. *Knowledge Management Research & Practice, 21*(2), 216–228. https://doi.org/10.1080/14778238.2020.1794993

Laihonen, H., & Kokko, P. (2020). Knowledge management and hybridity of institutional logics in public sector. *Knowledge Management Research & Practice, 21*(1), 14–28. https://doi.org/10.1080/14778238.2020.1788429

Laihonen, H., Kork, A.-A., & Sinervo, L.-M. (2023). Advancing public sector knowledge management: towards an understanding of knowledge formation in public administration. *Knowledge Management Research & Practice, 22*(3), 223–233. https://doi.org/10.1080/14778238.2023.2187719.

Laihonen, H., & Lönnqvist, A. (2010). Knowledge-based value creation: Grasping the intangibility of service operations in Finland. *International Journal of Knowledge-Based Development, 1*(4), 331–345. https://doi.org/10.1504/IJKBD.2010.038042

Laihonen, H., & Mäntylä, S. (2018). Strategic knowledge management and evolving local government. *Journal of Knowledge Management, 22*(1), 219–234. https://doi.org/10.1108/JKM-06-2017-0232

Lerro, A., & Carlucci, D. (2007). Intellectual capital and regions: Origins, theoretical foundations and implications for decision-makers. *International Journal of Learning and Intellectual Capital, 4*(4), 357–376. https://doi.org/10.1504/IJLIC.2007.016333

Lipsky, M. (1980). *Street-level bureaucracy: Dilemmas of the individual in public services*. Russell Sage Foundation.

Lönnqvist, A., Käpylä, J., Salonius, H., & Yigitcanlar, T. (2014). Knowledge that matters: Identifying regional knowledge assets of the Tampere region. *European Planning Studies, 22*(10), 2011–2029. https://doi.org/10.1080/09654313.2013.814621

Manes Rossi, F., Citro, F., & Bisogno, M. (2016). Intellectual capital in action: Evidence from Italian local governments. *Journal of Intellectual Capital, 17*(4), 696–713. https://doi.org/10.1108/JIC-01-2016-0011

Martin-Sardesai, A., & Guthrie, J. (2018). Human capital loss in an academic performance measurement system. *Journal of Intellectual Capital, 19*(1), 53–70. https://doi.org/10.1108/JIC-06-2017-0085

Massingham, P. R., & Tam, L. (2015). The relationship between human capital, value creation and employee reward. *Journal of Intellectual Capital, 16*(2), 390–418. https://doi.org/10.1108/JIC-06-2014-0075

Matos, F., Vairinhos, V., & Matos, A. J. (2018). Intellectual capital management and trust in public administration in European countries. In B. Kożuch, S. J. Magala, & J. Paliszkiewicz (Eds.), *Managing public trust* (pp. 273–289). https://doi.org/10.1007/978-3-319-70485-2_17.

Melo, N. A. P., & De la Gala Velásquez, B. (2022). The mediating role of structural capital in the relationship between human capital and performance in the public administrations of Mexico and Peru. *Estudios Gerenciales, 38*(164), 320–333. https://doi.org/10.18046/j.estger.2022.164.5087

Meritum. (2001). *Guidelines for managing and reporting on intangibles, intellectual capital report*. Final Report of the Meritum Project.

Moore, M. (1995). *Creating public value: Strategic management in government*. Harvard University Press.

Moore, M. (2014). Public value accounting: Establishing a philosophical basis. *Public Administration Review, 74*(4), 465–477. https://doi.org/10.1111/puar.12198

Mouritsen, J., Bukh, P. N., Flagstad, K., Thorbjørnsen, S., Johansen, M. R., Kotnis, S., Larsen, H. T., Nielsen, C., Kjærgaard, I., Krag, L., Jeppesen, G., Haisler, J., & Stakemann, B. (2003). *Intellectual capital statements – The New Guideline, Danish Ministry of Science Technology and Innovation, Copenhagen*.

O'Connor, A., Roos, G., & Vickers-Willis, T. (2007). Evaluating an Australian public policy organization's innovation capacity. *European Journal of Innovation Management, 10*(4), 532–558. https://doi.org/10.1108/14601060710828817

Osborne, S. (2018). From Public service-dominant logic to public service logic: Organizations capable of co-production and value co-creation? *Public Management Review, 20*(2), 225–231. https://doi.org/10.1080/14719037.2017.1350461

Osborne, S. (2021). *Public service logic: Creating value for public service users, citizens, and society through public service delivery*. Routledge.

Petty, R., & Guthrie, J. (2000). Intellectual capital literature review: Measurement, reporting and management. *Journal of Intellectual Capital, 1*(2), 155–176. https://doi.org/10.1108/14691930010348731

Rajala, T., Kokko, P., Laihonen, H., & Pekkola, E. (2024). Manifestations of hybrid accountability in horizontal network governance. In G. Grossi & J. Vakkuri (Eds.), *Handbook of accounting and public governance – exploring hybridizations* (pp. 68–94). Edward Elgar. https://doi.org/10.4337/9781800888456.00014

Ramírez, Y., Tejada, Á., & Sánchez, M. P. (2022). Determinants of online intellectual capital disclosure by Spanish local governments. *Journal of Intellectual Capital, 23*(2), 249–289. Scopus. https://doi.org/10.1108/JIC-03-2020-0086

Roos, G., Edvinsson, L., Roos, J., & Dragonetti, N. C. (1997). *Intellectual capital: Navigating the new business landscape*. Macmillan Publications.

Salonius, H., & Lönnqvist, A. (2012). Exploring the policy relevance of national intellectual capital information. *Journal of Intellectual Capital, 13*(3), 331–342. https://doi.org/10.1108/14691931211248891

Serrano Cinca, C., Mar Molinero, C., & Bossi Queiroz, A. (2003). The measurement of intangible assets in public sector using scaling techniques. *Journal of Intellectual Capital, 4*(2), 249–275. https://doi.org/10.1108/14691930310472857

Sinervo, L. M., & Laihonen, H. (2024). New development: Public managers between a rock and a hard place – social-financial sustainability in local government. *Public Money & Management, 44*(6), 559–564. https://doi.org/10.1080/09540962.2024.2351133.

Ståhle, P., & Bounfour, A. (2008). Understanding dynamics of intellectual capital of nation. *Journal of Intellectual Capital, 9*(2), 164–177. https://doi.org/10.1108/14691930810870283

Sveiby, K. (1997). *The new organizational wealth: Managing & measuring knowledge-based assets*. Berrett-Koehler.

Teece, D. J., Pisano, G., & Shuen, A. (1997). Dynamic capabilities and strategic management. *Strategic Management Journal, 18*(7), 509–533. https://doi.org/10.1002/(SICI)1097-0266(199708)18:7<509::AID-SMJ882>3.0.CO;2-Z

Torfing, J., Andersen, L. B., Greve, C., & Klausen, K. K. (2020). *Public governance paradigms. Competing and co-existing*. Edward Elgar.

Torfing, J., & Triantafillou, P. (2013). What's in a name? Grasping new public governance as a political-administrative system. *International Review of Public Administration, 18*(2), 9–25. https://doi.org/10.1080/12294659.2013.10805250

Vakkuri, J., & Johanson, J.-E. (Eds.). (2020). *Hybrid governance, organisations and society: Value creation perspectives* (1st ed.). Routledge. https://doi.org/10.4324/9780429286247

Vakkuri, J., & Meklin, P. (2006). Ambiguity in performance measurement: A theoretical approach to organisational uses of performance measurement. *Financial Accountability & Management, 22*(3), 235–250. https://doi.org/10.1111/j.0267-4424.2006.00401.x

Veltri, S., & Puntillo, P. (2020). On intellectual capital management as an evaluation criterion for university managers: A case study. *Journal of Management and Governance, 24*(1), 135–167. https://doi.org/10.1007/s10997-019-09461-5

Veltri, S., & Silvestri, A. (2015). The Free State University integrated reporting: A critical consideration. *Journal of Intellectual Capital, 16*(2), 443–462. https://doi.org/10.1108/JIC-06-2014-0077

Wall, A. (2005). The measurement and management of intellectual capital in the public sector: Taking the lead or waiting for direction? *Public Management Review, 7*(2), 289–303. https://doi.org/10.1080/14719030500091723

Wiig, K. M. (2002). Knowledge management in public administration. *Journal of Knowledge Management, 6*(3), 224–239. https://doi.org/10.1108/13673270210434331

Yigitcanlar, T., & Lönnqvist, A. (2013). Benchmarking knowledge-based urban development performance: Results from the international comparison of Helsinki. *Cities, 31*, 357–369. https://doi.org/10.1016/j.cities.2012.11.005

Harri Laihonen is a Professor of Health and Social Management at the University of Eastern Finland. He has specialized in knowledge management and performance management and is interested in improving the understanding of organizational performance in different organizational settings and designing performance management systems for public sector organizations, networks, and service systems. Professor Laihonen is actively participating in university-industry collaboration and applies action-oriented research approaches to gain an understanding of timely management issues.

Paula Pusenius is a doctoral student of Health and Social Management at the University of Eastern Finland. She has specialized in knowledge management and healthcare management, having solid practical experience as a knowledge management specialist, as a manager in healthcare, and as a management consultant. Her interests are capabilities, intellectual capital, and sustainable development in a changing environment, especially in the public sector, which has wicked problems to examine and multiple interests to reconcile.

Part III

Intellectual Capital Meets Artificial Intelligence: Reimagining the IC Landscape

Intellectual Capital and the Era of Raising AI

Bror Salmelin

Abstract

The focus of this chapter is to give a snapshot of the challenges intellectual capital and fast-developing AI bring to organisational operations. Knowledge management is the key when building intellectual capital and AI leads to high risks in developing the structural, human and relational capital components. The corruption of information together with deepfake technologies sets high demand on understanding and developing the IC assets and use of them in any organisation.

The skill set needed includes new professions like prompt engineering, but also new types of actions ensuring data set integrity in using AI tools for enhancing the capabilities of analytics and especially synthesis of the organisation's internal information (data sets and human knowledge).

Using AI for organisational information intense services needs to be well traceable, e.g. due to liability issues which stem from misinformation generated by the AI, even if the original data sets would be non-corrupted in the first place.

AI develops fast, and to have organisations grow into the use of it requires a clear development strategy for the take-up. When we understand the operative principles of AI systems and tools, we simultaneously will understand the role of verifying the quality of the AI implies in the IC of organisations, being a powerful tool to speed up the processes of using the multilayer IC in a safe(r) manner.

B. Salmelin (✉)
Industry Commons Foundation, ICF, Stockholm, Sweden
e-mail: bror@salmelin.eu

A. Kianto et al. (eds.), *Futurizing Intellectual Capital*, Knowledge Management and Organizational Learning 15, https://doi.org/10.1007/978-3-031-80197-6_10

1 Introduction

The chapter highlights the new elements focusing on the intellectual capital (IC) value as a strategic asset in the emerging AI era. Using AI enables analysing and pseudo-synthesising data in a much more efficient manner than ever before. However, the generative AI might mislead us into thinking that the core of IC is somehow changing. It is kept in mind that some important characteristics have to be taken into account when we intend to use AI as a tool to support knowledge intensive work. Knowledge management is the key when building intellectual capital, and AI leads to high risks in developing structural, human and relational capital (Edvinsson & Malone, 1997).

Most of the generic artificial intelligence approaches are based on large language models (LLM) and are based on large amounts of texts and other material taught to the system. This leads to the output generated by AI leading to most likely sequences of words, i.e. most probable historic word sequences, rather than creating or synthesizing new information. This also means the AI-generated contents need to be verified by the user as the large material used to teach the system might be wrong or wrongly interpreted.

AI development is very fast and is extending to media, such as text to image or text to video, which might create interesting new avenues in selected areas, e.g. in creating commercials or artwork for everyday use. This might look like creativity, but in essence, we still work with content probabilities, where the prompts (the commands for AI) determine the quality of the output to a high degree.

AI is a great tool, but using it requires skills to get the best of it, like for any tool. One needs to understand the philosophy and methods behind the surface. In the following chapters, I will try to highlight some of the central issues which need to be taken into account.

The key question is how the underlying pseudo-rich information produced by AI can be managed and used efficiently and correctly to enhance the IC in various organisations. How is proper KM and understanding the nature of AI processes affecting leading to new skills needed in organisations, and how to focus the AI-related activities best to enhance the IC of any given organisation.

2 AI Developments in Practice

AI enhances knowledge management by improving information retrieval, knowledge discovery, content curation, personalization, automation, decision support, collaboration, communication and continuous learning. By leveraging AI technologies, organizations can unlock the full potential of their knowledge assets and drive innovation, efficiency and competitive advantage.

Even if AI stems from the 1980s, the recent computational capacity and methods developed regarding neural network computation have led to the wide use and commercialisation of AI platforms. Most of them are based on large language models (LLM) and thus generative pre-trained transformers (GPT) which are based on the semantic relationships between words in sentences (natural language processing). Text-based GPT models are pre-trained on a large corpus of text which can be from the Internet. Some topical subsets can, e.g. be corporate internal sources when developing topical language models. The pre-training consists in predicting the next token (a token being usually a word, subword or punctuation). Throughout this pre-training, GPT models accumulate knowledge about the world and can then generate human-like text by repeatedly predicting the next token. Typically, a subsequent training phase makes the model more truthful, useful and harmless, usually with a technique called reinforcement learning from human feedback (RLHF). Current GPT models are still prone to generating falsehoods called "hallucinations", although this can be reduced with RLHF and quality data. They are used in chatbots, which allow one to ask a question or request a task in simple text. The design of the text is called prompt engineering and affects the quality of the query output significantly.

Most popular GPT models and services include platforms like Gemini (formerly Bard), ChatGPT, Grok, Claude, Copilot and LLaMA.

AI-based models and applications are currently in extremely fast developing stage. Multimodal models and applications suggesting contents for specific areas are blooming. Due to the fast-changing landscape, I will not go into depth about the application offerings, as the same issues arise in them as in the general use of AI systems. Examples offered include Book Writers, Prompt creators, Content reviewers, Content rewriters, Content summarizers and Content translators.

Multimodal GPT models can process different types of data (modalities) such as images, videos, sound and text, which has raised interest in the visual content industry, like advertising and media production. Data to image or even video productions with near to real-world image quality is now possible in the newest versions of the tools.

It is proposed that the journey towards general AI systems (AGI) will be surprisingly short. It is predicted to happen in a few years, accelerating the use of AI into increasingly wide use in different fields of life and work. It is thus increasingly important to understand the properties of AI systems including their strengths and weaknesses.

At the time of writing this chapter, the development of AI is extremely rapid, with new tools emerging almost weekly. Besides normal text-based tools, we see text-to-image and text-to-video applications enabling rich interactions and support in creativity. We have multilingual solutions enabling fluent real-time translations from several languages, even including video-level interactions. This creates great opportunities for a wide use of non-structured intellectual capital. At the same time, however, the risk of unreliable information in the IC networks rises significantly. Risk management needs to rise to entirely new levels.

As the AI platforms are mostly taught in English, it has raised the question if the quality of the responses is better in English than in other languages, e.g. Finnish. For example, the ChatGPT does not translate to English more than the bare instructions. Words represent ideas, and in similarly structured languages, the connections remain alike. Problems might arise only if the structure of the language is strongly different from the English and the training material poor in that very language. Normally the output quality is at a quite constant level.

A recent language model (Poro) (Tivi, 2024) is using novel methods of interlinking in the teaching process words from less resource-rich languages (like in this case Finnish) to English, enabling the efficient use of multilingual prompts. The Poro language model uses 34 billion parameters, managing the Finnish-English connections and is taught by using 1000 billion words of text data.

3 Example of AI Deliverable

A good example of current AI capability is the following generated by the simple prompt "Artificial Intelligence and Knowledge Management". Here I used one of the most popular tools, ChatGPT, which is based on large language models (LLM).

And this is the response:

"Artificial intelligence (AI) and knowledge management (KM) intersect in various ways, often enhancing each other's capabilities. Here's how AI contributes to knowledge management:

Information Retrieval: AI-powered search engines and knowledge bases enable users to quickly access relevant information. AI algorithms can analyze large volumes of data, identify patterns, and retrieve the most relevant knowledge assets based on user queries.

Knowledge Discovery: AI techniques such as natural language processing (NLP) and machine learning (ML) can sift through unstructured data sources like documents, emails, and social media posts to discover insights and patterns that humans might overlook. This helps in extracting valuable knowledge from vast amounts of information.

Content Curation: AI algorithms can curate and organize content by categorizing, tagging, and summarizing documents, articles, and other knowledge assets. This enhances the accessibility and usability of knowledge repositories, making it easier for users to find relevant information.

Personalization: AI-powered knowledge management systems can personalize content recommendations based on user preferences, browsing history, and behavior patterns. By analyzing user interactions, AI algorithms can deliver tailored knowledge resources, improving user engagement and satisfaction.

Automation: AI automates routine knowledge management tasks such as content classification, indexing, and maintenance. This frees up human resources to focus on higher-value activities such as knowledge creation, sharing, and collaboration.

Decision Support: AI systems can provide decision support by analyzing data, generating insights, and recommending courses of action. In knowledge management contexts, AI-powered analytics tools can help organizations make informed decisions based on data-driven insights derived from internal and external knowledge sources.

Collaboration and Communication: AI facilitates collaboration and communication by enabling knowledge sharing and exchange across individuals, teams, and organizations. AI-powered collaboration platforms integrate features such as chatbots, virtual assistants, and knowledge graphs to facilitate seamless communication and collaboration among users.

Continuous Learning: AI algorithms can learn from user interactions and feedback to improve knowledge management systems over time. By analyzing usage patterns and user feedback, AI-powered systems can adapt to changing user needs and preferences, continuously enhancing the quality and relevance of knowledge resources".

By using different prompts, of course, the output by the ChatGPT is different. Here I used a prompt which tackles one fundamental dimension of IC, the quality of information and its use. Example of prompting AI and intellectual capital is below:

"AI has a profound impact on intellectual capital, enhancing its creation, utilization, and protection. Here's how:

1. Creation: AI enables the rapid analysis of vast amounts of data, leading to insights that can fuel innovation and the generation of new intellectual capital. Whether it's through natural language processing, machine learning algorithms, or other AI techniques, systems can uncover patterns and connections that humans might miss, contributing to the creation of new ideas, products, and services.
2. Utilization: AI helps in extracting value from intellectual capital by automating tasks, improving decision-making, and optimizing processes. For instance, AI-powered analytics can sift through intellectual property databases to identify relevant patents or assist in managing knowledge repositories, making valuable information more accessible to organizations.
3. Protection: Intellectual capital often needs protection from theft or misuse. AI plays a crucial role here by augmenting traditional methods of intellectual property protection. Machine learning algorithms can detect anomalies and patterns indicative of unauthorized access to sensitive data or infringement of intellectual property rights. AI can also assist in the automated monitoring of trademarks, patents, and copyrights to ensure compliance and mitigate risks.

Overall, AI contributes to the enrichment, exploitation, and safeguarding of intellectual capital, thereby enhancing its value and impact on organizations and society."

As can be seen from the deliverables above, the AI produces well-readable and comprehensible content and can easily provide lists or summaries of rather specific topics. This is based on the nature of the data taught to the system and the list type of information asked in the prompt. However, as also can be seen, the output is very close to what one could a priori expect and thus might well operate as a stimulus (for human beings) for brainstorming, deeper thinking and analysis on the topic concerned.

In the same manner, AI has proven very useful in synthesising big numerical and statistical data sets, which then can be used almost in real time as the basis for analyses. In these cases, it is extremely important, however, that the user of the outcome is sufficiently knowledgeable about the topic and can detect the obvious (eventual) mistakes or poor quality of the result the AI system has provided.

This kind of list, like tables produced by AI, can be very helpful in stimulating the creative processes as background or touch on the topic, helping cover the whole area, e.g. one is writing about. Because of the nature of LLM, the product received from the AI system often is of mediocrity quality and does not necessarily provide new perspectives on the topic. This again highlights the use of LLM-based AI as a supportive tool for human knowledge work.

4 Intellectual Capital Management in the Artificial Intelligence Era

The IC assets of organisations need to be protected and need to include even more strongly the soft components of knowledge, like tacit knowledge, behavioural connections and trust. Organisations need to have guardians to protect their core assets from not being contaminated when using AI tools, and they need to clearly understand the nature of AI as a helper when analysing large amounts of data and information more effectively than at present, as well as enhancing the possibilities to use AI to larger groups by natural language prompts. It is noteworthy that when using AI tools, the control of data flows as well as data protection is of extreme importance.

Proper knowledge management is essential when we look at the intellectual capital of any entity, organisation or even individual. If knowledge management is poorly organised, the knowledge assets are eroded, as information gets eroded, and the interlinkage of the information components thus becomes unreliable. From the basic building blocks, the erosion of reliable information affects them all, and that is why the focus on AI related to knowledge management is essential. Intellectual capital is the result of mental processes that form a set of intangible objects that can be used in economic activity and bring income to its owner, usually, an organisation covering the competencies of its people (*human capital*), the value relating to its relationships (*relational capital*) and everything that is left when the individuals leave (*structural capital*) (Edvinsson & Malone, 1997). Human capital erosion is related not only to poor data but also, e.g. related to deepfake technologies, making various statements unreliable. This is directly reflecting to the relational capital. The IC assets from a structural capital perspective are essentially dependent on the non-corrupted information available at any moment, in all the fields of operation of the organisation.

This highlights the importance of any organisation having its AI and KM strategy to ensure the maintenance and development of the IC assets in any given field.

Strictly speaking, the current AI systems do not comply with the European GDPR regulation either as it is not ensured that personal data is treated according to the regulations. This can be the case, e.g. when using AI for administrative or healthcare applications. Again, this highlights the importance of the use of AI systems as a complementary tool to help professionals in their work.

Generative AI is often trained on unlicensed copyrighted works, including in domains such as images or computer code. The output is then used under the rationale of "fair use". Also, website owners who do not wish to have their copyrighted content be AI indexed can add code to their site, not wanting the website to be indexed by a search engine which is currently available to certain services such as OpenAI. Experts disagree about how well, and under what circumstances, this rationale will hold up in courts of law. Copyright violations might be the reason for the increased number of lawsuits.

A large part of the knowledge base of organisations is tacit. In these cases, efficient use of AI might help in finding the expertise, i.e. the persons dealing with specific topics in an organisation, again supporting the networking in large companies, e.g. consulting companies. Likewise, browsing rapidly intellectual assets like patent portfolios or previous tasks done is an area where AI systems can be very useful on a company's internal level.

Prompt engineers could be the new profession to achieve the quality standards to extract good quality outcomes from AI systems, which are rapidly mushrooming now. We currently see also commercial prompt engineering (AI-based) software offerings grow. Prompt engineering skills together with AI/KM understanding on all strategic levels of an organisation will increase significantly in importance.

AI will be part of the lifeblood of organisations, and the importance of managing the risks and seizing the opportunities remains at the heart of the IC management of all kinds of organisations and inter-organisational relationships.

5 What Is Artificial Intelligence in IC?

AI enables natural language prompts which make data analysis a tool for large masses, but in all cases, it is crucial to understand that AI which is based on LLM (large language models) is essentially behaving like a syntax parrot. It repeats what it has been learnt to and uses language probabilities to predict its outcome. This principle is true also when we move towards other media than words only (e.g. images, music, etc.). Hence very wide or focussed topical material is essential when teaching the AI system.

Machine learning applications will be biased if they learn from biased data. The developers may not be aware that the bias exists. Bias can be introduced by the way training data is selected and by the way a model is deployed. Many AI systems are very complex leading to that their designers cannot precisely explain how they reach their decisions. Particularly this is true with deep neural networks, in which there are a large amount of non-linear relationships between inputs and outputs.

The core of intellectual capital is the capture of knowledge beyond data and information. Knowledge also includes the element of tacit knowledge which turns knowledge into wisdom, experience and insight. This is beyond the reach of AI as it is based on the past data taught to the system. The characteristic of AI enables analysis of the data, but as the result is as good as the data and is based on LLM, the user must be aware of the risks of poor or even misleading outcomes of the AI.

6 Artificial Intelligence Feeding into Intellectual Capital

The intellectual capital assets need to be seen from the perspective of managing creativity and the ability to make synthesis for decisions in rapidly changing conditions.

Typical application areas currently in science include classification, regression, clustering, forecasting, generation, discovery and the development of new scientific insights. Managing large volumes of often incomplete data is a strong application for AI-based tools.

So far AI systems are not fit for serendipity, as they are (again based on the training data) simplifying the problem and providing the likely correct answer without case-specific thinking. This bias is also coming from the cases taught, as the values and ethics appearing in the data are directly affecting the outcome the AI is proposing. Even riskier is that it is quite easy to feed misinformation by feeding the data to the AI tools and thus spreading fast the wrong conclusions. AI is a semantic parrot, not more.

In some experiments by trying to guide the outcome of the AI towards more emotional contents, also emotional prompting is used. This has even led to the general audience thinking that AI can be genuinely creative and emotional, but at the same time forgetting that the result is a combination of the data taught and purpose-oriented prompting. So, nothing emotional, nothing creating new information at the end.

AI as a crawling tool in large clouds of data may help in continuously updating a priori assigned tasks, like "live business models" or "live marketing strategies". In essence, the structure where the updated information is fed into must be open for AI based continuous updates of data and information, integrating the new data into its contents seaminglessly. The tree for the input may be considered as a structure based on the organisational IC and strategic needs, and the AI output must be controlled for quality and consistency before being used on this strategic level.

An interesting dimension of using AI for knowledge management is the possibility of using multilingualism, even in real time. AI can provide translations in real time in conversations, which means that, e.g. in global organisations everyone can be in the same information-sharing sphere and even have dialogues with each other in their own mother tongues. This makes it easier to capture the tacit knowledge of an organisation as well, as often the tacit knowledge is transferred in natural language oral conversations rather than in written, instructional format.

On the other hand, this real-time multilingualism together with deepfake videos can be seen from the other side of the coin: it can be harmful and be used in misleading form. Current deepfake videos and voices require only very short clips of the original person; only a few seconds of the original material is enough to find the spectrum of the voice. Hence, intra- and inter-organisationally, the use of AI needs to be followed carefully leading to common organisational practices to ensure the authenticity of the contents.

7 Prompt Engineering

Prompts are the commands or requests initiating a query or other process to create information or, e.g. media contents by using AI. They are central when using generative pre-trained models (GPT). Prompt engineering is crucial when formulating queries in order to obtain precise and correct results using AI.

What is essential are precision and clear instructions as vague prompts may lead to very unpredictable or unwanted results. The prompt has, if possible, to be engineered based on the application-specific terms increasing the possibility of relevant results and narrowing the output to the desired field. The use of specific terminology might help in better understanding of the query by the model used.

Prompt engineering might lead to several iterative rounds of prompts, making the outputs more precise, and also more focussed on the issue desired. It makes sense to test different prompts to seek the best results, but also to verify the accuracy and correctness of the material the use of AI produced.

Prompts should provide sufficient context and a priori information for the AI model to generate better, more expected and precise results. It is noteworthy that depending on the material taught to the AI system, there might be a rather strong bias of the outcomes too. For example, politically, this has been proven to be the case. The design of the prompt should be intuitive making it easy for users to interact with the AI model, thus achieving more meaningful responses.

Google introduced 23.2.2024 (Google blog, 2024) a new paradigm for generative AI, *generative interactive environments* (Genie), whereby interactive, playable environments can be generated from a single image prompt. Genie can be prompted with images it has never seen before, such as real-world photographs or sketches, enabling people to interact with their imagined virtual worlds essentially acting as a foundation world model. This is possible despite training without any action labels. Instead, Genie is trained from a large dataset of publicly available Internet videos. The initial focus is on videos of 2D platformer games and robotics, but the method is general and should work for any type of domains and is scalable to ever larger Internet datasets. This might be a promising beginning of mastering tacit knowledge as well.

Prompt engineering is likely to grow to a new profession when targeting the wide use of AI, especially in professional and client service applications. Currently we already see commercial applications where prompts for business applications are proposed, like for marketing, information sharing and retrieval among others.

8 Liability

When using AI to extract information, it is important to consider not only the quality of information but also the liability issues which might be caused by false or weak information the system has provided. It is, again, important to notice that the quality of the output is solely dependent on the quality and spectrum of information taught to the AI system. This leads to liability issues for not only the provider of the AI system but also the user of the results the system has provided.

As AI becomes more complex, questions arise about who is accountable for the actions and decisions of these systems. This involves the identification not only about the algorithms but also all parties involved in the service offering, and at the end, the end user needs to be aware of the limitations of the AI system providing the content.

As in all complex software systems, the existence of bugs is highly likely, causing erroneous functionality and in AI even possibly dangerous or at least harmful outputs.

According to arstechnica.com (16.2.2024) (arstechnica.com, 2024) in 2023, a customer of Air Canada was asking online about cancellation and refunding issues regarding his flight. He used the official Air Canada site and their AI-driven chatbot. Following in detail the instructions received, he progressed with a claim. To his great surprise, the (human) client service denied the request as the written contractual documents stated differently than the chatbot advised to do. When bringing the claim to the court, the ruling was clear, stating that Air Canada was responsible for the wrong information provided by the chatbot, and the refund requested needed to be paid. This was the case even if the chatbot service was provided by one subcontractor of Air Canada, not the company itself. The service provider to the customer was responsible for the poor functionality of the AI-based chatbot service. It was also ruled that the client could not be held responsible for the false information, as he used the official route to gather information on how to proceed with the claim.

It is at least currently dangerous to let LLM-based AI systems act directly with the customer queries, and therefore many bots are limited to give guidance by using only a limited set of answers.

Users and operators of AI systems have also their responsibility to use these novel technologies and services provided by AI systems ethically and responsibly. This includes issues like bias in training data or algorithms. Training data selection, model development and algorithmic transparency might mitigate the risk of poor results and thus legal liabilities as well.

Critical users of the AI-provided information and contents should be aware of how the data is generated and also to which extent it is generated from open data sources. Not all teaching data collections are open source, as companies are now competing heavily with data-rich AI systems. In the near future, we will also see much wider offerings increasingly "small" AI GPT systems, which might be topic- or even organisation-specific. They exist already but are not yet mainstream.

9 AI and Creativity

AI as a tool enables the efficient use of large information sources and has significant benefits as assistive AI for knowledge-intensive work. This is shown, for example, in the Harvard Business School paper from 2023 (Dell'Acqua et al., 2023). In the experiment they established a performance baseline on a similar task, and subjects were randomly assigned to one of three conditions: no AI access, GPT-4 AI access or GPT-4 AI access with a prompt engineering overview. They suggested that the capabilities of AI create a "jagged technological frontier" where some tasks are easily done by AI, while others, though seemingly similar in difficulty level, are outside the current capability of AI.

For each one of a set of 18 realistic consulting tasks within the frontier of AI capabilities, consultants using AI were significantly more productive (they completed 12.2% more tasks on average and completed tasks 25.1% more quickly) and produced significantly higher quality results (more than 40% higher quality compared to a control group). Consultants across the skills distribution benefited significantly from having AI augmentation, with those below the average performance threshold increasing by 43% and those above increasing by 17% compared to their own scores. For a task selected to be outside the frontier, however, consultants using AI were 19 percentage points less likely to produce correct solutions compared to those without AI.

According to NESTA (podcast 2019) (NESTA, 2019), creative roles themselves are less likely to be automated, as well as the importance of creativity across the economy. It is essential that creative organisations make full use of the opportunities of technologies, encouraging research and development, especially in the cross-disciplinary sectors.

In the same podcast, Mark Davis from Autodesk states that new AI design tools flip the traditional solution-oriented design process. Instead, designers define the constraints of the design problem, and then the AI rapidly generates hundreds and thousands of possible models, which can be optimised for specific metrics and that have applications in everything from spatial design to spacecraft. Both the speed at which they are generated and the types of design that result go far beyond what human designers typically produce.

IBM in their recent research blog (22.2.2024) (IBM blog, 2014) by Michele Dolfi is presenting a new tool for large-scale information processing and management. Deep Search is a technology that uses AI to collect and convert the data in large documents into something searchable, and it is now integrating with watsonx.ai, IBM's enterprise studio for AI builders to train, validate, tune and deploy AI models at scale. A new feature of Deep Search, called Document Question Answering (DocQA), was presented at the 2024 AAAI conference in February 2024. The system enables users to upload their own documents and interact with them with the help of a conversational assistant.

One of the most promising applications of Deep Search technology is in the domain of environmental, social and governance (ESG) reports. These reports have become increasingly important in recent years, being one of the tools companies use to highlight their efforts in climate sustainability and social responsibility. They are essential for investors, regulators and other stakeholders to assess a company's impact. However, extracting accurate and relevant information from these reports can be a time-consuming and labour-intensive process.

McKinsey in their blog from August 2023 (McKinsey blog, 2023) tells about their experience about their internal generative AI solution (Lilli) as a researcher, a time saver and as an inspiration. It is a very good example on how especially large companies can benefit from the use of AI tools to find relevant connections and information in their internal network primarily, connected with outside complementary knowledge. Lilli is a platform that provides a search and synthesis of the firm's internal stores of knowledge to bring insights, quickly and efficiently, to the client process. McKinsey has a knowledge base in its 100,000 internal documents and transcripts as well as in their network of experts in more than 70 countries.

A user can type in a question and Lilli can scan the entire landscape of knowledge, identify between five to seven of the most relevant pieces of content, summarize key points, include links and even identify experts in the appropriate fields. The platform includes two modes: one for searching McKinsey's reserves of knowledge and a second option for external sources.

When an engagement kicks off, creating the initial project plan is an important first step. This includes searching for the most salient research documents and identifying the right experts, which can be an overwhelming task for people who are new to our firm. Even for senior colleagues, the work typically takes 2 weeks of researching and networking.

The very first news channel (Channel1 in Los Angeles) using AI in news creation and presenting with avatars is launched as I write this text. As all is generated in real time, it is possible to produce news in any language, and the avatars and even the clips can be processed to use any language the end user prefers. This also means that the clips used in the news can be modified with deepfake technologies, leading to the question about what is real, what is true and how dependable the news is. It highlights the ethical dimension of AI use and services very much. Similarly, these techniques can be used in business intelligence reporting. We can create business plans which update themselves in real time using vastly wider information sources than ever before possible.

All this shows the power of assistive AI to search and synthesize large amounts of even unstructured information, but it is essential to understand over and over that the output is still based on LLM and thus the material the system is trained with. The prompt design becomes essential, and as stated too narrow prompts limit the variety of solutions which the system provides for further elaboration, and too wide prompts might lead to suggestions too far from the desired.

10 Conclusion

AI is strongly developing due to recent developments in computational capacity. Technically the recent development areas of AI are in deep learning, i.e. exploration of different techniques improving the efficiency and scalability of the AI tools and enhancing the material fed into the AI in specific application areas.

AI has been studied for tens of years, but real commercial breakthroughs have recently happened when mainly LLM-based tools and platforms have been published. It is evident that many major players including Microsoft and Google are strongly investing in it, as many newer companies like Nvidia.

What is likely to happen is that embedded AI in services will grow rapidly, e.g. in the form of bots, which again raises the importance of the quality and correctness of the services, and not least the liability of the end services throughout the value chain.

We have recently seen the applications of AI systems moving beyond data and written information to other media, images and even near-reality video. This brings AI to virtual and extended reality applications and even to the world of metaverse.

As the use of AI and AI-based tools is increasing, it also has led to increased awareness of the ethics and liability issues related to the use of AI. Even some dystopias are presented. At the same time, the first legislative measures are debated, in order to securing safe and ethical use of the AI. This is strongly related to ethical guidelines development, but also to the interest in developing AI models and algorithms that could at least partially be interpretable and explainable by humans.

AI and Metaverse cannot be separated, and thus it is fair to say that we currently are at the edge of new computational, connected and extended space. It is the same as some 20 years ago when we saw the emergency of Internet, which now is an integral part of our communications, services and life tools. This implies directly research on IC coverage, taking into account the mesh-up of the various current (clear components) defined in IC. The boundaries are blurring, and highly interfering. We also need to find descriptive methods to classify the quality of the knowledge as base for IC. As stated before, the use of AI can produce superficially nice and often correct output, but at the end the reliability and correctness of the connections of information might be well questionable.

Addressing AI-related liabilities and quality classification requires international cooperation and collaboration to develop common standards, norms and best practices for the responsible use of AI technology across borders. International organizations, industry consortia, and policymakers play a crucial role in fostering global consensus and coordination on AI governance and liability issues.

AI is a great tool, but using it requires skills to get the best of it, like for any tool. One needs to understand the philosophy and methods behind the surface.

AI as such does not create new information and thus no new intellectual capital, but it is a very good tool to extract from existing data streams and dependencies. The quality of the outcome by AI is totally dependent on the data it has been taught which. AI development needs, like the Internet to be followed carefully to harness its power to strengthen its role as a powerful information management and presentation tool. It creates enormous potential for numerous applications extracting and presenting knowledge and creating entirely new ways of interacting between the various actors in the metaverse.

References

arstechnica.com, article 16.2.2024.

Dell'Acqua, F., McFowland, E., Mollick, E. R., Lifshitz-Assaf, H., Kellogg, K., Rajendran, S., Krayer, L., Candelon, F., Lakhani, K. R. Navigating the jagged technological frontier: Field experimental evidence of the effects of AI on knowledge worker productivity and quality (September 15, 2023). Harvard Business School Technology & Operations Mgt. Unit Working

Paper No. 24–013, Available at SSRN: https://ssrn.com/abstract=4573321 or https://doi.org/10.2139/ssrn.4573321.

Edvinsson, L., & Malone, M. S. (1997). *Intellectual capital: Realizing your company's true value by finding its hidden brainpower.* HarperBusiness. ISBN 9780887308413. OCLC 36024079.

Google blog 23.2.2024.

IBM blog 22.2.2024.

McKinsey blog, August 2023.

NESTA, podcast series 2019.

Tivi, article, 1.3.2024.

Bror Salmelin continues his work on modern innovation approaches as independent thought leader and as Industry Commons Foundation board member. ICF is an actor for value creation in industry and society by open innovation approaches. He is a former Advisor for Innovation Systems at the European Commission where he was responsible for Open Innovation and modern innovation systems. He was actively contributing to innovation policies related to new instruments, entrepreneurship and SME. He is also creator of the Open Innovation Strategy and Policy Group (OISPG), an industry-led group advising on strategies for open innovation. He, together with Martin Curley, created the concept of Open Innovation 2.0. He developed the approach of European Network of Living Labs, which is grown to a 450+ sites innovation network for collaborative innovation. Before joining the European Commission in 1998, he was the Deputy of the ICT Section in Technology Development Centre. He worked in Los Angeles as vice consul establishing business and research contacts between US and Finnish organisations. Bror Salmelin is a member of New Club of Paris. His current main interest areas include Industrial and Societal Commons, Open Innovation 2.0, modern innovation practises, innovation ecosystems and strategic development on organisational and methodological levels.

From a Data-Driven to Information-Driven Management Paradigm: Reflections on Generative AI and Intellectual Capital Management

Henri Hussinki and Josh Morton

Abstract

This chapter explores the emergence and transformative impact of generative artificial intelligence (Gen AI) on organizational intellectual capital (IC) management and the shift from a data-driven to an information-driven management paradigm. It contributes to future IC research and practice by outlining several implications that Gen AI will have on an organization's IC management. First, regarding human capital, it challenges organizations to develop and retain a specific breed of information engineering experts, sets demand for personnel reskilling including prompt engineering, and emphasizes the central role of collaboration between technical Gen AI experts and domain experts. Second, the chapter argues that organizations must pay attention to certain facets of their structural capital, including the controlled generation of new information through established business processes and the design and maintenance of adaptable information systems. Further, there is a need for an information-driven culture, which drives the utilization of Gen AI outputs in practice. Third, it emphasizes an increasing need to augment an organization's proprietary information with extra-organizational information, as higher volumes of complementary information improve Gen AI performance. This development will lead to a market of commercialized information products, where organizations may operate as clients and providers or participate through different networks and ecosystems.

H. Hussinki (✉)
LUT Business School, Lappeenranta-Lahti University of Technology LUT, Lahti, Finland
e-mail: henri.hussinki@lut.fi

J. Morton
Leeds University Business School, University of Leeds, Leeds, UK
e-mail: j.morton1@leeds.ac.uk

A. Kianto et al. (eds.), *Futurizing Intellectual Capital*, Knowledge Management and Organizational Learning 15, https://doi.org/10.1007/978-3-031-80197-6_11

1 Introduction

The turn of the decade has witnessed a surge in organizations' investments in different data-related resources, such as data analytics tools, technologies, and skills, as well as data management and governance initiatives. Remarkably, it was estimated in 2023 that organizations' investments in data analytics are expected to surpass their investments in all other combined software categories (International Data Corporation, 2022), and this has also been evidenced in more recent industry surveys (e.g. Davenport & Bean, 2024). One of the main drivers of these investments has been the urge for organizations to become more data-driven. The data-driven paradigm, including data-driven culture and data-driven decision-making, i.e. the extent to which an organization considers its data a tangible asset and makes its decisions based on the insights extracted from data (Brynjolfsson et al., 2011; Gupta & George, 2016; Mittal et al., 2023), assumes that organizations can create and capture benefits by systematically utilizing data analytics outputs to make better, more consistent, and quicker decisions (e.g. Lepenioti et al., 2020). The tenet is that data contains facts about an organization and its external environment, and the more fact-based and rational the decisions are, the less room there is for potential human error, including assumptions, beliefs, and estimations. In addition, when data collection and use are automated for routine-like processes and decisions, the share of manual human work decreases in simple work tasks, enabling organizations to reassign some of their personnel to tasks that benefit from human involvement (e.g. complex tasks that require creativity).

In the midst of this digital revolution, the academic research community, and wider society, have started discussing the next era of the digital revolution: Gen AI, such as large language models (LLMs). Gen AI refers to advanced machine learning models that are trained to generate new data/information, such as text, images, or audio, making them distinct from other AI models that are designed to make predictions or classifications or to fulfil other specific functions (Hacker et al., 2023). Gen AI models are often referred to as foundation models (Bommasani et al., 2021), LLMs (Ganguli et al., 2022), or large generative AI models (Hacker et al., 2023), all of them having the same general meaning. According to McKinsey and Company's (2023) survey of C-suite executives, 2023 was Gen AI's "breakout year" as it was found that one-third of participating organizations are using Gen AI regularly in at least one business function, while 40% of executives stated how they will increase their investment in AI because of advances in Gen AI specifically. Thus, Gen AI is already revolutionizing different facets of work and capabilities in organizations.

Compared to the conventional data analytics systems that perform exceptionally well in the framework of a particular task or dataset and in processing structured data to identify, for example, patterns or correlations, Gen AI models can *theoretically* make use of all an organization's unstructured data (information) that is created either by humans or information systems. These models are capable of performing tasks that are not strictly pre-defined, as well as processing text-based information as an input and creating seemingly new information, such as summaries, presentations, and reports, as an output. Referring to the knowledge pyramid, a popular metaphor in the knowledge management and IC research tradition, different knowledge dimensions can be portrayed as a data-information-knowledge-wisdom (DIKW) hierarchy (Ackoff, 1989). Data resides at the bottom of this hierarchy, as a machine-readable component of organizational knowledge, without clear meaning or purpose from the perspective of the organization's personnel. Information, in turn, is a human-readable form of organizational knowledge with meaning and purpose, making it more extensive and logically stronger than data (Frické, 2009, 2019). It therefore comprises insights that are more actionable for the organization's personnel.

Gen AI has the potential to revolutionize knowledge work and initiate a paradigm shift from data-driven to information-driven culture and decision-making. In this paradigm, experts can query Gen AI with different natural language text describing the task that AI should perform, known as prompt engineering. This allows the organization's personnel to gain insights about institutional information, use it to augment their personal knowledge, and make well-informed decisions based on it (Miikkulainen, 2024; Wessel et al., 2023). In sum, the data-driven paradigm builds upon highly specific structured datasets and analytics tasks and highlights the role of the insights extracted from structured data in organizational decision-making, whereas the emerging information-driven paradigm seeks actionable insights from unstructured data and involves new technologies that are very liberal in terms of data and task specificity. This enables a plethora of different experts to engage and succeed with it. Therefore, the proposed benefits of Gen AI are estimated to dwarf the benefits gained from data-driven management (Colson, 2019). Suddenly, therefore, organizations have found themselves in a situation where they might have more value potential in their information than in their data.

However, organizations that have been investing vastly in developing their data analytics capabilities are not *practically* ready to reap the benefits of Gen AI, as information engineering for Gen AI is a different craft from data management or data engineering. Information engineering for Gen AI involves the art of identifying, capturing, organizing, storing, and serving an organization's proprietary information—not directly for an organization's personnel, but for its organization-specific Gen AI model, the one that effectively enables the personnel to know everything organizations know (Dwivedi et al., 2023). In response, organizations need to equip themselves with new kinds of management practices, including re-assessment of their IC management. IC management is defined as the management of an organization's intangible assets for better value creation and improved organizational performance (Kianto et al., 2014), including the alignment of an organization's IC with its vision (Sullivan, 1999). In the context of the successful use of Gen AI, this means a re-assessment of what dimensions of IC could be the key inputs for Gen AI, how Gen AI contributes to an organization's IC, and what type of IC management is required to unlock the value creation potential of Gen AI.

In light of the above, this chapter discusses why the emerging transition from a data-driven to an information-driven management paradigm is likely to continue at an accelerating pace and what implications this has for an organization's key IC and its management. To conclude the chapter, a research agenda for Gen AI and IC management is provided with the aim of inspiring further avenues of work for scholars interested in this domain.

2 The Paradigm Shift from Data-Driven Management to Information-Driven Management

Based on contemporary scholarly debates (e.g. Brynjolfsson et al., 2023; Noy & Zhang, 2023) and burgeoning focus in the mainstream media, it is apparent that individuals, organizations, and even societies have strongly expressed their interest in the Gen AI hype and, in turn, reaping the potential benefits it might offer. Even Gen AI sceptics may have thought, perhaps deservedly, in 2022 (when Gen AI entered the mainstream) that it was a prime example of a momentary fad. However, such sceptics may now, just 2 years later, reconsider their stance and accept that this new technology has revolutionary potential and is seemingly here to stay. The drivers of the information-driven paradigm shift, where Gen AI has a major role, can be summarized in five key areas: 1. the relatively high value density of information, 2. the learning ability and scalability of Gen AI, 3. the shift from open Gen AI to organization-specific Gen AI, 4. organizations' recent switch of focus from technology to data, and 5. the Gen AI's ability to augment human and organizational capabilities in solving complex problems. These are also summarized in the table below (Table 1).

First, Gen AI offers a new way of augmenting human and organizational capabilities, as it can process unstructured or semi-structured data, including natural language text created by humans. When pre-trained (especially on large datasets) and fine-tuned on domain-specific tasks, Gen AI excels at understanding and generating human-like text, making it suitable for tasks involving language understanding and generation (Brynjolfsson et al., 2023). From the DIKW hierarchy standpoint (Ackoff, 1989), data represents the machine-readable subset of organizational knowledge that needs to be enriched with meaning and purpose. This takes place usually through data analysis or analytics, to make data useful and understandable for humans. Because Gen AI can process information (unstructured data) that is more extensive and logically stronger than structured data (Frické, 2009, 2019), it opens opportunities for organizations to efficiently process their proprietary knowledge and better understand what they already know. However, the information-processing capability of Gen AI does not make traditional data analytics irrelevant or superfluous but rather complements it, as they are designed to augment the human and organizational capabilities in different areas: traditional data analytics performs well when the problem is well-defined and when there is specific data available, whereas Gen AI can learn from the retrieved unstructured data and provide new information for users. Along these lines, Gen AI can tap into a more extensive and logically stronger level of organizational knowledge than traditional data analytics can, making it an intriguing option for organizations as they aim to amplify their data capabilities.

Second, traditional data analytics is often designed for specific tasks such as classification, regression, clustering, or anomaly detection, and the focus, in general, is on solving well-defined problems. For example, this could be testing hypotheses that are developed based on an in-depth understanding of the phenomenon and its context (Davenport & Harris, 2017). In comparison, Gen AI exhibits the

Table 1 The drivers of Gen AI use

Drivers of Gen AI use	Illustrative research questions
1. The relatively high value density of information	Gen AI can tap into an extensive and logically strong level of organizational knowledge Gen AI can learn from the retrieved unstructured data and provide new information for users
2. The learning ability and scalability of Gen AI	Gen AI exhibits the capability to find patterns and relationships in the data on its own Anyone who can ask questions and write sentences can also prompt Gen AI to some extent, which leads to potentially rapid engagement of entire organizations with it
3. The shift from open Gen AI to organization-specific Gen AI	Organization-specific Gen AI models are strictly limited to processing only an organization's own data, which continues to make them more reliable and trustworthy
4. Organizations' recent switch of focus from technology to data	Organizations have realized that "data tweaking" brings better results than "algorithm tweaking", which suits the Gen AI context where the technology and algorithms are commodity products
5. Gen AI's ability to augment human and organizational capabilities in solving complex problems	Gen AI has potential beyond the current understanding as it can augment human capabilities in complex problem-solving Organizations will increase their investments in Gen AI as they learn more about the benefits it brings along to complex tasks such as decision-making

capability "to find patterns and relationships in the data on its own, without being [explicitly] told what to look for" (Hacker et al., 2023, p. 1113). This is possible through a variety of techniques that allow Gen AI to perform a wide range of language-related tasks, including text completion, summarization, translation, querying, and more. Efficient use of traditional data analytics poses substantial analytics skill requirements for its end users, and those tasks are usually conducted by a small group of an organization's data specialists (e.g. data analysts and data scientists). In comparison, Gen AI use is not associated with similar scalability bottlenecks, as in theory, anyone who can ask questions and write sentences can also prompt Gen AI to some extent. Therefore, the strength of Gen AI is the potentially rapid engagement of entire organizations with it.

Third, traditional data analytics relies mainly on an organization's internal data sources and assets, offering high levels of reliability and interpretability as the data sources are well-known and the relationships between input features and output are often understandable and explainable. In contrast, the early-stage Gen AI models, which were trained based on openly available Internet data, were accused of generating potentially biased, prejudiced, or harmful content (Hacker et al., 2023) and left Gen AI with a stigma of being untransparent and inexplicable (Dwivedi et al., 2023). However, as the use of *organization-specific* Gen AI models, which are strictly limited to processing only an organization's own data, grows more popular, *these reliability and interpretability issues become manageable from the organization's perspective and something that the organization's business and IT management have control over.* In other words, the Gen AI-related reliability and interpretability issues will become an organization's information engineering issues, such as identifying, capturing, organizing, storing, and serving the relevant valuable information to the organization-specific Gen AI model.

Fourth, data-driven organizations have already started to move on from the "algorithm tweaking" approach to the "data tweaking" approach. Since the data-driven management paradigm came to fruition in the 2010s, organizations started to develop their data analytics capability in many ways, for instance, by improving the data quality, acquiring, and developing technological resources, hiring and training data experts, and putting effort into underlining the importance of data-driven decision-making. However, at some point, organizations understood that some of the data capability initiatives and investments were more profitable than others. Most notably, organizations have learned that breakthroughs through technology emphasis are far less likely than major achievements through emphasis on data (Bean, 2022; Wixom et al., 2023). Therefore, *organizations have adopted a fitting mindset for reaping Gen AI benefits, as it involves an off-the-shelf commodity technology that is available to all organizations (less algorithm tweaking), and its potential organizational benefits come down to how well an organization can identify, capture, organize, store, and serve its proprietary information for this new technology (more data tweaking).*

Fifth, Gen AI research and practice have only scratched the surface of the Gen AI potential for organizations (Bommasani et al., 2021). Since the emergence of Gen AI, the empirical contexts of the nascent academic Gen AI research have been characterized by a lack of information complexity (e.g. customer chats; see Brynjolfsson et al., 2023) or lack of task complexity (e.g. relatively short, self-contained, and no requirement for context-specific knowledge—see Noy & Zhang, 2023). However, there are potentially more Gen AI benefits beyond transactional gains in simple and repetitive tasks, as Gen AI can augment human capabilities in complex problem-solving (Dwivedi et al., 2023). *As organizations start using Gen AI in more complex tasks and understanding the related (potentially major) benefits, it will increase other organizations' strategic investments in Gen AI.*

In sum, the five drivers of the paradigm shift, including the relatively high value density of information, the learning ability and scalability of Gen AI, the shift from open Gen AI to organization-specific Gen AI, an organizations' recent switch of focus from technology to data, and the Gen AI's ability to augment human and organizational capabilities in solving complex problems, will greatly influence why organizations will continue adopting Gen AI at an increasing pace. Next, this chapter moves on to discuss the implications of this paradigm shift for IC management in organizations.

3 Implications for Intellectual Capital and Its Management

IC research has an established tradition to portray IC as a third-order construct (Fig. 1) that consists of three second-order constructs, including human capital, structural capital, and relational capital, and various first-order constructs that involve, for instance, personnel skills, organization's databases, and knowledge accessed through customer relations (Cabrilo & Dahms, 2018; Inkinen, 2015). Human capital refers to the knowledge resources embedded in an organization's personnel, structural capital concerns the intra-organizational knowledge resources other than those embedded in personnel, and relational capital comprises the extra-organizational knowledge resources that can be accessed through relationships with different stakeholders (e.g. Hussinki et al., 2017).

The tripartite categorization of IC emerged more than 20 years ago (e.g. Bontis, 1998), and it has shown characteristics of timelessness and robustness to portray an organization's key IC in different times and conditions. Therefore, the strong emergence of Gen AI is not expected to change the actual structure of an organization's

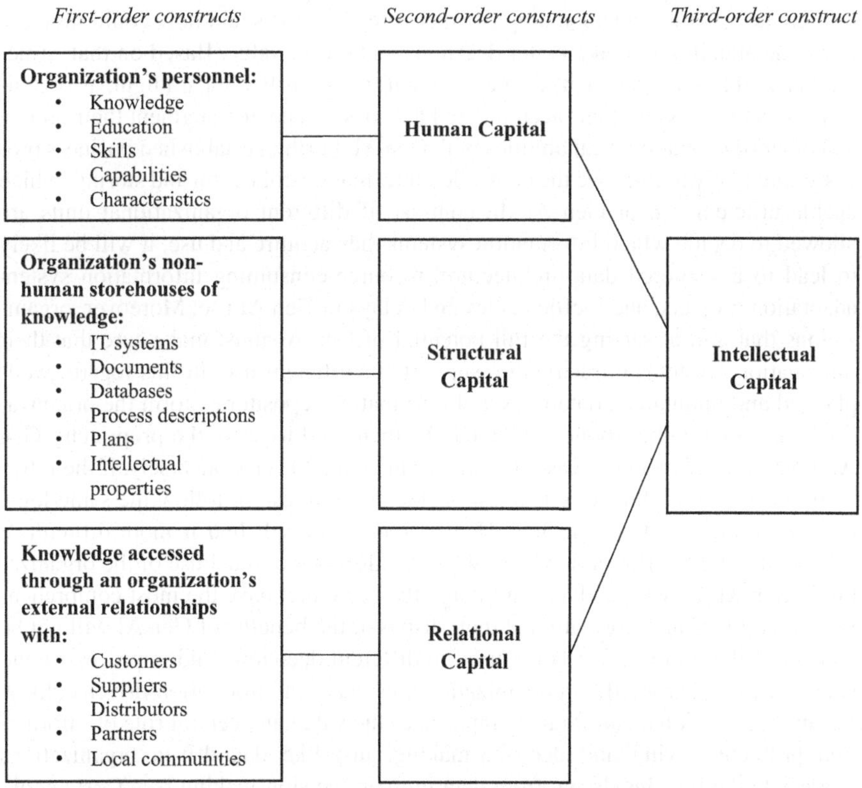

Fig. 1 Intellectual capital as a third-order construct (source: Inkinen, 2015)

IC but will instead have Gen AI-specific implications for the relative importance of the second-order constructs of IC, contents of the first-order constructs, as well as managerial implications on IC management in the era of Gen AI.

3.1 The Relative Importance of Intellectual Capital Dimensions and Their Contents

With the sudden emergence of Gen AI, information becomes a potentially more valuable asset than an organization's structured data as all the documents and other text-based information objects created by either personnel or information systems can be combined, processed, and presented as seemingly new information with this new technology (Dwivedi et al., 2023). The situation shares similarities with the beginning of the data-driven era in the early 2010s when the availability of new analytics technologies made organizations realize that the "side product" of their operations (data) that comprised previously unnoticed value potential became a source of better understanding of an organization's current operations and a possible corner piece of their future operations. This time around the focus is also on data, but growingly on unstructured data and how organizations could make use of it to create a better understanding of what it really knows and how could they use this understanding to make better decisions and create value. Based on that, structural capital has an emphasized role in the information-driven paradigm, as organizations can process all their accumulated text-based data and augment their human and other organizational capabilities with Gen AI. Further, established business processes are likely to improve the controlled information collection and storing, which enable efficient use of Gen AI. In contrast, if different organizational units are allowed to decide which information systems they acquire and use, it will be likely to lead to a scattered data architecture, resource-consuming information system adaptation projects, and inefficiencies and delays in Gen AI use. Moreover, organizations that aim at seizing the full potential of Gen AI must make sure that their information (system) infrastructure supports its efficient use. In this regard, well-planned and maintained databases and information repositories form the organization's information backbone, which can be then used to serve the proprietary Gen AI model for different use cases (Bommasani et al., 2021). Conversely, if the information (system) architecture is questionable and it does not follow the same logic of how an organization operates, Gen AI end users will find it more difficult to retrieve the right "information sets" which leads to suboptimal use of the organization's Gen AI model. Lastly, even though the personnel have the most comprehensive and up-to-date information at their disposal, the benefits of Gen AI will not be realized if this information is not used in different decision-making processes and situations. In other words, an organization must have an information-driven culture, i.e. an organizational culture that emphasizes the value and central role of information problem-solving and decision-making, just like data-driven organizations appreciate the insights drawn from data in their decision-making (see Cosic et al., 2015; Gupta & George, 2016).

Organizations can improve their chances for Gen AI value creation by matching their proprietary information resources (structural capital) with personnel who can "engineer" and serve this information for an organization's Gen AI model. Before the relevant information can be served, it must be first identified, captured, organized, and stored, encompassing a whole spectrum of information engineering activities (Hicks et al., 2002; Hussinki, 2024). To identify relevant information and its suitability for an organization's Gen AI model, an organization must possess an extensive understanding of what this new technology can and cannot do, as well as a deep understanding of what sources contain valuable, relevant, and up-to-date information on an organization and its operations. This *combined* understanding allows organizations to focus on the right types of information that can be processed with Gen AI to provide insights to the personnel, including decision-makers. Therefore, cross-functional collaboration and knowledge sharing between Gen AI experts and context experts will be required to help an organization actively combine its technological and contextual understanding and reach the required level of Gen AI maturity. Inevitably, some Gen AI and information engineering specialists, who possess this ambidextrous ability, will establish themselves as key organizational assets just as data scientists and data engineers became in the wake of the data-driven management paradigm. These key experts are needed not only to increase an organization's technological and human Gen AI maturity but also to disseminate their knowledge throughout organizations to improve their Gen AI literacy. In sum, personnel with AI and information engineering know-how will have a highlighted role in the era of Gen AI, as they can develop organizational practices and act as a catalyst for an organization's Gen AI literacy. However, other personnel and their contextual understanding will also be needed to help the Gen AI experts flourish.

The emergence of Gen AI and the related information-driven paradigm will have implications also for an organization's relational capital, as the highlighted role of text-based input information leads organizations to scavenge for supplementary information from a plethora of extra-organizational information sources and through different types of relationships, such as client-provider, network participation, and ecosystem involvement. The practices and dynamics of relational capital acquisition and accumulation will therefore change, as organizations increase their efforts in seeking "Gen AI-ready" information from, for instance, different providers' information catalogues, other (open) Web-based sources, networks, and ecosystems, which potentially also impacts the degree of personal contacts required to access the information. Consequently, it is very likely that information monetization, i.e. the transformation of an organization's proprietary information into commercial information products, will gain ground in the same fashion we have witnessed with data monetization in the data-driven era. However, the potential quality and reliability issues of extra-organizational information sources may hinder this development in the early stages, given that the objective is to get as accurate and reliable information for decision-makers as possible. Nevertheless, information accessed through customers, suppliers, distributors, partners, supply chains, networks, and ecosystems will remain the core of what an organization should know about themselves and the surrounding environment to make better decisions. Only the means to access this information will be likely to change, but it remains to be seen how significant the change will be.

3.2 Reaping Benefits for Intellectual Capital Management

To reap Gen AI-related benefits, organizations will have to start paying attention to their information assets in a similar fashion as they have learned to pay attention to structured data assets; what is relevant, what has value potential, and what should be retained for further use? Organizations must work out answers to these questions, as it will also allow them to identify the information that should be the focus when commencing the information engineering activities that aim at serving an organization's proprietary information for its Gen AI model. Fostering collaboration between Gen AI experts and domain experts is key when organizations identify relevant information sources and develop Gen AI models. Domain experts know what data sources contain relevant and valuable information, and Gen AI experts know how to feed it into the Gen AI model, so combining this understanding is key to achieving desirable outcomes.

Organizations must also invest in information engineering experts who possess the know-how on how to capture and organize institutional information in a way that is usable by Gen AI models. Specifically, information engineers handle the generation, distribution, analysis, and use of information, data, and knowledge in systems and are employed by most industries due to the widespread need for such expertise (Roberts, 2018). As the need for Gen AI and information engineering talent grows higher, this expertise will become even more coveted in the labour market. This includes designing databases and information repositories that can be easily accessed and processed by Gen AI, an information system architecture that facilitates seamless integration between source systems and the Gen AI model, and establishing robust data pipelines and architectures that enable the efficient collection, cleaning, and storage of relevant data. In addition, as Gen AI models become more efficient when pre-trained, an organization's information engineers should be able to develop mechanisms for pre-training organization-specific Gen AI models based on contextual peculiarities and information needs. Also, as these needs and an organization's operational conditions evolve, information engineering should design adaptable systems capable of incorporating new data and retraining models. Further, organizations must also consider the challenges in retaining such talent and the knowledge and know-how they represent. Because organizations cannot force personnel to stay, and it is always a possibility that people change jobs and move to new employers, organizations are more likely to retain this ambidextrous competence by constructing and embedding it in wider social contexts, such as teams and competence units, which could still function even if some specialist turnover takes place.

Lastly, Gen AI models have the potential to provide more relevant and accurate information to (at least some of) its users if the organization's proprietary information is coupled with information from well-curated external information sources.

Therefore, the organizational IC management should focus on identifying and accessing the best possible extra-organizational information sources to give the Gen AI model more input information to work with. In addition, organizations should also prepare themselves for the very likely growing demand for commercialized information products, to reap benefits not only from using Gen AI but also from monetizing their information for other organizations that adopt and use Gen AI.

4 Research Agenda for Gen AI and Intellectual Capital Management

4.1 Gen AI and Structural Capital

To conclude, we present a comprehensive research agenda to encourage further work on the role of Gen AI in the context of IC. The nexus between Gen AI and IC is not only theoretically compelling but also ripe with practical implications. Firstly, organizational information is dynamic instead of static, and it accumulates and changes when basically anything happens within or outside an organization. Unstructured data tends to get outdated quite quickly, as its version control is quite difficult and information systems are filled with document drafts. Gen AI cannot recognize the difference between outdated and up-to-date information without exceptionally advanced prompting skills, and sometimes not even if those skills were available. Therefore, it would be paramount for future research to uncover the processes and practices that help organizations to keep their information base relevant and up to date, as the performance of a Gen AI model is dependent on the quality of information it is served. For instance, one future research endeavour in this regard could be to study how established business processes impact different facets of information quality and the successful use of Gen AI. Another avenue for future research is to analyse whether information life cycle models could help organizations retain valuable and relevant information and eliminate outdated information. Secondly, early studies on Gen AI research hint at a spectrum of benefits that Gen AI can deliver, particularly in streamlining repetitive operational-level tasks to reap efficiency gains (e.g. Brynjolfsson et al., 2023; Noy & Zhang, 2023). This presents one fruitful area for further exploration in relation to IC, especially how Gen AI augments an organization's structural capital in terms of, for instance, more efficient business processes.

4.2 Gen AI and Human Capital

The transformative potential of Gen AI is not confined to mere operational efficiencies and can augment human capabilities in solving complex problems (Dwivedi et al., 2023). Therefore, research can go beyond the state of the art by focusing on the extensive benefits related to Gen AI use especially as organizations begin to deploy Gen AI in more complex tasks (Davenport & Bean, 2024), including those relevant to human capital augmentation. Another key area for future research is the most effective collaboration skills and mechanisms in terms of combining the technical Gen AI and contextual expertise. There are various options for organizations to chase that desired future state, such as the development of "unicorns" who possess both technical and contextual understanding, establishing team-level combinations of cross-functional experts, or the increase of organization-wide Gen AI literacy. However, it remains currently an open research question of which practices are the most suitable in the context of Gen AI use.

As a further area, it is foreseeable that Gen AI can have a pivotal role in strengthening an organization's structural capital through the extraction of insights from an entity's proprietary knowledge. Therefore, Gen AI does not only help organizations to make use of their existing structural capital more efficiently, but it also cumulates their human capital as personnel applies the Gen AI-generated information in work tasks and through that infuses decision-making processes (Mittal et al., 2023). Improved decision-making is likely to lead to better organizational performance, so it would be relevant and potentially very impactful for research to examine the effects of Gen AI use in the relationship between structural capital, human capital, decision-making (primary performance outcome), and organizational performance (secondary performance outcome). One of the key additions to the Gen AI-enhanced IC framework (Fig. 2) is information engineering. It is highly plausible that an organization's capability to identify, capture, organize, store, and serve its proprietary information to its Gen AI model makes a difference between inefficient and efficient Gen AI use. However, empirical studies in various contexts are required to test this hypothesis. Lastly, it is pertinent and potentially transformative to craft research that examines the multifaceted effects of Gen AI on the dynamics between IC and organizational strategy. This has rich potential to unearth the nuanced interrelations and potential causal linkages in how Gen AI could be a driver for organizational change and performance. This also offers the potential to uncover the deployment of Gen AI for strategizing (Morton et al., 2022) as a core component of, for example, competitive differentiation, value creation, or business model innovation.

4.3 Gen AI and Relational Capital

The strong emergence of Gen AI is likely to have an impact on how and from which sources organizations collect information in the future. Gen AI-driven organizations are eager to identify and access such information sources that are relevant and reliable, complement and augment their intra-organizational information base, and offer information that is ready to be used immediately. However, it is currently unclear which extra-organizational information sources and what kind of relationships between the information provider and client present significant additional value. Therefore, one particularly interesting area for future research could be to find out the types of relationships, for instance, buyer-seller, network participation,

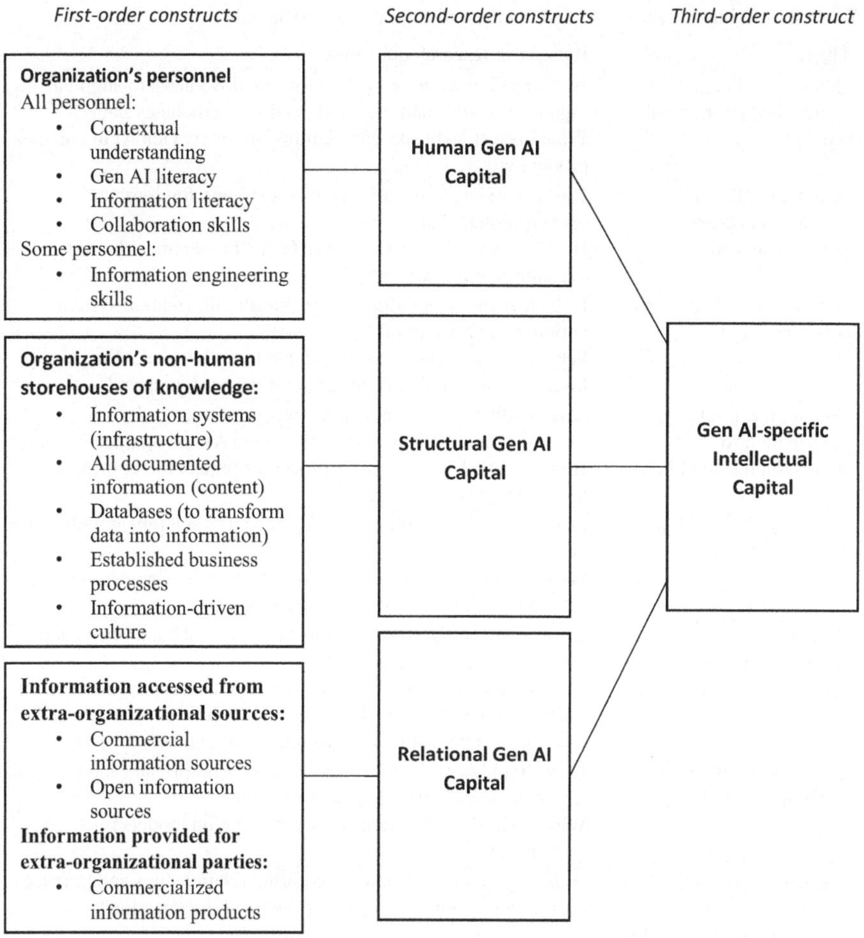

Fig. 2 Gen AI-specific intellectual capital (source: authors)

and ecosystems, which provide a competitive edge through information acquiring or sharing. Related to this new information commercialization marketplace, future research could also develop guidelines on the steps organizations could take to monetize their proprietary information and generate sustainable income streams by actively participating in this market as providers.

Below is a brief table (Table 2) to summarize the main themes we have suggested as a starting point for a research agenda. The table also details some illustrative research questions for each theme.

Table 2 An illustrative Gen AI and intellectual capital research agenda

Themes	Illustrative research questions
Gen AI, intellectual capital, and operational efficiency	How can Gen AI be optimized for repetitive tasks to augment organizational capabilities and maximize efficiency gains? What operational tasks can be transformed by Gen AI to enhance productivity?
Gen AI, intellectual capital, and complex problem-solving	How does Gen AI enhance problem-solving for complex organizational challenges? How can organizations integrate Gen AI to augment human decision-making capabilities?
Gen AI's contribution to structural capital	How does the integration of Gen AI into information systems enrich structural capital? What processes can be implemented to utilize Gen AI in improving the quality of insights for decision-makers?
Structural capital's contribution to the successful use of Gen AI	How do different organizational practices, such as information life cycle models, impact the use of Gen AI and attained benefits? How do established business processes impact the information quality and use of Gen AI?
Gen AI's effect on human capital	How does Gen AI influence learning and development within an organization? What approaches can be employed to leverage Gen AI-generated information for employee task performance?
Human capital's contribution to the successful use of Gen AI	How do information engineering skills contribute to the benefits gained from Gen AI use? How does the Gen AI-AI-generated structural capital cumulate human capital, and how does this lead to different primary and secondary organizational performance outcomes?
Gen AI's effect on relational capital	How should organizations monetize their proprietary information for other Gen AI-driven organizations? What kind of information commercialization models is sustainable?
Relational capital's contribution to the successful use of Gen AI	Which types of information-acquiring relationships and practices provide an information edge for the focal organization?
Gen AI, intellectual capital, and strategy	What is the impact of Gen AI use on a firm's intellectual capital and performance metrics? How does the use of Gen AI in IC management correlate with competitive advantage and financial success?

5 Conclusion

This chapter argues that Gen AI is positioned at the forefront of a potentially significant shift in IC management. Gen AI models, particularly LLMs, are transitioning from intriguing novelties to robust realities throughout organizations and in organizational knowledge work. Consequently, they promise a new era where information is not merely collected but actively generated and utilized to drive key processes. Specifically, we have explored the transformative role of Gen AI in shifting organizational paradigms from data-driven to information-driven management and the potential implications for IC management. Gen AI liberates organizations to comprehensively access and utilize their proprietary information, enhancing the utility of unstructured data—from human-generated text documents to system-generated content—and emphasizing the value of structural capital. We have also discussed the critical importance of developing expertise in information engineering for Gen AI, which not only augments an organization's human capital management but also necessitates the retention of professionals who deeply understand both the technology and its applications. Moreover, the effective utilization of Gen AI for value creation hinges on collaborative efforts among context experts, Gen AI specialists, and robust information system architectures, all working together to streamline data integration, cleaning, and storage processes. Finally, we posit that while Gen AI reshapes the mechanisms through which organizations engage with external information sources, the essence of relational capital—encompassing interactions with customers, suppliers, and market partners—remains vital. Collectively, these insights, along with our research agenda, underscore the pivotal influence of Gen AI in modernizing organizational capabilities and driving future growth and innovation.

References

Ackoff, R. L. (1989). From data to wisdom. *Journal of Applied Systems Analysis, 16*(1), 3–9.

Bean, R. (2022). Why becoming a data-driven organization is so hard. *Harvard Business Review*. Retrieved from: https://hbr.org/2022/02/why-becoming-a-data-driven-organization-is-so-hard

Bommasani, R., Hudson, D. A., Adeli, E., Altman, R., Arora, S., von Arx, S., et al. (2021). On the opportunities and risks of foundation models. *arXiv*. preprint arXiv:2108.07258.

Bontis, N. (1998). Intellectual capital: An exploratory study that develops measures and models. *Management Decision, 36*(2), 63–76.

Brynjolfsson, E., Hitt, L. M., and Kim, H. H. (2011). Strength in numbers: How does data-driven decision making affect firm performance?. Available at SSRN 1819486.

Brynjolfsson, E., Li, D., & Raymond, L. R. (2023). Generative AI at work. *Working Paper 31161. National Bureau of Economic Research.*

Cabrilo, S., & Dahms, S. (2018). How strategic knowledge management drives intellectual capital to superior innovation and market performance. *Journal of Knowledge Management, 22*(3), 621–648.

Colson, E. (2019). What AI-driven decision making looks like. *Harvard Business Review*.

Cosic, R., Shanks, G., & Maynard, S. B. (2015). A business analytics capability framework. *Australasian Journal of Information Systems, 19*, S5–S19.

Davenport, T. H., & Bean, R. (2024). Five key trends in AI and data science for 2024. *MIT Sloan Management Review*.

Davenport, T. H., & Harris, J. (2017). *Competing on analytics: The new science of winning*. Harvard Business School Publishing Corporation.

Dwivedi, Y. K., Kshetri, N., Hughes, L., Slade, E. L., Jeyaraj, A., Kar, A. K., et al. (2023). "So what if ChatGPT wrote it?" Multidisciplinary perspectives on opportunities, challenges and implications of generative conversational AI for research, practice and policy. *International Journal of Information Management, 71*, 102642.

Frické, M. (2009). The knowledge pyramid: A critique of the DIKW hierarchy. *Journal of Information Science, 35*(2), 131–142.

Frické, M. (2019). The knowledge pyramid: The DIKW hierarchy. *Ko Knowledge Organization, 46*(1), 33–46.

Ganguli, D., Hernandez, D., Lovitt, L., Askell, A., Bai, Y., Chen, A., et al. (2022, June). Predictability and surprise in large generative models. In *Proceedings of the 2022 ACM conference on fairness, accountability, and transparency* (pp. 1747–1764).

Gupta, M., & George, J. F. (2016). Toward the development of a big data analytics capability. *Information & Management, 53*(8), 1049–1064.

Hacker, P., Engel, A., & Mauer, M. (2023, June). Regulating ChatGPT and other large generative AI models. In *Proceedings of the 2023 ACM conference on fairness, accountability, and transparency* (pp. 1112–1123).

Hicks, B. J., Culley, S. J., Allen, R. D., & Mullineux, G. (2002). A framework for the requirements of capturing, storing and reusing information and knowledge in engineering design. *International Journal of Information Management, 22*(4), 263–280.

Hussinki, H. (2024). Generative artificial intelligence: The new era of knowledge management. In *Translating knowledge into innovation dynamics, proceedings of the 19th international forum on knowledge asset dynamics*. in press.

Hussinki, H., Ritala, P., Vanhala, M., & Kianto, A. (2017). Intellectual capital, knowledge management practices and firm performance. *Journal of Intellectual Capital, 18*(4), 904–922.

Inkinen, H. (2015). Review of empirical research on intellectual capital and firm performance. *Journal of Intellectual Capital, 16*(3), 518–565.

International Data Corporation. (2022). International data corporation. 4 Ways to unlock transformative business outcomes from analytics investments. InfoBrief, sponsored by Alteryx August 2022 Doc. #US49458122.

Kianto, A., Ritala, P., Spender, J. C., & Vanhala, M. (2014). The interaction of intellectual capital assets and knowledge management practices in organizational value creation. *Journal of Intellectual Capital, 15*(3), 362–375.

Lepenioti, K., Bousdekis, A., Apostolou, D., & Mentzas, G. (2020). Prescriptive analytics: Literature review and research challenges. *International Journal of Information Management, 50*, 57–70.

McKinsey and Company. (2023). *The state of AI in 2023: Generative AI's breakout year*. McKinsey and Company Industry Report.

Miikkulainen, R. (2024). Generative AI: An AI paradigm shift in the making? *AI Magazine, 45*(1), 165–167.

Mittal, N., Perricos, C., Sterrett, L., & Dutt, D. (2023). *The generative AI Dossier: A selection of high-impact use cases across six major industries*. Deloitte AI Institute Industry Report.

Morton, J., Amrollahi, A., & Wilson, A. D. (2022). Digital strategizing: An assessing review, definition, and research agenda. *Journal of Strategic Information Systems, 31*(2), 101720.

Noy, S., & Zhang, W. (2023). Experimental evidence on the productivity effects of generative artificial intelligence. Working Paper. Massachusetts Institute of Technology.

Roberts, S. (2018). *Introduction to information engineering*. Oxford Information Engineering.

Sullivan, P. H. (1999). Profiting from intellectual capital. *Journal of Knowledge Management, 3*(2), 132–143.

Wessel, M., Adam, M., Benlian, A., Majchrzak, A., & Thies, F. (2023). Call for papers: Generative AI and its transformative value for digital platforms. *Journal of Management Information Systems*. In Press.

Wixom, B. H., Beath, C. M., & Owens, L. (2023). *Data is everybody's business: The fundamentals of data monetization*. MIT Press.

Henri Hussinki, D.Sc. (Bus. Adm. & Economics), is an Assistant Professor (tenure track) of Business Analytics at the Business School, LUT University, Finland. Henri's research and teaching work focus on information systems (IS) business value, through lenses of IS-related organizational capability frameworks, and his in-depth research background is in the realms of knowledge management (KM) and intellectual capital (IC). Prof. Hussinki has made significant contributions to the state-of-the-art KM and IC literature through his actively cited publications in the top outlets of these research areas, such as the Journal of Knowledge Management, Journal of Intellectual Capital, Critical Perspectives on Accounting, and Accounting, Auditing and Accountability Journal.

Josh Morton is an Associate Professor of Strategy and Technology at Leeds University Business School, University of Leeds, UK. His research focuses on strategy practice, digital strategy and digital innovation, strategic agility, and open forms of organizing. He has worked closely with organizations on a number of research and consultancy projects, many of which are ongoing, including with Accenture, Deloitte, IBM, CILIP, Microsoft, Meta, and Wikimedia, amongst others. His work has been published in a number of outlets, including the Journal of Strategic Information Systems, California Management Review, and Harvard Business Review. He is also an Associate Fellow at the digital futures at work research centre (Digit).

IC-Related Risks and AI: Friends and Foes!

Susanne Durst

Abstract

This chapter aims to identify positive and negative risks related to the three IC dimensions that may arise in connection with the increasing use of AI-based tools. From the perspective of smaller companies, it will be made clear not only how manifold these risks related to IC are, but that they need not be negative per se. More precisely, in this chapter positive and negative risks for each IC dimension are identified and described. The findings presented in this chapter are likely to be valuable for different target groups. The chosen approach can not only give academics new food for thought but also provide practitioners with an alternative way of thinking about IC risks (the IC dimensions) in connection with the use of AI. This alternative way of thinking is reinforced by viewing AI as augmentation and substitution, which allows for a more detailed discussion of the topic.

1 Introduction

Digital transformation (DT) has begun to permeate every aspect of people's lives, or at least that is the impression it can give, and artificial intelligence (AI), viewed as a specific subset of technologies that supports DT, is said to have transformative power and will consequently shape industries and societies (Gruetzemacher & Whittlestone, 2022). In an AI-driven world, knowledge is no longer limited to the human intellect but extends to algorithms and machine learning models (Alavi &

S. Durst (✉)
Department of Business and Economics, Reykjavik University, Reykjavík, Iceland

LUT Business School, Lappeenranta-Lahti University of Technology LUT, Lappeenranta, Finland
e-mail: susanned@ru.is

A. Kianto et al. (eds.), *Futurizing Intellectual Capital*, Knowledge Management and Organizational Learning 15, https://doi.org/10.1007/978-3-031-80197-6_12

Westerman, 2023). The latter can process vast amounts of data at lightning speed to generate insights and solutions, challenging our usual notions of knowledge generation and its management. The traditional methods of knowledge creation, sharing, and storage, based on interactions with a variety of different people and/or the study of physical documents, have been turned upside down by the ongoing digital transformation and the advent of AI.

The perception and relevance of knowledge are also being challenged by these developments. For example, knowledge identification and capture have evolved to use AI tools to efficiently extract, analyze, and interpret information and knowledge (Jarrahi et al., 2023). Knowledge documentation and storage may also become less important as the introduction of ChatGPT in November 2022 can be used not only as a tool to generate information and knowledge but also as an external knowledge storage (external retention) base. Conversely, this could reduce costly measures in organizations in this regard or even make them completely redundant. The question of whether "knowledge is power" continues to apply and is also open to debate in this environment (Farbman, 2023).

If we now move to a risk perspective, an AI-driven world harbors a variety of both negative and positive risks. Among the potential downsides (negative risks) of these developments, the increased need for data protection and security must be mentioned. Furthermore, the increasing use of AI in intellectual capital (IC)-based processes raises concerns that human expertise and creativity could be lost. (Over-) reliance on AI-generated content can also lead to procedures that miss the necessary critical evaluation of the accuracy of the information generated by the AI tools. The fact that AI tools provide quick answers and summaries might also lead to the consequence that people are less motivated to engage in deeper learning (Lähteenmäki, 2023). Among the potential upsides (positive risks), language translation and cross-cultural communication are continuously facilitated by these tools, which should make it easier to work with people in different regions of the world. The use of virtual assistants and chatbots can also improve business models and processes, especially in smaller companies. These examples already make it clear that an AI-driven age has an impact on all three classic IC dimensions.

Hence, this chapter aims to illustrate how risks related to IC (i.e., its three dimensions, namely, human capital, structural capital, and relational capital), created or amplified by the increased use of AI-based tools and solutions, can impact organizations and their ability to cope with current and future challenges. IC risks are considered in this chapter as positive and negative risks, stressing that a risk can be both a threat and an opportunity. Additionally, this chapter focuses on smaller organizations, as they are not only more susceptible to risks (Durst et al., 2021), often ill-prepared for risk management (De Araújo Lima et al., 2020) but at the same time make up the majority of companies in all economies.

The ideas and thoughts presented in this chapter seem to be valuable for different target groups. Academics studying IC and related fields should get new food for thought, while practitioners an alternative way of thinking in relation to IC/knowledge and their relevance in an IA-driven era. The main messages of this chapter are (i) that a forward-looking and impactful IC theory is holistic and integrative and (ii) is able to look at IC from a neutral perspective in order to be closer to reality. Conversely, this significantly strengthens IC practice, as such an approach allows a more balanced discussion in terms of value creation and value destruction.

The chapter is organized as follows. In the next sections, the main concepts are presented. This is followed by a section that proposes several concrete positive and negative risks associated with the three IC dimensions and is presented from the perspective of a smaller company. This section presents some ideas as how to approach these risks as well. The chapter ends with a discussion and conclusion.

2 Theoretical Background

2.1 Risks Related to IC

In this chapter, risk is understood as a measure of the estimated or expected likelihood and severity of positive and negative impacts from, or in any way related to, IC-related activities that could affect the functioning of an organization at any level.

Regarding the negative impacts, some researchers (e.g., Harvey & Lusch, 1999; Abeysekera, 2006; Brunold & Durst, 2012) have argued that to do proper IC management, organizations have to address the negative sides of IC as well, i.e., IC as a negative risk or a liability. Or as Stam (2009) put it, IC is the difference between intellectual assets and intellectual liabilities. The reasoning makes sense. It is therefore all the more surprising that the possible negative sides of IC or knowledge are still little researched (Durst & Zieba, 2020; Zieba et al., 2022). Against the backdrop not only of developments in connection with AI but also a global poly-crisis, i.e., the simultaneous occurrence of several catastrophic events, it has become all the more important to do more here, both at the research and corporate level.

Following the three IC dimensions, IC/intangibles-related risks can be classified into three types: human capital risks, relational capital risks, and structural capital risks (Brunold & Durst, 2012). Human capital risks are associated with organization members and their activities inside and outside the organization. These risks cover staff turnover or long-term absence of key members but also knowledge sharing and hiding, etc. For example, the departure of an employee with relevant knowledge and expertise may mean that the company is no longer able to offer products and services of the desired quality or is only able to do so to a limited extent. Relational capital risks refer to the consequences of relationships the company has with internal and external stakeholders. Let's go back to the example of the person who is about to leave the company. This departing employee will most likely also take their contacts and relationships with them, which can make the old company weaker and the new company stronger. Finally, structural capital risks arise from the organization's structures, infrastructure, processes, and culture. Examples could be weak or underdeveloped strategic foresight or organizational inertia. Regarding the latter, organizational inertia, for example, could increase the threat that the company is unwilling to make necessary adjustments to the business to prepare for present and future adversities.

Viewing risk as something positive (an opportunity) is uncommon in common parlance, but common in the insurance industry as well as project management, for example. A neutral perspective allows a more balanced view and emphasizes that a risk per se does not have to be negative.

2.2 Artificial Intelligence

Existing literature makes a distinction between weak (traditional) AI and strong (generative) AI. According to Martinez (2019, p. 1027), "weak AI is the concept that whatever the program is meant to do, it is merely trying to replicate or duplicate that function, and for most tasks that is sufficient." The related systems are built to accomplish specific tasks. On the other hand, strong or generative AI is viewed as the next phase where machines can think like humans without being programmed by humans (Hoffmann, 2023). While this chapter was being written, generative AI is a type of AI that can create something new from the information that is provided by human beings.

The use or integration of AI in organizations can be viewed from two angles: AI as augmentation/complementary resource and AI as replacement/substitute (Raisch & Krakowski, 2021; Krakowski et al., 2023). The first perspective takes a positive stance and sees the use as an enrichment for the company, its members, and their activities, while the second perspective focuses more on the negative consequences that can result from its use. This subdivision corresponds very well with the consideration of positive and negative risks and is therefore considered useful for the subsequent presentation of the different types of IC risks, positive and negative risks with regard to AI.

2.3 Small- and Medium-Sized Enterprises

Smaller companies, or small- and medium-sized enterprises (SMEs), are defined both qualitatively and quantitatively in the literature. Qualitative definitions usually emphasize the close relationship between the owner and the business; the aspect of independence, i.e., the business is not part of a larger company; and the relative freedom of the owner from external control in its strategic and operational decisions (Durst & Bruns, 2018). Among the quantitative definitions that are more popular, the EU definition of SMEs is often used. This definition is based on three criteria: number of employees, annual turnover, and annual balance sheet. These criteria help to determine whether the company is a micro-, small-, or medium-sized enterprise. The EU definition includes micro-, small-, and medium-sized enterprises that employ fewer than 250 people and have either an annual turnover of no more than 50 million euros or an annual balance sheet total of no more than 43 million euros (European Commission, 2020). In recent years, the EU definition has been adjusted to reflect the fact that smaller companies operating in different sectors vary in size, i.e., companies in trade and distribution have higher turnover figures than companies in manufacturing.

The smaller a company is, the more difficult it is to understand and overcome the challenges associated with AI. Smaller companies generally lack not only the financial resources but also the knowledge and experience to familiarize themselves with this rapidly developing field and keep up to date. This could jeopardize the company's sustainable development. At the same time, it is also known that smaller companies only have rudimentary risk management (Falkner & Hiebl, 2015; Crovini et al., 2021). However, as the development of AI cannot be stopped, smallness must not be used as an excuse for inaction. Quick and well-considered decisions are needed. This also applies to the other challenges facing these companies, such as the shortage of skilled labor, geopolitical risks, or climate change and its consequences, to name a few.

To avoid the mistake that SMEs are viewed as a generic term and thus overlooking their heterogeneity, in this chapter the focus is on small firms as defined by the EU. This focus appears reasonable considering that small firms are big enough to address certain business challenges micro firms are not, but they are not big enough to handle them in a way medium-sized firms can be due to their structures, resources, etc. which are closer to those found in large companies already (Fernández et al., 2019).

In sum, in this chapter, risks related to IC are considered in conjunction with the increased use or integration of AI-based tools and solutions in organizations. These risks are viewed from both sides as positive and negative risks, the emphasis is being put on small firms, and AI is viewed both as replacement/substitute and as augmentation/complementary resource.

3 Risks Related to IC Triggered by AI Adoption in Small Firms

This section lists and presents some possible positive and negative risks related to the three IC dimensions that could be triggered by AI adoption. The lists of risks (six in total) are divided into ones viewing AI as augmentation and ones seeing AI as replacement. All lists are prepared with a small firm setting in mind. The content presented is based on the author's many years of work in the areas of risks associated with IC/intangible assets, knowledge (risk) management, and small business management.

3.1 AI from the Perspective of Positive IC Risks: AI as Augmentation/Complementary Resource

Tables 1, 2, and 3 provide an overview of possible positive risks related to the three IC dimensions from the perspective of AI as an augmentation/complementary resource.

Table 1 Positive risks related to human capital

Positive risks related to human capital	Description
Skill enhancement	In a small organization, where employees often have multiple roles and functions, improving skills can be particularly beneficial as it allows them to better manage the different tasks, increasing the overall efficiency of the business
Increased productivity	Small firms often operate with limited financial and non-financial resources, and increased productivity through AI can significantly impact their ability to compete with (larger) competitors through better-qualified organization members
Innovative capabilities	Innovation is often a key differentiator for small businesses. AI tools can enable small businesses to constantly innovate and compete in the marketplace by streamlining processes and encouraging creative problem-solving
Employee satisfaction	In small organizations with close-knit members, the positive impact of AI on employee satisfaction can contribute to a positive work culture, which in turn leads to greater loyalty and motivation among individual members
Diversity and inclusion	Small businesses benefit from diversity of thought and skills. AI tools can help foster a diverse workforce and create an inclusive environment, where each organization member contributes their skills and expertise in the best possible way
Health and well-being	AI-driven tools that assist in workload management can be especially crucial for small firms where each member's contribution is significant. This can lead to a healthier and more sustainable work environment (healthier and stronger individuals)
Data-driven decision-making	Small companies may lack the necessary resources for in-depth data analysis. AI tools can democratize access to data insights and enable informed decision-making even with limited resources
Employee empowerment	In smaller firms, each member's contribution is vital. AI tools can empower employees by providing them with tools to excel in their roles and functions, contributing to a sense of ownership and empowerment
Job creation	Small businesses can use AI tools to continuously improve their operations and processes. This can free up resources to create new jobs focusing on areas such as customer retention, innovation, and strategic planning which, in turn, allows the small company to grow in terms of more demanding tasks and projects

3.2 AI from the Perspective of Negative IC Risks: AI as Replacement/Substitute

Tables 4, 5, and 6 provide an overview of possible negative risks related to the three IC dimensions from the perspective of AI as a replacement/substitute.

Tables 1, 2, 3, 4, 5, and 6 not only contain a list of various positive and negative risks associated with IC from a small firm perspective, but it is also clear that many of these risks are interconnected and influence (reinforce) each other. This applies to both the positive and negative risks. It also becomes clear that some risks might overlap, i.e., they can be assigned to different dimensions, depending on the initial situation, i.e., the individual (HC dimension) or the group (culture—SC dimension).

Table 2 Positive risks related to relational capital

Positive risks related to relational capital	Description
Customer engagement	AI tools can enhance customer interactions through personalized recommendations and efficient customer service, leading to improved customer satisfaction and loyalty. This could further strengthen small companies, as they are known for their proximity to customers
Reputation	AI-driven analytics can help small firms better understand customer sentiments and market trends, enabling them to make more informed decisions that positively impact their (brand) reputation
Stakeholder communication	AI-supported communication tools can optimize interaction with internal and external stakeholders, including customers, suppliers, and partners, and lead to more effective and transparent communication
Global collaboration	As many small businesses are also looking to expand or operate globally, AI tools can facilitate communication and collaboration across borders without the need for a large physical presence, enabling cost-effective global operations
Strategic partnerships	AI tools can assist small firms in identifying potential strategic partners or collaborations, strengthening the small firm's network, and creating opportunities for sustainable growth
Market positioning	The use of AI for market research and analysis can help small companies identify niche markets and position themselves strategically in them
Customized offerings	AI-supported insights into customer preferences enable small companies to make their products or services (even) more individual and create personalized offers that appeal to their target groups
Feedback and improvement	AI tools can automate the collection and analysis of feedback, enabling small firms to quickly respond to customer needs and continuously improve their products or services
Supply chain optimization	AI in supply chain management can improve efficiency, reduce costs, and enhance relationships with supply chain actors, ensuring a more reliable and responsive network. This could be particularly helpful for small companies, as they are often the weakest partners in these supply chains
Employee collaboration	AI-supported collaboration tools can also strengthen internal relationships and promote teamwork and knowledge sharing between the employees of a small company
Adaptability	Small businesses that utilize AI tools are in a better position to adapt to market changes and new trends, creating a more agile and responsive environment that strengthens relationships with various stakeholders

For example, employee satisfaction may have a positive impact on the organizational culture (structural capital) and a positive impact on employee motivation (human capital). At the same time, a frightened employee (human capital) can have a negative impact on the organizational culture (structural culture) and a negative impact on the company's business relations (relational capital). The differentiation between AI as a complementary resource or as a substitute broadens the discussion and enables different perspectives and implications.

Table 3 Positive risks related to structural capital

Positive risks related to structural capital	Description
Enhanced IC management	AI tools can enhance IC management within small firms, ensuring that valuable IC is efficiently and permanently identified, assessed, developed, accessible, and utilized across the organization
Process optimization	Implementing AI in the small firms' workflow processes can lead to increased efficiency and productivity, allowing small firms to optimize their operations and allocate scarce resources more effectively
Innovation culture	AI can foster a culture of innovation by automating routine tasks, freeing up time for organization members to focus on creative problem-solving and strategic thinking
Competitive intelligence	AI-driven analytics can provide small firms with valuable insights into market trends, competitor strategies, and emerging opportunities, enabling them to stay competitive and make better (i.e., more informed) decisions
Operational resilience	Integrating AI in operations can enhance the resilience of small firms, making them better equipped to adapt to changes, disruptions, and unforeseen challenges in the business environment
Cost reduction	AI tools can automate repetitive tasks, reducing the need for manual labor and minimizing operational costs for small firms, allowing them to allocate the freed resources in other business areas
Quality control	AI-based quality control systems can improve the ongoing consistency and reliability of products or services, contributing to a continued positive reputation and stakeholder satisfaction
Risk management	AI-powered data analysis can enhance small firms' ability to identify, analyze, and mitigate different types of risks, improving their overall approach to risk management
Strategic planning	AI tools enable data-driven decision-making and help smaller companies to develop and execute more informed strategies for sustainable business development
Continued training and development	AI can facilitate personalized training programs and ensure that the organization members acquire and continuously improve the necessary skills and competences needed to adapt to the changing demands of the business landscape

4 Conclusion

All organizations must be ready to become more AI-driven. As, with any change, risks are to be expected, this refers to both positive (risk as an opportunity) and negative ones (risk as a threat). Approaching these risks is a challenge for small companies in particular. The content presented in this chapter draws attention to IC-related risks in this context. Such a focus could enable decision-makers in small companies to better manage the positive and negative IC challenges associated with AI and ultimately operate successfully and sustainably in the long term.

The focus of this chapter is seen as a relevant and necessary complement to IC theory, as it invites alternative (in the sense of more holistic and balanced) thinking. By looking at the IC dimensions from a risk perspective that looks at both the

Table 4 Negative risks related to human capital

Negative risks related to human capital	Description
Job displacement	The automation of certain tasks through AI could lead to job displacement for those employees involved in routine and repetitive activities, potentially causing job insecurity and morale issues
Resistance to change	Employees in small firms may face challenges in adapting to new AI technologies, leading to resistance and a lack of enthusiasm for incorporating these tools into their daily workflow
Skill gaps	The implementation of AI may require new skill sets that current organization members might not possess. Small firms may face challenges in upskilling their workforce, potentially resulting in a skills gap The need for specialized skills in AI may create skill gaps within the organization, making it challenging for small firms to find and retain skilled staff with the required expertise
Burnout	While AI can streamline processes, the expectation of increased productivity may lead to higher workloads for organization members, potentially contributing to burnout and stress
Lack of personalization	AI-driven processes may depersonalize certain aspects of work, reducing the human touch in interactions with stakeholders, e.g., customers, and employee engagement, which however is crucial for small firms building and maintaining close relationships
Ethical concerns	Issues related to AI ethics, such as bias in algorithms or privacy concerns, may arise. Organization members may be uncomfortable with the ethical implications of using certain AI tools in their daily work
Loss of human touch	Small firms often thrive on personal relationships. Over-reliance on AI for stakeholder interactions may lead to a loss of the human touch, impacting the quality of relationships
Job redefinition	The introduction of AI may redefine job roles, requiring people to take on different and new responsibilities. This can lead to uncertainty and a need for continuous adaptation among the small firm workforce

negative and positive sides, the possible contributions of each IC dimension (sub-dimension) to companies and their activities can be more clearly identified. Considering AI both as a complementary resource and as a substitute encourages further alternative thinking that should be stimulating for future IC research. This in turn may also enable more precise recommendations for IC practice. Ultimately, IC can become more relevant in companies.

One main message of the chapter is that knowledge matters even more in the era of AI. As only a knowledgeable person can assess the advantages and disadvantages of using AI-based tools in their work/company and act accordingly, less knowledgeable people can run the risk of making the wrong decisions or no decisions at all. Moreover, in order to make the best possible use of IC, the members of small firms should be aware of the positive and negative risks that can arise from the use of AI-based tools and solutions for the various IC dimensions. This understanding requires constant training for everyone in the organization. Small companies in particular, which by definition usually have few employees, should ensure that all

Table 5 Negative risks related to relational capital

Negative risks related to relational capital	Description
Depersonalization of customer interactions	Over-reliance on AI for customer interactions may lead to a depersonalized experience, reducing the quality of relationships with customers who value a human touch
Communication barriers	The introduction of AI tools may create communication barriers between the small firm and its stakeholders, especially if there is a perception that the technology is replacing human interaction
Communication breakdown	AI tools may alter communication dynamics within a small organization. Lack of effective communication about the integration of AI can lead to misunderstandings, fear, and decreased morale among employees
Trust issues	Certain stakeholders may be hesitant to trust AI-driven processes, especially if there are concerns about data security, privacy, or the accuracy of automated decision-making
Customer privacy concerns	The use of AI in data analytics may raise concerns about customer privacy. If this is not handled transparently, it could lead to a loss of trust not only among customers but also among other stakeholders
Resistance from stakeholders	Customers, suppliers, or partners may resist engaging with the small firm if they perceive that AI is negatively impacting the quality of relationships or if they feel uncomfortable with the level of AI integration
Ineffective conflict resolution	AI tools may struggle to effectively navigate complex interpersonal conflicts or handle delicate situations, potentially leading to misunderstandings and strained relationships between the people involved
Misalignment with stakeholder values	If AI-driven processes conflict with the values or preferences of critical stakeholders, it can negatively impact the relational capital as this group may feel the small firm does not understand or respect their needs
Loss of personal connection	The introduction of AI in stakeholder interactions may result in a loss of the personal connection that is often a strength of small firms, potentially impacting long-term relationships
Customer service challenges	Over-reliance on AI for customer service may lead to difficulties in addressing unique or complex customer inquiries that require a human touch and personalized approach, a typical strength of small firms
Cultural insensitivity	AI tools, if not properly designed, may lack cultural sensitivity, leading to misunderstandings or unintended offense, particularly in a small firm dealing with diverse stakeholders

members of the organization use AI and are constantly trained to do so. This technology allows every member to make an active contribution, and this should also be used to tackle current and future challenges the company could face together. Recognizing this advantage clearly lies with the company leadership. As there are usually fewer hierarchies in small companies, it can be assumed that this approach is easier to implement.

Table 6 Negative risks related to structural capital

Negative risks related to structural capital	Description
Resource intensiveness	The implementation of AI tools and solutions can be resource-intensive for small firms, including the costs associated with acquiring and maintaining the technology, potentially further straining limited budgets
Dependency on external vendors	Small firms may become overly reliant on external vendors for AI solutions, leading to potential challenges if these vendors face disruptions, go out of business, or increase service costs
Data security concerns	Small firms may lack robust cybersecurity measures, making them more susceptible to data breaches or cyberattacks, especially if AI involves handling sensitive information and knowledge
Complexity in implementation	The complexity of implementing AI-based structural changes may overwhelm small firms with limited technical expertise, leading to operational inefficiencies and potential setbacks
Over-emphasis on technology	Focusing too much on AI implementation may divert attention from other critical aspects of structural capital, such as process optimization and IC management, potentially causing imbalances in the organization
Over-reliance on automation	Small firms may over-rely on AI-driven automation, neglecting the importance of human judgment and creativity in certain decision-making processes, which can impact overall business agility
Lack of customization	Off-the-shelf AI solutions may not fully align with the specific needs and processes of small firms, leading to challenges in customization and potentially suboptimal outcomes
Training costs	Implementing AI requires training. Small firms may face challenges in allocating resources for comprehensive training programs, potentially hindering the successful integration of AI
Deterioration of the business climate and corporate culture triggered by job insecurity among employees	The fear of job displacement due to automation may create anxiety among employees, affecting morale and potentially leading to a decline in organizational performance

Although in this chapter AI is viewed from a substitution/replacement perspective as well, it is recommended that AI in small businesses is rather seen as a complement to, not a replacement for, people, in other words, as another complementary resource that small companies could add to their existing resources in order to continuously improve. Hence AI means a technology resource and could support small firms in overcoming its smallness and the related consequences. Seeing AI from this view while at the same time still being aware of the positive and negative risks of IC dimensions is also likely to positively contribute to the small firm's overall IC management as it becomes more balanced and ultimately more powerful.

The author of this chapter hopes that a small contribution has been made to the advancement of IC theory and practice by emphasizing and elaborating on the importance of integrating positive and negative risks into the IC discussion.

References

Abeysekera, I. (2006). The project of intellectual capital disclosure: Researching the research. *Journal of Intellectual Capital, 7*(1), 61–77.

Alavi, M., & Westerman, G. (2023). How generative AI will transform knowledge work. *Harvard Business Review*. November 7, 2023, https://hbr.org/2023/11/how-generative-ai-will-transform-knowledge-work

Brunold, J., & Durst, S. (2012). Intellectual capital risks and job rotation. *Journal of Intellectual Capital, 13*(2), 178–195.

Crovini, C., Ossola, G., & Britzelmaier, B. (2021). How to reconsider risk management in SMEs? An advanced, reasoned and organised literature review. *European Management Journal, 39*(1), 118–134.

De Araújo Lima, P. F., Crema, M., & Verbano, C. (2020). Risk management in SMEs: A systematic literature review and future directions. *European Management Journal, 38*(1), 78–94.

Durst, S., & Bruns, G. (2018). Knowledge management in small and medium-sized enterprises. In J. Syed, P. A. Murray, D. Hislop, & Y. Mouzughi (Eds.), *The Palgrave handbook of knowledge management*. Springer.

Durst, S., & Zieba, M. (2020). Knowledge risks inherent in business sustainability. *Journal of Cleaner Production, 251*, 119670. https://doi.org/10.1016/J.JCLEPRO.2019.119670

Durst, S., Palacios Acuache, M. M. G., & Bruns, G. (2021). Peruvian small and medium-sized enterprises and COVID-19: Time for a new start! *Journal of Entrepreneurship in Emerging Economies, 13*(4), 648–672.

European Commission. (2020). Directorate-general for internal market, industry, entrepreneurship and SMEs, user guide to the SME definition, Publications Office. 10.2873/677467. Accessed 17 March 2022.

Falkner, E. M., & Hiebl, M. R. W. (2015). Risk management in SMEs: A systematic review of available evidence. *Journal of Risk Finance, 16*(2), 122–144. https://doi.org/10.1108/JRF-06-2014-0079

Farbman, Z. (2023). AI is knowledge, and knowledge is power. https://www.forbes.com/sites/forbestechcouncil/2023/11/29/ai-is-knowledge-and-knowledge-is-power/. Accessed 2 Feb 2024.

Fernández, E., Iglesias-Antelo, S., López-López, V., Rodríguez-Rey, M., & Fernandez-Jardon, C. M. (2019). Firm and industry effects on small, medium-sized and large firms' performance. *BRQ Business Research Quarterly, 22*(1), 25–35.

Gruetzemacher, R., & Whittlestone, J. (2022). The transformative potential of artificial intelligence. *Futures, 135*, 102884.

Harvey, M. G., & Lusch, R. F. (1999). Balancing the intellectual capital books: Intangible liabilities. *European Management Journal, 17*(1), 85–92.

Hoffmann, C. H. (2023). A philosophical view on singularity and strong AI. *AI & Society, 38*, 1697–1714. https://doi.org/10.1007/s00146-021-01327-5

Jarrahi, M. H., Askay, D., Eshraghi, A., & Smith, P. (2023). Artificial intelligence and knowledge management: A partnership between human and AI. *Business Horizons, 66*(1), 87–99.

Krakowski, S., Luger, J., & Raisch, S. (2023). Artificial intelligence and the changing sources of competitive advantage. *Strategic Management Journal, 44*(6), 1425–1452.

Lähteenmäki, J. (2023). The impact of AI on human motivation: Is automation making us lazy? https://www.linkedin.com/pulse/impact-ai-human-motivation-automation-making-us-lazy-l%C3%A4hteenm%C3%A4ki/. Accessed 2 Feb 2024.

Martinez, R. (2019). Artificial intelligence: Distinguishing between types & definitions. *Nevada Law Journal, 19*(3) Article 9. Available at: https://scholars.law.unlv.edu/nlj/vol19/iss3/9

Raisch, S., & Krakowski, S. (2021). Artificial intelligence and management: The automation–augmentation paradox. *AMR, 46*, 192–210. https://doi.org/10.5465/amr.2018.0072

Stam, C. D. (2009). Intellectual liabilities: Lessons from the decline and fall of the Roman empire. *The Journal of Information and Knowledge Management Systems, 39*(1), 92–104.

Zieba, M., Durst, S., & Hinteregger, C. (2022). The impact of knowledge risk management on sustainability. *Journal of Knowledge Management, 26*(11), 234–258. https://doi.org/10.1108/JKM-09-2021-0691

Susanne Durst is a Full Professor of Management at Reykjavik University, Iceland, and a Visiting Professor at LUT University, Finland. She received her doctorate in Economics from Paris-Sud University, Paris 11, Paris, France, in 2011, and her Habilitation (Venia Docendi) certificates in Business Management from University of Skövde, Skövde, Sweden, in 2015, and in International Business and Entrepreneurship from Lappeenranta-Lahti University of Technology, Lappeenranta, Finland, in 2021. Her research interests include knowledge (risk) management, innovation management, responsible digitalization, and sustainable business development in the context of smaller entrepreneurial organizations. Her work has been recognized through different awards, including Emerald Literati Awards "Outstanding Paper" in 2020 and 2023 and has been published in international peer-reviewed journals.

Part IV

Reenvisioning Intellectual Capital: Rethinking Economic Models, Value, and Progress in the Knowledge Era

Considerations Toward the Development of a Foundational Theory of Intellectual Capital

Anthony K. P. Wensley and M. Max Evans

Abstract

This chapter aims to move intellectual capital (IC) research and practice one step closer toward the development of a foundational theory, which can be used to test scholarly research hypotheses and expound practical organizational strategies that bring about enhanced organizational value and, where appropriate, competitive advantages. The history and research into IC and knowledge management (KM) are examined for possible theoretical foundations since both disciplines initially sprang from similar concerns regarding the part knowledge played in the creation of value by organizations. Such a review demonstrates that there are many considerations that need to be reflected on in any foundational theory of IC. Theories and principles in economics are also explored as they might provide a natural basis for such an IC theory. However, in critically reviewing several Theories of the Firm, it is concluded that they provide a very limited articulation into the part played by knowledge in the creation of value by firms and, by extension, organizations in general. Thus, the conclusion of this chapter is that, at present, there is no adequate theory which explains the process by which organizational knowledge underpins the creation of value by organizations. However, the conclusion is not wholly negative since some possible ways forward are discussed.

A. K. P. Wensley
University of Toronto, Toronto, ON, Canada
e-mail: anthony.wensley@utoronto.ca

M. M. Evans (✉)
McGill University, Montréal, QC, Canada
e-mail: max.evans@mcgill.ca

A. Kianto et al. (eds.), *Futurizing Intellectual Capital*, Knowledge Management and Organizational Learning 15, https://doi.org/10.1007/978-3-031-80197-6_13

1 Introduction

This chapter is intended to present a challenge to intellectual capital (IC) researchers to open their minds to a variety of issues which, in the authors' opinion, have been overlooked and under-researched over the 30 years or so that IC has been the object of dedicated research. It should be noted that several of the highlighted issues are grounded in knowledge management (KM) research, which evolved contemporaneously with IC research and had similar research agendas until the most recent 15–20 years. Since KM addresses itself to the investigation of all aspects of relating to the management of knowledge and IC relates, to some extent, to organizational knowledge, it can be argued that the two research agendas should have communalities. In addition, theories concerning the way knowledge "functions" with respect to organizations should relate to the theoretical frameworks and theories that can be developed for KM and IC. Examining communalities and differences between these two research agendas have considerable value to both disciplines and represents an important way of "futurizing research in IC."

This chapter investigates the extent to which one approach to theorizing about the structure and functioning of organizations, the Theory of the Firm, can provide a basis for IC research. However, Theories of the Firm, as they currently exist, typically do not make use of the concept of IC, per se. They do, however, make use of concepts such as knowledge and knowledge resources which, on the surface, provide a link to both KM and IC research. Thus, unpacking various approaches to developing Theories of the Firm may provide insight into how firms themselves might change at the macro- (e.g., structure and boundaries) and micro-level (e.g., tasks, jobs, and processes) in response to a variety of different technological and social changes. Furthermore, examining Theories of the Firm that describe organizational knowledge (or the part organizational knowledge plays within and across organizations) may also provide further insight for IC research.

The chapter provides a brief review of the Theories of the Firm proposed by Coase (1937), Williamson (1991), Kogurt and Zander (1996), and other researchers in Strategic Management (Spender & Grant, 1996). Considering these theories, some important questions are posed relating to knowledge-intensive firms/organizations, organizational knowledge, IC, and other concepts which have either been taken for granted by researchers (or practitioners) or used without adequate articulation of the concepts themselves. An attempt is then made to provide a broader inquiry into several issues and concerns examining the nature, value, and function(s) of knowledge and IC in organizations.

Ultimately, it is argued that current Theories of the Firm cannot presently be adapted to provide appropriate theoretical underpinnings for either IC or KM research. As will be discussed, not only do these theories fail to adequately articulate the nature and functions of knowledge but also, in the case of IC, are not able to incorporate the components of IC as they are articulated in the IC literature.[1]

[1] The most popular IC framework builds on the work of early IC scholars (e.g., Bontis, 1998; Bontis et al., 2002; Edvinsson & Malone, 1997; Sullivan, 1998) who describe three dimensions or

Although it is often stated that the effective management of IC is central to the ability of a firm to create value and achieve competitive advantage, this remains basically a nostrum. There is no theory capable of answering why IC adds value or how it does so. The importance of a theory of IC is fundamental since developing a better understanding of the nature and functions of organizational knowledge represents a fundamental way of advancing IC research. Such a development will allow IC researchers to test hypotheses aimed at managing IC (and its components) in ways that improve firm performance or enhance the firm's value through the establishment of competitive advantage. In a familiar positivistic approach to theory interpretation, the creation of an appropriate theory also allows for the making of some testable predictions about the future of IC and the form and function of knowledge-intensive organizations. It is fully recognized that several researchers (e.g., Kianto et al., 2023) have provided impressive normative theory for IC and KM. However, without a better-developed positive theory, the extent to which IC or KM theory can be advanced is quite limited.

Furthermore, at this stage of the development of IC and KM research, it may be premature to try to develop a coherent and comprehensive theory, whether based on economic principles or theories from other disciplines. There is far more work to be done to clearly articulate relevant concepts in KM and IC research before any theory can be proposed. Thus, research directed toward futurizing IC should focus on conceptual foundations and descriptions, as well as explore the links between IC and value creation in firms. This, of course, does not dismiss the extensive research that has been completed to date with respect to IC theories, KM theories, and research in both disciplines, more broadly. The authors are indebted to more colleagues, researchers, and practitioners than can be named or cited.

2 Intellectual Capital and Knowledge Management Research: Rethinking Perspectives and Communalities

It is important to begin by considering the evolution of KM and IC research, in general, and to trace their theoretical foundations. As noted above, in many ways IC research and KM research sprang from the same root, at around the same time, and claim common precursors. However, in the last 15–20 years, they have drawn apart.

As Lambe (2023) notes:

[O]ver the past 25 years the main intellectual capital (IC) movement has evolved into a specialized discipline focused on value measurement and value accounting. It has developed journals, conferences, and publications that sit largely apart from their KM counterparts. pp. 302–303.

In the above quote, Lambe (2023) identifies some generalizations about the value-based focus of IC research. Although these are generalizations, definitions of IC generally agree that IC creates "value" to the organization. The principal source of value may be the IC itself, or the IC may act as means by which the organization

components of IC: human capital, structural capital, and social capital.

gains a competitive advantage (e.g., Bontis, 1996, 1998; Edvinsson & Malone, 1997; Stewart, 1997; Sveiby, 1997). IC researchers largely explain IC as a combination of organizational knowledge and knowing capabilities (e.g., processes) that enable organizations to derive value from organizational knowledge (Bontis, 1998; Nahapiet & Ghoshal, 1998).

In contrast, the focus of much KM research was epistemological or technological where knowledge was treated in a similar fashion to data or information. Discussions were largely supply-side and somewhat technology-centric, as they focused on technologies and processes to capture, process, and share knowledge. A second generation of KM research brought with it more of a consideration of human involvement and focused on the production, management, and utilization of knowledge (McElroy, 2003). This research did not classify all knowledge as inherently valuable but rather tried to explain how organizational knowledge can be turned into valuable knowledge through dynamic capabilities that facilitate the acquisition, combination, and sharing of knowledge to support decisions and processes that create value for the organization. Unlike IC research, this perspective tends to separate knowledge from the creation of value. Although both IC research and KM research recognize that organizational knowledge or IC is fundamental to the creation of value, the nature of this value and the manner in which this occurs are not explored in detail.

Both the KM and IC research literature are replete with terms that have been appropriated from other disciplines. For example, the KM research literature commonly refers to *knowledge* and, on occasion, *knowledge capital*, *knowledge assets*, and *knowledge resources*. Similarly, the IC research literature refers to *intellectual capital*, *intangible assets*, and *intellectual resources* and often directly mentions organizational *knowledge*. It is important to exhibit care in such appropriation because their use, and hence meaning, in KM and IC research does not map precisely to their use and meaning in their originating discipline. This may lead to inappropriate assumptions or insufficient analysis with respect to divergences in meaning and use in different contexts. For example, the pragmatic focus of IC research led to the adoption of the term, capital, which was drawn from economics. Since it was generally accepted that organizations created value through the management of capital, the use of this term in IC research added credibility and relatability. However, many of the characteristics of traditional capital (labor and physical capital) were not mirrored in IC. Thus, such appropriation has led to difficulties linking IC research to economics and in particular economic theories of the firm. For example, explanations as to how capital (in an economic sense) plays a part in the creation of economic value give relatively little insight as to how IC plays a part in creating value (economic or otherwise).

It is also important to note that neither KM nor IC research has been able to establish well-grounded theoretical foundations. Although links to research in economics and accounting exist, no convincing attempts have been seen to explicate the economic or accounting functions of knowledge. Furthermore, economics and accounting researchers have little to say about organizational knowledge, in any specific sense.

Perhaps, rather than appropriating concepts from economics or accounting, it might be more productive to review the part KM and IC have played historically in the creation and maintenance of organizations, as well as the creation of value within and between organizations. It often seems that IC and KM researchers consider that IC and KM concepts arose only recently. The following section examines the interactions between knowledge, IC, and organizations in a broad historical context.

3 A Discursion into the History of Knowledge, Intellectual Capital, and Organizations

Historically, knowledge has been seen as a basis of power or as a source of value. Francis Bacon noted this as early as the sixteenth century (Azamfirei, 2016). Individuals who possessed knowledge were often respected and powerful figures in society. As such, questions about individual and organizational knowledge, and its management, have been relevant for many centuries, if not millennia. In fact, it may be argued that the history of human culture runs parallel to the history of (human) knowledge and its effective management.

In earlier times the principal way of representing knowledge was through what might be considered routines, which were passed on, initially through observation and mimicry and later through pictorial representation and language. In this context, the type of knowledge concerned was practical knowledge, which informed physical performance as distinct from, say, spiritual knowledge. As language evolved, along with its representation in some fixed form, knowledge could be passed from one generation to another. It became possible to represent knowledge externally, and to some extent explicitly, allowing institutions to curate and share knowledge in different domains. Though, even at an early stage, it became clear that there were limitations with respect to representing knowledge, particularly pertaining to the performance of actions or routines.

Moreover, knowledge had limited value without curation. Initially, curation amounted to collecting physical representations of knowledge in particular locations, such as monasteries and libraries, which drastically restricted the access and sharing of these physical artifacts. However, access increased with the development of Codex and other technologies like indices, but even sharing explicit knowledge was still difficult, because it required someone to copy representations from one physical medium to another similar physical medium. Thus, a scroll would be copied to another scroll or CODEX. Such copying was often inaccurate for a variety of reasons including, but not limited to, simple transcription errors, errors arising from the physical decay of the recording medium, and translation errors. These errors were often not captured since there were no formal processes of review or formal ways of establishing reliable representations. Although critical analyses of the texts were sometimes developed, quite often texts were accepted unchallenged. More troubling, those individuals doing the copying were not "skilled in the art" or knowledgeable in the subject of the text.

Over time, social structures, such as the family, and then small groups, provided a context for the creation, representation, and transmission of largely tacit knowledge. By the Middle Ages, guilds provided formal structures and frameworks for apprenticeships where masters of (largely artisan) crafts formally passed on "industry" knowledge in the form of technologies (e.g., tools) and processes. It is interesting to note that guilds often deliberately restricted the creation of explicit knowledge and focused on the management and sharing of tacit knowledge. Focusing on tacit knowledge allowed guilds to control access to knowledge but also created challenges for the creation of new knowledge or the revision of existing knowledge.

As societies became more complex, and knowledge more abundant, public and private institutions focused more on the preservation and efficacious dissemination of knowledge. If this same historical perspective is examined, from an IC research viewpoint, it can be argued that human capital[2] has been relied on for centuries, largely in the form of "know-how." However, as representational approaches were developed, this allowed for the augmentation of this human capital. The evolution of increasingly rich communications and relational networks both enhanced social and relational capital[3] and, in the process, enhanced the value of human capital. Furthermore, as organization systems were developed to acquire, curate, and disseminate knowledge, structural capital[4] was being created with the stakeholders and communities involved.

It is difficult to argue with the fact that knowledge lies at the heart of current society. The creation, retention, transfer, and application of knowledge are essential to the smooth running of society. The complex interweaving of institutions and organizations would not be possible without knowledge. However, to handle the complexities involved, knowledge must constantly be revised and applied in conditions of uncertainty (Spender, 1996).

Through their interaction with knowledge, knowledge processes, knowledge embedded in information systems, organizational routines, procedures, and other stakeholders, individuals become better able to act on knowledge. By being exposed to a broad range of (curated) knowledge and knowledge routines and processes, individuals become better able to handle complex tasks, solve complicated problems, and identify novel opportunities. Furthermore, these interactions may result in the creation of new knowledge and learning that facilitates improved performance (or value) in the future. However, expanding knowledge is not necessarily a panacea. As knowledge expands inevitably, individuals focus on more specialized

[2] Human capital is embedded in the knowledge, skills/abilities/competencies, education/training, innovativeness/creativity/intuition, attitudes, and beliefs of a firm's employees (Bontis, 1998, 2000; Bontis et al., 2002; Edvinsson & Malone, 1997; Roos & Roos 1997).

[3] Social capital is embedded in the relationships the organization has developed with key stakeholders that lead to competitive advantage (Bontis, 1996; Edvinsson & Malone, 1997, Stewart, 1997).

[4] Structural capital is embedded in a firm's systems, processes/routines, organizational design, and culture (Bontis, 1998; Brooking, 1997; Edvinsson & Malone, 1997; Martín-de-Castro et al., 2011; Stewart, 1997; Sveiby, 1997). Examples include intellectual property (e.g., patents, trademarks, trade secrets, etc.), ICTs, and other non-human capabilities.

knowledge domains. This results in the need to orchestrate knowledge possessed by many different individuals to solve complex problems. Tantalizingly it may also lead to knowledge being ignored or forgotten at both the individual level and the organizational level.

The creation, preservation, protection, curation, and dissemination of knowledge have also been influenced by a wide variety of socio-legal and technological factors. For example, the increasing focus on individualism and the value of the individual have led to the adoption of a perspective of knowledge as belonging to individuals and organizations. This perspective is clearly witnessed in the IC concept of human capital, where individual beliefs, assumptions, values, and skills are referred to. KM adopts a similar perspective in their descriptions of individual or personal knowledge. This individual perspective exists alongside a much older perspective that knowledge belongs to society, and it represents a valuable resource to society. One can see evidence of these two different perspectives in the creation and evolution of laws to offer protections for knowledge, both for the individual creator and for those in society who require access. Patent laws were essentially created to provide incentives for individuals to create knowledge and articulate it in such a manner that others can use the knowledge to the benefit of society. Typically, such knowledge is related to the "useful arts."

Intellectual property laws also provide some interesting insights that reverberate through the fields of KM and IC. Most obviously, patent laws address the application of knowledge in the production of some specific product or process. From an IC perspective, patents represent both knowledge and the manner (i.e., processes and applications) by which such knowledge can be valorized. In fact, patent laws require patents to provide sufficiently rich and detailed descriptions of actions required to produce the relevant outcome (i.e., procedural knowledge). Unfortunately, or perhaps inevitably, in most cases, this is not possible as there is often a significant amount of contextual or tacit knowledge that cannot be represented in a patent description or in a prototype provided by the individual or organization. This signifies an important challenge to IC researchers when considering patents a constituent of IC. Patents derive their value from a complex interaction of human capital, relational capital, and structural capital. It is also interesting to note that many economists, in investigating the contribution of organizational knowledge to the creation of economic value, use the number of patents as a proxy for organizational knowledge.

Patent law is also a reminder of how knowledge does not come in discrete units. Knowledge is embedded in webs of other knowledge and in information systems. This should alert to the dangers of referring to capturing, storing, and sharing knowledge, as the use of such locutions can mislead individuals into thinking of knowledge as an object rather than as a constituent of complex, dynamic webs of meaning and value.

In the above, reference has been made to the co-evolution of knowledge, organizations, and society. Clearly, more of an IC lens could have been put on this review though it would have become much more difficult to contain since the concept of IC has expanded way beyond knowledge to include processes, routines, beliefs, and so on. Hence, to the extent that the above discussion refers to IC, it mostly addresses one component, human capital. Furthermore, it can be argued that the relative importance of the components of IC fluctuates with changes in technology and society. Exploring these interactions in a historical context may provide insights into the future importance and influence of components of IC.

Adopting a historical perspective, however, does not provide a workable theoretical perspective for either exploring KM or IC. Hence, the following section steps back from a historical and evolutionary view of knowledge to examine existing Theories of the Firm, as both KM and IC lack sufficient self-developed theoretical grounding. Reference will be made to theories that are primarily derived from economics. However, it will be noted, in a limited fashion, that other disciplines such as sociology can also provide potential sources of theoretical grounding.

4 Why Do Firms Exist in the First Place?

The existence of organizations and firms is a feature of modern societies. However, the nature of the institutions that are present and their demarcation varies between societies, particularly when seen from a historical perspective. Thus, researchers have sought to explain why particular types of organizations have come about and develop theories relating to different organizational types. Although several disciplines provide theories related to the functions and evolution of organizations, this section will largely view organizations from an economic perspective. It should also be made clear that much of the theorizing about organizations tends to focus on business organizations. Within this discipline and context, several prevalent Theories of the Firm have been proposed, most notably the Transactions Cost Theory, the Resource-based Theory of the Firm, and the Knowledge-based Theory of the Firm. All three of these theories are relatively new, with the oldest based on research originally published in the 1930s. Many of the theories discussed below could be considered *positive* theories to the extent they seek to explain why firms exist in the first place. Ideally, such positive theories should be used to identify how organizational performance can be improved, thus using positive theories as a vehicle for developing *normative* theories.

Ronald Coase's (1932) work recognized the "need" for Economists to establish some explanation for the existence of firms, as in classical economics there was no compelling explanation for their existence since economic transactions are processed in the marketplace and, through the price system, the markets are efficiently cleared. Any out-of-equilibrium states are corrected through the mechanism of price. Since all production is coordinated through markets, there is theoretically no need for firms. However, one rationale for their existence is related to the costs associated with entering into market transactions, which may be mitigated when firms participate in productive or cooperative activities.

During his lifetime Coase engaged in spirited discussions with other economists with respect to both the interpretation of his own theorizing and how it related to those theories developed by other economists. Rather than enter an extended analysis of the various disputes, it is generally safe to say that Coase argued that the determination of price is not necessarily a costless task or that there are likely to be various market failures and inefficiencies that can be addressed through other non-market mechanisms.

Coase's work led to what is now referred to as Transaction Cost Economics (TCE) propounded by Williamson (1991). This approach proposes that firms exist to minimize transaction costs. Essentially, an argument is developed to explain why some transactions take place within organizations rather than through the market. To the extent that there are situations where firms face lower transaction costs than those individuals face transacting through the marketplace, firms will represent the preferred approach to coordinating production.

Attempts have been made to use TCE to explain and predict the effects of radically changing communication and computing costs. It seems clear that TCE provides some explanation for the evolution of such phenomena as outsourcing, ex post. As Information, Communication, and Technology (ICT) needs become more standardized, and the costs associated with communication and computing drop, firms that specialize in ICT services can provide services much more cheaply than non-specialist firms. However, TCE does not seem to provide a very good explanation as to why managers, a priori, developed strategies, which embraced outsourcing. Not only is this because there is little evidence that managers were primarily motivated to outsource because of a detailed analysis of transaction costs nor were such detailed transaction costs available to them. Even if they had attempted to develop detailed costs, there is little guidance as to how to determine, in each instance, the transaction costs involved. One critical problem in determining transaction costs relates to the allocation of overhead costs and infrastructure costs. Perhaps even more basically there is a problem as to what constitutes a transaction in the first place. Thus, it is difficult to see how TCE could provide guidance to practitioners on developing strategies to improve performance or competitiveness, except in a very general sense.

As previously mentioned, classical economics considers that all transactions should take place through the market with price conveying all the necessary information to adequately clear markets. However, over the last decades, situations were identified where prices may not have adequately conveyed complete information about transacted products and services. One set of examples relates to situations where the suitability of a particular product or service is not adequately communicated through price or other information provided by the seller because they are motivated to overstate the performance or quality of the product or service. In these situations, the most famous initial discussion was presented by Ackerlof (1970) and represents an example of market failure.

Another concern with attempts to use economic theories as the basis of developing IC or KM theory is that, generally speaking, economists have had a somewhat limited approach to conceptualizing production. The idea that value is created by organizations combining economic factors through a production function is very much rooted in a physical understanding of the transformation(s) that take place in production. This approach is largely limited in its applicability to the manner in which KM or IC contributes to the creation of value.

A Theory of the Firm that emerged in the 1990s rests on assumptions that firms exist to manage resources that are not solely traditional economic resources. The objective of management is to acquire or create and leverage value from these resources. This theory is generally referred to as the Resource-Based Theory of the Firm or RBV (Barney, 2001). In a very general sense, it is argued that the transformation of these resources represents the core rationale for the firm. To be successful, the firm needs to be able to determine what types of transformation lead to the creation of value and for whom. The firm must also ensure that the value derived from the transformation(s) exceeds the costs entailed because of the transformation(s). To the extent that the firm seeks competitive advantage and, hence, sustainability, some or all the resources must have certain characteristics of value, rarity, and non-substitutability.

One of the challenges is that resource characteristics are difficult to ascertain, and they are dependent on many other factors. For example, oil had little value until the mass production of the internal combustion engine and the "invention" of oil refining. One can likely determine the value of a particular resource in a static sense, but dynamically it will depend on a wide variety of firm and market factors. Rarity poses a similar problem. For example, oil became more abundant as drilling technologies improved or when certain social, legal, and political changes occurred. The same can be said for gold and other extractive metals. Furthermore, more efficient ways to use a rare resource decrease the effective rarity since a reduced quantity of the resource is needed to create a certain level of output. On the other hand, new uses for resources may increase rarity as is now seen with lithium, cobalt, manganese, nickel, and graphite used in the development of batteries. Finally, non-substitutability is also not immune from a variety of factors. Alternative, more efficient, processes of production may result in products or services that satisfy similar needs, or environmental conditions may change the attractiveness of certain resources or processes. For example, COVID and its attendant lockdowns made air cargo competitive as the cost of surface transportation, such as container shipping, rose drastically.

In the above discussion, the value of resources is intimately related to knowledge, both individual and organizational. One way in which this observation has been operationalized has been through the Knowledge-Based Theory of the Firm (KBV). KBV is essentially a restricted version of the RBV, and hence it has similar foundations and challenges. Instead of physical resources alone, KBV additionally focused on the knowledge resources of the firm. The identification and classification of these knowledge resources are central to KBV and have been the focus of much KM research over the last two and a half decades. However, the IC research literature does not seem to have explored the applicability of KBV as extensively. Neither KM nor IC research categorizes knowledge, or IC, in such a way that is directly translatable into KBV. Additionally, neither seems to link knowledge (a "resource") to RBV through being able to identify what knowledge is rare, non-substitutable, and valuable. In this context, rare would seem to mean, known only by a few. What non-substitutability means in the context of knowledge has not been explored, and its value may well be difficult to define in discrete terms. In addition, as noted above, part of the problem is the appropriation of the term "resource" without an adequate investigation of whether failure to fully articulate the traditional meaning of the term obfuscates important differences between traditional economic resources and knowledge considered as a resource.

KBV has been further extended to take account of the fact that knowledge alone does not carry value without the existence of capabilities that allow firms to transform knowledge into value—so-called knowledge capabilities. Typically, these capabilities are not static; they need to embrace change over time and are thus dynamic capabilities. In the context of KM research, these capabilities may be viewed as KM processes. To the extent that IC research recognizes these capabilities, they are intertwined with the various IC components and rarely made explicit. Even in the case of KM, the precise way in which knowledge capabilities add value to knowledge is not made clear.

One of the most tantalizing non-economically based Theories of the Firm, developed by Kogurt and Zander (1996), considers that firms arise from the creation of social/legal spaces where individuals work cooperatively to effectively manage risks and complete complex tasks. These individuals "donate" their time, skills, knowledge, and energy and, in return, achieve the satisfaction of working on complex problems collaboratively. Thus, a feeling of identity, belonging, and community is developed, all creating and reinforcing a purpose for an organization to exist. From this perspective, the development of an organization's IC is heavily reliant on the organization's ability to recruit appropriate individuals and support them with efficient and effective cognitive and social structures. Furthermore, this theory reinforces the challenge of trying to either value IC, in isolation, or determine its current and future strategic significance without a broader understanding of the richness of organizational context.

In the preceding review, it is instructive to observe that IC has not been directly articulated in any of the theories of the firm from the TCE theory to the RBT or the KBT. Even when knowledge plays a part in these theories, it is not articulated very clearly or in a manner which maps well to the components of IC. It is certainly a challenge for IC researchers to investigate the extent to which existing components of IC can be mapped into the categories of knowledge that have been identified by economists. However, given the relative paucity of the analysis of knowledge in an economic context, this may be a daunting task.

In the above, reference has often been made to considering that the overall objective of firms, and many different types of organizations, is to create value. In the following section, the contribution of knowledge to the creation of value is explored.

5 Where Does Knowledge "Fit In"?

There is considerable discussion of the role of knowledge in organizations. As noted earlier, Kogurt and Zander (1996) argue that knowledge lies at the heart of organizations, as they are social institutions for the creation and utilization of knowledge. However, when one reviews the extensive research examining the importance of knowledge to firms or, at a greater extent, theories such as the Knowledge-Based Theory of the Firm, there is a relative paucity of detailed discussion about the nature of knowledge and no real engagement with IC and its components. Although many researchers, particularly in economics, note distinctions between explicit and tacit knowledge and identify knowledge as a productive resource, there is relatively little in-depth discussion into the nature of these categories of knowledge, their other relevant characteristics, or the way they facilitate the creation of value.

Unlike other knowledge-based institutions, firms typically have an underlying economic justification for creating and sharing knowledge. The problem with this perspective is that assessing and utilizing knowledge to add value require an understanding of how the added value is determined. Unfortunately, it is difficult post hoc to explicate past knowledge that may have allowed an organization to create value, in an economic sense. Even more challenging is to establish the value of knowledge ex ante. When it comes to deciding what to invest in, with respect to knowledge, organizations need to base their decisions and strategies on predictions of potential future trajectories of that knowledge. Given that the full richness of knowledge cannot be articulated, it would seem impossible to make any reliable future projections. Similar arguments can be made for determining the value of any component or type of IC though these may be more complex given their multifaceted composition. For example, when structural capital is considered, it may consist of databases, networks, organizational routines, particular organizational structural components, and so on. None of these components can be easily valued individually or in combination.

Another central issue that needs to be addressed is the overall purpose behind the development of different categories of knowledge. Lambe (2023, p. 255) notes, in the context of knowledge auditing, "What is our purpose here, the purpose against which we need to evaluate the quality of our typologies of knowledge? We want to know what knowledge the organization has and what knowledge it needs to do its work." As other researchers also note, over the past decades, a wide variety of different categories of knowledge have been proposed, with the most popular one dividing knowledge into tacit and explicit knowledge. This categorization is attractive because of its simplicity and the intellectual heritage it brings with it, most notably the work of Polanyi (1966). However, there has been much discussion over how Polanyi's (1966) distinction between tacit and explicit should be interpreted (e.g., Tsoukas, 2005a, 2005b). Furthermore, Lambe (2023) suggests that tacit knowledge is often not open to subcategorization, whereas explicit knowledge is subcategorized in many ways. In KM research it is commonly classified by format, stakeholder/owner, KM function/process, or organizational department/functional area.

The paradox with tacit knowledge is that it is tacit—it cannot be expressed linguistically with any degree of precision or completeness. To some extent, it can be displayed and observed through action, as well as through outcome of the tacit knowledge. For example, to determine an individual's knowledge or skill to play the violin, they must play the violin to assess the quality of their playing. If distinctly different levels of performance can be identified, then this would suggest that there are different levels of tacit knowledge. This is further evidenced by the way traditional crafts classified their members as they progressed through their apprenticeship to became masters. There might even be a place for the concept of collective tacit knowledge to the extent that groups are able to perform more complex tasks than individuals through the combination of their tacit knowledge (e.g., teams that perform complex surgeries or financial trading groups). There are also challenges to determining whether two individuals have "shared" their tacit knowledge. Two individuals may reach the same level of performance but not share the same tacit knowledge. In one sense this may not matter, but when the context of performance changes, the performance of the two individuals may diverge if they do not share the same tacit knowledge.

Unfortunately, it is difficult to see how tacit knowledge can be systematically or accurately classified, captured, or shared. The best researchers and practitioners may be able to do is identify different levels of what might be termed the "possession of tacit knowledge" by an individual. Lambe (2023) notes that, in a practical setting, it is possible to ask individuals about tacit knowledge but not provide any detailed guidance or classification of the term, compared to explicit knowledge. For example, in a research study examining a tax department knowledge audit of a large oil and gas company, Lambe (2023) reported finding 15 "distinct explicit knowledge types, while tacit knowledge (or "people") was a single category without any further differentiation" (p. 255). Interestingly, over the last 35 years, Robert Sternberg and his colleagues at Yale have developed and tested a cognitive psychological theory of tacit knowledge (as well as concomitant research methods), but these have simply not been widely adopted by organizational researchers in economics, IC, or KM (Frissen et al., 2019).

A commonly proposed third category of knowledge is that of "embedded" or "encapsulated" knowledge (e.g., Evans et al., 2014; Van den Berg, 2013). These terms have been used to characterize knowledge which is "represented" by organizational procedures, routines, and what has been termed business logic. Encapsulated knowledge may also be object-based where the value is derived from the object's design and functionality (van den Berg, 2013; Wiig, 1993; Gorga, 2007; Boisot, 1998). Patents and prototypes were previously mentioned as examples, but other examples could include products, tools, code, models, and technical drawings (Choo, 2006; van den Berg, 2013; Wiig, 1993; Kogurt & Zander, 1992). What makes this unique is that the substantive knowledge that went into the design and development of embedded or encapsulated knowledge is often hidden, but users can still gain utility from its functional use (Gorga, 2007; van den Berg, 2013).

From an IC perspective, there is clear value for the organization in the functional use of the encapsulated knowledge, as well as in the substantive knowledge embedded in the object, procedure, process, patent, etc. This is, of course, assuming that the embedded knowledge can be extracted or reverse engineered. Moreover, like the other "types" of knowledge, encapsulated or embedded knowledge will be dependent on several codependent IC components. For example, human capital is required as individuals apply their past knowledge, skills, and experiences in the creation of organizational knowledge and the functional use of such knowledge. Structural capital provides the supportive infrastructure and processes for this knowledge to be created and leveraged for value, and social capital encompasses the interconnected networks of relationships and shared perspectives needed to accomplish this effectively. Furthermore, social capital encompasses the trust required leading up to these interactions and during them, especially when faced with incomplete or not fully specified conditions or information.

It is also clear that, when focusing on value, the distinction between tacit, explicit, and embedded knowledge is important. Distinctively different processes need to be put in place to enable the creation of value depending on the nature of the underlying knowledge. As noted above, knowledge becomes valuable through the orchestration of its articulation, cooperation, and combination. IC researches proposing IC components that combine tacit, explicit, and embedded knowledge together face considerable challenges linking these IC components to value creation.

Although there has been limited discussion or research directed toward developing a theory of IC or KM, researchers in these fields have produced an impressive body of research that deserves attention.

6 A (Very Short) History of Researching Knowledge and Intellectual Capital

The need to keep pace with the expansion of knowledge and the need to develop more and more complex skills are hardly new, but one can make a plausible claim that these demands have become increasingly acute as the twentieth century progressed. Thus, practitioners sought to find ways of identifying and measuring knowledge or skills. Initially, this involved attempting to classify knowledge in a variety of ways and then developing ways to identify, measure, and value these categories in various organizational contexts. In the early years, KM and IC research tended to complement each other, with IC research focusing on inventorying and measuring knowledge and KM focusing on empirical and conceptual analyses of the interactions between different "types" of knowledge and between these "types" of knowledge and different organizational groups or individual stakeholder characteristics. There are also many examples of studies examining the impact of organizational knowledge on individual, group, and overall organizational performance. It is here where it seems a divergence takes place between IC and KM conceptual structures and aims, as well as their respective research literature. In a general sense, it could be argued that the overarching aim of both KM and IC research is to be able to examine the firms' current and future strategic objectives to determine what knowledge and skills (i.e., human capital) are presently available, what infrastructures are needed to support them (i.e., structural capital), and what relationships are needed (i.e., social/relational capital). A similar aim would be needed to achieve future strategic objectives. If gaps are found, strategies should be developed to fill these gaps.

As noted above, in the 1990s practitioners became aware of the Strategic Management literature and related Theories of the Firm, like RBT and KBT, but these theories did not give much guidance in the way of assessing present or future knowledge or IC capabilities (see, e.g., Spender & Grant, 1996). As such, there was also little guidance with respect to developing strategies to fill knowledge or IC gaps. Furthermore, the ways in which the components of IC were defined made the "fit" with concepts such as "resource" in RBV or "knowledge" in KBT to be essentially impossible.

Another discipline that appeared to provide some guidance was accounting. In the 1980s and 1990s, accounting researchers became increasingly concerned with the extreme divergence between the market value of some firms, particularly in information technology, and their value as reported using traditional accounting principles. For example, firms were often in possession of assets that were not physical assets, such as goodwill or patents. To address this, some researchers looked to earlier work by economists and introduced new concepts such as intangible assets, intellectual assets, and IC, which were meant to account for what traditional capital could not. From the standpoint of the typical rationale accounting profession, this provided a more "accurate" valuation of a firm, which was necessary for supporting managerial decision-making (managerial accounting) and potential investment (financial accounting). For publicly traded companies, this was typically calculated by taking a firm's market value and subtracting its book value. However, using market value as a measure is largely problematic because it constantly fluctuates. If book value were to remain relatively stable, then the value of the firm's IC (i.e., intangible assets) becomes directly tied to market value fluctuations. This is troublesome as it would seem unlikely that IC should be so volatile. As is noted above, IC components are defined to include such a wide range of sub-components; their composite valuation would seem to be extremely challenging. No one valuation approach will likely work for any of the sub-components of IC. In addition, market fluctuations can be based on innumerable factors, most of which have little to do directly with a firm's IC. For private companies, valuing intangible assets or IC is even more imprecise, as market value is not available and existing methods of valuation (e.g., comparing valuation ratios, EBITDA, discounted cash flow analysis, internal rate of return, etc.) do not directly account for it. It can be argued that ex post accounting provides a limited explanation for the value of IC and ex ante accounting provides no guidance as to what components of IC to invest in.

The next section will explore in more detail the part knowledge plays in the creation of value and some of the inherent complexities, which cannot be finessed.

7 Knowledge and Value

The chapter has previously alluded to the fact that the concept of knowledge is used in a very disordered way in both KM and IC research. It has been noted that whatever knowledge is, its principal value lies in the actions and skills that it supports, whether individually or collectively. In a business context, this is more pragmatic as it can be broadly applied and measured through to the firm's ability to create value in the environment within which they operate. Often relatively little effort has been expended in organizations to examine the foundations of the knowledge that is used in decision-making. This is a key omission given that knowledge does not have an intrinsic value—and its value is established *in use*. Since that use, in a managerial context, is in decision-making, the omission of a detailed discussion of decision-making from KM and IC research would seem to be a serious oversight.

To a certain extent, IC research has sought to identify ways in which the various components of IC can be enhanced. However, as was previously noted, the components of IC do not have inherent value, and their value essentially derives from their coordinated use in decision-making. It is likely that the nature of the coordination will vary considerably with the nature of the tasks that individuals engage in. A similar point can be made with respect to KM where not only is the type of knowledge important to ways in which value may be created but to some extent the very nature of the knowledge. For example, distinctly different approaches may be necessary to articulate and combine knowledge in the financial services industry or the healthcare industry.

Knowing that individuals in the organization possess the required knowledge or skills, alone, has little value to an organization. Knowledge, in an organizational setting, has value only to the extent that it can be leveraged and that it can improve performance or some other factor related to competitive advantage. On an individual basis, knowledge can improve the performance of specific tasks and assist in planning and decision-making tasks. Economic benefits depend on the needs of the organizational stakeholders (i.e., consumers of knowledge) and the value those stakeholders place on the satisfaction of those needs. Moreover, the extent to which a product or service satisfies the needs of the stakeholders will depend on their ability (or knowledge) to use the product or service. Thus, for example, value decreases if the stakeholders must exert considerable effort to "learn" or acquire knowledge on using the product or service.

Interestingly, one might argue that in many cases it may be easier to put a value on tacit knowledge than explicit knowledge. For example, the value of the work of an expert craftsperson is easier to assess than the value of a textbook dealing with, say, Tensor Calculus. This could be because, for many people, the immediate applicability of Tensor Calculus is not obvious. For explicit knowledge to be judged as valuable, there typically needs to be a known application or challenge that it can be applied to yield an economic benefit (or minimize individual or organizational costs). As noted above, the value of knowledge is largely in the actions or skills that it supports. Value will also depend on context and on such variables as the presence of other knowledge, technology, and organizational culture.

Moreover, even if it were possible to identify certain knowledge as valuable, at a particular point in time, the dynamic nature of an organization's internal and external environment will inevitably change the value of their existing knowledge. Failure to respond to new challenges may highlight organizational voids or missing knowledge. Inappropriate actions may be based on knowledge which has been insufficiently validated or only has limited temporal or contextual validity. Highly valued knowledge may be degraded, and new or previously undervalued knowledge become more valuable. Moreover, even if it were possible to assess the value of all individual knowledge in an organization, this valuation would still ignore the added value created through the combination of that individual knowledge and the facilitation of it through social and technological organizational systems. Using an IC lens, similar issues can be raised with respect to IC components whose value may fluctuate because of internal or external developments. It is interesting to note that even though all the components of IC may initially contribute to an organization's ability to add value, at a later stage, one or more may positively impede value creation.

Given that it has been argued that there is no extant theory underpinning IC or KM, the next section will examine the extent to which IC or KM can be managed.

8 Is Knowledge Management or Intellectual Capital Management Possible and to What Extent?

Perhaps the most germane insight that this chapter can offer to IC (and KM) researchers is that it is impossible to properly manage something, whether knowledge or IC, when its nature, quality, and value are ill-defined. This should not be taken as suggesting that firms ignore attempts to improve the quality and value of their individual and organizational knowledge through better network/community structures, procedures, routines, artifacts, and supporting technologies. However, the notion that all aspects of organizational knowledge can be accurately valued and managed is to trust too much in rationalism.

Spender (1996) tantalizingly refers to his concern that it is not the presence of knowledge that is to be managed, it is its absence. Since firms are often insufficiently active in reviewing what they think they know, it is important to systematically revise knowledge and remove inaccurate and false knowledge. Spender (1996) also suggests organizations should look to the future to identify knowledge needed for operational and strategic planning, especially knowledge that is not currently possessed. One of the best ways to do this is to recruit individuals who have general organizational knowledge and specific domain knowledge (when it can be identified). If one element is missing, provide them with an environment which proactively encourages them to acquire the skills and knowledge needed by them (and potentially their coworkers), to be successful. A proactive environment will be one that combines appropriate values, rewards, and infrastructure for them to be successful. Increasingly they should become better judges of what skills to develop and what knowledge to acquire and share. It should also be noted that the culture should be one in which continual questioning is encouraged because, as noted above, organizational knowledge needs to be recognized as being uncertain, revisable, and even potentially false.

9 Wherefore IC Research and Practice?

Given the above concerns, it is important to consider some productive paths that IC research and practice might take. First, value has been a recurring theme throughout this chapter. From a theoretical perspective, there needs to be a more grounded investigation of how IC adds value in a measurable way. Although there has been relatively little progress in incorporating IC into different Theories of the Firm, this should not result in the abandonment of such attempts. Although, through the years, much empirical research has shown that IC (and its components) contribute to firm performance and the creation of value, little is known of how. Identifying ways in which IC may be further articulated, as well as the manner in which it can contribute to the creation of value and the achievement of competitive advantage, would be an indispensable theoretical and practical contribution. Without this knowledge, the practical advice given to firms about where to concentrate their IC investments will tend to remain very general.

Thoughtful proposals have been made concerning the futurizing of IC theory (e.g., Kianto et al., 2023). These proposals both identify and argue cogently with respect to the impact of several key trends such as digitalization, gig work, remote work, and others on IC theory (and practice). However, without an articulated theory of value, the extent and importance of these impacts are difficult to determine. This does not necessarily mean that valuable insights may be available for practitioners, but it does limit the ability to evaluate different investments in IC or articulate how the return on such investments can be improved.

Although this chapter has primarily focused on economic theories, this does not exclude the incorporation of theories that approach value from a non-economic perspective. However, these theories are even less developed from an IC perspective than existing economic theories.

A note of humility is appropriate here. As indicated above, the value of knowledge, even in a scientific context, is often fluid and difficult to define. Perhaps the challenges facing the development of an IC theory may make such development essentially unattainable. However, more nuanced explanations of how IC contributes to creating value have merit and can lead to extended inquiry and more focused insights into IC and its function in the creation of organizational creation of value.

10 Conclusion

Based on the concerns noted above, the overall conclusion is that it may not be possible, nor desirable, to develop a Theory of the Firm in the context of IC (or KM). Perhaps the most compelling reason is that the ability of any theory to explain and predict the interactions of knowledge with organizations and markets, as well as the effect on organizational value, is likely to be remarkably limited.

As previously suggested, given a variety of conceptual and pragmatic challenges, it is difficult to identify where knowledge "fits" into either the Transaction Cost Theory of the Firm, the Resource-Based Theory of the Firm, or the Knowledge-Based Theory of the Firm. It should also be noted that currently there does not appear to be another sufficiently mature Theory of the Firm, in particular, or theory of organization, in general, that addresses knowledge in a sufficiently rich way as to be of use in developing a foundational IC theory. It is also noted that although these "theories" have been used as justification that knowledge is important and valuable there is little pragmatic or practical guidance that organizations can use to identify or value their knowledge. Identifying which current knowledge is valuable for present performance is critical. Even more so is having the ability to identify what knowledge will be valuable in the future. These tasks are still beyond the capability of any extant Theory of the Firm and perhaps out of reach of any theory.

References

Ackerlof, G. A. (1970). The market for lemons. *Quarterly Journal of Economics, 84*, 488–500.

Azamfirei, L. (2016). Knowledge is power. *The Journal of Critical Care Medicine, 2*(2), 65–66.

Barney, J. B. (2001). Is the resource-based "View" a useful perspective for strategic management research? *Academy of Management Review, 26*(1).

Boisot, M. H. (1998). *Knowledge assets: Securing competitive advantage in the information economy*. Oxford University Press.

Bontis, N. (1996). There's a price on your head: Managing intellectual capital strategically. *Business Quarterly, 60*(4), 40–78.

Bontis, N. (1998). Intellectual capital: An exploratory study that develops measures and models. *Management Decision, 36*(2), 63–76.

Bontis, N. (2000). *Managing organizational knowledge by diagnosing intellectual capital. Knowledge management: Classic and contemporary works*. MIT Press.

Bontis, N., Crossan, M. M., & Hulland, J. (2002). Managing an organizational learning system by aligning stocks and flows. *Journal of Management Studies, 39*(4), 437–469. https://doi.org/10.1111/1467-6486.t01-1-00299

Brooking, A. (1997). *Intellectual capital: Core assets for the third millennium enterprise*. International Thomson Business Press.

Choo, C. W. (2006). *The knowing organization: How organizations use information to construct meaning, create knowledge, and make decisions* (2nd ed.). Oxford University Press.

Coase, R. H. (1937). "The Nature of the Firm," *Economica*, pp 386–405. Reprinted in Coase, R. H. 1988. The firm, the market and the law. Chicago University Press, pp 55–57. 1946.

Edvinsson, L., & Malone, M. S. (1997). *Intellectual capital: Realizing your company's true value by finding its hidden brainpower* (1st ed.). HarperBusiness.

Evans, M. M., Dalkir, K., & Bidian, C. (2014). A holistic view of the knowledge life cycle: The knowledge management cycle (KMC) model. *Electronic Journal of Knowledge Management, 12*(2), 85–97.

Frissen, I., Evans, M. M., & Wensley, A. K. P. (2019, September). How to measure tacit knowledge: Lessons from 35 years of psychological research. In *Proceedings of the 20th European conference on knowledge management (ECKM 2019)* (pp. 344–351). Academic Conferences and Publishing International.

Gorga, E. (2007). Knowledge inputs, legal institutions and firm structure: Towards a knowledge-based theory of the firm. *Northwestern University Law Review, 101*(3), 1123–1206.

Kianto, A., Cabrilo, S., & Hussinki, H. (2023). Futurizing intellectual capital theory to uncover pertinent and unexplored horizons. In C. Bratianu, M. Handzic, & E. Bolisani (Eds.), *The future of knowledge management* (pp. 67–90). Springer Nature.

Kogurt, B., & Zander, U. (1992). Knowledge of the firm, combinative capabilities, and the replication of technology. *Organization Science, 3*(2), 383–397.

Kogurt, B., & Zander, U. (1996). What firms do? Coordination, identity and learning. *Organization Science, 7*(5) September-October 1996.

Lambe, P. (2023). Principles of knowledge auditing. *MIT Press, 2023.*

Martín-de-Castro, G., Delgado-Verde, M., López-Sáez, P., & Navas-López, J. E. (2011). Towards 'an intellectual capital-based view of the firm': Origins and nature. *Journal of Business Ethics, 98*, 649–662.

McElroy, M. W. (2003). *The new knowledge management: Complexity, learning, and sustainable innovation*. KMCI Press; Butterworth-Heinemann.

Nahapiet, J., & Ghoshal, S. (1998). Social capital, intellectual capital, and the organizational advantage. *Academy of Management Review, 23*, 242–266.

Polanyi, M. (1966). *The tacit dimension* (1st ed.). Doubleday and Company.

Roos, G., & Roos, J. (1997). Measuring your companies intellectual performace. *Long Range Planning, 30*(3), 413–426.

Spender, J. C. (1996). Making knowledge the basis of a dynamic theory of the firm. *Strategic Management Journal, 17*(52) Winter Special Issue, 45–62.

Spender, J. C., & Grant, R. K. (1996). Knowledge and the firm. Special issue. *Strategic Management Journal, 17*(52) Winter 1996.

Stewart, T. A. (1997). *Intellectual capital: The new wealth of organizations*. Bantam Doubleday Dell Publishing Group.

Sullivan, P. H. (1998). *Profiting from intellectual capital: Extracting value from innovation (Ser. Intellectual property series)*. Wiley.

Sveiby, K. E. (1997). *The new organizational wealth: Managing and measuring knowledge-based assets*. Berrett-Koehler Publishers.

Tsoukas, H. (2005a). What is organizational knowledge? In H. Tsoukas (Ed.), *Complex knowledge: Studies in organizational epistemology*. Oxford University Press.

Tsoukas, H. (2005b). Do we really understand tacit knowledge? In H. Tsoukas (Ed.), *Complex knowledge: Studies in organizational epistemology*. Oxford University Press.

van den Berg, H. A. (2013). Three shapes of organizational knowledge. *Journal of Knowledge Management, 17*(2), 159.

Williamson, O. E. (1991). Comparative economic organization: The analysis of discrete structural alternatives. *Administrative Science Quarterly, 36*(2), 269–296.

Wiig, K. M. (1993). *Knowledge management foundations: Thinking about thinking: How people and organizations create, represent, and use knowledge*. Schema Press.

Anthony K.P. Wensley is an Emeritus Associate Professor at the University of Toronto, Canada. He was the Founding Director of the Institute of Communication, Culture, Information and Technology at the University of Toronto and a faculty member of the Department of Management and the Rotman School of Business at the University of Toronto. He has published widely in the fields of Knowledge Management, Information Systems and Intellectual Property. He is active in a wide variety of academic organizations including IAKM, IEEE, and ACM. He is also has been the Executive Editor of the Wiley journal *Knowledge and Process Management* (KPM) for over 25 years.

M. Max Evans is an Associate Professor at the School of Information Studies at McGill University in Montréal, Canada. His research focuses on organizational information and knowledge management, with a specific interest in affective, cognitive, social, and technological factors influencing information and knowledge sharing; interpersonal and organizational trust; and the development of emotional intelligence. Max is the co-founder of the Knowah Research Lab on human knowledge sharing, an Associate Editor with Knowledge and Process Management (Wiley), and a member of several academic associations including IAKM, CIRMMT, AGE-WELL, and Responsible AI.

Futurizing Intellectual Capital: New Economic Models and the Venue of AI Requests for an Update

Günter Koch

Abstract

The purpose of this paper is to open a series of discourse issues on the future of Intellectual Capital Reporting (ICR) modeling and how these would involve new aspects of what intellectual capital models in the future shall be conceived. It does, however, not (yet) provide a new ICR scheme.

Three economic reference models will be lined out to open the discussion: (1) the Degrowth (or post-growth) economy, (2) the Solidarity Economy, and (3) the Economy for the Common Good (ECG). Since the change towards a new economic model is argued to be near impossible under current circumstances, the governing capitalistic model—although a need for its replacement is claimed—will be assumed for further discourse in this paper.

The core subject then is on the insight that nature and its treatment, e.g. its regeneration, are accountable in the traditional sense, and this naturally has an impact on the modeling of future Intellectual Capital Reports.

A further new paradigmatic definition of the term "intellectual capital" is discovered when this capital is materialized in the form of artificially generated intelligent (AI) statements. The point is being made by debating the distinction between intellectual capital produced by humans from the intellectual capital produced by intelligent machines.

G. Koch (✉)
Humboldt Cosmos Multiversity, Tenerife, Spain

Humboldt Cosmos Multiversity, Vienna, Austria

A. Kianto et al. (eds.), *Futurizing Intellectual Capital*, Knowledge Management and Organizational Learning 15, https://doi.org/10.1007/978-3-031-80197-6_14

1 Introduction: Alternative Economic Models to Address the Sustainability Crisis

To lay the grounds, this contribution starts with a discussion of three economic forms that see themselves as an alternative to the prevailing market-based capitalist economic system: (1) the Degrowth (or post-growth) economy, (2) the Solidarity Economy, and (3) the Economy for the Common Good (ECG). In contrast to the capitalist economic system, these three approaches share the view that the market-based capitalist economic system does more harm than good to human life, coexistence, and its foundations and must therefore be reorganized according to the conviction of representatives of these three alternative models. A special aspect that will be introduced here is the question of the extent to which alternative economic models offer new possibilities for valuing intellectual capital beyond the capitalist reference system.

Given the major challenge of saving the planet's climate, the unresolved question is identified to remain: Is the capitalistic model sufficient to tackle the climate crisis through a holistic, if not total, approach? And what does a shift towards alternative models mean for the definition of "intellectual capital"? The question that arises from such a critical consideration is whether the idea of intellectual property valued in monetary terms and owned by private owners can be maintained.

In the search for alternative economic models that are better suited to the requirements of our time, namely, the management of a series of so-called "grand challenges"—first and foremost the climate catastrophe—one primarily encounters proposals that aim to supplement existing models with dimensions that, like the underlying economic parameters, reflect a characterization of an economic unit based on financial data—whether macro- or microeconomic. If we look at the historical discussion of the modeling of intellectual capital as published by the pioneers of such models more than 20 years ago (RICARDIS, 2006), it becomes apparent that their authors assumed, without questioning the existing and practiced models in the economy at the time, that it was merely a matter of adding additional dimensions of observation.

Since then, macroeconomists have set out to propose new economic models with the claim that these new dimensions can ultimately be used to describe economic activity. Three of these approaches, which are characterized by the fact that they have found a large number of supporters and promoters, also politically, will be presented here as examples to set the discourse space:

1. *The Degrowth (or post-growth economy)*
2. *The Solidarity Economy*
3. *The Economy for the Common Good (ECG)*

1.1 The Degrowth (or Post Growth Economy)

This economic movement involves challenging the conventional paradigm of continuous economic growth as a necessity for prosperity and well-being. Instead, proponents argue for a shift towards sustainable and equitable forms of economic organization that prioritize human well-being and ecological sustainability over GDP growth.

Key features of the Degrowth or post-growth economy include the following:

- Sustainable use of resources, emphasizing the need to live within ecological limits and promoting sustainable resource management practices to ensure the long-term viability of ecosystems and natural resources
- Reduction of consumption particularly in affluent societies, to alleviate pressure on natural resources, reduce waste, and mitigate environmental degradation
- Social equity and distributional justice, aiming to reduce inequalities within and between societies to ensure a more just and fair distribution of resources and opportunities
- Promoting localized economies and production systems to enhance community resilience, reduce dependence on global supply chains, and support local businesses and livelihoods
- Advocating for policies that prioritize well-being over economic growth, including shorter working hours, greater leisure time, and a re-evaluation of societal priorities beyond purely economic metrics
- Alternative economic metrics, i.e. proposing alternative indicators of progress and well-being "Beyond GDP", such as measures of social cohesion, environmental quality, and subjective well-being, to better capture the multifaceted dimensions of human flourishing

The key proponents of the Degrowth "economic philosophy" include Serge Latouche (Latouche, 2013), Giorgos Kallis (Kallis, 2018), and Tim Jackson (Jackson, 2009). Several institutions are profiled in doing research in this domain, which are (1) The Center for the Advancement of the Steady State Economy (CASSE) based in the USA; (2) The International Research and Degrowth (R&D) Network, a volunteer network of scholars and activists dedicated to advancing research and advocacy on degrowth and related topics and R&D facilitates collaboration and knowledge exchange within the degrowth community (DEGROWTH); (3) parts of the European Parliament which in a conference titled "Beyond Growth" in May 2023 marked their position (Kallis et al., 2024); and (4) last but not least the World Capital Institute (WCI), which runs a discourse platform on alternative economics mainly inspired by its former president Javier Carrillo (Carillo & Koch, 2021).

1.2 The Solidarity Economy

The Solidarity Economy is an economic framework that emphasizes solidarity, cooperation, and social justice as central principles for organizing economic activities. It seeks to create an alternative to mainstream capitalist economies by prioritizing community well-being, equitable distribution of resources, and democratic decision-making. The Solidarity Economy encompasses a diverse range of practices and initiatives, including cooperatives, community currencies, fair trade networks, social enterprises, and mutual aid organizations.

Features of the Solidarity Economy include the following:

- Cooperation and solidarity, emphasizing collaboration, mutual support, and solidarity among individuals, communities, and organizations, rather than competition and individualism
- Democratic governance, promoting participatory decision-making processes that empower stakeholders and ensure the equitable distribution of resources and benefits
- Social and environmental justice, prioritizing the needs and rights of marginalized and vulnerable groups while also addressing environmental sustainability and ecological resilience
- Equitable distribution, fostering economic practices that aim to reduce inequalities and ensure fair access to resources, opportunities, and benefits for all members of society
- Encouraging sustainable production and consumption patterns that respect ecological limits and promote environmental stewardship
- Supporting local economies and self-reliant communities to enhance resilience, reduce dependence on external actors, and promote cultural diversity

Promoters of the Solidarity Economy include a diverse array of individuals, organizations, and movements spanning the globe. These are some of the key promoters and organizations associated with the Solidarity Economy movement including:

- The Solidarity Economy Network (SEN), active in the USA.
- The Intercontinental Network for the Promotion of Social Solidarity Economy (RIPESS) which facilitates collaboration, knowledge exchange, and advocacy among solidarity economy practitioners worldwide
- The UN's Inter-Agency Task Force on Social and Solidarity Economy (UNTFSSE).
- Cooperative movements, such as the Mondragon Corporation in Spain (Mondragon) or in the Emilia Romagna region in Italy (Emilia Romagna).

1.3 The Economy for the Common Good (ECG)

The essence of the concept of the "Economy for the Common Good" (ECG) revolves around redefining the goals and metrics of economic activity to prioritize the well-being of people and the planet over mere financial profit. The Economy for the Common Good proposes a radical shift in economic thinking and practice towards a more ethical and sustainable framework.

Members of the World Capital Institute (WCI) and The New Club of Paris (NCP) such as Günter Koch (Koch & Tim Goydke, 2019) or José Carlos Ramos (Ramos) engaged in the scientific foundations of the Economy for the Common Good by discussing the following concepts; a key promoter is the founder of the European movement of the Economy for the Common Good, Christian Felber (Felber, 2019):

- The "Common Good Balance Sheet" is not a balance sheet after its classical definition, but rather than a model for reporting on a company's contributions to societal well-being, environmental sustainability, social justice, and democratic participation. This is done through the creation of a Common Good Balance Sheet, which evaluates a company's impact on various social and environmental factors.
- The ECG advocates for transforming the market economy into one that is guided by ethical principles, such as solidarity, fairness, sustainability, and respect for human rights. This entails fostering cooperation and collaboration among businesses, government, civil society, and citizens to advance common goals.
- ECG proposes legal and institutional reforms to incentivize ethical behaviour and discourage practices that harm the common good. This may include changes to taxation, corporate governance, and related regulations.

Many prominent scientists, amongst them Nobel Prize winners, have worked on this subject, as are:

- Elinor Ostrom, who was awarded the Nobel Memorial Prize in Economic Sciences for her "Analysis of Economic Governance", especially "The Commons" (Ostrom, 1990).
- Jean Tirole, Professor of Economics at the Toulouse Capitol University. In 2014, he received the Nobel Memorial Prize in Economic Sciences for his analysis of market power and regulation (Tirole, 2019).
- Mariana Mazzucato, Professor at University College London where she is the founding director of the UCL Institute for Innovation and Public Purpose (IIPP). One of her latest publications has the title "Governing the Economics of the Common Good—From Correcting Market Failures to Shaping Collective Goals" (Mazzucato, 2023).
- Jean Gadrey, a French economist known for his work on alternative economic paradigms and social progress indicators. He has engaged with the ECG concept and its implications for rethinking economic priorities (Gadrey, 2002).

- Lorenzo Firamonti who has explored alternative measures of progress and well-being, aligning with the principles of the ECG movement in his work on "gross national happiness" and beyond GDP indicators (Fioramonti, 2017).
- Katherine Trebeck and Jeremy Williams, who have focused on issues of sustainability, inequality, and alternative economic models, including the ECG framework. Their book *The Economics of Arrival* discusses the need for rethinking economic growth paradigms (Trebeck & Williams, 2019).
- Kate Raworth, known for her work on "Doughnut Economics", her ideas overlap with the principles of the Economy for the Common Good, particularly in advocating for a more holistic approach to economic thinking that considers social and environmental factors (Raworth, 2018).

1.4 The Conclusion from the Discussion on Alternative Economic Models

The current discussion presented here as an example to describe both the macro- and microeconomic alternatives to the currently prevailing, namely, capitalist economic model, shows that all of these "new" models are ultimately based on ethics-based political convictions, the aim of which is to bring about a major social transformation—possibly in line with Karl Polanyi's idea of a "Great Transformation" (Polanyi, 1944)—aimed at saving our planet.

The problem, however, is that the "currently prevailing economic model", as the author calls it, is so cemented in all its legal, financial, and, above all, monetary policy determinations that it would take an asteroid impact of the kind that occurred during the Mesozoic era and thus the beginning of the Palaeozoic era to fundamentally change this stable edifice. To describe it impressively according to Mark Fisher's theory of "capitalist realism" (Fisher, 2009) or—complementary—"socialist realism", the statement he adopted from Frederic Jameson (Jameson, 2014) or Slavoj Žižiek (Žižiek, 2014) should be quoted here, which says: "It is easier to imagine an end to the world than an end to capitalism".

- Based on this insight, the further explanations in this paper assume that to model a future ecological, i.e. sustainable economy geared towards the regeneration of nature, it is actually proposed to pursue the approach that existing economic models and thus also the question of how intellectual capital can be redefined will have to be answered by *expanding* existing models as introduced in the previous discussion.

2 Regulatory References to Address the Sustainability Crisis

The discussion began in the European community in 2011 with the Commission adopting its renewed strategy for Corporate Social Responsibility (CSR), which combines horizontal approaches to promote CSR and Responsible Business Conduct (RBC), with more specific approaches for individual sectors and policy areas. Following up on its strategy, the Commission published a Staff Working Document (SWD) in March 2019 which gives an overview of the Commission's and the European External Action Service's (EEAS) progress in implementing how the economy can be changed in its behaviour by its stakeholders, first and foremost companies, in such a way that the Paris climate targets (IPCC) in particular can be achieved. This has subsequently led to a veritable flood of regulatory measures, the end of which is not in sight. EFRAG (European Financial Advisory Group) has made a name for itself as the EU Commission's think tank for preparing regulatory standards, having already implemented a series of draft regulations and continuing to work on corresponding proposals (EFRAG).

The European Union's already comprehensive regulatory density in terms of sustainable management, especially to achieve the climate targets, is being expanded by equally intended proposals from other supranational organizations such as the UN or the OECD and their thought leader institutions and presented in the form of standardization proposals—see the two images below, which are illustrative enough and will not be subject to further discussion here (Figs. 1 and 2).

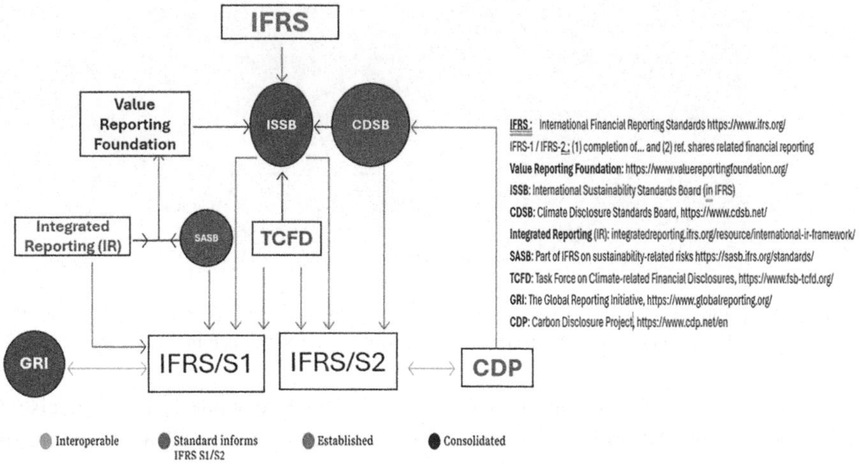

Fig. 1 Compilation from the NaWIS project (Nachhaltiges Wirtschafts-Spiel für KMUs (NaWiS 4 KMUs)), conducted in Austria under the funding of the National Funding Agency FFG (NaWiS)

Characteristic	Nature-related assessment and disclosure approaches						
	CDP disclosure system	European Sustainability Reporting Standards (ESRS)	Global Reporting Initiative (GRI) Standards	International Sustainability Standards Board (ISSB) Standards	Natural Capital Protocol	Science Based Targets Network (SBTN) target setting guidance	Taskforce on Nature-related Financial Disclosure (TNFD) framework
Type of approach	Climate and nature reporting platform	Sustainability reporting standards	Sustainability reporting standards	Standards for sustainability-related financial disclosures	Measurement and valuation framework	Guidance on target setting	Risk management and disclosure framework
Voluntary or mandatory	Voluntary	Mandatory[2]	Voluntary	Voluntary[4]	Voluntary	Voluntary	Voluntary
Coverage of nature	Climate, forests and water security questionnaires cover specific nature-related issues	Cover nature and other sustainability issues, include dedicated environmental standards	Cover nature and other sustainability issues, include topic standards on specific environmental issues	Cover nature and other sustainability issues, include dedicated climate standards	Overarching nature coverage	Overarching nature coverage	Overarching nature coverage
Status	New guidance to be released in 2024.	Expected to be in force from January 2024 for the first group of companies.	Release of revised GRI Biodiversity Standard expected in early 2024, other nature-related standards available.	ISSB Standards (IFRS S1 and IFRS S2) issued in June 2023. The CDSB Framework Application Guidance for Biodiversity-related Disclosures and Water-related Disclosures were published in 2021. The SASB Standards were last revised in June 2023.	Current version released in 2016. An Integrated Capital Protocol (replacing Natural Capital Protocol and Social and Human Capital Protocol) will be released in 2024.	First release of SBTs for nature in May 2023, next updates planned for 2024.	TNFD Framework v1.0 released in September 2023.
Target report preparers	Businesses and financial institutions	Businesses and financial institutions as specified in the EU CSRD	Businesses, financial institutions and other organizations	Businesses and financial institutions	Businesses and financial institutions	Businesses	Businesses and financial institutions
Target report users	Financial institutions/investors, public/civil society	Financial institutions/investors, businesses, governments, civil society, EU institutions	Financial institutions/investors, businesses, governments and regulators, civil society, and any other interested party	Investors, lenders and other creditors	Businesses and financial institutions	Businesses and financial institutions	Financial institutions/investors, businesses, regulators, financial service providers, public/civil society
Definition of materiality	Environmental, social and financial materiality	Environmental, social and financial materiality	Environmental and social materiality	Financial materiality	Flexible	Environmental and social materiality	Flexible
Availability of realm- or biome-specific guidance	Yes	Yes	No	No	No	Yes	Yes
Scope of sector-specific guidance	Sector-specific disclosure requirements for selected sectors	Sector-specific disclosure requirements for selected sectors	Sector-specific disclosure requirements and guidance for selected sectors	Sector-specific guidance for all sectors	Sector-specific guidance for selected sectors	Selected sector-specific guidance	Sector-specific guidance and disclosure requirements for selected sectors
Coverage of value chain	Direct operations, upstream and some downstream	Direct operations, upstream and downstream	Direct operations and upstream and downstream (downstream is optional in the GRI Biodiversity Standard)	Direct operations, upstream and downstream	Direct operations, upstream and downstream	Direct operations and upstream (downstream may be covered in future releases)	Direct operations, upstream and downstream
Use of location information in the assessment	Yes	Yes	Yes	Yes	Flexible – tailored to the choice of the business	Yes	Yes
Assessment of business dependencies and impacts on nature	Both dependencies and impacts	Both dependencies and impacts	Impacts, limited assessment of dependencies	Both dependencies and impacts	Both dependencies and impacts	Impacts only (dependencies may be covered in the future)	Both dependencies and impacts
Disclosure on business dependencies and impacts on nature	Both dependencies and impacts	Both dependencies and impacts	Impacts only	Both dependencies and impacts (subject to financial materiality, except for certain climate impacts)	Disclosure optional	Impacts only (dependencies may be covered in the future)	Both dependencies and impacts
Assessment of nature-related risks and opportunities	Both risks and opportunities	Both risks and opportunities	Not covered	Both risks and opportunities	Both risks and opportunities	Not covered	Both risks and opportunities
Disclosure on nature-related risks and opportunities	Both risks and opportunities	Both risks and opportunities	Not covered	Both risks and opportunities	Disclosure optional	Not covered	Both risks and opportunities
Disclosure of nature-related targets	Yes	Yes	Yes	Yes	Disclosure optional	Yes	Yes
Engagement with rights-holders and relevant stakeholders required/recommended	Yes	Yes	Yes	Yes	Yes	Yes	Yes

Fig. 2 Adoption from the NaWIS project report (Nachhaltiges Wirtschafts-Spiel für KMUs (NaWiS 4 KMUs)), conducted in Austria under the funding of the National Funding Agency (NaWiS)

Concerning these many and varied regulatory processes underlying the decision of the EU Commission, the framework of its so-called Green Deal, a dictum of fundamental importance for the discussion here is that the model it propagates is based on two essentials, namely, "dual materiality".

The concept of "dual materiality" is central to the European Commission's Green Deal Model (GreenDeal), particularly in the context of required sustainability reporting and corporate accountability. Dual materiality recognizes that businesses have a responsibility not only to their financial stakeholders but also to society and the environment. It emphasizes the interconnectedness of financial performance (financial materiality) and environmental, social, and governance (ESG) factors (non-financial materiality). Thus, the two complementary materialities are as follows:

1. *Financial materiality*, which refers to the traditional focus on financial performance and the impact of economic activities on a company's bottom line. Financial materiality considers factors such as revenue, profits, costs, and shareholder value. It is concerned with the financial risks and opportunities that affect the company's ability to create value for its investors.
2. *Non-financial materiality*. This encompasses environmental, social, and governance (ESG) factors that are relevant to a company's long-term sustainability and societal impact. Non-financial materiality includes considerations such as carbon emissions, resource usage, labour practices, human rights, diversity, community relations, and corporate governance.

The two materialities are claimed to complement each other in several ways:

- *Interdependence*. Both financial and non-financial performances are interconnected, e.g. poor environmental practices can lead to financial risks such as regulatory fines, supply chain disruptions, or reputational damage. Conversely, strong ESG performance can enhance financial performance by improving operational efficiency, reducing costs, attracting investment, and enhancing brand reputation.
- *Long-term value creation*, i.e. sustainable value creation requires consideration of both financial and non-financial factors. By integrating ESG considerations into business strategies and decision-making processes, companies can better manage risks, seize opportunities, and create long-term value for all stakeholders.
- *Transparency and accountability*: companies are encouraged to provide transparent and comprehensive reporting on both financial and non-financial performance. This enhances accountability to investors, regulators, customers, employees, and the broader society, fostering trust and credibility.
- *Fulfilling regulatory compliance and standards*: related frameworks and reporting standards are increasingly incorporating dual materiality principles, requiring companies to disclose both financial and non-financial information. This reflects the growing recognition of the importance of ESG factors in assessing a company's overall performance and impact.

The key finding for the axiom on which this paper is based, namely, that every economic model of our time, however sophisticated, is based on the dominant capitalist model, inevitably means that any new and future modeling of non-financial aspects—and this includes all future models of Intellectual Capital Reporting—must ultimately be adapted as an extension of the capitalist, i.e. financially dominated, basic model.

3 The Basis for a Renewed Intellectual Capital Reporting Model: The Accounting Recognition of Externalities

Externalities are the positive or negative effects of economic activities that are not reflected in the accounting and w.r.t. market participation in the prices of goods or services being traded. They can affect parties not directly involved in the transaction and in today's traditional accounting systems are usually overlooked. Examples of externalities that businesses may need to account for include carbon emissions, air and water pollution, habitat destruction, social inequality, labour exploitation, and public health impacts. By capturing these externalities in their accounting systems, businesses can better understand their true costs and benefits, leading to more sustainable and responsible decision-making.

Capturing externalities in a business accounting system involves identifying, quantifying, and incorporating these impacts into financial reporting and decision-making processes. The tough challenge here is how to internalize externalities, which need external costs (negative externalities) to be assigned to a monetary value to them and thereby include them as part of the company's cost structure. For example, costs associated with pollution control measures or compensation for environmental damage can be included in the company's expenses. In contrast, positive externalities, such as social or environmental benefits generated by the company's activities, can be recognized and valued as part of the company's assets or revenues. This may involve recognizing the value of ecosystem services, community development initiatives, or sustainable product innovations. Incorporating externalities into accounting systems enables companies to identify and manage potential risks associated with their operations, such as regulatory non-compliance, reputational damage, or supply chain disruptions. Finally, companies will enhance transparency and accountability by reporting on their externalities in sustainability reports, annual filings, or integrated reporting frameworks which the Intellectual Capital Report is a core of. This provides stakeholders with a comprehensive understanding of the company's impacts and performance beyond financial metrics.

In addition to the many aspects to be considered in the course of updating and thus enriching reporting systems, including the Intellectual Capital Report (ICR) of an organization, one question is of central importance, namely, how it should not only be possible to provoke sustainable management through various methods and criteria extensions, e.g. through the circular economy, but also how the consumption of our planet's natural resources and the associated environmental effects can be reversed. In other words, the central challenge is how we can give back to nature what we have previously and continuously taken from it. Or, to put it even more clearly, how can nature be regenerated?

Based on the previously introduced thesis that the capitalist economic model is currently irrevocable, the question of how to regenerate nature can only be answered logically by assigning an economic value to nature as an externality that has hitherto been viewed in this way. This attempt is currently being made with the creation of a new ISO standard with the planned number 14054 (ISO 14054). From the introductory text, the objective can be concluded (quote): "Natural capital accounting is a systematic way of collating financial, socio-economic and environmental information about an organization's impacts and dependencies on nature and presenting it in formats that are familiar to decision-makers. Such accounts enable organizations to see all the information in one place, think about their impacts and dependencies in a holistic way, and prioritize 'material impacts and dependencies'...There are two key natural capital accounting outputs prescribed – each with supporting schedules: a) a Natural Capital Balance Sheet (NCBS) shows an organization's dependency on natural capital assets. It mimics a financial balance sheet so far as it shows the (natural capital) asset values and (natural capital maintenance) liabilities... An NCBS documents the asset values to the organization and the rest of the society, when financial accounts only show the former... b) a Natural Capital Income Statement (NCIS) shows the organization's impacts on natural capital assets. It mimics a financial income statement so far as it shows the positive impacts (the enhancements) and negative ones (degradations). Like its financial counterpart, NCIS looks at the past performance during the financial year to date".

Thus, Natural Capital Accounting (NCA) as defined in ISO 14054 involves incorporating the value of natural resources and environmental impacts into the financial accounting of companies. This approach recognizes the financial implications of environmental dependencies and impacts, leading to more comprehensive balance sheets. Here are the concrete financial and non-financial items that are expected to be included in the balance sheet under NCA:

Financial Items

1. Natural resource assets:
   - Renewable resources: The value of renewable resources such as forests, fisheries, and agricultural land
   - Non-renewable resources: The value of non-renewable resources like minerals, oil, and gas reserves
2. Environmental liabilities:
   - Restoration costs: Estimated costs for the restoration of damaged ecosystems or degraded land
   - Decommissioning costs: Costs associated with decommissioning operations, such as closing mines or dismantling oil rigs
3. Environmental provisions:
   - Provisions for pollution control: Future costs for pollution control measures, such as waste management and emission reduction technologies
   - Compliance costs: Expected costs for compliance with environmental regulations and standards
4. Revenue from ecosystem services:
   - Carbon credits: Revenue from selling carbon credits or participating in carbon trading schemes
   - Payments for ecosystem services (PES): Income from schemes where companies are paid for conserving or enhancing ecosystem services

Non-financial Items

5. Environmental impact metrics:
   - Carbon footprint: Quantitative data on the company's greenhouse gas emissions
   - Water usage: Metrics on water consumption and management practices
   - Biodiversity impact: Data on the impact of operations on local biodiversity and ecosystems
6. Resource use efficiency:
   - Energy efficiency: Metrics on energy consumption and efficiency improvements
   - Material use: Data on the use of raw materials and efforts to minimize waste and enhance recycling
7. Ecosystem condition and trends:
   - Habitat condition: Information on the condition and trends of habitats affected by the balance author's operations
   - Species populations: Data on the populations of key species within affected ecosystems
8. Sustainability indicators:
   - Sustainability certifications: Achievements in obtaining sustainability certifications such as ISO 14001 or FSC (Forest Stewardship Council)
   - Environmental performance indexes: Ratings and scores from environmental performance indexes or assessments
9. Stakeholder engagement:
   - Community impact reports: Information on the social and environmental impacts on local communities
   - Partnerships and initiatives: Details of partnerships with environmental organizations and participation in sustainability initiatives

By integrating these new financial and non-financial items, companies in the future will much better manage their environmental impacts, dependencies, and associated risks, leading to more sustainable business practices and improved long-term financial performance.

In the context of Natural Capital Accounting (NCA) as defined in ISO 14054, several non-financial items included in the balance sheet are relevant to be included and transferred to an Intellectual Capital Report (ICR). These items reflect the intangible assets related to environmental sustainability and corporate responsibility, which are critical for the intellectual capital. Here are the non-financial items suggested to be included in a future ICR. Referring to the classical model structure of an ICR in its classical version defining the three major categories which are human, structural, and relational capital, these may be the criteria added to the classical ICR model (if not already included):

1. *Human capital:*
   - Employee expertise and training: Knowledge and skills of employees in implementing and managing environmental sustainability practices

   - Leadership in sustainability: The strategic vision and leadership demonstrated in sustainability initiatives
2. *Structural capital:*
   - Processes and systems: Internal processes, systems, and technologies developed for environmental management and resource efficiency
   - Innovation and R&D: Research and development efforts focused on sustainable technologies and practices
3. *Relational capital:*
   - Stakeholder relationships: Relationships with environmental organizations, regulatory bodies, and local communities
   - Reputation and brand: The company's reputation and brand value derived from its sustainability practices and achievements

By incorporating these non-financial items into their Intellectual Capital Report, companies can much better communicate their intangible assets related to sustainability, which are crucial for long-term value creation and competitive advantage.

- One conclusion for any redesign of an Intellectual Capital Report must be that the dimensions to be considered in becoming part of a new ICR model must inevitably reflect the discussion of how to integrate natural capital and its restoration into it. At this point, one could argue that nature, conceived as capital, has a material and thus a tangible quality, while intellectual capital is characterized precisely by the fact that it is immaterial and intangible. However, this position cannot be upheld in an age in which digitalization means that virtually every tangible object can be understood also by being represented as a "digital twin". The thesis that introduces the following section is that models of intellectual capital include virtually all human-generated intellectual products, including the construct of natural capital, within the scope of intellectual capital. The concluding question then arises from the discussion of what is currently the hottest topic, namely, whether and how knowledge generated by machines, i.e. by artificial intelligence, should be subject to capture and evaluation by an intellectual capital model as well.

4 Finally: A Little Discourse on Intellectual Capital Assets Created by an Artificial Intelligence

Asking ChatGPT (ChatGPT) about how it would evaluate the contribution being produced by an Artificial Intelligence System, the answer was: "The value of an AI-generated object that qualifies as intellectual capital can be expressed in non-monetary terms using various criteria that extend beyond capitalistic metrics. Intellectual capital encompasses intangible assets that contribute to an organization's value, innovation, and competitive advantage, and its evaluation can consider non-financial dimensions".

As we have learned in the previous sections, particularly from the discussion of "double materiality", the two dimensions, i.e. the financial capitalist and the non-financial non-capitalist, are interdependent. Thinking radically from the perspective of the capitalist, the assumption that hitherto believed external or non-financial objects cannot be monetized is invalid in the long run. With this radical approach, it could be argued that ultimately every object, even external objects that can be traded and priced in the corporate world, has a measurable (financial) value.

For an Intellectual Capital Report, which ultimately reflects the knowledge, expertise, and performance potential of an organization, the quasi-non-financial arguments for involving results from artificial intelligence-produced propositions could be:

- Any AI-generated object, i.e. a result from, e.g. a generative artificial invention process, needs to be evaluated, if and how it contributes to an organization's intellectual advancement, i.e. its knowledge creation, absorption, and increase in innovation potential.
- Also such results must be analysed if they align with an organization's vision, mission, strategic objectives, and company values, especially conforming to the long-term commitments to comply with Sustainable Development Goals.
- Shorter term, any AI-produced asset must prove its positive impact on society and the environment, i.e. to what extent it addresses positive societal challenges, the application of ethical practices, minimizing negative environmental footprints, and similar.
- Another test shall be if and how an AI-generated object will contribute to building and maintaining positive relationships with stakeholders, including employees, customers, suppliers, and communities. Consider its role in enhancing trust, collaboration, and mutual value creation.
- A further evaluation must be done if the AI-generated object aligns with and reinforces the culture of the organization and its values, ethics, and principles, such as diversity, transparency, and integrity.
- Another aspect of checking on an AI-generated object's value would be identifying its role in facilitating learning, skill development, and professional growth within the organization and its impact on enhancing employees' capabilities, knowledge sharing, and collaborative problem-solving.
- An AI-generated object to become included in an ICR may be checked if it contributes to the organization's reputation, brand equity, and market positioning. Regarding its customers, the question would be if the AI object will help to build trust, credibility, customer loyalty, and general positive perception among its stakeholders.

5 To Pull the Loose Ends Together

This article is intended to address the different new aspects that need to be considered for the design of new models for Intellectual Capital Reporting.

The discourse extends to which non-financial aspects outweigh classical financial criteria in terms of their relevance for the valuation of companies. The founding fathers of the New Club of Paris (NCP) already discussed this insight more than 25 years ago concerning the valuation of an organization's intellectual capital, but even then, in two essentially distinguishable directions—capitalist and non-capitalist—the first one also associated with the claim of intellectual property, whereas the second favours the freedom of open access. During that historic founding period, the famous "Stiglitz-Sen-Fitoussi Report" (Stiglitz et al., 2008) fueled the discussion if and how the performance of an economy can be measured "beyond the GDP" metric.

Taking the prevailing capitalist model as an accepted point of reference, one approach to defining what is capital (and therefore an organization's intellectual capital) can be by extending the definition beyond the historic financial definition. Thus the current major concerns of saving the planet by tackling sustainability and regeneration measures can also be appropriately modeled by defining "natural capital" and capturing it in accounting, as is currently being done, for example, in a new accounting framework in the preparation of a new ISO standard 14054 (ISO 14054) (quoting from the introductory text: "Natural capital accounting is a systematic way of collating financial, socio-economic and environmental information about an organization's impacts and dependencies on nature and presenting it in formats that are familiar to decision-makers").

In essence, these are the new insights gained from this discussion:

1. Economic models for describing the realities of our economic status beyond the predominant capitalistic system, as discussed currently, are either incomplete or unrealistic to implement, and thus elements constituting intellectual capital are simply extensions including new criteria of relevance for the management for sustainability and regeneration.
2. Non-financial models and financial ones applying to the same object are interdependent. In the course of gaining new insights through science on the nature of the nature we are living within, metrification of so far non-measurable characteristics will continue and become more and more sophisticated, thereby making it possible to map so far non-financial criteria to eventually receive a financial, i.e. economic value. Thus, externalities and so far non-quantifiable issues will be incorporated sooner or later in integrated reporting systems.
3. The basic insight through the classes of economists being discussed here is nature is accountable!

4. A surplus discussion is on objects and statements being generated by an "AI intelligence", and being subjects of the business economy reporting of enterprises for sure will become part of the intellectual capital stock of an organization if such artificially generated statements are authorized by checking them against the agreed ethical standards as, e.g. discussed by the community engaged in "Digital Humanism" (Werthner et al., 2024), as well as against principles and values of the organization authorizing AI-generated statements.
5. Finally: The discussion conducted here is meant to stimulate ideas on a new ICR model but, however, is not providing such a model yet. However, the elements already listed in this article can serve as a starting point for the design of new ICR models (and standards).

References

Carrillo, F. J., & Koch, G. (2021). *Knowledge for the anthropocene*. Edward Elgar Publishing Ltd.

Felber, C. (2019). *Change everything: Creating an economy for the common good*. Zed Books Ltd.

Fioramonti, L. (2017). *Wellbeing economy: Success in a world without growth*. Pan Macmillan South Africa.

Fisher, M. (2009). *Capitalist realism: Is there no alternative?* Zero Books Publisher.

Gadrey, J. (2002). New economy, New Myth. Routledge. ISBN 9780415301428.

Jackson, T. (2009). *Prosperity without growth*. Routledge—Taylor & Francis Group.

Jameson, F. (2014). *Representing 'Capital': A reading of volume one*. Verso Books.

Kallis, G. (2018). *Degrowth (economy: Key ideas)*. Agenda Publishing. ISBN-10:1911116800.

Kallis, G., Mastini, R., & Zografos, C. (2024). Perceptions of degrowth in the European Parliament. *Nat Sustain, 7*, 64–72. Retrieved March 2024. https://doi.org/10.1038/s41893-023-01246-x

Koch, G., & Tim Goydke, T. (2019). *Economy for the common good—a common standard for a pluralist world?* Tredition Publisher. ISBN-10:3347184319.

Latouche, S. (2013). Degrowth as a way out of the crisis. Centre de Cultura Contemporània de Barcelona. Retrieved March 2024 from https://www.cccb.org/en/multimedia/videos/serge-latouche/210803.

Mazzucato, M. (2023). *Governing the economics for the common good*. University College London, Institute for Innovation and Public Purpose. Also retrieved March 2024. https://doi.org/10.1080/17487870.2023.2280969

Ostrom, E. (1990). *Governing the commons: The evolution of institutions for collective action*. Cambridge University Press.

Polanyi. (1944). *The great transformation: The political and economic origins of our time*. Beacon Press. ISBN-10:080705643X.

Raworth, K. (2018). *Doughnut economics: Seven ways to think like a 21st-century economist*. Cornerstone Publisher. ISBN: 9781847941398.

RICARDIS—Reporting Intellectual Capital to Augment Research, Development and Innovation in SMEs Report to the Commission of a High Level Expert Group (2006). Retrieved March 2024 from https://ec.europa.eu/invest-in-research/pdf/download_en/2006-2977_web1.pdf.

Stiglitz, J.E., Sen, A., Fitoussi, J.-P. (2008). Report by the commission on the measurement of economic performance and social progress.. Retrieved March 2024 from https://www.economie.gouv.fr/files/finances/presse/dossiers_de_presse/090914mesure_perf_eco_progres_social/synthese_ang.pdf

Tirole, J. (2019). *Economics for the common good*. Princeton University Press.
Trebeck, K., & Williams, J. (2019). *The economics of arrival: Ideas for a grown-up economy policy*. Press University of Bristol.
Werthner, H., Ghezzi, C., Kramer, J., Nida-Rümelin, J., Nuseibeh, B., Prem, E., & Stanger, A. (2024). *Introduction to digital humanism—an open access textbook*. Springer. https://link.springer.com. https://doi.org/10.1007/978-3-031-45304-5
Žižiek, S. (2014). In Trouble in paradise. Penguin, UK.

Günter Koch, co-founder of the New Club of Paris, once headed the European Software Institute ESI and the Austrian Research Centers. He invented an intellectual capital model which turned into a reporting model imposed to Austrian universities. As today's Chairman of the Steering Committee of the World Capital Institute, he engages in developing alternative economics models.

The Future of Intellectual Capital in the Era of Artificial Intelligence: Analysis from the Perspective of Value Creation

Ante Pulic

Abstract

In this chapter, the future of intellectual capital (IC) is considered from several key points of view. As we are witnessing the inflation of the use of the term "capital," its origin should first be clarified. Furthermore, bearing in mind the emergence and rapid spread of AI in business, it is necessary to define its position within IC. After having a precise picture of what "capital" can be and whether AI is intellectual capital, the whole area should be placed within economic theory. Mainstream economic theory, even after more than 50 years, has not covered IC either at the macro or micro level. However, IC fits perfectly into complexity economics. Finally, in the last part of this chapter, a measurement system suitable for the knowledge-based economy and which connects the micro- and macroeconomic levels is presented.

1 Introduction

> "When you can measure what you are speaking about,
> and express it in numbers, you know something about it;
> But when you cannot measure it,
> When you cannot express it in numbers,
> Your knowledge is of a meager and unsatisfactory kind."
> **Lord Kelvin,**
> Lecture to the Institution of Civil Engineers, May 3, 1883

A. Pulic (✉)
Libertas International University, Zagreb, Croatia
e-mail: apulic@libertas.hr

A. Kianto et al. (eds.), *Futurizing Intellectual Capital*, Knowledge Management and Organizational Learning 15, https://doi.org/10.1007/978-3-031-80197-6_15

It is not usual to start a serious scientific work in this way, but it seems appropriate for an introduction. My grandson, although he knows what I do, has never asked me anything related to my field of interest, that is, economics. He graduated from high school in economics. When I once asked him why he never asked for help or an explanation of a topic, he replied that there was simply no need. He solves tasks by searching the Internet; if something needs to be clarified, he simply consults with his friends via WhatsApp. He was born in 2005. At that time, there was nothing that is widely used today: neither smartphones nor tablets, nor AppStore, nor Facebook, nor TikTok, nor Dropbox, and nor Cloud. It just goes to show how fast technology is developing, and for his generation, it is quite normal to use all the tools available to them. And now generative AI has come to all this. When I compare the period in which I attended school, which is from the 1950s to the 1970s, I only remember color TV and the appearance of the IBM System/360 (I did not mention the moon landing; it had no impact on my student life). From then until the 1990s, the advent of the PC, which I bought in 1982, had a huge impact on me and after that, until 2000, the Internet and everything that came with it. In other words, more changes have taken place in the last 20 years than in the period 1950–2000.

But it seems that these, from my perspective, extra-fast changes leave no trace at all in the field of economic theory. There are still remnants of the pre-industrial and industrial era mentalities. In contrast to economics, physics underwent a major transformation; new phenomena were discovered that could not be explained by Newton's laws of classical mechanics. Electromagnetism appeared at the beginning of the nineteenth century, and thermomechanics developed until the end of the nineteenth century. The theory of relativity and quantum mechanics marked the beginning of the twentieth century.

And what happens to economics during that time? As the great economist Leontieff (1951) pointed out in the 1950s, the nineteenth-century physicist James Clerk Maxwell would struggle to understand twentieth-century physics, but his contemporary, the economist John Stuart Mill, would fit in with twentieth-century economics without any difficulty. He said, "Physics, applying the method of inductive reasoning from quantitatively observed events, has moved to entirely new premises. The science of economics, in contrast, remains largely a deductive system resting upon a static set of premises, most of which were familiar to Mill and some of which date back to Adam Smith's *Wealth of Nations*." Unfortunately, the economic theory is still stuck in place. Forty years later, McCloskey (Floud and McCloskey, 1994) said: "It is in fact something of a scientific scandal that economists have not explained modern economic growth." Fourteen years later, in 2008, when the great financial crisis broke out, Her Majesty the Queen asked the London School of Economics, "Why didn't you see this coming?" Unfortunately, she did not receive an answer. "The profession didn't have a good answer because it didn't want to admit weakness" (Constable, 2016).

Although it has a short history, something similar is happening in the field of intellectual capital (IC). It started at the end of the twentieth century with a lot of hope and enthusiasm. However, in the last 20 years, i.e., approximately from 2005 to the present day, no significant progress has been made either in theory or, even more importantly, in implementation in practice. The research field is full of various studies; new types of capital have appeared, such as customer, relational, innovation, entrepreneurial, and so forth. I would even say that some authors have utopian verbal exhibitions that have nothing to do with IC and its role in value creation. And the worst thing is that very, very little of it is usable and even less applicable in everyday business.

Generally speaking, I see measurement as a major problem in the entire field of IC. Lord Kelvin is right: You can't manage something that you don't know what the result is. And this is exactly what has been happening with IC throughout this 20-year period. Therefore, in order to make a significant shift, it is necessary to do the following:

1. In order to measure something, it must be precisely defined, and the field of IC is full of vague definitions. An example can be taken of what is called 'customer capital."? It is „the value of the relationships that a company has with its customers" (Cambridge Business English Dictionary). And now the question arises: how to accurately measure the "customer capital" defined in this way? So far, in all these 20 years, there is not even close to a precise answer. It is similar to some other IC components.
2. In recent times, the term artificial intelligence (AI) has appeared, which is already used in business processes, and this trend will accelerate. However, there are almost no texts dealing with the relationship between AI and IC. So far, existing works mainly deal with AI from the point of view of intellectual property (which is only a small part of IC). That's why the emergence and spread of AI in business deserve special attention and an appropriate place in the IC structure.
3. After having a crystal clear picture of what IC is and the position of AI in it, that whole area should find a place in the economic theoretical ecosystem. The existing neoclassical economic theory does not mention knowledge and intellectual capital as key value creators, neither on a macro- nor a micro-level nor in any specific context. This is a valid reason for rethinking traditional economic theory.
4. Finally, an IC measuring model should be proposed, tested, and validated in a real business environment. "Whoever does not manage processes does not manage the company either" is the famous saying of Joseph M. Juran (1970). When all the literature is analyzed, it is difficult to find even a couple of works in which the problem of measuring the efficiency of IC in business processes (and in them creating value) is considered. Almost everything written about IC measurement has only gone down to the company level. To be able to understand how IC creates value in an organization as a whole, we need first to understand how IC contributes to value creation in business processes, which business processes make or break value in an organization and measure IC efficiency in business processes.

Only on these premises will the field of IC have a future and become a serious theory within the entire new economic theoretical ecosystem.

2 Capital and Intellectual Capital

Every banker and every commercial man
knows that there is only one kind of capital, and that is money.
Every commercial and financial transaction is based on the truth of this proposition.
Every balance sheet is made out of this well-established fact.
And yet every economist bases his teaching on
on the hypothesis that capital is not money.
Alfred Mitchell Innes (1914)

In order to be able to know what we are talking about and to be able to express it precisely, we must have a clear and accurate understanding of the key terms that appear in this paper. That is why it is necessary to first define what intellectual capital is. At the beginning, it must be noted that today there is inflation in various capitals. For example, here is a list of different capitals arranged chronologically by their origin (Hodgson, 2014):

"natural capital" (Johnson, 1909); "health capital" (Grossman, 1972); "religious capital" (Azzi & Ehrenberg, 1975); "linguistic and cultural capital" and "symbolic capital" (Bourdieu, 1977);

"reputational capital" (Veljanovski & Whelan, 1983); "social capital" (Bourdieu, 1986); "organizational capital" (Tomer, 1987); "academic capital" (Bourdieu, 1988); "cultural or consumption capital" (Becker & Murphy, 1988); "cognitive capital" (Rescher, 1989); "symbolic capital" (Bourdieu, 1990); "environmental capital" (Hartwick, 1991); "intellectual capital" (Thomas A. Stewart, 1991); "network capital" (Sik, 1994); "personal capital" (Dei Ottati, 1994; Becker, 1996); "political, social, and cultural capital" (Mouzelis, 1995); "resource capital and institutional capital" (Oliver, 1997); "spiritual capital" (Verter, 2003); "individual trust capital (relational capital)" (Castelfranchi et al., 2006); "collective trust capital" (Castelfranchi et al., 2006); "street capital" (Sandberg & Pedersen, 2009); and even "erotic capital" (Hakim, 2011).

Joseph A. Schumpeter (1954) insisted that the term *capital* should be applied to financial assets alone.

"The word capital had been part of legal and business terminology long before economists found employment for it. With the Roman jurists and their successors, it denoted the 'principal' of a loan as distinguished from interest and other accessory claims of the lender. In obvious relation to this, it later came to denote the sums of money or their equivalents brought by partners into a partnership or company, the sum total of a firm's assets, and the like. Thus the concept was essentially monetary, meaning either actual money, claims to money, or some goods evaluated in money."

However, there have been two approaches to defining a "capital" used in economics and related social sciences (Hodgson, 2014):

- One is the post-Smithian trend that considers "capital" as "any relatively permanent thing or attribute that leads to the satisfaction of desires. According to this definition, capital has existed since the dawn of humanity and is not limited to a certain method of production."
- The second option advocated by Hobson, Sombart, Weber, Mitchell Innes, Fetter, and Schumpeter is to restore the meaning of capital "which appeared in Europe until the thirteenth century in the context of trade and investment. Capital is then defined as a monetary fund that a person or company will invest in. (...) In both cases, capital is measured as an amount of money. Capital is money or the realizable monetary value of assets owned and assets that can be collateralized."

The last word in the last quote is what makes the essential difference between these two approaches. If the owner of the factory does not have sufficient money to operate his business, he can go to the bank and use his business assets (buildings and machines) as collateral to fully secure the bank loan. You cannot get a bank loan by using any of the previously mentioned capitals as security because such assets cannot be collateralized. Therefore, it is completely wrong to call something "assets" if that cannot be expressed in money as capital. Finally, Piketty (2014) defines capital in a way to include cash, bonds, stocks, and assets that can be collateralized, such as buildings, land, machinery, and intellectual property.

Despite such a precise definition of capital, two terms have become widely used in the economy: *social capital* and *human capital*. After knowing what capital is, it is important to clarify social and human capital.

Social relations are called *social capital*. No reasonable person will deny that these relations influence and have economic effects. The problem is whether they should be subsumed under capital or treated as capital. Social capital has the same problem as the other capitals listed above: the problem of measurability. Bowles (1999) criticized the term "social capital," stating that "'Capital' refers to a thing possessed by individuals; even a social isolate like Robinson Crusoe had an axe and a fishing net. By contrast, the attributes said to make up social capital—such as trust, commitment to others, adhering to social norms, and punishing those who violate them—describe relationships *among* people." Given that "social capital" cannot be owned, borrowed, or sold, it is quite clear that it cannot be priced or used as collateral. Therefore, its advocates would do better to use more appropriate and comprehensible terms such as "culture," "networks," "trust," or just "wealth," anything else but not "capital."

"Human capital" was first introduced into the literature by Fisher (1897) in an article entitled "Senses of 'Capital" and published in a respected economic journal at the time. He went down in economic history because he proposed that all factors of production, i.e., land, buildings, machinery, and labor, should be treated as capital. "Human capital" was suggested as a production factor by Schultz (1960, 1971) and Becker (1964). However, the term "human capital" has the same problem as "social capital" and cannot be seized as collateral. There is a big difference between the "capital" of the employees and the "capital" of the factory owner. Admittedly, both are assets, but only one of them is recognized as collateral.

Summarizing all previously discussed, the term "capital" can be used for an asset that fulfils three conditions:

- It is measurable.
- It can be expressed in money.
- It can be collateral.

If we now look at all the "capital" terms listed before, we can conclude that none of them meet the stated conditions and, in fact, should not be referred to as "capital." Only intellectual capital (IC) as a term justifies the use of the term "capital." Here is the explanation.

The basis of IC is actually "human capital" (HC). The value of HC can be calculated based on salaries and other benefits received by employees. Thus, HC can be precisely measured, and it is possible to express it in money. It remains to be seen whether HC can be collateral. Most of the relevant literature that deals with the term "capital" was created in the period from the nineteenth to the twentieth century, in the period of the industrial era dominated by capital and manual labor. It is easy to understand that economists from that period could not predict the transformation of the industrial economy into a knowledge-based economy, dominated by intellectual and knowledge-based work.

Given this reality, the approach of financial institutions to collateral has also changed. For a long time, an employee can get a loan for, for example, an apartment or house based on his salary, and the property serves as a mortgage. A special example is startups, or micro-enterprises, where the necessary financial resources are obtained only on the basis of a well-developed business idea. Many of them grow into global companies, and their founders and employees become owners. Furthermore, according to research by Massolution (2015), there are more than 600 crowdfunding platforms around the world, and the collected funds reach billions of dollars annually. All of these are examples of circumstances in which intellectual work and intellectual assets become collateral and therefore meet all the conditions to be named "capital."

Another component of IC is structural capital (SC). The content of that part of IC consists of patents, licenses, copyrights, software, franchises, business organizations, strategies, documents, business processes, and databases. All its components are measurable, can be expressed in money, and serve as collateral, so it meets the conditions to be referred to as "capital."

In a nutshell, the term "capital" can be used for:

- Mass of living human labor engaged in the value creation process and valued in money—HC,
- Mass of inanimate labor included in the value creation process and valued in money—SC,

which together form the IC.

3 Intellectual Capital and Artificial Intelligence

I definitely belong to the camp of opinion about artificial intelligence as an increase in human abilities and capacities.
Satya Nadella

It can already be seen that AI, after its rapid popularization in just a few years, will have a "deeper" impact on all aspects of individual and social life than has been the case with other innovations so far. Although other disruptive innovations have had a significant impact on human work, this one will, by all odds, be the most significant. If we can draw some parallel with the past, then we could say: what the appearance of the steam engine was for the physical; now the appearance of AI will be for mental work. Judging by the transformation brought about by industrialization, it is clear what kind of transformation awaits the field of intellectual capital.

Given that what can and cannot be "capital" was defined in the previous part, now it remains to be seen what happens with AI and its place in IC. In order to do this, it is first necessary to determine what AI is. In the last few decades, numerous definitions of AI have emerged. However, most agree that the basis was created by Alan Turing's paper entitled "Computing Machinery and Intelligence." It offers a famous test where the examiner tries to distinguish between computer and human responses.

The needs of this text are met by the definition from one of the leading textbooks in the field of AI, "Artificial Intelligence: A Modern Approach." The authors, Stuart Russell and Peter Norvig (2021), list four potential goals or definitions of artificial intelligence, which distinguish computer systems based on rationality and thinking versus acting:

Human Approach
- Systems that think like humans

Systems that act like people

Ideal Approach
- Systems that think rationally

Systems that act rationally

Alan Turing's definition would fall into the category of "systems that act like humans." If this "human" approach to artificial intelligence is followed, it is obvious that it belongs to the field of IC. As a part of IC, it is quite understandable that AI is integrated into all aspects of human activity, including business and, in fact, the entire economy. In this expansion, two forms appear: enterprise AI (EAI) and generative AI (GAI). The difference between them can be briefly described as follows: EAI is used as an application that takes over routine business activities. On the other hand, GAI uses existing content on the web and generates completely new content in all forms: text, images, audio, and video. For businesses looking to leverage AI technologies to improve their operations, it's essential to know the key differences between them.

Enterprise AI has a focus on improving business processes, operations, performance, and efficiency. It is based on the use of data analysis, machine learning, and automation tools to solve problems and various tasks more rationally. In particular, expert knowledge about certain business processes and activities is transferred into an AI product that better contributes to the creation of added value for its users. A significant benefit of EAI is that once it is loaded with all the necessary data and networked with other processes, it continues to improve itself. It supplements its database with data from undertaken activities. There, data on the behavior of their customers, their characteristics, preferences, paying power, and taste are automatically generated and classified, and after that, new knowledge is derived, which fine-tunes the procurement and logistics, production and marketing, distribution, and sales chains. There are no more unnecessary stocks; marketing, sales, and distribution are improved; and time and money are saved.

Generative AI is based on huge amounts of data from which it creates new content such as texts, images, and music. The main characteristic of the content created by GAI is that it is indistinguishable from human-made content. This is precisely where the enormous potential lies for all activities that require creativity, innovation, and knowledge processing. In particular, it enables new applications that were previously impossible or impractical to automate, such as realistic virtual assistants, personalized education and services, and digital art. With these possibilities, GAI has significant implications for scientists and practitioners.

Generative artificial intelligence will have significant economic implications in a variety of industries and markets. It can increase efficiency and productivity by automating many tasks that were previously performed by humans. It can reduce costs and open new opportunities for growth and innovation (Eloundou et al., 2023). For example, translation between different languages based on artificial intelligence is responsible for significant economic gains (Brynjolfsson et al., 2017). The digital transformation made possible by GAI presents challenges and opportunities for economic policy. It will certainly have a significant impact on future work patterns and, indirectly, on employee capabilities. It will affect the sharing and distribution of content, and so I can expect implications for the exploitation and protection of intellectual property. The concentration of power in the hands of a few companies over AI innovation can result in a monopoly over AI capabilities and hinder future innovation, fair competition, and scientific progress. All of these future impacts are important to understand and provide meaningful guidance for shaping economic policy (Feuerriegel et al., 2023).

After looking at these two sides of the same coin, it can be concluded: "While enterprise AI addresses business-centric challenges, generative AI is a master of creativity. The magic happens when these realms intersect, potentially leading to innovative solutions that marry efficiency with ingenuity" (Dixit, 2024).

AI systems already outperform most humans in some tests of creativity. Thus, one study revealed that in the task of searching for business innovations, AI offered better ideas than students. Furthermore, a well-known consulting company tested AI by giving one group of business consultants to solve tasks with the help of GPT-4 and another to solve the same tasks by themselves. The results showed that the first group completed 12 percent more tasks, 25 percent faster, and even 40 percent better (Dell'Acqua & McFowland, 2023).

At the company level, there are many examples where AI helps solve routine administrative tasks. Thus, the human resources (HR) staff gets more time for tasks that need their professional processing. Likewise, the application of AI in measuring employee productivity in real time is already in operation. AI provides information about the work time spent solving tasks and the rate of their execution. This not only provides information on productivity but also identifies areas that can be improved. As traditional employee reward measures can be biased and unreliable, now, with the help of AI, they seem much more objective (Czarnitzki et al., 2022).

These are just some of the examples that show that HC and AI are not in a fight for dominance but in cooperation with each other. AI is at an advantage when dealing with huge amounts of data that need to be processed for repetitive tasks. HC gets rid of such types of jobs and focuses on those that are oriented toward creativity, innovation, and general decision-making with a higher level of demands. It is also the joint creation of HC and AI value that leads to increased productivity and sustainable business.

Now it can be established that there is no doubt that AI is an integral part of IC. Not only that, the examples presented show that it will have an increasingly significant impact on the mass of value created. However, in order to fulfil the conditions to be "capital," it must have value and be collateral, which means that it must be expressed in money. That is why the question of how much artificial intelligence costs is being asked today by companies of all sizes, from start-ups to large companies. The answer is simple: it depends on the problem it solves. The range is available from 0 to the level decided by the management. If a customized solution is desired, then the amounts are higher, and if ready-made AI software is used, various forms of subscriptions are paid. Regardless of which variant the company chooses, it is always more or less complex software. Another component of using artificial intelligence in the enterprise is specialized hardware that can process large amounts of data. This hardware is generally more expensive than standard computer hardware, so the costs of setting up and running an AI system can be significant.

Based on everything presented and viewed from an accounting point of view, it can be concluded that AI satisfies all requirements to be treated as a capital and as it is a software working based on the training data set, AI should be considered as an integral part of SC.

The entry of AI into the SC changes the current situation, rather than its structure. Namely, all its components, such as infrastructure, databases, organization, software, and IP, were only supported by HC in the value-creation process. One could even say that they were passive participants. However, by incorporating AI, structural capital becomes an active participant in the value-creation process. Therefore, I would suggest the following distinction for SC:

- The passive, which provides support for HC in value creation;
- The active AI, which independently performs some of the tasks previously performed by HC.

So, AI is definitely a part of SC and, as such, an integral part of IC. The ratio of the active and passive parts of the SC will depend on the speed with which AI is further developed and implemented. In this context, a question can be raised about the future of HC. It is quite certain that the advancement of AI will reduce the need for HC. Namely, there are already examples where some business processes take place without the participation of HC. These are, for example, parking lots, parcel machines, robotaxis, and similar simple forms of value creation. In such and similar business processes, however, there is some operator or other form of HC participation in the background. So, at least for now, there are no examples of SC itself creating value.

However, predictions also announce such a possibility. Mustafa Suleyman (2024), the co-founder of DeepMind, Google's AI division, spoke on a panel at the World Economic Forum in Davos about when artificial intelligence will be so advanced that it will be able to pass the so-called Turing Test. Successfully passing that test would mean that the technology has reached advanced capabilities that only humans have today; that is, for some experts, it would be proof that general artificial intelligence has been developed. Or, more specifically, AI will become capable enough to act as an entrepreneur, project manager, and inventor who will be able to manufacture, advertise, and sell their products at a profit. Currently, AI does not have these capabilities, but he believes that they will have them by the end of this decade: "I'm pretty sure that within the next five years, certainly before the end of the decade, we are going to have not just those capabilities, but those capabilities widely available for very cheap, potentially even in open source. I think that completely changes the economy."

4 The Future of IC as Part of Complexity Economics

Everything is energy, and that is all there is to it.
There can be no other way.
This is not philosophy.
This is physics.
Albert Einstein
The law of conservation of energy tells us
that we can't get something for nothing,
but we refuse to believe it.
Isaac Asimov

The last sentence from the previous part, "I think it completely changes the economy," is a thought-provoking sentence. AI will not completely change the economy because significant changes have been happening for, at least, the last 70 years. These changes will now occur in a wide range of activities; they will be more visible and faster, so they will also seek scientific explanations. That is why it is necessary to see the current state of economic science and determine the position of IC in this new economic environment.

Economic theory has been based on the trinity of land, labor, and capital for centuries. Only about 60 years ago was "technical progress" added to that. However, none of these factors of the production function dominantly creates value today. What creates value today is "knowledge" incorporated into IC. But that IC today is not covered either at the macro-economic or micro-economic level. It is not there either as a component of the national GDP or in the balance sheet and PLO of the company. It is simply incredible that for half a century there has been an IC that is not covered by existing economic theory.

Even Alan Greenspan, the former chairman of the US Federal Reserve and one of the most highly respected figures in economic policymaking, once remarked to his Federal Reserve colleagues, "We really do not know how [the economy] works. The old models just are not working" (Beinhocker, 2006).

That is why there are two economies today: one is the mainstream economy, and the other is the real one that works every day. What is today's economic reality are companies and markets, which are exceptional dynamic systems in constant development and interaction. The following table shows what kind of two worlds we are talking about (Table 1).

The foundation on which Complexity Economics rests is the awareness that economic systems are complex, open, and dynamic structures and, as such, are subject

Table 1 Characteristics of complexity and traditional economics

	Complexity economics	Traditional economics
Dynamics	Open, dynamic, non-linear systems, far from equilibrium	Closed, static, linear systems, in equilibrium
Agents	Individually modelled, use inductive rules to make decisions; have incomplete information; they are subject to errors and biases; they learn and adapt over time	Modelled collectively; use complex deductive calculations to make decisions; they have complete information; they do not make mistakes and have no prejudices; no need to learn or adapt (they are perfect)
Networks	It explicitly models interactions between individual agents; networks of relationships change over time	It assumes that agents interact only indirectly through market mechanisms
Emergence	There is no distinction between micro- and macroeconomics; macro patterns are the emergent result of micro-level behavior and interactions	Micro- and macroeconomics remain separate disciplines
Evolution	The evolutionary process of differentiating selection and amplification renews the system and is responsible for its growth and complexity	No mechanism for endogenous novelty creation or growth in order and complexity

Source: Krause (2009)

to the second law of thermodynamics. This means that the economic system is not something abstract but a real physical system composed of matter, energy, and information, and energy is needed for its functioning (Jakimowicz, 2020).

In his work, Alam (2005) recognizes energy as the basis of all economic activities. He explicitly states, "The economy is a manifestation of energy applied, directed, amplified, and modified by the intervention of people and capital goods. The conclusion is inevitable: the economy is an energy system. Extracts and applies energy to activities that produce goods and services or support consumption activities."

After presenting the characteristics of complexity economics and traditional economics, I think there should be no doubt as to which of these two economies belongs to the area of IC. By all its characteristics, IC is part of complexity economics. Even more, I think IC is its main driving force.

The connection between economics and physics has always existed. The emergence of neoclassical economics is firmly methodologically linked to thermodynamics, i.e., its first law. A number of key discoveries from then until today have resulted from the application of physics methods in economics. Unfortunately, mainstream economics still ignores this. The problem lies in the fact that Walras, Jevons, and other builders of traditional economics were not familiar with the second law of thermodynamics, which arose in the second half of the nineteenth century. In addition, they also lacked the concept of closed and open systems. A detailed understanding of open systems emerged only gradually during the twentieth century, accelerating with the work of the Russian-born chemist Ilya Prigogine in the 1960s and 1970s. Finally, at the beginning of the 1970s of the last century, Georgescu-Roegen (1971) wrote in his work that if the universe cannot avoid the Second Law, then neither can the economy. What does the Second Law say?

"A fundamental rule that determines the fate of the universe. The second law of thermodynamics says that hot things always cool unless you do something to stop them. It expresses a fundamental and simple truth about the universe: that disorder, characterized as a quantity known as entropy, always increases."[1] There has never been an exception to the Second Law.

Translated into the language of economics, this means the following:

First, "All products and services with economic value are produced by thermodynamic irreversible transformations." Simply said, you can't make an omelet without breaking the eggs.

Second, "All economic transformations that create value reduce entropy locally within the economic system and increase entropy globally." Any process that creates value must be both irreversible and reduce entropy (Georgescu-Roegen, 1971).

Seen from the level of everyday business, this would mean:

[1] https://www.newscientist.com › definition › second-law-t.

- Company entropy can be defined as available energy that has not been used to create value.
- The company needs to be understood as a subsystem of a wider system (the macro economy) that transmits the effects of its actions to that higher level.
- The company as a sub-system has three constituent parts of each system: matter, energy, and information. The function of the company is to reduce entropy through its actions. The results of this activity are transferred to the wider environment: the sector in which it operates and the national economy.
- More successful business leads to a decrease in entropy. Inadequate management of resources and non-productive performance of work duties are reflections of organizational disorganization, and the consequence is an increase in entropy.
- Work can be performed more or less efficiently, which corresponds to the structure of the company's organization. Each individual efficiency also shows the individual level of entropy.
- An increase in the level of organization means better organization and a decrease in entropy. The dynamics of entropy reflect the quality of the business operations of companies and the national economy (Zhou et al., 2013). Short and clear, entropy is a measure of organizational and work order in the economy. Or even simpler, higher efficiency, lower entropy.

Many scientists believe that the second law of thermodynamics is the basis for understanding all transformational processes in nature and society. As an example, Atkins (2010) states that "the second law is of central importance in the whole of science because it provides a foundation for understanding why *any* change occurs." This explains the use of entropy and the second law of thermodynamics not only in classical thermodynamics but also in statistical mechanics, information theory, biology, linguistics, musical creativity, economics, business, and knowledge management (Bratianu, 2019). Therefore, it could be concluded that complexity economics driven by IC means a definitive break with traditional economics, just as modern physics broke with Newtonian physics.

5 More Efficient HC and AI: Lower Entropy

If your theory is found to be against
the second law of thermodynamics I can give you no hope;
there is nothing for it but to collapse in deepest humiliation.
Sir Arthur S. Eddington
New Pathways in Science (1927)

In order for a company to be efficient, it must deliver low entropy. This leads to the next important question: how can companies and the economy measure entropy? The starting point has to be value creation. To understand economic value creation, it is necessary to analyze the dominant ways of value creation in history. These are the following:

- Agricultural production until approximately 1800;
- Industrial production until around 1970;
- Creation of services since 1970.

What we all have in common is that value has always been created through extraction, collection, and transformation by using information. In order to create value, it is necessary to extract seeds, coal, oil, and data, collect them, and finally transform them using information or knowledge of how to do it. For example, in agriculture, it was not only necessary to know where to dig but also to have the appropriate skills to manage tools. In industry, it is not only important what to produce but also how to operate complex machines. In the field of services, the hairdresser does not only work with his hands; he must have information not only about current fashion trends but also about the latest cosmetic products that he combines in his work. This is how we get the universal model of value creation presented in Fig. 1.

The collected resources (input) are combined with existing information and **transformed** into mass-added value and outcomes on the market (output). Transformation is a process that involves one or more changes (e.g., processing in any form, physical or mental) to a particular unit so that it appears and is used in a different state. In other words, value has always been created through transformation. The only thing that changes is the level of complexity of these transformations. It is quite understandable that transformations in the era of agricultural production were much simpler than those in industrial production. The transformations taking place in today's economy are realized to the greatest extent by the use of knowledge in all its forms. Or, quite specifically, value is created through the organization's business model, where inputs of financial, physical, and intellectual capital, through business activities and interactions, are transformed and turned into results and outcomes that, in the short, medium, and long term, create or destroy **value** for the organization, its stakeholders, society, and the environment (International Integrated Reporting Council, 2013).

If we now return to the practical sphere, we see that all these levels of transformation are actually the incorporation of knowledge into products and services, and in economic reality, this manifests itself as value addition. "Value-added products or services are worth more because they have been improved or had something added to them" (Cambridge Advanced Learner's Dictionary and Thesaurus).

Added value is an objective indicator of business success since output and input, the two categories from which it derives, are taken from the market. On the contrary, profit is an indicator based on numerous subjective transactions and calculations. A simple calculation of value added (VA) is possible at different business levels, from

Fig. 1 Universal model of value creation

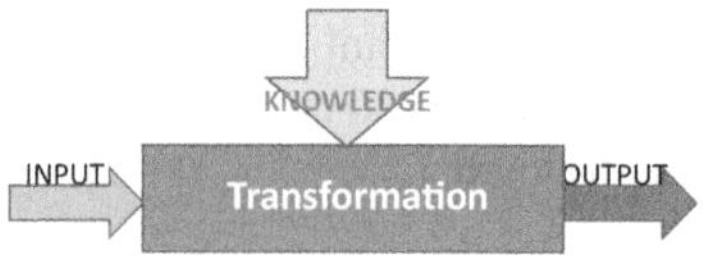

intra-company processes to company units, at company, regional, and national levels. Furthermore, it can be calculated whenever necessary and, in accordance with classic business reports, on a weekly, monthly, quarterly, and annual basis. This makes it a universal unit that applies to the entire economy.

Neither income nor profit, the basic indicators of an industrial economy actually show whether and how much value has been created. Even traditional economic theory doesn't know how much value the company has created. Here is just one example of the stated statement Fig. 2.

As you can see, the main indicator is operative profit (OP), which is used by many managers for decision-making but has no relation to value added. For the same added value of 950 million (red line), the companies showed profits ranging from 10 to 600 million.

The use of added value in business brings various advantages that can be summarized in three groups:

- Usefulness for employees and management because it shows their key role in the process of value creation, shows their productivity, which enables them to be rewarded more objectively,
- Advantages for investors because they get a completely realistic insight into the company's ability to create value. It shows them a far better insight into productivity and business success than is the case with profit (shown in Fig. 2)
- Enables the connection of the microsphere—companies—with the macroeconomic level, which enables the state administration to operate more efficiently (Saho, Pramanik, 2017).

Value added was also recognized by the Government of the United Kingdom (The Value Added Scoreboard, 2009) and states quite precisely: "The importance of Value added measures the amount of wealth created by a company and is of particular importance since it reflects the ability of companies to provide their customers

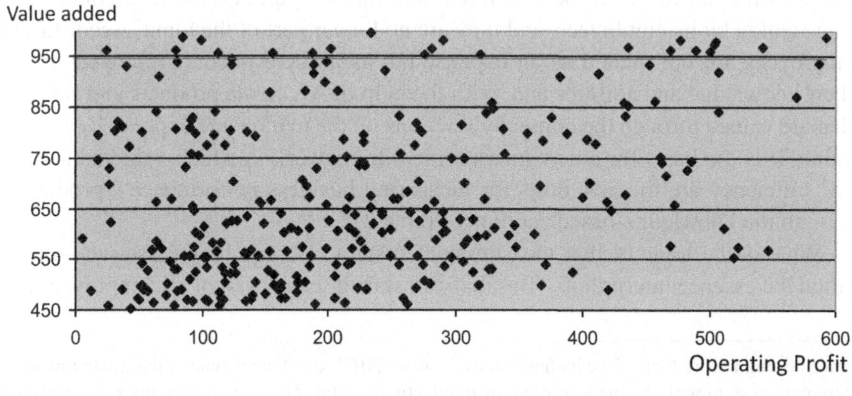

Fig. 2 The relationship between VA and profit. Source of data: The Value Added Scoreboard (2009)

with what they want and are prepared to pay for. As such, it provides a broader perspective on a company's economic contribution than operating profit."

On the other side of the world, the government of Singapore (A Guide to Productivity Measurement, 2011) is encouraging companies to use VA to improve operations and increase productivity. Their agency issued a manual in which it states:

"Why use added value? Value added is a better measure of output for the following reasons:

1. *It measures the real output of the organization.* Revenue measures the dollar value of the output generated by the organization. Value added, on the other hand, shows the net wealth created by the organization. It is the difference between sales (what the customer pays the organization for products or services) and purchases (what the organization pays suppliers for materials and services to generate the sale). It provides a customer-centric perspective and focuses on the real value created by the organization.
2. *It is practical.* Added value is measured in financial units, which allows the aggregation of different outputs.
3. *It is easy to calculate.* Added value can be easily derived from an organization's profit and loss statement. There is no need to set up a separate data collection system.
4. *It is an effective communication and motivational tool.* Added value provides a common link between employers and employees to achieve the goal of increasing the economic pie shared by both parties. The higher the value created by the collective effort, the greater the wealth distributed to those who have contributed to it.
5. *It is applicable to both production and service industries.* Added value is calculated in the same way for both production and service activities. Unlike physical indicators, value-added can measure the output of service activities, which is often intangible."

From the above, it can be concluded that human capital (HC) of a company is represented by its employees, and they are no longer part of the input. Accordingly, employees are not treated as an expense but as an investment. Employees invest their knowledge and abilities and, with the help of AI, create products and services that are valued through the company's actions on the market and expressed in added value. It is the basis for a new measurement framework in which value-added and HC efficiency are the new units for measuring business performance—productivity—in the knowledge-based economy (Table 2).[2]

What is the logic of that measurement system? Here is how those who understood the essence interpret it: "To satisfy all stakeholders (first of all, employees and

[2] Even though more than 25 years have passed since VAIC's existence, many still equate this measurement system with the measurement of intellectual capital. That is why I mention again **that it is not about measuring IC but about measuring its efficiency**.

Table 2 Statements of value added intellectual coefficient (VAIC)

Sales	OUT
Costs	- IN =
Value added	VA
Human capital (all incomes of employees)	HC
Structural capital (SC)	VA - HC
Human capital efficiency (HCE)	VA/HC
Structural capital efficiency (SCE)	SC/VA

shareholders), it is necessary to create value-added (VA) for paying personnel wages (HC) and the gross operating profit (SC or EBITDA). (…) It links value creation for stakeholders (SCE) with the productivity of knowledge workers (HCE). It appears that the variable on which value creation for shareholders (SCE) depends is knowledge workers productivity (HCE). The higher the productivity of knowledge workers (HCE), the higher the value created for stakeholders (SCE)" (Iazzolino et al., 2013).

Given that higher efficiency, i.e., higher HCE and higher SCE, means lower entropy, this change can be expressed as:

$$\Delta S = 1 / \mathrm{HCE}$$

According to all that has been stated, it appears that the value-added intellectual coefficient (VAIC) is a suitable measurement system for Complexity Economics because it provides precise information on:

- Efficiency of HC
- SC efficiency and therefore AI efficiency
- Entropy changes ΔS

The key to everything is HCE; once that is known, everything else is defined, including both SC and AI efficiency and ΔS. All business performance indicators used so far, such as return on equity (ROE), return on assets (ROA), earnings per share (EPS), debt-to-equity ratio (DER), debt-to-asset ratio (DAR), and current ratio (CR), rested on capital. Now, a new measurement system is entering the scene, which is dominated by knowledge and not capital. It complements the existing measurement system, which did not include intellectual capital and its key contribution to value creation.

6 It Works in Reality: From the Process to the National Economy

Knowledge is of no value unless you put it into practice.
Anton Chekhov
Measurement is the key to success;
It is the catalyst that propels progress.

Steve Maraboli

This section will demonstrate the VAIC measurement model implemented on different levels (process, micro, macro) in real economic environment. First is an example of one company, Singapore Airlines, which has been using VAIC components for its annual report for years (Fig. 3).[3]

From the above statement, it can be seen that, compared to the previous year, the HCE (marked in red) increased to 2.67 and the entropy decreased to ΔS 0.37. This is understandable because 189.2% more value was created than in the previous period.

The presented results of Singapore Airlines operations are actually the sum of what was created in their business processes. The creation of value begins in the processes, and therefore the measurement of business efficiency should start from there as well. That's why Juran was right when he said, "Whoever doesn't manage processes doesn't manage the company either" (Juran, 1970).

The large ellipse in Fig. 4 represents the highest level of the business environment; it can be a company, sector, national, or global economy. If we take a company, then we can say that the five ellipses within the main ellipse represent different parts or units of the company—branches, stores—depending on the nature of the company's operations.

	2022/23 $ million	2021/22 $ million
Total revenue	17,774.8	7,614.8
Less: Purchase of goods and services	(9,946.4)	(4,751.3)
	7,828.4	2,863.5
Add:		
Interest income	412.6	45.9
(Loss)/Surplus on disposal of aircraft, spares and spare engines	(7.3)	85.9
Dividends from long-term investments	4.0	4.0
Other non-operating items	(58.4)	(49.5)
Share of profits of joint venture companies	34.8	28.2
Share of losses of associated companies	(59.5)	(157.9)
Total value added for distribution	8,154.6	2,820.1
Applied as follows:		
To employees:		
- Salaries and other staff cost	3,055.8	1,473.6
To government:		
- Corporation taxes	480.0	(155.5)
To suppliers of capital:		
- Interim and proposed dividends	1,128.9	-
- Finance charges	419.9	391.6
- Non-controlling interests	6.5	13.9
Retained for future capital requirements:		
- Depreciation, amortisation and impairment	2,035.6	2,058.5
- Retained profit/(loss)	1,027.9	(962.0)
Total value added	8,154.6	2,820.1
Value added per $ revenue ($)	0.46	0.37
Value added per $ employment cost ($)	2.67	1.91
Value added per $ investment in property, plant and equipment ($)	0.24	0.08

Fig. 3 Statements of value added and its distribution

[3] Singapore Airlines, Annual Report and Sustainability Report 2022–2023, p. 55.

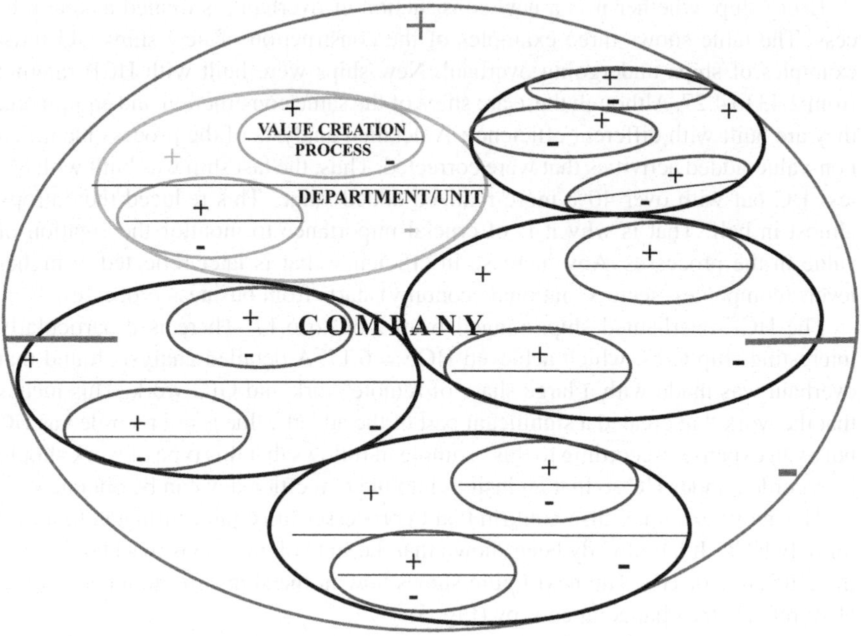

Fig. 4 Universal efficiency structure

Within these units or parts, there are more and less efficient processes. The goal of value creation management is to examine the reasons for inefficiency and improve efficiency by removing them. This can be done in various ways, through reorganization, outsourcing, knowledge and IC management, improving customer service or logistics, more innovative products and services, better education and training of employees, and so on. Step by step, by eliminating inefficient areas in business processes, the efficiency of value creation can be increased in parts of the company and consequently also at the company level. Table 3 shows how it looks in the business of a shipyard.

Table 3 HCE in processes

	New building			Overhaul			**Total**
	WB224	WB225	WB227	DMB81	Kraljica	Cres	
Value added VA	2,057,609	1,881,441	2,811,716	435,934	366,304	484,904	8,037,907
Human capital HC	785,365	774,725	657,875	162,260	134,805	78,613	2,593,643
HCE	2.62	2.43	4.27	2.69	2.72	6.17	3.10
Entropy change (ΔS)	0.38	0.41	0.23	0.37	0.37	0.16	0.32

Every ship, whether it is a new construction or overhaul, is treated as one process. The table shows three examples of the construction of new ships and three examples of ships undergoing overhaul. New ships were built with HCE ranging from 2.43 to 4.27. Although these are ships of the same construction and equipment, they are built with different efficiency. A detailed analysis of the process identified non-value-added activities that were corrected. Thus, the last ship was built with 8% less HC but with over 40% more realized added value. This reduced the entropy almost in half. That is why it is of crucial importance to monitor the creation of value in the processes. Any increase in efficiency that is later reflected at higher levels (companies, sectors, national economy) starts from business processes.

The HCE-overhauled ships ranged from 2.69 to 6.17. There is a particularly interesting ship Cres, which achieved HCE = 6.17. A detailed analysis found that overhaul was made with a large share of remote work and GIG work. This means that the work that created a significant part of the added value is not recorded as HC but as an expense. According to this example, it follows that this type of work should be recorded under HC so that an insight into the real efficiency can be obtained.

The above examples also confirm that in processes, it is quite sufficient to monitor only HCE. It has already been shown that the state of entropy is reached through the efficiency of HC. The next figure shows how in the shipyard the movement of HCE reflects the change in entropy (Fig. 5).

In the initial year of application of this method of business improvement, HCE was slightly above 1, which resulted in almost maximum entropy. As the HCE increased each year, the entropy decreased. In the last year, HCE decreased a little, and this was immediately reflected in the change in entropy.

One can say that everything that happens at the process level also happens at higher levels. This shipyard is part of a larger business system. It is about the ISKRA Group, a multinational company with about 1500 employees. The group's operations in 2023 were carried out with the shown efficiencies.

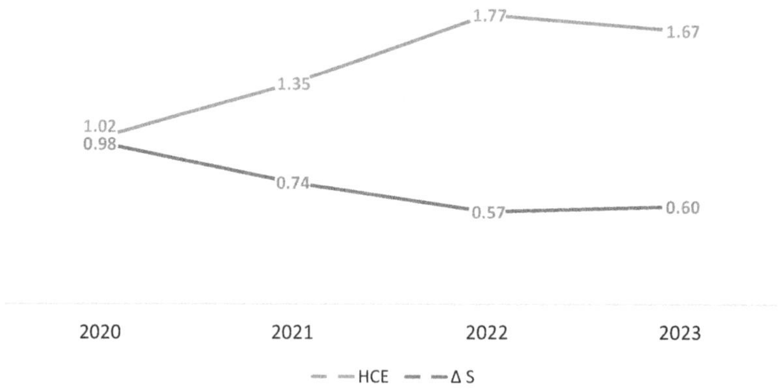

Fig. 5 Movement of HCE and entropy

As presented in Fig. 6, there are parts and companies with different levels of efficiency: 1.86 is the average at the level of the entire group, and individual efficiencies range from 1.67 to 2.85.

The goal of management should be to increase efficiency in those companies that work below the group average by improving the efficiency of their processes.

All this is also shown at the sector level, where companies operate with higher or lower efficiency. The average efficiency of the sector provides an indication of the level of efficiency of the company. Figure 7 presents the results of the operations in different sectors of the Croatian economy.[4]

If the national economy is observed, the efficiency of value creation is the result of the business performance of all companies divided by sector. In this way, the state administration has a tool for locating those parts of the economy whose operations are not efficient and can think about interventions to improve the situation. In this

Fig. 6 HCE in the ISKRA GROUP

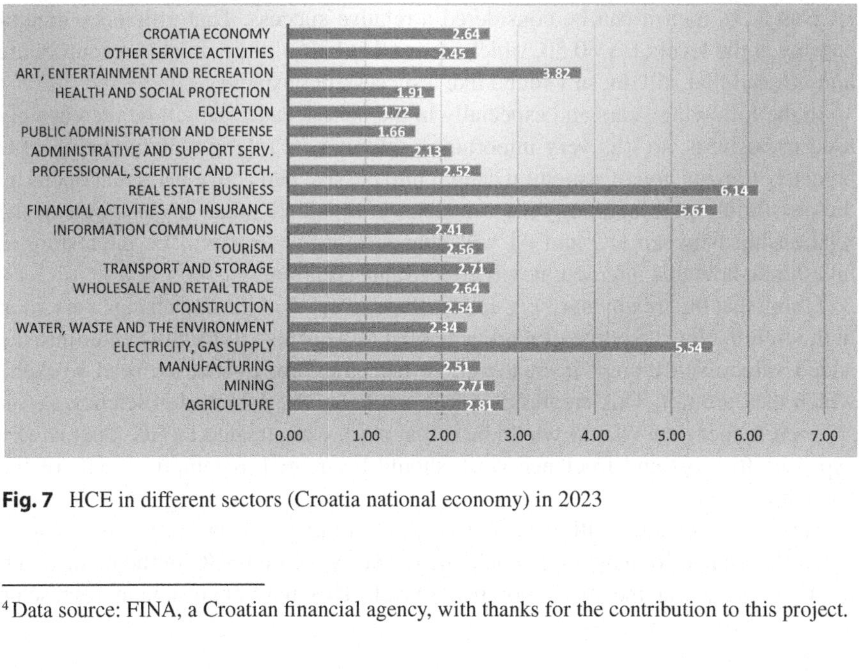

Fig. 7 HCE in different sectors (Croatia national economy) in 2023

[4] Data source: FINA, a Croatian financial agency, with thanks for the contribution to this project.

example, these are public administration and defense, education, and health and social protection.

7 Conclusion

"In God we trust; all others bring data."
W. Edwards Deming

The aim of this chapter was to identify the main obstacles to the development of IC theory, present some new ideas, and offer potential solutions. Everything presented should serve as a basis for the further progress of IC theory and its wider application in practice. I would highlight the following as the most important contribution to this chapter:

If you can't express something in numbers, your knowledge is insufficient; if it can't be measured, it can't even be improved (Lord Kelvin). That is why I first mention measuring the efficiency of HC in processes. I think that this is crucial for wider application in practice and makes a great contribution to increasing business efficiency. The level of business processes is crucial in the analysis of value creation because it is the place where value and entropy are created.

The introduction of the concept of entropy into everyday business was considered another significant step forward. Namely, entropy is all around us; it accompanies us even when we cook dinner and when we drive a car. That is why it is important to know that this phenomenon also exists in the realm of business. It is necessary to have information about the level of entropy in business processes and the company in order to increase the responsibility of management. If the achieved HCE is 2.00, then it can be considered a relative success. That efficiency creates entropy at the level of ΔS 0.50, which means that half of the available resources are unused, and that still doesn't sound like a successful business.

In the following years and especially in the next decade, AI will be increasingly used in business, so it is very important to monitor its role in value creation. It is precisely the division of structural capital into passive and active parts that opens up the possibility of calculating AI's contribution to added value. In this context, the relationship between HC and AI will change rapidly, so it will be interesting to investigate how this interaction will affect value creation.

I think that the treatment of gig and freelance work will have to change very soon in the future. Now this type of work is treated as a cost, so it does not enter into the added value even though it creates it. In fact, they are treated as hired workers, which they are not. This creates a wrong picture of the achieved efficiency, i.e., it shows it higher than what it would be if that work were treated as HC. That is why expenses for gigs and freelance work should be treated as temporary HC of the company.

Finally, this chapter will leave a mark on the future of IC because it is placed in a new theoretical framework. Namely, there was no place for IC in the mainstream economy, either at the micro- or macrolevel. This new environment represents

Complexity Economics, which in all its characteristics corresponds to what IC is. On the other hand, treating IC as an integral part of that contemporary economic framework not only complements Complexity Economics but becomes its driving force.

All these emphases actually point to the emergence of a new era, which I would call **knowlism**. Let me explain a little. The term "lism" is first associated with capitalism and then with other historical socioeconomic formations, from feudalism to the present day. All of them were related to the designation of a belief system or ideology, but above all to the dominant way of value creation. Therefore, according to everything presented, it can be concluded that all the conditions for the emergence of a new era—knowlism—have been met. This new epoch has its own theoretical framework and its own measurement system, VA, HCE, and ΔS. Knowlism implies an epoch, a value system, and an ideology, having in focus knowledge as the creator of all values.

References

A Guide to Productivity Measurement. (2011). Published by SPRING Singapore.

Alam, M. S. (2005). *The economy as an energy system* (p. 02115). Department of Economics, Northeastern University.

Atkins, P. (2010). *The laws of thermodynamics: A very short introduction*. Oxford University Press.

Azzi, C., & Ehrenberg, R. (1975). Household allocation of time and church attendance. *Journal of Political Economy, 38*(1).

Becker, G. S. (1964). *Human capital: A theoretical and empirical analysis, with special reference to education*. University of Chicago Press.

Becker, G. S., & Murphy, K. M. (1988). A theory of rational addiction. *Journal of Political Economy, 96*(4).

Becker, G. S. (1996). *Accounting for Tastes*. Harvard University Press.

Beinhocker, E. D. (2006). The origin of wealth: Evolution, complexity, and the radical remaking of economics.

Bourdieu, P. (1977). *Outline of a theory of practice, translated by Richard Nice*. Cambridge University Press.

Bourdieu, P. (1986). The Forms of Capital. In J. G. Richardson (Ed.), *Handbook of Theory and Research for the Sociology of Education*. Greenwood.

Bourdieu, P. (1988). *Homo Academicus*. Stanford University Press.

Bourdieu, P. (1990). *The logic of practice, translated by Richard Nice from the French edition of 1980*. Stanford University Press and Polity Press.

Bowles, S. (1999). "Social Capital" and community governance. *Focus: Newsletter for the Institute for Research on Poverty, 20*(3).

Bratianu, C. (2019). Exploring knowledge entropy in organizations. *Management Dynamics in the Knowledge Economy, 7*(3). https://doi.org/10.25019/MDKE/7.3.05

Brynjolfsson, E., Rock, D., & Syverson, C. (2017). *Artificial intelligence and the modern productivity paradox: A clash of expectations and statistics*. National Bureau of Economic Research.

Castelfranchi, C., Falcone, R., & Marzo, F. (2006). Being trusted in a social network: Trust as relational capital. *Lecture Notes in Computer Science, 3986*.

Constable, J. (2016). Energy, entropy, and the theory of wealth, delivered on February 11, 2016, as part of Newcastle University's "Insight" series of public lectures.

Czarnitzki, D., Fernández, G. P., & Rammer, C. (2022). *Artificial intelligence and firm-level productivity*. ZEW-Centre for European Economic Research.

Dei Ottati, G. (1994). Trust, interlinking transactions and credit in the industrial district. *Cambridge Journal of Economics, 18*(6).
Dell'Acqua, F., McFowland, E.. (2023). Experimental evidence of the effects of AI on knowledge worker productivity and quality,. Harvard Business School Technology & Operations Mgt. Unit Working Paper No. 24-013, https://ssrn.com/abstract=4573321.
Dixit. (2024). Enterprise AI vs. Generative AI. https://www.linkedin.com/pulse/enterprise-ai-vs-generative-vivek-dixit-e0otc/
Eloundou, T., Manning, S., Mishkin, P., & Rock, D. (2023). GPTs are GPTs: An early look at the labor market impact potential of large language models. arXiv:2303.10130.
Feuerriegel, S., Hartmann, I., Iainesch, C., Zschech, P. (2023). Generative AI. https://www.researchgate.net/publication/370653602_Generative_.
Fisher, I. (1897). Senses of 'Capital' https://www.jstor.org/stable/2957240.
Floud, R., McCloskey, D. (1994). The economic history of Britain, 1700–present, 2nd, Cambridge UP, Cambridge.
Georgescu-Roegen. (1971). *The entropy law and the economic process*. Harvard University Press.
Grossman, M. (1972). On the concept of health capital and the demand for health. *Journal of Political Economy, 80*(2).
Hakim, C. (2011). *Honey money: The power of erotic capital*. Allen Lane.
Hartwick, J. (1991). Degradation of environmental capital and national accounting procedures. *European Economic Review, 35*(2-3).
Hodgson, G. M. (2014). *What is capital?* Hertfordshire Business School, University of Hertfordshire.
Iazzolino, G., Laise, D., Migliano, G. (2013). Measures of value creation: A comparison between VAIC and EVA, IFKAD Conference Paper,
International Integrated Reporting Council. (2013). Value creation background paper for IR.
Jakimowicz, A. (2020). The role of entropy in the development of economics. *Entropy, 2020*(22), 452.
Johnson, A. S. (1909). *Introduction to economics*. Heath.
Juran, J. M. (1970). *Quality planning and analysis*. McGraw-Hill.
Krause, S. (2009). https://blog.stevekrause.org/2009/10/origin-of-wealth-by-eric-beinhocker.html.
Leontieff, W. (1951). *Input-output economics* (2nd ed.). Oxford University Press.
Massolution. (2015). The crowdfunding industry report. http://www.crowdsourcing.org/editorial/global-crowdfunding-market-to-reach-344b-in-2015-predictsmassolutions-2015cf-industry-report/45376.
Mouzelis, N. (1995). *Sociological Theory: What Went Wrong? Diagnosis and Remedies*. Routledge.
Oliver, C. (1997). Sustainable comparative advantage: Combining institutional and resource-based views. *Strategic Management Journal, 18*(9).
Piketty, T. (2014). *Capital in the twenty-first century*. Harvard University Press.
Rescher, N. (1989). *Cognitive Economy: The Economic Dimension of The Theory of Knowledge*. University of Pittsburgh Press.
Russell S., & Norvig P. (2021). Artificial Intelligence, a Modern Approach, 4th edition.
Saho, B. B., & Pramanik, A. K. (2017). Value added: Technique for corporate performance measurement under social perspective. *KINERJA, 21*(1).
Sandberg, S., & Pedersen, W. (2009). *Street capital: Black cannabis dealers in a white welfare state*. Policy Press.
Schultz, T. W. (1960). Capital formation by education. *Journal of Political Economy, 68*(4).
Schultz, T. W. (1971). *Investment in human capital: The role of education and research*. The Free Press.
Schumpeter, J. A. (1954). *History of economic analysis*. Oxford University Press.
Sik, E. (1994). Network capital in capitalist, communist and post-communist societies. *International Contributions to Labour Studies*.
Suleyman, M. (2024). https://www.businessinsider.com/google-deepmind-ai-could-run-businesses-in-five-years-2024-1.

Stewart, T. A. (1991). Brainpower: How intellectual capital is becoming America's most important asset. *Fortune*.

The Value Added Scoreboard. (2009). Department for Business Innovation and Skills, a ministerial department of the United Kingdom Government, the value added scoreboard was issued in the period 2004–2008. Nowhere and never was it explained why this analysis was not continued.

Tomer, J. F. (1987). *Organizational capital: The path to higher productivity and well-being*. Praeger.

Veljanovski, C. G., & Whelan, C. J. (1983). Professional negligence and the quality of legal services-An Economic Perspective. *Modern Law Review, 46*(6).

Verter, B. (2003). Spiritual capital: Theorizing religion with Bourdieu against Bourdieu. *Sociological Theory, 21*(2).

Zhou, R., Cai, R., & Tong, G. (2013). Applications of entropy in finance: A review. *Entropy, 2013*, 4909–4931.

Ante Pulic started working at the University of Zagreb in 1983 and deals with topics in microeconomics. From 1989 to 1999, he was also a guest professor at UNI Graz, Austria. In 1995, he co-founded the Austrian Intellectual Research Center (AICRC). In that period, he publishes the book *Elements of the Information Economy–Beyond Smith and Keynes* (BOHLAU Verlag), which announces the transition to a knowledge-based economy. Within the framework of the AICRC in 1998, at the Second World Congress on the Management of Intellectual Capital, Hamilton, Canada, he promoted the VAIC (value added intellectual coefficient) method of measuring the efficiency of intellectual capital. In addition to his work at the university, he actively participates in the promotion and implementation of the measurement system for monitoring the efficiency of intellectual capital. Based on experience and further research, in 2004, he published the highly cited article "Intellectual capital—does it create or destroy value?" (Emerald). He participates in congresses and conferences around the world (on all continents except Africa) with his speeches and presentations. At the Fourth Symposium on China-ASEAN Entrepreneurs Exchange (Beijing 2008), he announces and then publishes "The Principles of Intellectual Capital Efficiency: A Brief Description." After retirement, he continues to work at Libertas International University, Zagreb, where he participates in doctoral studies.

Effective Intellectual Capital Management as the Enabler of Future Value and Success in a Knowledge Economy

Stefan Güldenberg

Abstract

When Leif Edvinsson first coined the term intellectual capital in the early 1990s, he wanted to overcome the one-dimensional focus on financial capital and shareholder value, in particular. Just as IQ scores were developed to measure the likelihood of mastering our lives and ultimately succeeding, IC scores were developed to measure the likelihood of business future success and survival in an increasingly turbulent environment.

This paper aims to challenge our outdated and backward-looking understanding of value and success by linking the IC framework with the attention-based view of the firm, system dynamics, organizational learning, and sensemaking. Properly applied, IC can not only help to accelerate the necessary sustainable transformation of our businesses and society but also redefine what we teach in business schools about corporate value, role models, and successful careers for the next generation. If we stop defining value and success in financial terms only, we will open the doors to many more opportunities to shape our own destiny and the future viability and resilience of organizations and our society at large.

1 Introduction

Our mental models about success determine where we focus our attention on;
where we focus our attention on determines what we do, learn, measure, and manage;
what we do, learn, measure, and manage determines what we create as future values;
what we create as future values determines our destiny and survival as human beings.

S. Güldenberg (✉)
EHL Hospitality Business School, HES-SO, Lausanne, Switzerland
e-mail: stefan.guldenberg@ehl.ch

A. Kianto et al. (eds.), *Futurizing Intellectual Capital*, Knowledge Management and Organizational Learning 15, https://doi.org/10.1007/978-3-031-80197-6_16

1.1 Best Practice: Transforming Money into Future IC

Ruth Gottesman believes in the power of transforming tangible into intangible capital. It is the largest donation of its kind in the history of the United States: Former professor Ruth Gottesman is relieving students in New York of the burden of high tuition fees with a generous donation. If you want to study in the USA, you have to raise a lot of money—a former professor at Albert Einstein College of Medicine (AECOM) now wants to make it easier for some students. Gottesman is donating one billion dollars to the faculty in New York to pay the tuition fees for all students.

Gottesman is making this donation from the estate of her late husband David "Sandy" Gottesman. The former Wall Street investor died in September 2022. "I am very grateful to my late husband Sandy for leaving me this fortune, and I feel blessed to have the great privilege of making this donation to such a worthy cause," she was quoted in a joint statement with the university (Goldstein, 2024).

Gottesman came to the medical school in 1968. During her time at the school, she researched learning disabilities in children and developed a literacy program for adults. She is currently chair of the Einstein Board of Trustees and sits on the board of the affiliated hospital.

The gift will reimburse all current full-time students for their fees for the spring term 2024, and all future students will also be able to attend the university free of charge. Tuition at the school is approximately $60,000 per year, leaving many students with more than $200,000 in debt upon graduation.

The "gift is intended to attract a talented and diverse pool of individuals who might not otherwise have the means to attend medical school," the university said. The university is attended by around 1100 students. It is located in the Bronx, an area that the University of Wisconsin Population Health Institute ranks last in New York State for population health.

1.2 Worst Practice: A Lot of Sunk Costs and No Future IC

In fierce contrast to Ruth Gottesman, Vladimir Putin believes more in the power of tangible than intangible capital: Since Putin's reign, Russia has lost a considerable part of its intellectual elite, lost its personal reputation, and destroyed the future viability of Russian civil society. Every day that the war in Ukraine drags on claims human lives, promotes the outflow of intellectual capital, and consumes vast amounts of financial resources.

RAND researchers estimate the military costs of the war to date at 132 billion dollars (Shatz & Reach, 2023). The losses in gross domestic product for 2022 alone amount to around 100 billion dollars, and the destruction of financial capital for the entire year to 322 billion dollars. In the long run, the Russian economy and the standard of living of the Russian population will fall dramatically; the country will be set back by years, if not decades, not least due to the loss of its intellectual elite and the loss of independence and scientific freedom of its universities. In addition, the rewriting of history textbooks in schools is damaging the intellectual development and growth opportunities of the next generation.

Putin is proving incapable of escaping his mental models from the past: He finds himself in a similar situation to numerous decision-makers in politics and business before him. The sunk cost fallacy: The human tendency to rationalize the commitment in the event of failure instead of reducing losses applies to this war in particular (Gloe, 2023). The sunk cost fallacy is a psychological phenomenon in which people continue to invest in a project or endeavor despite clear evidence that the costs exceed the benefits (Parayre, 1995). If Putin perceives significant sunk costs associated with the Ukraine war, such as financial investment or loss of reputation, he may be inclined to continue the conflict in order to justify or recoup these costs, even if this becomes strategically impossible.

Like so many political leaders before him, Putin is thinking about his legacy and his place in history. "He has three advisors," his Foreign Minister Lavrov once said in response to an oligarch why he was not asked for advice before the invasion of Ukraine: "Ivan the Terrible. Peter the Great. And Catherine the Great" (Seddon et al., 2023). Building a strong, prosperous Russia and leaving a mark on the world stage are important personal motives for his success. However, as Yves Doz rightly pointed out in an interview (Fisher, 2002), the reason for the failure of many leaders is not that they make fundamentally wrong decisions but that they cling too long to decision-making patterns that were successful in the past, but which inevitably lead to failure today due to a changed world situation—in Putin's case, the mistaken belief that size and access to material resources make future success of nations possible.

Authoritarian leaders are always trying to convince their followers that sacrifice is part of a journey that will ultimately lead to a better outcome (Gloe, 2023). In their logic, it is better to continue the struggle at an even higher cost than to admit that the sacrifices made so far have been in vain. The escalation is accelerating: the more sacrifices, the more important it becomes to achieve success. As Senge (1990) has already stated, such an escalation, be it in a ruinous price war or in a military arms race, can only be overcome if both sides agree on a common, sustainable strategy. Subjective judgements can thus be overcome.

1.3 Implications for Organizations and Nations: A Mindshift among our Leaders is Needed

According to Edvinsson and Malone (1997), intellectual capital (IC) is based on the use of a company's brainpower to realize its true value. As a consequence intellectual capital measurement and management require an important mindshift of our leaders from a backward to a forward-looking approach, from a focus on financial metrics to non-financial metrics, from a view of the organization as a money-making machine to a view of the organization as a brain and living organism. With its system-oriented perspective, IC management focuses on the relationships in between the environment, nations, organizations, and people. It determines how the people living and working perceive their environment and the nation/organization itself. This organizational perception is in turn externalized via the IC measurement and management system and thus gains transparency. Transparency is the necessary anchor for the strategic learning of organizations. The focus here is on actively sharing assumptions about the corporate environment, the wealth of nations, the organization itself, and the people working in it.

At the core of IC measurement and management systems lies the idea to develop a strategic map that shows the path to be taken into the future and at the same time provides orientation for all stakeholders. As shown below, the existing traditional performance management systems are only able to do this to a very limited extent due to their focus on financial key figures only. This applies in particular to knowledge-based organizations and resourced-based strategies. Even newer performance measurement systems, which replace financial measures by process measures, like efficiency and productivity, still have disadvantages that result from the traditional, industrially orientated management logic. This contribution will therefore develop a research agenda of IC measurement and management based on a system dynamics perspective, which will be presented and discussed at the end of this chapter.

2 The Three Cornerstones of the Knowledge Economy: Human Capital, Structural Capital, and Relational Capital

Initially, this development was only noticed by a few, but from the middle of the twentieth century, the production factor of capital gradually began to lose its function as a scarce resource step by step. At the end of the Second World War, an unprecedented accumulation of capital began, which has continued unabated to this day. Total global monetary assets will soon break through the 500 trillion-dollar barrier (Czímer et al., 2022). It can be concluded from this that global poverty will no longer be seen as an economic scarcity problem in the future, but rather as a distribution problem.

With capital relatively easily available, management's attention has once again shifted to an already familiar critical factor of production: labor, but this time not manual work but knowledge work, the innovative and creative potential of people. As a result, mastering human interaction and making people grow will become a key management capability. The great leaders of the future are the ones who have access to or rights of disposal over knowledge and intellectual potential, and there are many strong indications that this is already the case today:

- The richest people in the world are no longer the *Rockefellers*, *Krupps*, and *Rothschilds*, but *Bernard Arnault and family*, *Elon Musk*, *Jeff Bezos*, and *Mark Zuckerberg* (Forbes, 2024). All of the later have made their fortune in the area of intangibles (brand capital, human capital, innovation capital, relational capital, and structural capital).

- Knowledge entrepreneurs are more in demand today than ever before, even more so than good business ideas: Venture capitalists invest primarily in people and only secondarily in ideas.
- The "war of talents" shows that access to intangible capital, the so-called high potential, is more important today than access to tangible capital.
- Today, the financing of new developments for traditional industrial products does not fail due to the construction of new production capacities or the cost of materials or labor, but due to knowledge-intensive research and development. Accordingly, the proportion of knowledge in these products has increased from the previous 10–20% to over 50%. On average, knowledge now accounts for over 60% of value creation in companies (Güldenberg et al., 2021). Today, a single company is less and less able to bear these development costs; strategic alliances, innovation platforms, and ecosystems are needed.

This chapter analyzes three main IC elements (human capital, structural capital, relationship capital) from the macroeconomic towards the micro (organizational and individual) level.

2.1 Human Capital: Reaching the Limits of Population Growth But Not Human Growth

The Club of Rome's report on the limits to growth already anticipated this, even if the focus was not on the limits of the knowledge economy and intangibles but on the limits of the industrial age and tangible resources: They examined the five basic factors that determine and, in their interactions, ultimately limit growth on this planet: population increase, agricultural production, nonrenewable resource depletion, industrial output, and pollution generation (Meadows et al., 1972).

In November 2022, the world's population has passed the eight billion marks. Almost all forecasts agree that we will reach the world population peak in this century, which is good news in terms of sustainability but will lead us also in the age of unknown as we never have experienced human de-growth as humankind before.

Researchers from the Earth4All initiative draw two possible scenarios for the future (Dixson-Declève et al., 2022):

1. In the first, the world will continue to develop economically in a similar way to the last 50 years. The population will then grow more slowly until 2050, reaching its maximum of around 8.6 billion in 2046 and shrinking to 7.3 billion by 2100.
2. In the second scenario, the peak could even be reached as early as 2040 with 8.5 billion people and fall back to around 6 billion by the end of the century if, among other things, there were greater investment to combat poverty.

In the meantime, 50 out of 240 countries worldwide have already reached or exceeded the population peak. The average number of children per woman is primarily linked to the level of education of the female population of reproductive age: Fertility rates fall when girls have access to education and women are economically empowered and have access to better healthcare. Slower population growth—despite all regional differences—offers many opportunities, especially for developing countries. In addition to combating poverty and hunger, this applies above all to the issue of education: Fewer birth increases the attention per child. If the average family size decreases, both families and societies will be able to invest more in each child, improve the quality of education, and develop the human capital of the population. So human de-growth is not necessarily leading to human capital de-growth. The opposite might be the case.

2.2 The Triple A of Structural Capital: Algorithms, Artificial Intelligence, and Attentiveness

The value of an organization and thus its strategic success are determined by the behavior of the organization. However, the behavior in turn results from the underlying dynamic capabilities and structures of the organization (Teece et al., 1997). Simon (1947) differentiates between the cognitive structures of employees and the structural influences of the organization on individual attention. Ocasio (1997, p. 189) formulated this idea most consistently, following Simon (1947):

"An attention-based theory views firms as systems of structurally distributed attention in which the cognition and action of individuals are not predictable from the knowledge of individual characteristics but are derived from the specific organizational context and situations that individual decision-makers find themselves in."

Ocasio (1997) understands strategy as a pattern of organizational behavior, namely, a pattern of decisions that define and make transparent the key strategic goals of the organization and determine the ways to achieve these goals. Ocasio develops this understanding further into a view of strategy as a pattern of organizational attention, understood as a pronounced focus of the organization's time and energy on a selected collection of strategic issues, problem areas, opportunities, and threats as well as a selected bundle of resources, skills, projects, and routines.

This interplay is formulated by Ocasio (1997, p. 188) in the following three interrelated premises:

1. "What decision-makers do, depends on what issues and answers they focus their attention on (**Focus of Attention**).
2. What issues and answers decisions-makers focus on, and what they do, depends on the particular context or situation they find themselves in (**Situated Attention**).
3. What particular context or situation decision-makers find themselves in, and how they attend to it, depends on how the firm's rules, resources, and social relationship regulate and control the distribution and allocation of issues, answers, and decision-makers into specific activities, communications, and procedures (**Structural Distribution of Attention**)."

Due to their limited cognitive capacities, people can only pay attention to a certain number of activities and implement them with their mental energy. They must consciously or unconsciously set priorities. The degree of available attention and mental potential determines the extent of successfully implemented activity.

This level of attention can be improved through various measures. The first important step is to focus attention and reduce distraction. This can be done either by the person themselves, which requires a great deal of discipline and willpower, or by specifically shaping the context of thought and action in which the person moves.

Algorithms, artificial intelligence, automation, and routinization can all be used to increase the level of attention (Glaser et al., 2024). This applies both to individuals and to organizations based on the division of labor. However, automation and routinization require long-term learning processes. The more these learning processes take place, the more the individual or the organization can regain attention. The available cognitive capacity grows and creates space for coping with new tasks.

A third way to increase the level of attention is to link the focus of attention to one's own cognitive strengths (structural intelligence). Structural intelligence itself is therefore always the result of the own historical development path and learning history (March, 1999). This is why every company, like every person, has its own, organization-specific intelligence. For this reason, it is also possible, in line with Gardner's (1998) approach, to identify and further specify organizations with the help of intelligence types. One could also try to make intelligence types measurable and assessable.

This third option is closely related to the second option: in those areas where employees find learning easier due to their structural predisposition or their previously acquired knowledge base, they are able to transform consciously controlled thought and action processes into unconsciously automatic ones more quickly. They create free cognitive capacities again.

Organizations exist because they are "more intelligent" than the individual or the sum of individuals who only interact with each other via the market. This generates economic value for the organization. This economic value leads to the organization attracting new employees. This applies in particular to highly qualified and intelligent people who have previously worked either via the market or in less intelligent organizations. Intelligent organizations therefore attract intelligent people, which ideally increases the overall organizational intelligence.

The raison d'être of an organization in a knowledge economy is primarily to further increase its cognitive capacity. However, this requires targeted management of the attention of employees and the organization:

> "Paying attention is no trivial task. Indeed much of the process of mastering any domain involves continual refinement in the capacity to pay attention, while simultaneously performing. [...] I believe all organizations must develop their own practices and disciplines for cultivating attentiveness" (Senge, 2000, p. xiv).

2.3 Relationship Capital, Strategic Preparedness, and Control

The Internet went down for more than 12 hours in Australia on November 8, 2023 (Haskell-Dowland et al., 2023). Chaos was the result in many places. In Australia, a continent-sized country with a population of around 26 million, a lot of work was left undone: a nationwide outage of the mobile, telephone, and Internet network at communications provider Optus not only affected ten million private customers. Trains also came to a temporary standstill, while hospitals, media, and payment systems also experienced problems.

Millions of people were unable to make calls or use the Internet via their cell phones or landlines. Only the SOS function was still available on cell phones. Optus was late to respond. At around 6.45 a.m., it said it was "aware of an issue affecting Optus' mobile and NBN services" and was working to restore services. At 8:30 a.m., the company promised via X (formerly Twitter) to provide updates as soon as possible and apologized. After that, however, there were hours of radio silence in the truest sense of the word. In addition to more than ten million private customers, i.e., almost 40 percent of the Australian population, 400,000 companies and individual businesses were also affected. Hospitals and doctors' surgeries were unavailable, and trains in Melbourne were temporarily at a standstill, causing panic, especially among high school students who were due to arrive on time for their exams. Newspapers such as the Sydney Morning Herald and The Age (Melbourne) could not be delivered on time, a number of cab drivers from Uber could not access the app, and other cab providers and many food delivery companies were also unavailable.

One man said that he initially thought he had been fired by his employer in the morning after neither his work phone nor his laptop worked. Another reported that he and his small company had already suffered a loss of earnings of around 1500 dollars in the morning. One woman said that the automatic feeding system for her cat had broken down, while a café owner complained that his payment terminal was no longer working. "Customers can't pay their bills," he said and complained: "People are back in the Stone Age."

This case clearly shows the financial damage that can occur when existing structural and relational capital suddenly and unexpectedly fails. In addition to cultivating attentiveness and managing the limits of growth, risk management and strategic preparedness are of central importance in the knowledge economy in order to manage future success and survival.

According to Simon (1993), the three key skills that ensure the survival and strategic preparedness of a company include:

The Ability to Anticipate the Shape of an Uncertain Future

This ability involves less the targeted quantitative forecasting of developments and much more the ability to anticipate qualitatively relevant changes in the environment:

"Anticipating the future means detecting, preferable prospectively, novel features in the environment that may affect the firm significantly in the future, and determining at what point in time attention should be focused on them and energy devoted to dealing with them. The available management time and attention are never sufficient to deal with all the contingencies that may arise; relative priorities for attention, planning and action need to be revised continually. [...] Anticipating the future is less like forecasting, as that term is usually used, than it is like carrying out what the military calls intelligence operations" (Simon, 1993).

Senge et al. (2004) go one step further here and see presencing (sensing the presence) as a new type of learning that, in contrast to Kolb's (1984) classic learning cycle, is based on past experiences, tries to bring the future into the present, and let it emerge there already, to make it perceptible and tangible as an experience:

"We've come to believe that the core capacity needed for accessing the field of the future is presence. We first thought of presence as being fully conscious and aware in the present moment. Then we began to appreciate presence as deep listening, of being open beyond one's preconceptions and historical ways of making sense. We came to see the importance of letting go of old identities and the need to control and, as Salk said, making choices to serve the evolution of life. Ultimately, we came to see all these aspects of presence as leading to a state of 'letting come', of consciously participating in a larger field for change. When this happens, the field shifts, and the forces shaping a situation can shift from re-creating the past to manifesting or realizing an emerging future" (Senge et al., 2004).

The Ability to Generate Alternatives

Classical economic theory assumes that decision-makers in companies are aware of all possible alternatives and choose the best of these alternatives based on economic rationality. Simon (1947) has challenged this view with his bounded rationality approach by stating that people can never be aware of all possible alternatives due to their limited cognitive capacity and are therefore already satisfied with relatively good solutions, but do not necessarily always make the optimal decision.

If the reason for the existence of organizations is to expand the limited cognitive capacities of humans, then a promising lever could be to increase the number of consciously perceived alternatives in organizations as part of IC measurement and management.

The Ability to Implement New Plans Quickly and Effectively

In order to implement strategic plans quickly and effectively in an organization, it is essential to disseminate the thinking and assumptions on which these plans are based throughout the organization:

"To be effective, a mission statement or a description of the organization's comparative advantage must become part of the mind-set of every member of the organization who is responsible for making or helping to make decisions of any consequence. Only if this conception of mission and guidelines is evoked whenever the occasion for decision arises, will decisions be shaped by it. A new member of the organization has not been assimilated successfully until he or she has acquired the concept of what the organization is seeking to accomplish and how it proposes to go about it" (Simon, 1993).

In intelligent organizations, in contrast to traditional industrial organizations, almost every employee is directly or indirectly involved in the decision-making process. Therefore, in contrast to the past, the strategy must also be communicated to all these employees. This places enormous demands on the tools of strategic performance measurement and control.

3 From Financial Management to IC Management: From the Past Towards the Future

Strategic performance measurement and management have the task of measuring and assessing the value and strategic performance of a company. It is therefore the core system of sensemaking of every company, which ultimately defines its success. Every company thinks and acts through its performance measurement system, even if many decision-makers may not be very aware of this fact: It determines the performance measurement and evaluation of top management and all employees and influences the setting of strategic priorities.

The performance measurement system can be seen as a strategic map that deliberately reduces reality in order to enable successful decision-making and action (Csaszar et al., 2024). Maps can differ fundamentally depending on the underlying objective: For example, there are road maps, hiking maps, flight maps, and weather maps. However, all good maps have two things in common:

1. They provide orientation: They help us to concentrate our perception on the essentials in a complex environment and to find our path, which lies in the future.
2. They are rational models of reality: They never depict reality one-to-one; firstly, because this would not be possible and, secondly, because it would not be particularly helpful for the underlying objective (orientation function). Too much detail would exceed the cognitive and capacities of people the organization and would make decisions impossible.

But how do our current strategic orientation maps in companies look like? What success do they focus our attention on? Do these variables help us to get strategically prepared? And what is defined as a company's success?

Classic approaches to performance measurement answer these questions by usually defining various financial indicators as success. These start with turnover, profit, or EBIT and range from traditional return ratios such as ROI or EBITDA to shareholder value performance indicators (ROCE, EVA, DCF, CFROI, etc.). The major disadvantage of all these financial indicators is that they are only insufficiently able to depict the resource of knowledge and its significance in the context of the new rules of the knowledge economy with sufficient accuracy (Lev, 2003). This inevitably leads to mismanagement within strategic performance measurement, which in turn has a negative impact on the company's financial success in the long term. One example of this is the problem of underinvestment in research and development.

Eccles (1991) noted this change already in his "Performance Measurement Manifesto":

> "At the heart of this revolution lies a radical decision: to shift from treating financial figures as the foundation for performance measurement to treating them as one among a broader set of measures. Put like this, it hardly sounds revolutionary. Many managers can honestly claim that they – and their companies – have tracked quality, market share, and other non-financial measures for years. Tracking these measures is one thing. But giving them equal (or even greater) status in determining strategy, promotions, bonuses, and other rewards is another. [...] Finally, many managers worry that income-based financial figures are better at measuring the consequences of yesterday's decisions than they are at indicating tomorrow's performance."

Today, more than 30 years later, the first tentative signs of change can be observed.

According to North and Güldenberg (2011), the reasons and disadvantages for the persistent adherence to existing financial performance measurement systems can be summarized in several categories:

1. **Managers often measure the wrong things:** Decision-makers measure what is easy to measure without questioning what the results of these measurements are. They become prisoners of their convenience and bounded rationality: Financial indicators are the easiest measures to collect in today's organizations. Mathematical calculability usually dominates the cause-and-effect chain and not strategic relevance. Thereby managers tend to forget about intangibles, synergies, and interrelationships, which are what characterize every organization and its raison d'être.
2. **Managers measure too often with the wrong yardstick:** Temporal yardstick are very often far too short. They measure statically and not dynamically. They only see a series of snapshots instead of recognizing the entire film. This means that decision-makers' perceptions miss out on dynamic processes that are essential for their strategic decisions and business understanding, such as time delay effects or feedback loops. In addition, they measure with absolute rather than relative numbers. By definition, however, absolute values can only ever be control-oriented and never learning-oriented, because it is only from the relative interplay with other values that it is possible to draw conclusions. This leads to distorted perception and operational blindness. The focus on internal mediocrity obscures the view of possible strategic potential.
3. **Managers do not measure what is important:** Intangible assets are generally not measured at all or are measured too little. As a result, decision-makers are essentially guided by tangible assets when making strategic decisions. They know too little about their organizational knowledge base and its strategic value. They do not know in which areas they possess a knowledge advantage over their competitors. They do not know how widespread this knowledge is on the market. They do not know how well their knowledge management system works and what strategic contribution it makes. They know nothing about the quality and

nature of their organizational learning capability. They know nothing about the extent and strategic superiority of their intellectual capital.

4. **Managers measure, but they don't know what for:** Decision-makers use numerous key figures but find it difficult to link these metrics to their strategy. That's why they try to exercise operational control via key figures instead of learning strategically from them. They find it difficult to interpret and learn from strategic gaps. They therefore concentrate on correcting them. In doing so, they overlook strategic opportunities and risks.

The above analysis calls for an urgent change. In order to achieve this change, a redefinition of IC research as well as IC practice is highly needed. In the following two chapters, a research agenda and practical implications for further action are developed.

4 Redefining IC Measurement and Management: A Research Agenda

This chapter summarizes the previous points of criticism in order to generate a research agenda for IC measurement and management.

4.1 In Search of a More Dynamic IC Measurement and Management

Existing IC measurement and management tools take too little account of the dynamic dimension of knowledge. They inevitably become selective and episodic. They present knowledge as something that can be photographed and thus measured at a certain point in time or even just once a year, as in the case of IC statements. As a consequence, decision-makers perceive the development of their company as if it were a photo album, a colorful, disjointed, and unintegrated collection of snapshots. To do justice to the dynamic nature of knowledge as a resource, however, you need a movie rather than images. This is the only way to achieve meaningful strategic control. A greater focus on dynamic complexity also requires a reduction in structural complexity. It is therefore important that managers concentrate on a few strategically but highly relevant decision variables and observe these so intensively that they can recognize patterns of behavior over time ("time-path") (Warren, 2002).

This is not supported by most inductive-analytical IC measurement models today. Their structural complexity, which results from an exuberant and incoherent collection of key figures, measures, and target values, overwhelms human perception. As a result, the dynamic complexity that is so crucial is covered up and no longer visible. Although the balanced scorecard goes one step further in this respect by limiting the number of key figures to around 15–20 and fundamentally understanding strategy as a cause-and-effect chain in its strategy map, it is structured exclusively hierarchically and statically in the Kaplan and Norton (1996) proposal and, in contrast to the system-dynamic representation via causal loops, conceals important information such as self-reinforcing and balancing processes, delay effects, and the distinction between the underlying dynamic structure and the resulting behavioral level. So far no distinction is made between knowledge as a stock variable and knowledge as a flow variable, which means that steering interventions cannot be targeted at the learning and development perspective underlying the balanced scorecard. What we therefore urgently need is not more IC categories, measures, and statements, but more research on dynamic IC frameworks that enable decision-makers to learn better and faster (Kianto et al., 2020).

4.2 In Search of a More Integrated IC Measurement and Management

Existing IC measurement and management tools focus too much on the individual key figures and too little on their relationship to the strategy, on the overall strategic picture. Their greatest strength is therefore also their greatest danger: the reduction of complexity to a few key figures, which leads to false conclusions. For example, what is the strategic significance if companies invest over 3% in research and development, staff turnover is 20%, or employees receive an average of 5.8 days of further training per year? What strategic conclusions can be drawn from this? What about the future potential and strategic performance of this organization?

In addition, the path dependency (path-dependency) of knowledge is not incorporated into the design of the control systems (Teece et al., 1997). Knowledge cannot simply be created in a context-free space; it must be capable of being linked to existing knowledge (absorption capacity) (Cohen & Levinthal, 1990). This also means that strategic knowledge gaps cannot be filled at will. Corporate strategy is dependent on existing intellectual capital and knowledge and not vice versa. What we therefore urgently need is a stronger integration of IC into strategy research (e.g., Cabrilo & Dahms, 2018).

4.3 In Search of a More Indirect IC Measurement and Management

Existing IC measurement and management tools focus very strongly on the direct measurement of knowledge via input and output variables. As a rule, these represent inventory variables such as investments in research and development, turnover, and profit. However, this does not allow any statement to be made about the strategically relevant processes of knowledge generation and knowledge transfer. On the contrary, empirical studies confirm that there is no statistically significant correlation between these input variables (such as investment in research and development) and the output achieved (such as the number of innovations or patents) (Kandybin & Kihn, 2004). It therefore depends on the process variables in between. However, these variables are significantly influenced by intangibles (such as culture, motivation, loyalty, reputation, attention, and trust).

IC measurement must include process variables if it is to become more meaningful and relevant. However, as these process variables cannot be directly quantified, models and assumptions must be used to assess them at least indirectly. For example, a suitable indicator for employee motivation could be the number of sick days, attentiveness could be measured by the number of accidents at work, and loyalty by the extent of criminal activity by employees within the company. Even if these indicators do not appear to have much to do with IC at first glance, they can provide more insight into the strategic performance of a company than the input- and output-focused indicators mentioned above. What we therefore urgently need is a stronger process focus of IC research in the tradition of Roos and Roos (1997).

4.4 In Search of a More Interactive IC Measurement and Management

Existing IC measurement and management tools remain too much in the realm of diagnosis and do not make the leap to an interactive strategic performance management system that supports the organizational learning process. Simons (2000) himself, for example, classifies the Balanced Scorecard, which comes closest to addressing the link to organizational learning processes, as a diagnostic and not an interactive management system.

IC measurement and management tools are therefore still today too often used as performance evaluation instruments in the good tradition of classic financially oriented control systems. They focus exclusively on: Where do we have an unplanned deviation, and who is to blame, or what can we do now to close this gap? These questions, which are very often not asked explicitly but usually implicitly, immediately prevent any organizational learning process and trigger defensive routines (Argyris, 1985). Instead, it is important to understand that it is the emergence of deviations, of surprises, that enables learning and can reveal new strategic opportunities for the company: Drucker says "I'm not saying that every surprise is an opportunity, but every surprise is something to be taken seriously" (Drucker & Senge, 2000, originally from Drucker, 1999). What we therefore urgently need is more research on how IC tools are actually integrated and applied in organizations in line with Roos et al. (2001).

5 Practical Implications for Rethinking IC Management in Organizations

Mental models are the basis of strategic thinking and learning. IC management must be guided by these. The following five principles of strategic management of knowledge in companies should provide orientation so that IC management can be successfully implemented in practice (an earlier version of these five principles was already published in Güldenberg, 1999).

5.1 Strengthen Dynamic Thinking: Presenting the Relevant Strategic Control Variables over Time

Existing knowledge-oriented management tools do not take enough account of the dynamic dimension of knowledge. Integrating system dynamics and thus the causal loop language into the design of knowledge-oriented management systems can help to emphasize this dynamic aspect more strongly (see, e.g., Kianto, 2007).

5.2 Strengthen Networked Thinking: Depicting the Relevant Internal and External Cause-Effect Chains (Feedback Loops)

Existing strategic management tools focus too much on the individual key figures and too little on their inter-relationships, in the overall context. In connection with the dynamic nature of strategic management systems, it is therefore important to make the underlying dynamic system structure (feedback loops) visible. Only the connection between the dynamic structure and behavior of the system over time enables an understanding of how the overall system functions and thus opens up the insight for effective intervention and control (Warren, 2002).

5.3 Strengthening Thinking in Models: Differentiation and Equal Consideration of Stock and Flow Variables

Existing strategic management tools focus too much on input and output variables. As a rule, these represent stock variables, such as investments in research and development, turnover, and profit. However, the so-called flow variables are much more important for strategic management, especially in knowledge-based companies. They generally represent the process that lies between input and output. Care should therefore be taken to ensure that a sufficient number of flow variables are taken into account in the underlying strategic management model. However, flow variables also always require thinking in models, as the assumptions about the black box that lies between input and output must now be revealed and made transparent (Roos & Roos, 1997).

5.4 Strengthen Strategic Thinking and System-Oriented Action: Directly Linking Feedback Loops to Knowledge Strategy, Knowledge Management Strategy, and Strategic Success

Existing strategic management tools promote too much the illusion of a possible direct and one-dimensional management based on knowledge. For this reason, IC management must go beyond the pure key figure level and make the underlying dynamic structure and interconnectedness of the measured influencing variables transparent. In this context, it is important to realize that IC measurement itself has never an absolute and static value but is always a reflection of current strategic thinking and is therefore subject to constant adjustments and changes. Like a good map, it must therefore be continuously adapted and actively changed if it is to continue to be useful for organizational sensemaking and strategic preparedness.

Secondly, it is important to recognize that the types of interventions in the system are always determined by the system itself. In the following, we summarize this under the term "acting in accordance with the system" (Güldenberg, 1999). The belief in direct and one-dimensional top-down control must therefore be replaced by thinking in terms of influencing levers, whose change can stimulate the overall dynamics of the system in a certain direction. These levers can vary in power depending on their integration into the system.

5.5 Strengthening Strategic Learning: The Three Pillars of Organizational Intelligence Are Organizational Structure, Organizational Learning Capability, and Organizational Knowledge Base

Existing strategic management tools remain too much tied up in diagnosis and do not make the leap to an interactive strategic performance management system that supports the organizational learning process. However, this is an important prerequisite for IC management. IC management systems must therefore be designed in such a way that they focus managers' and employees' attention on learning opportunities. This includes both strategic learning opportunities within the organizational knowledge base and the improvement of the organizational learning capability as a whole. Above this is the premise of organizational intelligence, which essentially states that it is about recognizing one's own organization-specific intelligence and structure in order to use this to build a sustainable strategic competitive advantage. A good IC performance management system must therefore not block or slow down organizational learning, but on the contrary must promote and accelerate strategic learning processes. This is achieved by increasing organizational attentiveness, which focuses on the aspects of knowledge dynamics and path dependency.

6 Conclusion

What kind of IC measurement and management tools will define effectively the future value and success of our organizations in a knowledge economy? While we cannot answer this question, this contribution tries to redefine strategic performance management for today's companies as a central component of strategic thinking, learning, and action in a knowledge economy. In doing so, the weaknesses of financial performance measurement tools have been outlined, and the need for action toward more advanced IC measurement and management frameworks has been highlighted. Organizations exist today not because they are more efficient than the market but because they are more intelligent. Intelligent organizations therefore attract intelligent people, which ideally increases the overall organizational intellectual capital. This is why we must concentrate more on measuring intellectual capital instead of shareholder value, on measuring national intellectual capital instead of gross national product, on measuring brainpower instead of purchasing power.

At the same time, the limitations of existing IC measurement and management tools have been critically discussed. These limitations include a too selective, static, and episodic view; they often remain too separated from strategy. IC statements count too often inputs and outputs of knowledge, instead of focusing on meaning and processes. IC statements remain too much in the realm of diagnosis and do not make the leap to an interactive strategic performance management system that supports the organizational learning process. That is why this contribution proposed a research agenda for a redefined IC measurement and management. What we urgently need here is not more IC categories, measures, and statements but more research on dynamic IC frameworks, a stronger integration into strategy research, a stronger process focus of IC research, and more empirical research on how IC tools are actually integrated and applied in organizations. As a conclusion five principles have been proposed that should guide the implementation of IC measurement and management tools in order to improve the existing strategic performance management in organizations.

References

Argyris, C. (1985). *Strategy, change, and defensive routines*. Pitman.

Cabrilo, S., & Dahms, S. (2018). How strategic knowledge management drives intellectual capital to superior innovation and market performance. *Journal of Knowledge Management, 22*(3), 621–648.

Cohen, W. M., & Levinthal, D. A. (1990). Absorptive capacity: A new perspective on learning and innovation. *Administrative Science Quarterly, 35*(1), 128–152.

Csaszar, F. A., Hinrichs, N., & Heshmati, M. (2024). External representations in strategic decision-making: Understanding strategy's reliance on visuals. *Strategic Management Journal*, 1–36.

Czímer, B., Dietz, M., László, V., & Sengupta, J. (2022). The future of banks: A $20 trillion breakup opportunity. In: McKinsey quarterly. 20 Dec 2022. https://www.mckinsey.com/industries/financial-services/our-insights/the-future-of-banks-a-20-trillion-dollar-breakup-opportunity.

Dixson-Declève, S., Gaffney, O., Ghosh, J., Randers, J., Rockström, J., & Stoknes, P. E. (2022). *Earth for all: A survival guide for humanity*. New Society Publishers.

Drucker, P. F. (1999). *Management challenges for the 21st century*. Routledge.

Drucker, P. F., & Senge, P. M. (2000). Meeting of the minds. *Across the board, 37*(10), 16–21.

Edvinsson, L., & Malone, M. S. (1997). *Intellectual capital realizing your company's true value by finding its hidden brainpower*. Harper Business.

Eccles, R. G. (1991). The performance measurement manifesto. *Harvard Business Review, 69*(1), 131–137.

Fisher, L. M. (2002). *Yves* Doz: The thought leader interview. *Strategy + Business, 29*(4), 115–123.

Forbes. (2024). The world's real-time billionaires. *Forbes, 4*(3), 2024. https://www.forbes.com/real-time-billionaires/#8f8e44f3d788

Gardner, H. (1998). A multiplicity of intelligences. *Scientific American, 9*(4), 19–23.

Glaser, V. L., Sloan, J., & Gehman, J. (2024). Organizations as algorithms: A new metaphor for advancing management theory. *Journal of Management Studies*. Forthcoming. Open Access 17.1.2024: https://onlinelibrary.wiley.com/doi/10.1111/joms.13033

Gloe, D. V. (2023). Putin is trapped in the sunk-cost fallacy of war: Moscow is grasping for meaning in a meaningless invasion. *Foreign Policy Magazine*. 14 Mar 2023. https://foreignpolicy.com/2023/03/14/putin-ukraine-war-sunk-cost-fallacy/

Goldstein, J. (2024). $1 billion donation will provide free tuition at a Bronx Medical School. *The New York Times*. 26 Feb 2024. https://www.nytimes.com/2024/02/26/nyregion/albert-einstein-college-medicine-bronx-donation.html

Güldenberg, S. (1999). Measuring in the knowledge age: The perspective of the living and learning organization. *Journal of Strategic Performance Measurement, 3*(6), 6–15.

Güldenberg, S., Ernst, E., & North, K. (2021). *Managing work in the digital economy—challenges, strategies and practices for the next decade*. Springer.

Haskell-Dowland, P., Gregory, M. A., & Ahmed, M. (2023). Optus blackout: What is a 'deep network' outage and what may have caused it? 8 Nov 2023. https://www.abc.net.au/news/2023-11-08/optus-deep-network-outage-what-is-the-cause/103080080.

Kianto, A. (2007). What do we really mean by the dynamic dimension of intellectual capital? *Journal of Intellectual Capital, 4*(4), 342–354.

Kianto, A., Ritala, P., Vanhala, M., & Hussinki, H. (2020). Reflections on the criteria for the sound measurement of intellectual capital: A knowledge-based perspective. *Critical Perspectives on Accounting, 70*, 102046.

Kaplan, R. S., & Norton, D. P. (1996). *The balanced scorecard: Translating strategy into action*. Harvard Business School Press.

Kandybin, A., & Kihn, M. (2004). Raising your return on innovation investment. Resilience Report, Strategy + Business, Booz Allen Hamilton, 35, 5 Nov 2004.

Kolb, D. A. (1984). *Experiential learning: Experience as the source of learning and development*. Prentice Hall.

Lev, B. (2003). Corporate earnings: Facts and fiction. *The Journal of Economic Perspectives, 17*(2), 27–50.

March, J. G. (1999). The pursuit of organizational intelligence, Malden/MA und Oxford/UK.

Meadows, D. H., Meadows, D. L., Randers, J., & Behrens, W. (1972). *The limits to growth: A report for the Club of Rome's project on the predicament of mankind*. Universe Books.

North, K., & Güldenberg, S. (2011). *Effective knowledge work: Answers to the management challenge of the 21st century*. Emerald Group Publishing.

Ocasio, W. (1997). Towards an attention-based view of the firm. *Strategic Management Journal, 18*(Summer Special Issue), 187–206.

Parayre, R. (1995). The strategic implications of sunk costs: A behavioral perspective. *Journal of Economic Behavior & Organization, 28*(3), 417–442.

Roos, G., Bainbridge, A., & Jacobsen, K. (2001). Intellectual capital analysis as a strategic tool. *Strategy & Leadership, 4*(29), 1–26.

Roos, G., & Roos, J. (1997). Measuring your company's intellectual performance. *Long Range Planning, 30*(3), 413–426.

Seddon, M., Miller, C., & Schwartz, F. (2023). How Putin blundered into Ukraine—then doubled down. *Financial Times, 23*(2), 2023. https://www.ft.com/content/80002564-33e8-48fb-b734-44810afb7a49

Senge, P. M. (1990). *The fifth discipline: The art and practice of the learning organization.* Doubleday/Currency.

Senge, P. M. (2000). Foreword. In T. H. Johnson & A. Bröms (Eds.), *Profit beyond measure: Extraordinary results through attention to work and people* (pp. ix–xvi).

Senge, P. M., Scharmer, C. O., Jaworski, J., & Flowers, B. S. (2004). *Presence: Human purpose and the field of the future.* Crown Currency.

Shatz, H. J., & Reach, C. (2023). *The cost of the Ukraine war for Russia.* RAND Corporation. 18 Dec 2023. https://www.rand.org/pubs/research_reports/RRA2421-1.html

Simon, H. A. (1947). *Administrative behavior, a study of decision making processes in administrative organizations.* Macmillan.

Simon, H. A. (1993). Strategy and organizational evolution. *Strategic Management Journal, 14*(Winter Special Issue), 131–142.

Simons, R. L. (2000). *Performance measurement & control systems for implementing strategy.* Prentice Hall.

Teece, D. J., Pisano, G., & Shuen, A. (1997). Dynamic capabilities and strategic management. *Strategic Management Journal, 18*(7), 509–533.

Warren, K. (2002). *Competitive strategy dynamics.* Wiley.

Prof. Dr. Stefan Güldenberg is a Full Professor at EHL Hospitality Business School, HES-SO, Lausanne, Switzerland, and Academic Director at EHL's Graduate School. He serves as the current President of The New Club of Paris, a think tank and agenda-setter for the knowledge economy. His research and teaching focuses on strategic management, sustainable leadership, learning organizations, and knowledge management. He is the Editor-in-Chief of the Swiss Journal of Business (Die Unternehmung) and at the Editorial Board of several other scientific journals, including EURAM Sparks, the Journal of Knowledge Management, and the Journal of Digital Economy. Before joining EHL he has worked as a Professor at the University of Liechtenstein and the Vienna University of Economics and Business (WU Vienna). Visiting Professorships abroad led him, among others, to Harvard University, MIT, and the National University of Singapore. He has more than 30 years of working experience in strategy research, strategy consulting, as a knowledge entrepreneur, and platform founder. His two latest book publications are on *Managing Work in the Digital Economy: Challenges, Strategies and Practices for the Next Decade* (together with E. Ernst and K. North) and *Cross-Border Life and Work: Social, Economic, Technological and Jurisdictional Issues* (together with P. Droege, M.J. Menichetti, and S. Seidel).

Being Critical About Intellectual Capital in 2024: Chocolate as a Manifesto for Social Change

John Dumay

> *We must use our experiences and lessons learned from the past and think of how we can combine people, relationships, systems, physical and natural capitals to build a better society for everyone. Then maybe the research we have been doing in accounting that considers ways to measure, value, manage, and report on IC might be worthwhile after all.*
>
> *(Dumay et al., 2020, p. 8)*

J. Dumay (✉)
Macquarie University, Sydney, NSW, Australia

Nyenrode Business Universiteit, Breukelen, The Netherlands

Aalborg University, Aalborg, Denmark
e-mail: john.dumay@mq.edu.au

A. Kianto et al. (eds.), *Futurizing Intellectual Capital*, Knowledge Management and Organizational Learning 15, https://doi.org/10.1007/978-3-031-80197-6_17

Abstract

Intellectual capital should be worthwhile to society, not just worth something to companies. In this chapter, we critically analyse the intellectual capital of the cocoa supply chain through the Chocolate Scorecard project. We find that the outcome of producing chocolate (manufactured capital) from cocoa beans and the downstream financial gains (Financial capital) comes with a heavy price because the chocolate companies and retailers are contributing to destroying human capital (farmers and their families) and natural capital (land and the forests). At the heart of the problem is the shared value business model that keeps companies rich, farmers poor, and their children have no choice but to work on the farms as modern-day slaves. However, chocolate companies can pay more and do more, as companies like Tony's Chocolonely and Godiva do. The changed business models positively impact people's lives (human capital) and the environment (natural capital), and this is certainly worthwhile.

1 Introduction

Several years ago, Dumay et al. (2018) identified a fifth stage of intellectual capital (IC) research. It advocates going beyond the fourth stage of research, which adds concern for society and the environment (Dumay & Garanina, 2013). The fifth stage of IC research removes boundaries, and the question researchers ask changes from "What is IC worth to investors, customers, society and the environment?" to "Is managing IC a worthwhile endeavour?"

Since writing the above quote, our research has extended into the fifth stage. This chapter presents a case study of the Chocolate Scorecard, a worthwhile research project. Here, I examine how human and natural capital are compromised to create financial value. As a result, we offer a critique of the shared value theory of economic development and a manifesto for continued change in how researchers conceptualise and undertake IC research to build a better society for everyone (Dumay et al., 2020, p. 8).

2 Getting Mad at Nestlé and Finding the Chocolate Scorecard

It was 8 March 2016—International Women's Day. An article by Esther Han (2016b), the Consumer Affairs editor at the Sydney Morning Herald, spurred me into action. The article was about a woman's dire predicament in the cocoa supply chain. Women working in the cocoa supply chain earned significantly less than men, women did the lowest paying jobs, and cultural gender biases meant that women didn't own land, were not properly trained, or had the same opportunities as men to earn a living.

The article then lamented how the big cocoa companies, who control 40% of world output, were coming to rescue the women. Han (2016b) outlined how Nestlé's Cocoa Plan, Mondelez's Cocoa Life program, and Mars' Women's Empowerment Plan will help by offering training and finance to help them grow more cocoa. However, the article does not mention paying women or men for their cocoa based on the profits of these giant cocoa companies in the mega millions of dollars.

Why would someone write something so favourable about the companies when it is clear they are not doing the right thing? The answer is in the disclaimer to the story—"The writer travelled to Ivory Coast as a guest of Nestlé". Greenwashing at its best—pay to have something good written to obfuscate bad practices. What made it worse for me was that Nestlé led the charge by paying a journalist to go to Africa. Unfortunately, Nestlé is often in the spotlight for alleged failings in its corporate responsibility that threaten its legitimacy and social license to operate (Perkiss et al., 2021)—from its marketing of baby formula in Africa (Husted, 2000), tax scandals (Sikka & Willmott, 2010), and failings in the nutritional value of food marketed to children (Smith & Westerbeek, 2007). However, it is one of the world's biggest food companies and has a long history of distancing itself from problems using impression management techniques (Perkiss et al., 2021).

I was mad and decided to do something about it!

Fortunately, I have two amazing colleagues who shared my anger, and we investigated Nestlé's discourse about their involvement in the cocoa supply chain. Our initial research discovered how the cocoa supply chain is riddled with serious issues such as child and forced labour and unsustainable farming practices. Nestlé used impression techniques to repair its legitimacy because child labour and unsustainable farming practices exist in its cocoa supply chain, and different stakeholders were attacking it to change those practices. The result is a paper we published in Critical Perspectives on Accounting that highlighted the unsustainability of the cocoa supply chain and "the plight of cocoa's child labourers" (Perkiss et al., 2021, p. 1).

When Critical Perspectives on Accounting published the paper, it caught the attention of the editor of my university's (Macquarie University) Lighthouse online magazine, which publishes articles about interesting and impactful research projects at the university. As a result, The Lighthouse website published an article about the paper that several Australian news media outlets picked up. Soon, several people reached out to me about the research that led to further collaboration on the impact of child and forced labour and other sustainability issues in the cocoa supply chain and modern slavery.

Two of those reaching out were Fuzz and Carolyn Kitto, the founders and co-directors from the non-government organisation (NGO) Be Slavery Free, an Australian coalition of civil society campaigning against modern slavery, human trafficking, and forced and child labour. Along with fighting to end modern slavery, Be Slavery Free also runs the annual Chocolate Scorecard. The Chocolate Scorecard is a resource for consumers seeking information about the chocolate they purchase, made from cocoa beans, from companies along the cocoa supply chain, and for investors and stakeholders seeking to understand a company's performance.

The result is a partnership with Macquarie University Business School, The University of Wollongong, The Open University UK, and the Be Slavery Free Chocolate Scorecard project. Be Slavery Free developed the current format of the Chocolate Scorecard in 2020 to evaluate the participating companies' performance in addressing human rights and environmental challenges and facilitate a productive dialogue to enhance their policies and practices towards improving the whole industry. Many companies use the scorecard to develop and improve their policies and practices, which positively impacts people, mainly farmers and their families in Western Africa, who rely on the chocolate supply chain for their livelihoods.

The Chocolate Scorecard is now in its fifth edition. The project is receiving considerable interest internationally as it is widely publicised in the international media, especially online. Reliable estimates for the Fourth Edition Chocolate Scorecard (2023) were that it had a media audience reach of more than one billion in 2023 based on an analysis using Coveragebook.com. Additionally, I have travelled in Australia and internationally to present our findings about the Chocolate Scorecard at conferences and seminars at many universities (Italy, the Netherlands, Denmark, Norway, Sweden, Finland, Belgium, the UK, and Sri Lanka). The research demonstrates the power of IC and sustainability accounting and how it can positively impact the people who depend on the cocoa supply chain for their existence.

3 The Intellectual Capital of the Cocoa Supply Chain

Cocoa is grown on cacao trees in tropical climates within 20 degrees of the equator. Originally from Central and South America, most of the chocolate we consume comes from cocoa beans grown in two West African countries, the Côte d'Ivoire and Ghana. The cocoa produced in these two countries accounts for about 70% of the world's production (Perkiss et al., 2021). Countries like Ecuador, Brazil, Vietnam, Indonesia, and Papua New Guinea also grow cocoa. However, I will stick mainly to the West African supply chain because most of the cocoa grown there is the raw material for mass-produced chocolate by big, powerful multinational companies such as Nestlé, Mars, Hershey, and Cadbury (Mondelez).

The intellectual capital of the cocoa supply chain is multifaceted and complex, as I summarize in Table 1. To present Table 1, I also draw on natural, manufactured, and financial capital as per the International Integrated Reporting Framework (International Integrated Reporting Council (IIRC), 2021). I use the IIRC framework as it helps complete the analysis because these are essential elements of the cocoa supply chain. It is essential to note that as we move downstream in the cocoa supply chain, the outcome is that companies are increasing profits, and governments are getting more tax. However, the outcome of producing chocolate (manufactured capital) and downstream financial gains (Financial capital) comes with a heavy price because the chocolate companies and retailers are contributing to destroying human capital (farmers and their families) and natural capital (land and the forests).

Cocoa beans come from the fruit pods of the cacao tree, which are typically grown on relatively small farm holdings that produce less than a tonne of beans per

Table 1 Capital and the cocoa supply chain in West Africa

	Natural capital	Human capital	Structural capital	Relational capital	Manufactured capital	Financial capital (€/kg finished product)
Farming cocoa beans	Land, water, trees	Farmers, their wives Child, adult, and forced labour	Tacit and explicit farming knowledge	Pisteurs Cooperatives Governments	Agrochemicals Fuel Farm tools Drying facilities Warehouses	Little or no profit or tax Poverty Farm gate pricing
Transportation and distribution	Land and sea	Pisteurs Wholesalers Government officials	Cocoa bean quality, grading and sorting	Cooperatives Cocoa exporters Government	Trucks, roads and warehouses Port and boats Fuel	Small profits €0.07 and tax €0.09
Processors	Cocoa beans, butter, liquor, powder.	Factory workers	Brands Recipes and formulas	Manufacturers Governments Shareholders	Factories and machines for grinding, processing	Some profit €0.08 and tax €0.02
Manufacturing	Milk, sugar, palm oil, hazelnuts	Factory workers Chocolatiers	Brands Recipes and formulas	Retailers Shareholders Governments	Factories and machines for manufacturing, packaging	More profit €0.29 and tax €0.07
Retailing	Fuel, water, energy	Retail workers Store managers	Brands Online retailing	Customers Shareholders Governments	Physical stores Packaging Finished products	The most profit €0.82 and tax €0.75

Source: Author's interpretation and Food and Agriculture Organization of the United Nations and Bureau d'Analyse Societale d'Interet Collectif (2023)

hectare (Suh & Molua, 2022). Productivity is low because monoculture is stripping nutrients from the soil, cocoa trees are getting older, climate change alters weather patterns, and the trees are more susceptible to pests and diseases (Trading Economics, 2024). While the farmers know how to grow cocoa traditionally, most do not have the knowledge or resources to increase their productivity.

The small farm holdings are mainly family-owned, or families work as sharecroppers. Typically, the farmer is male and works with his wife (or wives), who do most of the domestic work, and their children. Child labour is common because the farmers are poor and can't afford to pay for farm workers.

The work done by children is not simply doing a few chores on the farm and is a form of modern slavery because the children are doing work that adults should do. For example, spraying agrichemicals without proper personal protective equipment, using machetes to control weeds and harvest the cocoa pods, and helping dry and bag the cocoa beans. Unfortunately, there have also been cases of forced labour with children being abducted or transported from poorer neighbouring countries of Mali and Burkina Faso (Food Empowerment Project, 2016). In many cases, children have no choice but to work on the cocoa farms, do not get paid, and often miss out on going to school. Essentially, these children work under slave-like conditions.

The farmers and their helpers, including children, open the pods to expose white cocoa beans inside a sticky, sweet pulp (placenta). The beans and pulp are placed on banana leaves and then allowed to ferment for about a week, allowing enzymes in the beans to transform them into the dark cacao beans, chocolate flavours, and aromas we are familiar with. The farmers dry the beans in the sun and then put them into sacks for transport to local cooperatives.

However, farmers cannot sell their beans directly to the market as they are often unable to transport them. The farmers rely on Pisteurs, intermediaries who buy the cocoa from the farmers and transport it to cooperatives. However, while the government sets a farmgate price for cocoa, the farmer is not guaranteed to get that price as the Pisteur also needs to earn money and pay transport costs. After the farmer covers expenses, there is little or no profit. Hence, farmers and their families live in poverty (Food and Agriculture Organization of the United Nations and Bureau d'Analyse Societale d'Interet Collectif, 2023).

The cooperatives clean and quality-check the beans before selling some to local processing plants for grinding into cocoa butter, liquor, or powder. Alternatively, they might send the beans to a local port destined for export (Food and Agriculture Organization of the United Nations and Bureau d'Analyse Societale d'Interet Collectif, 2023). The companies make some profit, and the producing country governments collect taxes and export fees from these companies.

The beans then go to processing companies, mainly in Europe and America. The biggest of these is a little-known company called Bary Callebaut, which processes 14% of all cocoa bean production, has a 39% share of the processed cocoa products market, and makes considerable profit for its shareholders (Barry Callebaut, 2021). Most of the processing occurs outside the producing countries and by foreign companies. Therefore, most of the profit and taxes accrue to companies in the Global North.

Cocoa processors supply the chocolate manufacturing companies. The biggest of these are the brand names we often associate with chocolate: Mars, Ferrero, Mondelez (Cadbury), Hershey's, Nestlé, and Lindt. However, thousands of small and medium chocolate manufacturers and chocolatiers exist. These companies mix processed cocoa with other ingredients such as milk, sugar, palm oil, and hazelnuts and then package it to make the chocolate candy we all love. These companies sell and distribute their finished products to retailers and make considerable profits, and they pay taxes to their respective governments, again mainly in the Global North.

The last link in the cocoa supply chain is the retailers, big and small. It is this link where the most profit and taxes accrue. Compared to the producing countries' share of profit and tax, it is exponentially more. Therefore, the shareholders and governments of the countries that consume chocolate reap most of the financial benefits from the value chain. Hence, shareholders in the Global North become richer, cocoa farmers remain poor, and their farms become unsustainable because they are becoming less productive. At the same time, the governments in the Global North collect taxes to build schools, hospitals, and infrastructure. At the same time, the producing countries in the Global South struggle to find money to do the same. But how do you fix the problem and better share value in the supply chain?

4 Is Shared Value the Answer?

Looking at where the profits and taxes are prevalent in the cocoa supply chain, a simple solution seems apparent. Pay more for raw cocoa beans, so farmers and producing countries can have a greater share of the value created. That means that companies in the Global North make less profits, and their respective governments collect less taxes. However, this is not an approach that companies, governments, and even business schools advocate. Instead, their idea of shared value is to increase the efficiency and productivity of poor farmers so they can produce more for less (Porter & Kramer, 2011, 2019). As Porter and Kramer (2011, p. 65) from Harvard Business School advocate:

> Shared value, then, is not about personal values. Nor is it about "'sharing" the value already created by firms-a redistribution approach. Instead, it is about expanding the total pool of economic and social value. A good example of this difference in perspective is the fair trade movement in purchasing. Fair trade aims to increase the proportion of revenue that goes to poor farmers by paying them higher prices for the same crops. Though this may be a noble sentiment, fair trade is mostly about redistribution rather than expanding the overall amount of value created. A shared value perspective, instead, focuses on improving growing techniques and strengthening the local cluster of supporting suppliers and other institutions in order to increase farmers' efficiency, yields, product quality, and sustainability. This leads to a bigger pie of revenue and profits that benefits both farmers and the companies that buy from them.

Porter and Kramer (2011, p. 65) argue that while paying poor cocoa farmers more might lift incomes by 10 to 20%, their shared value model can lift incomes by up to

300%. However, they do not share their calculations of how this might happen or provide references to the "early studies" they claim proves their argument.

One chocolate company that believes in and advocates the shared value model is Nestlé. Nestlé has been spruiking shared value since 2007 when it entitled its sustainability report *The Nestlé Creating Shared Value Report* (Nestlé, 2007). Here is what Nestlé (2007, p. 1) had to say about shared value (emphasis in the original):

> For a business to be successful in the long term it has to create value, not only for its shareholders but also for society. We call this *Creating Shared Value*. It is not philanthropy or an add-on, but a fundamental part of our business strategy. Simply stated, in order to create value for our shareholders and our Company, we need to create value for the people in the countries where we are present. This includes the farmers who supply us, our employees, our consumers and the communities where we operate.
>
> As a necessary condition for Creating Shared Value, we need to demonstrate responsible behaviour – by assuring compliance and sustainability. This includes complying with Nestlé Business Principles, national laws and international norms, and ensuring that our actions are environmentally sound, socially just and economically viable.

Nestlé (2007) reported buying 370,000 tonnes of cocoa beans, powder, butter, and liquor, worth CFH 930 million in 2006, or about US$2011 per tonne (at 1.25 CFH to USD average closing price). This price reflects that Nestlé purchases raw and processed cocoa products as it was above the $US1600 a tonne price for raw cocoa beans. At that time, Nestlé (2007, p. 32) did not "own any cocoa farms or plantations" but was "committed to contributing to more sustainable cocoa growing through programmes run with other members of industry, governments in the producer countries of West Africa, and other partner organisations". Hence, in 2006 Nestlé appears to have little control over their cocoa supply chain.

Fast forward to Nestlé's (2023) *Creating Shared Value and Sustainability Report*, where there are no financial disclosures about how much Nestlé is paying for cocoa. However, they disclose how they are changing how they impact the cocoa supply chain through the Nestlé Cocoa Plan, which now covers 85.5% of farmers in their supply chain. The Nestlé Cocoa Plan has three pillars: "Better farming, aiming to improve livelihoods in communities. Better lives, aiming to improve social conditions for families. And Better cocoa, aiming to improve product sustainability". Hence, Nestlé now has considerably more impact on their supply chain than in 2006. However, the program is not without its critics, with The Chocolate Accountability Lab (2023) claiming that it has "failed to bring farmers out of poverty and have not stopped hazardous child labor on cocoa farms".

Nestlé (2023, p. 32) is also experimenting in the Ivory Coast with their income accelerator program, which "has empowered more than 10,000 farmers with skills and knowledge on good agricultural practices and environmental protection, and has enabled more children to register in school, to reduce child labor risks". In the income accelerator program, farming families are not paid more for their cocoa but get extra money for ensuring they enrol children in school, good agricultural practices such as pruning cocoa trees to increase yields, agroforestry activities that increase biodiversity and yields, and encouraging farmers to diversify their incomes and not rely 100% on cocoa. It reports that families can earn an extra €500 in 2 years for complying and reap additional income from increased yields of between 160 and 470 kg per hectare. However, there are still 150,000 farming families who are not part of the program, and Nestlé does not intend to reach all of them until 2030.

Despite almost two decades of espousing shared value that might increase income by up to 300%, the value remains with the manufacturers and retailers (Food and Agriculture Organization of the United Nations & Bureau d'Analyse Societale d'Interet Collectif, 2023). Still, the farmers in Ghana and Ivory Coast "earn, on average, below the World Bank's poverty line of $1.90 per day, and do not earn enough to be able to pay adult workers anything close to a fair wage" (The Chocolate Accountability Lab, 2023). But can companies like Nestlé pay fairly for the human capital that goes into producing cocoa?

Nestlé paid CHF 5.6 billion in income tax on its CHF 16.1 billion underlying trading profit based on a 17.1% profit margin in 2022, leaving its shareholders CHF 10.5 billion better off (Nestlé, 2022). However, the Ivory Coast, the world's largest exporter of cocoa beans, exported US$3.8 (~CFH 3.5 Billion) in 2021. Hence, Nestlé, one of the world's largest food and chocolate manufacturers makes more money from its operations than the Ivory Coast does from the raw materials that Nestlé relies on. It certainly can afford to pay more. However, if Nestlé does, it will likely pass the cost on to consumers (Poposki, 2024).

The shared value model also advocates for growing cocoa to be more sustainable. Of course, it is in the best interests of the entire supply chain to ensure a stable and sustainably produced cocoa supply. However, since 2023, cocoa prices have surged to record levels because cocoa yields are decreasing in Ivory Coast and Ghana. The drop in cocoa yields is because bad weather and disease are damaging the natural capital of the cocoa trees. Climate change impacts cocoa production due to long-term deforestation, changing weather, and rainfall patterns. Low incomes, increasing input costs, and low productivity drive farmers out of production, contributing to a decline in worldwide supply. While the price is increasing due to low supply, the farmers cannot benefit if there is nothing to sell (Courty, 2024).

Thus, the evidence shows that Porter and Kramer's (2011, 2019) shared value concept in the cocoa supply chain is not delivering its espoused benefits, and the upstream human capital suffers. While shared value is supposed to help increase productivity, it cannot fight climate change. In the future, there might be no value to share. Again, this is more evidence to show how chocolate companies manufacture chocolate for financial gain at the expense of farmers and the environment. While the IC of a company is valuable, making money should not compromise or diminish the value of human or natural capital (Dumay, 2020; Guthrie & Dumay, 2021).

5 How Do We Solve the Problems?

The simple solution seems to be paying more to the cocoa farmers, and consumers will need to pay more for their chocolate. However, this will not fix the environment. That is where the Chocolate Scorecard helps, as part of a wider ecosystem of people, civil society, and governments tackle the problems faced by farmers and the environment in the cocoa supply chain. The scorecard assesses how major chocolate companies and retailers, those who capture most of the value from the value chain, are performing against six key sustainability measures, which are also related to different IC elements.

Table 2 demonstrates that resolving the sustainability issues in the cocoa supply chain requires more than just paying farmers more money for their produce. First, we need to trace where the cocoa is coming from so it is possible to identify the issues. Second, we need innovative action to resolve the issues. Resolving the issues is where it all becomes complicated. Solving the sustainability issues in the cocoa supply chain is a wicked problem (Dumay, 2020).

Wicked problems are difficult to solve (Rittel & Webber, 1973). Rittle and Webber identify several conditions that make a problem "wicked". There is no definitive formulation, no stopping rule, and no test of a solution for wicked problems. In short, they have no solutions that we can all agree on. For example, how much is enough to pay farmers for their cocoa? Or is it possible to grow cocoa entirely organically? Hence, while we can address sustainability issues, can we define what sustainably produced cocoa or any other agricultural product is? If sustainability were not a wicked problem, we would already live in a sustainable world. However, cocoa is not sustainable, and we must take action to make it more sustainable. Otherwise, there might not be any cocoa (Courty, 2024; Han, 2016a).

Overall, the scorecard helps tackle these wicked problems. Be Slavery Free (2024) made the following observations after releasing the Fifth Edition Chocolate Scorecard in March 2024:

- Improvements in traceability are evident in response to European Union Deforestation Regulations (EUDR), yet achieving full EUDR compliance remains a work in progress. As companies focus on their supply chains, there is a risk that farmers may not receive the necessary support they require.
- Governments, NGOs, companies, and consumers must work together to ensure that farmers are supported in meeting the requirements for EUDR compliance and are compensated fairly for their efforts.
- Companies are increasingly aware of their responsibility to ensure farmers get a decent income from cocoa, but still, too many farmers remain in poverty. Without additional financial support, this will continue.
- Child labor responses are increasing in effectiveness, but the road to elimination is still fraught, mainly due to the lack of scale of programs.
- Environmental initiatives, such as climate targets, ending deforestation, and use of agroforestry, are gaining momentum, partly due to emerging legislation (particularly in the EU) requiring that companies care for the planet seriously.
- While many companies have policies on pesticide management, this hasn't resulted in enough action on the ground. Overall, we have not observed significant reductions in pesticide use.

- Child labour interventions need to be scaled up and eradicated in all supply chains. There needs to be traceability and a focus on addressing the root causes, such as poverty, that lead to its prevalence.
- Companies must work towards reducing their pesticide use and implementing more sustainable farming practices to protect the farmers (particularly the children) and the environment and ensure the long-term viability of cocoa.
- It will take a concerted effort from all stakeholders to achieve these goals, but the industry's and the planet's future depends on it.

While companies in the cocoa supply chain need to put much more effort into resolving these issues, the good news is that some companies are proving they can be more sustainable and pay farmers more for their cocoa. Ducth-based Tony's Chocolonely is an example of a chocolate company doing the right thing for cocoa farmers, and the environment is part of its business model. In the Fifth Edition Chocolate Scorecard, Be Slavery Free (2024) gave Tony's Chocolonely an Achievement Award for being the top-ranked company for all five scorecard editions. Their award relates to their sourcing principles, which include paying a living income price for 100% traceable cocoa beans. By paying the higher price directly to farmers, they are helping to end forced labour, child labour, and deforestation in the cocoa supply chain (Tony's Chocolonely, 2024).

While the Chocolate Scorecard measures companies' sustainability performance and what gets measured gets managed (Drucker, 1954; Dumay & Rooney, 2011), improvements are needed. However, improved sustainability and IC accounting methods—such as increased reporting and better disclosure techniques—have failed to improve these problems. Table 2 attests that Wicked problems are part of complex systems with multiple perspectives that are hard to resolve (Dillard & Vinnari, 2019). What is needed is the ability to bring people together with these multiple perspectives and have a dialogue about how to resolve these issues.

The Chocolate Scorecard is foremost a consumer advocacy resource for those seeking information about the companies and the chocolate they produce. The scorecard also provides information to investors and stakeholders seeking to understand a chocolate company's social and environmental performance. As such, it is a tool that challenges the legitimacy of the chocolate companies and publicly showcases where they can improve. The real power of the scorecard is when we invite the companies to discuss their performance. While we don't always agree on the way forward, at least we have a productive dialogue on what needs to change.

The dialogue impacts companies because they use it as feedback to identify ways to improve. For example, in 2020, "Chocolate maker Godiva was given The Rotten Egg Award for failing to take responsibility for the conditions with which its chocolates are made, despite making huge profits off its chocolate. Godiva rated poorly across the board" (Baskett, 2022). However, Godiva reached out to Be Slavery Free, where they introduced them to the Earthworm Foundation, an NGO specializing in helping companies with traceability. As a result, in the 2022 scorecard (third edition), Godiva's overall ranking improved because their sustainability performance improved (Baskett, 2022). Thus, sustainability and IC accounting are tools that help

Table 2 Sustainability measures and IC elements of the Chocolate Scorecard

Traceability and transparency (structural capital) A company that lacks knowledge of its cocoa's origin (an issue of traceability) cannot genuinely ensure that it is not tainted by extreme poverty, worst forms of child labour, child labour, forced labour, deforestation, or other abuses. Put simply, if you can't see it, you can't fix it. Without transparency on this traceability, civil society cannot hold companies accountable or discover ways to help them. Transparent traceability is a crucial bedrock for all other reforms and development
Living income (human and financial capital) A living income is not a reality for most cocoa farmers and their families in West Africa. Many live in poverty to extreme poverty, making them more vulnerable to hunger, malnutrition, health crises, and other social challenges, including exposure to child labour and forced labour. Some farmers already earn a living income, but this is not the case for the vast majority
Child and forced labour (human, manufactured, and financial capital) A report funded by the US Department of Labor (Sadhu et al., 2020) found the following: • 1.56 million children exposed to child labour in cocoa production (including approximately 790,000 children in the Ivory Coast and 770,000 in Ghana) • Cocoa production exposed 1.48 million children to at least one component of hazardous child labour • Between 2008/09 and 2018/19, exposure to agrichemicals became more common, with the proportion of children exposed to agrichemical products increasing approximately five-fold from 5% to 24% Despite voluntary corporate efforts promising to eradicate it, the prevalence of child labour has increased by 14% over the past decade. Poverty and extremely low incomes are linked to children's exposure to child labour and hazardous child labour, depriving them of their future and subjecting them to abuse. A significant increase in the number of children in child labour exposed to harmful pesticides (from 10% to 27%) along with an increase in injuries impacts on health and level of care needed (including hospitalization). Exposure of children to chemicals is the "worst form of child labor" (Sadhu et al., 2020)
Deforestation and climate (natural and relational capital) Cocoa is a major global driver of forest destruction. West Africa produces 75% of the world's cocoa, with Côte d'Ivoire and Ghana being the largest producers. These two countries have lost most of their forest cover in the past 60 years—around 94% and 80%, respectively, with approximately one-third of forest loss from cocoa growing. In 2018, these two countries also had the highest rise in primary forest loss of any tropical country. In 2020, the cocoa-growing areas of the Ivory Coast lost another 47,000 ha of forest Cocoa from almost anywhere, from Asia to Africa to Latin America, leads to deforestation, negatively impacting climate change. Forests absorb carbon, but when they die, they release carbon and no longer serve as a carbon sink. Forests are also a key habitat for some of the most endangered species in the world, including gibbons and great apes The cocoa supply chain contributes to global annual greenhouse gas (GHG) emissions, leading to severe climate change. To address this, the governments of Ivory Coast and Ghana, 35 leading cocoa and chocolate companies, and farmers have joined together to end cocoa-driven deforestation through the Cocoa & Forest Initiative (CFI), and subsequently, Colombia and Cameroon have developed similar initiatives. There is more to do, and CFI has not yet fulfilled its promises

(continued)

Table 2 (continued)

Agroforestry (natural, human, financial, and structural capital)
Though cocoa has been a major driver of deforestation worldwide, it can become the reverse—an agent of re-greening and re-wilding around the planet. Agroforestry, as opposed to pesticide-soaked monoculture, is a more ecologically sound way of growing cocoa and restoring farming landscapes. Scientific research demonstrates that robust agroforestry cocoa systems, carbon sequestration, soil and air moisture retention, and biodiversity are better for the planet. Studies show it is also better for farmers' food security and income diversification. When implemented correctly, it is a win-win for people, the planet, farmers, forests, and endangered species, including primates. Birds and animals may also return to agroforestry environments
Deforestation in Africa has destroyed much of the natural habitat of great apes, gorillas, chimpanzees, and bonobos. However, there is some evidence that primates can re-populate in agroforestry contexts. For example, in Madagascar, there is re-population for some of the 107 endemic species of endangered Lemur
Pesticides (manufactured, natural, and human capital)
As we face an insect mass extinction crisis, largely driven by chemicals used in agriculture, chocolate companies must reassess their current methods and adopt more sustainable cocoa farming practices. Farmers must reduce their dependency on harmful agrichemicals and instead invest in practices supporting and enhancing cocoa farming. Increased productivity via chemical inputs cannot be the primary means for companies sourcing increasing amounts of cocoa. Instead, the long-term sustainability of the industry, the health of the farming communities (who often rely on neighbouring rivers for drinking and bathing), soil health, and the planet's health must become a priority
To achieve this, companies must eliminate the most hazardous pesticides and move towards reducing the overall use of agrichemicals. They should support farmers in transitioning to agricultural practices that do not rely on dangerous chemicals while helping them maintain their yield and income through safer fertilization and pest control methods
Companies should emphasize non-chemical interventions such as grafting, pruning, hand pollination, and education around best agroecological practices and Integrated Pest Management (IPM) to increase yields for farmers

Source: Author's analysis and Be Slavery Free (2024)

foster dialogue and worthwhile change that impacts people's lives and not just the profitability of companies.

6 Conclusion

This chapter presented a case study of the Chocolate Scorecard, a worthwhile research project. Unfortunately, the companies in the cocoa supply chain human and natural capital are compromised to create financial value. At the heart of the problem is the business model and the so-called shared value theory of economic development that preferences increase farmer productivity instead of paying farmers more for their produce. The chocolate companies can pay more, and some, like Tony's Chocolonely, do. Additionally, companies can improve their sustainability performance. In Godiva's case, they improved their traceability (structural capital), and this helped them understand and identify their sustainability issues better. As their sustainability performance increases, this positively impacts peoples' lives (human capital) and the environment (natural capital).

There is still a long way to go in resolving the sustainability issues in the cocoa supply chain. However, as academic researchers, we can help improve society and the environment beyond the boundaries of individual companies—we can affect entire ecosystems (Dumay et al., 2010; Milne et al., 2008), such as the cocoa supply chain. The Chocolate Scorecard project serves as a manifesto for continued change in how researchers conceptualize and undertake IC research to build a better society for everyone. I have demonstrated how IC researchers can apply fifth-stage IC research principles to help build a better world beyond just managing IC to ensure that our research positively impacts society and the planet. It is a worthwhile endeavour.

References

Barry Callebaut. (2021). *Barry Callebaut with substantial sales growth and marked increase in net income*

Baskett, N. (2022). *Godiva and earthworm foundation work on traceability*. Retrieved 17 December 2023 from https://bartalks.net/godiva-and-earthworm-foundation-work-on-traceability/?unapproved=1201&moderation-hash=f8450dac0bdf3e0dfb5ee8453730fd53#comment-1201

Be Slavery Free. (2024). The 5th edition chocolate scorecard. Be slavery free. Retrieved 30 March 2024 from https://www.chocolatescorecard.com/

Courty, A. (2024). *Chocolate prices this Valentine's Day will be at a record high. What's behind the bittersweet hike?* Australian Broadcasting Commission. Retrieved 30 March 2024 from https://www.abc.net.au/news/2024-02-13/chocolate-prices-at-record-high-this-valentines-day/103446924.

Dillard, J., & Vinnari, E. (2019). Critical dialogical accountability: From accounting-based accountability to accountability-based accounting. *Critical Perspectives on Accounting, 62*, 16–38. https://doi.org/10.1016/j.cpa.2018.10.003

Drucker, P. (1954). *The practice of management*. Harper and Bros.

Dumay, J. (2020). Using critical KM to address wicked problems. *Knowledge Management Research & Practice*, 1–9. https://doi.org/10.1080/14778238.2020.1790310

Dumay, J., & Garanina, T. (2013). Intellectual capital research: A critical examination of the third stage. *Journal of Intellectual Capital, 14*(1), 10–25. https://doi.org/10.1108/14691931311288995

Dumay, J., Guthrie, J., & Farneti, F. (2010). GRI sustainability reporting guidelines for public and third sector organisations: A critical review. *Public Management Review, 13*(4), 531–548.

Dumay, J., Guthrie, J., & Rooney, J. (2018). The critical path of intellectual capital. In J. Guthrie, J. Dumay, F. Ricceri, & C. Nielsen (Eds.), *The Routledge companion to intellectual capital: Frontiers of research, practice and knowledge* (pp. 21–39). Routledge.

Dumay, J., Guthrie, J., & Rooney, J. (2020). Being critical about intellectual capital accounting in 2020: An overview. *Critical Perspectives on Accounting, 70*, 102185. https://doi.org/10.1016/j.cpa.2020.102185

Dumay, J., & Rooney, J. (2011). "Measuring for managing?" An IC practice case study. *Journal of Intellectual Capital, 12*(3), 344–355. https://doi.org/10.1108/14691931111154670

Food and Agriculture Organization of the United Nations, & Bureau d'Analyse Societale d'Interet Collectif. (2023). *German cocoa and chocolate value chains: Analysis of the distribution of value, costs, taxes, and net margins along the German cocoa and chocolate value chains*. https://www.nachhaltige-agrarlieferketten.org/fileadmin/user_upload/BASIC_German_Cocoa_and_Chocolate_Value_Chains_March_2023__changed_graphs_.pdf.

Food Empowerment Project. (2016). Child labor and slavery in the chocolate industry. http://www.foodispower.org/slavery-chocolate/

Guthrie, J., & Dumay, J. (2021). Wicked problems involve social justice, social change, climate change and the social economy. *Journal of Behavioural Economics and Social Systems, 3*(1), 11–16. https://doi.org/10.5278/ojs.bess.v3i1.6774

Han, E. (2016a). Bitter battle: Chocolate makers fighting to save the world's cocoa supply. *Sydney Morning Herald*. Retrieved 19 September, 2016, from http://www.smh.com.au/business/retail/bitter-battle-chocolate-makers-fighting-to-save-the-worlds-cocoa-supply-20160323-gnpfg4.html

Han, E. (2016b). Women cocoa farmers struggle with less pay, land and training compared with men. *Sydney Morning Herald*. Retrieved 27 January, 2017, from http://www.smh.com.au/business/retail/women-cocoa-farmers-struggle-with-less-pay-land-and-training-compared-with-men-20160229-gn6asl.html

Husted, B. W. (2000). A contingency theory of corporate social performance. *Business & Society, 39*(1), 24–48. https://doi.org/10.1177/000765030003900104

International Integrated Reporting Council (IIRC). (2021). *The international <IR> framework*. https://integratedreporting.org/wp-content/uploads/2021/01/InternationalIntegratedReportingFramework.pdf

Milne, M., Ball, A., & Gray, R. (2008, 6–8 July). Wither ecology? The triple bottom line, the global reporting initiative, and the institutionalization of corporate sustainability reporting. 2008 AFAANZ/IAAER Conference, Sydney, Australia.

Nestlé. (2007). *The Nestlé creating shared value report*.

Nestlé. (2023). *Creating shared value and sustainability report 2023*.

Nestlé S. A. (2022). *Annual review 2022*. https://www.nestle.com/sites/default/files/2023-03/2022-annual-review-en.pdf.

Perkiss, S., Bernardi, C., Dumay, J., & Haslam, J. (2021). A sticky chocolate problem: Impression management and counter accounts in the shaping of corporate image. *Critical Perspectives on Accounting, 81*, 1–31. https://doi.org/10.1016/j.cpa.2020.102229

Poposki, C. (2024). *Chocolate prices could soon be on the rise thanks to cocoa hike*. news.com.au. Retrieved 24 May 2024 from https://www.news.com.au/lifestyle/food/eat/chocolate-prices-could-soon-be-on-the-rise-thanks-to-cocoa-hike/news-story/2c67f54752c2d24ea2a9274d8d36aa38.

Porter, M. E., & Kramer, M. R. (2011). *Creating shared value: How to reinvent capitalism—and unleash a wave of innovation and growth*. Harvard Business Review.

Porter, M. E., & Kramer, M. R. (2019). Creating shared value. In *Managing sustainable business* (pp. 323–346). https://doi.org/10.1007/978-94-024-1144-7_16

Rittel, H. W. J., & Webber, M. M. (1973). Dilemmas in a general theory of planning. *Policy Sciences, 4*(2), 155–169. http://www.jstor.org/stable/4531523

Sadhu, S., Kysia, K., Onyango, L., Zinnes, C., Lord, S., Monnard, A., & Arellano, I. R. (2020). *NORC final report: Assessing progress in reducing child labor in cocoa production in cocoa growing areas of Côte d'Ivoire and Ghana*. https://www.cocoainitiative.org/sites/default/files/resources/NORC%202020%20Cocoa%20Report_English.pdf

Sikka, P., & Willmott, H. (2010). The dark side of transfer pricing: Its role in tax avoidance and wealth retentiveness. *Critical Perspectives on Accounting, 21*(4), 342–356. https://doi.org/10.1016/j.cpa.2010.02.004

Smith, A. C. T., & Westerbeek, H. M. (2007). Sport as a vehicle for deploying corporate social responsibility [Article]. *Journal of Corporate Citizenship, 25*, 43–54. http://simsrad.net.ocs.mq.edu.au/login?url=http://search.ebscohost.com/login.aspx?direct=true&db=buh&AN=25222911&site=ehost-live

Suh, N. N., & Molua, E. L. (2022). Cocoa production under climate variability and farm management challenges: Some farmers' perspective. *Journal of Agriculture and Food Research, 8*, 100282. https://doi.org/10.1016/j.jafr.2022.100282

The Chocolate Accountability Lab. (2023). *So-called sustainability programs are failing cocoa farmers and their families: how Nestlé and Mondelez greenwash—and labor wash—their chocolate products*. Retrieved 20 May 2024 from https://corpaccountabilitylab.org/cal-

blog/2023/2/15/so-called-sustainability-programs-are-failing-cocoa-farmers-and-their-families-how-nestl-and-mondelez-greenwash-and-labor-wash-their-chocolate-products.
Tony's Chocolonely. (2024). Tony's wins chocolate scorecard's achievement award. Tony's chocolonely. Retrieved 25 May 2024 from https://tonyschocolonely.com/int/en/our-story/news/tonys-wins-chocolate-scorecards-achievement-award
Trading Economics. (2024). *Cocoa*. Trading Economics. Retrieved 31 March 2024 from https://tradingeconomics.com/commodity/cocoa.

Dr. John Dumay is a Professor of Accounting and Finance at Macquarie Business School (Sydney, Australia) with affiliations at Nyenrode Business Universiteit and Aalborg University Business School. John is a critical scholar researching modern slavery, sustainability, and corporate disclosure and has over 150 peer-reviewed publications. John's research is highly cited, and a Stanford University study recognizes him as one of the top 2% of scientists globally. In 2020, 2022, and 2023, the Australian newspaper recognized John as Australia's leading Accounting scholar. He is an Associate Editor of *Accounting, Auditing and Accountability Journal* and *Meditari Accountancy Research* and a Deputy Editor of *Accounting & Finance.*

Visionary Intellectual Capital Landscapes: An Invitation for Discussion

Aino Kianto, Slađana Čabrilo, and Lina Užienė

Abstract

This chapter is an editorial overview and interpretation of the most critical topics concerning future development of intellectual capital (IC) theory, research and practice. Based on the 16 ground-breaking and future-oriented core chapters in this book, we identify eight emerging themes for futurizing the field of IC: 1) the need for multilevel approach towards IC; 2) an examination of IC dynamics; 3) redefining of value and economic models at the basis of IC; 4) a better recognition of sustainability and ethics in IC research; 5) a focus on the role of AI in IC; 6) a renewed emphasis on humans and culture; 7) a focus on non-rational and non-technological aspects of IC; and 8) an interdisciplinary approach towards research. We also compile a list of theoretical and practical highlights to futurizing IC, provided by the authors of the individual chapters in this book. The ideas presented in this chapter contribute to opening up new perspectives for the development of IC theory and practice, and inviting scholars and practitioners to a global and future-oriented discussion on IC.

A. Kianto (✉)
Lappeenranta-Lahti University of Technology (LUT), Lahti, Finland
e-mail: aino.kianto@lut.fi

S. Čabrilo
I-Shou University, Kaohsiung, Taiwan
e-mail: sladjana@isu.edu.tw

L. Užienė
Kaunas University of Technology, Kaunas, Lithuania
e-mail: lina.uziene@ktu.lt

A. Kianto et al. (eds.), *Futurizing Intellectual Capital*, Knowledge Management and Organizational Learning 15, https://doi.org/10.1007/978-3-031-80197-6_18

1 Overview

As editors of this volume, in this concluding chapter, we do our best to make sense of the future directions suggested in the wise and thoughtful contributions of the chapter authors of this book. However, we are very mindful of the fact that every reader will have their own interpretations and find their own inspirations, which may differ from ours. We hope this book is not an end to the discussion concerning futurizing intellectual capital (IC) but a beginning to a continuous global dialogue.

To inspire the future of IC research and practice, the authors of this book have provided a thorough and groundbreaking compilation of perspectives, which pave the way for future thinking about IC. The 16 chapters in the book represent the thinking of leading IC scholars and enthusiasts across the globe.

This collection of future-oriented chapters demonstrates how IC research and practice create significant value and may contribute to the global societal transformation through intellectual connectivity and companionship, between individuals, organizations, governments, nature, and technology. Chapters illuminate future IC research and practice by highlighting IC as a complex and multilevel, dynamic ecosystem that includes IC at the individual, team, process, organizational, and finally national levels.

In this book, the authors explore tacit IC, humanization of IC, emotional and spiritual capital, trust, connectivity and contactivity, areas of interconnectivity, and "ba" as a shared space for knowledge creation. It is notable that all of these issues are fundamentally human affairs that differentiate humans from machines.

Nevertheless, in the era of increasing artificial intelligence (AI), intellectual companionship between humans and machines has become essential for sustainable growth. As AI rapidly transforms industries and societies, points of intersection and overlap between IC and AI become extremely intriguing. The chapters address questions such as the following: Where does IC meet AI? Where are the boundaries of IC in the era of advanced technology? How can such emerging technologies as AI redefine the concept, model, measurement, management, and value of IC in knowledge-intensive ecosystems?

Finally, the chapters demonstrate a strong impetus toward fundamentally rethinking economic models, performance measurement, and the concept of value. The book offers critique and extension to existing economic theories and principles, as well as a re-evaluation of assumptions concerning value and its distribution, along with associated reporting practices. The chapters strengthen IC's theoretical foundations by highlighting the specific areas where the existing theories fall short and providing new suggestions, such as complexity theory, the knowledge management perspective, and the attention-based view of the firm. Overall, these chapters provide a groundbreaking review and discussion of the essential tenets of future IC research and practice.

To do justice to the brave new ideas on IC research and practice that the contributors have provided, we will give voice to them. Appendix compiles the theoretical and practical highlights of the chapters in the words of the authors themselves.

2 Editorial Insights into the Future of IC

We invite readers to study the table in Appendix with an open and curious mindset and to find what inspires them. However, we cannot resist the opportunity to share with the readers of this book our own editorial ideas for future emphases.

There are, in particular, eight strong themes that emerge from the chapters as key insights for futurizing IC theory and practice: a multilevel understanding of IC; IC dynamics; repositioning and re-constructing IC theory based on alternative economic models and a redefinition of "value"; sustainability, ethics, and social justice; the intersection of AI and IC; emphasis on humans and culture; the potentiality of widening the rationality and technology-based views of IC; and interdisciplinarity.

2.1 A Multilevel Understanding of IC

One important conclusion raised by the chapters is that IC is not related only to profit-seeking private firms or knowledge-intensive companies. Rather, as the wicked problems facing the planet and humanity concern everyone, it is more important than ever that we examine IC from a macro-perspective that addresses not only single firms but also other types of organizations, as well as ecosystems, networks, regions, and societies.

IC is created and applied in the context of interconnected webs of many types of actors and institutions and the interactions and relationships between them. This realization points to a multilevel IC model, where IC consists of affordances at the individual, team, organizational, and institutional levels, based on personal resources and individual IC, team climate and practices, organizational systems and culture, and infrastructural, ecosystem-level, and societal IC.

The contributions in this book clearly point out that single-level focus is not sufficient anymore and that IC must be addressed beyond organizations for the global societal transformation. In the future, to an increasing extent, it will be important to acknowledge the complex and interconnected nature of the global ecosystem and economic environments.

On the one hand, the multilevel IC model implies a need for improved recognition of individual-level IC and the fact that individuals in organizations differ in terms of what IC they possess, as well as what kind of IC is needed from them in their work roles. In addition, individuals contribute in various manners to value creation, and they can benefit from a variety of IC management methods. For example, the individual IC approach may help to evaluate the intellectual contribution of IC safeguards, freelancers, gig workers, and other unstandardized forms of employment in organizational, social, and global value creation. The small amount of literature on individual-level IC merits being extended, especially as concerns the emerging skills needed in the work life, such as resilience or AI and analytics skills, according to the World Economic Forum (2023) survey.

On the other hand, the multilevel approach to IC emphasizes groups, networks, and collectives as an intermediate level of knowledge-based value creation, as well as a mediator between individual contributions and organizational outcomes. At present, this socio-psychological group and team dimension seems to be the most overlooked layer in the emerging multilevel IC model.

The macrolevel of IC has hence far been discussed most notably under the auspices of the New Club of Paris (http://new-club-of-paris.org), which provides support for societal transformation into the knowledge society. The chapters in this book extend that discussion and demonstrate powerfully that sustainability is a fundamental goal and value for IC activities, and hence IC should not be considered cut off from the societal and natural ecosystems in which it exists.

From a future research perspective, a more explicit acknowledgment of the various levels of phenomena at play should offer many interesting possibilities. Questions range from IC components across individual, team, organizational, and societal levels to effective management methods and metrics.

2.2 IC Dynamics

Based on the chapters of this book, consideration of the dynamic dimension of IC (Kianto, 2007) is no longer a supplementary exercise but a mandatory element when dealing with research and development in any system. Nowadays, the need for agility, resilience, and renewal confronts everyone in the global system alike, and the complexity perspective allows examination of the interactions among systemic elements.

The chapters in this book have opened the floor for dialogue concerning the interactions and dynamics between IC elements at different levels, from individuals to teams, organizations, institutions, ecosystems, and nations. Even with these contributions, the dynamic approach to IC has not reached its full potential yet, and we expect to see significant advancements in this field in future research and development endeavors.

Enticing research gaps exist, for example, in terms of understanding what kinds of bundles of IC resources are needed and how to develop them, how IC is enacted in organizations, and how IC is renewed and applied to promote sustainability. Regardless of which dynamic perspective is applied to examine IC, it is clear that the static snapshot type of approach can only afford a limited and retrospective understanding of IC. The dynamic approach will help to understand the complex web of inter-relationships that build the IC ecosystem, as well as what kinds of interconnections and interactions exist between the different analytical levels under various contingencies and conditions. One may see enticing research trajectories in addressing, for example, the role that individual skills and emotional capital play in building customer satisfaction and a knowledge-friendly organizational culture or exploring the employee skills that matter the most for creativity or customer satisfaction. Multilevel empirical research seems to be lacking in the IC literature and could be applied to improve understanding of IC dynamics and the complex interactions among IC elements.

Furthermore, there is a mismatch between theory and methods regarding knowledge dynamics (Bratianu, 2023) and outcome complexity. When IC is considered from a multidimensional and dynamic perspective, it becomes clear that value created has no relationship with different knowledge-based resources independently; rather, it is associated with an integrated bundle of such knowledge assets. Therefore, interpreting IC should be based on the configuration thinking that considers causal conditions not as adversaries in the struggle to explain variation in the outcome but as potential collaborators contributing to the outcome (Ragin, 2008). It is possible to overcome the gap between theory and method by applying a configurational rather than a symmetric approach to IC (Cabrilo & Dahms, 2018). Asymmetrical techniques such as fuzzy-set qualitative comparative analysis (fsQCA) allow us to look beyond associations between single variables and a limited set of interaction terms, as well as to understand equifinality and causal asymmetry (Kumar et al., 2022); therefore, in the context of multilevel and dynamic IC, they can improve the explanatory power to IC theory and practice.

2.3 Alternative Economic Models and the Redefinition of Value

In this book, an essential question is often raised about the fact that the usual economic models, which have been functioning in the world for many years, no longer meet the needs of society or the planet and therefore require fundamental changes. The IC approach demands a radical questioning of economic theory and its foundational principles, as these are not able to accommodate and explain the current reality of IC-based value creation.

A few decades ago, the highly emphasized stage of economic development called the knowledge economy recognized IC as an essential factor for organizational and regional development, creating prosperity for business, the economy, and society. Unfortunately, this has been overshadowed recently by the prevailing capitalistic mindset that focuses on purely economic value creation. Chapters in the book propose alternative economic models that emphasize sustainable and equitable forms of economic organization and prioritize human well-being, environmental sustainability, solidarity, and the planet over GDP growth and financial gain.

Based on the discussions developed in this book, a whole series of important questions emerge that are worth exploring as central to the intersection of knowledge, value, well-being, and society. These new questions require an ecosystem and multilevel IC approach to society, future generations, and well-being that is based on ethical political convictions, sustainability, and the common good.

The issue of harnessing IC for well-being creation while preserving the interests of business, society, and the planet is crucial but hardly solvable. Ethical, sustainable, and common good-oriented IC management is vital in today's world and requires novel economic models, repositioning and re-constructing of IC theory, and novel approaches to measurement of value added.

A fundamental issue coming up across this book is that an essential questioning of what is valued, as well as who gets to decide what is valued, is needed across IC activities. Not only practitioners but also researchers should ask who gets to decide what is valued—and hence, strived for. This is very closely connected to the next theme, which considers sustainability, ethics, and social justice as critical values in the global ecosystem.

2.4 Sustainability, Ethics, and Social Justice

The future of IC research and practice should recognize sustainability as one of the critical factors for organizational, national, and societal success. This issue is fundamentally connected to the questions of what value is, what is valued and by whom, and who has the power to determine whose conception of value is adhered to. It is crucial for IC research and practice to be critical about what is supposed to be sustainable in order to develop global trust in the sustainable IC concept and its metrics. Although it has become obvious that a complex, dynamic, and multilayered IC ecosystem is not isolated from—but organically integrated with—nature and society, the IC research and practice that tackle issues of IC and sustainability together seem to be in an embryonic stage. One way to proceed may be to reconceptualize IC frameworks and metrics to address environmental, social, and governance (ESG) criteria and sustainable development goals (SDGs) more clearly (Alvino et al., 2021; Kianto et al., 2023). This approach may clarify how intangible assets contribute to sustainable business practices and sustainable regional competitiveness (Januškaitė & Užienė, 2018).

It can be anticipated that human knowledge can simultaneously contribute to the three pillars of sustainability, environmental, social, and economic. Therefore, future research should be more focused on intersections between the concepts of IC, sustainability, the circular economy, and open innovation. It is worthwhile to explore collaborative and coordinated efforts that combine the knowledge of multiple agents in innovation ecosystems to increase economic, societal, and environmental well-being. It is also relevant to use IC management to put into practice green innovations that optimize production and consumption to achieve a balance between economy, society, and the environment. We believe that addressing sustainability from the IC perspective requires cross-disciplinary insights from social sciences, economics, environmental science, and business management to develop holistic models and solutions.

Taken together, the themes of value and sustainability point to a new sphere of discussion for the IC field—namely, that of IC ethics. Until now, questions of justice have mainly been addressed from the limited approach of intangible property rights and knowledge protection mechanisms. Based on the chapters, there are other, wider questions which must be brought to the fore in IC activities, for example, ethical considerations related with AI usage, as well as fair and socially equitable distribution of value and societal justice. We further suggest considering ethical leadership, based on a leader's honesty, justice, credibility, and integrity (Brown & Treviño, 2006; Anderson & Sun, 2017), as one of the essential IC-related drivers of not only organizational well-being and success but also global trust and peace. Further research questions stemming from this stance include the following: How can societally transformative IC research be conducted? What is the role of IC and related resources in IC diplomacy for peace?

2.5 The Interplay Between IC and AI

AI is fundamentally changing humanity, organizations, economics, and value creation. These changes open up a new set of opportunities—and challenges. On the one hand, together with AI, new enriched forms and opportunities for more efficient use of IC arise, which speed up value creation by increasing access to intellectual resources. This supplements and enriches them with artificial assistance, which may lead to better performance and higher productivity. On the other hand, there are challenges, such as the risk that AI will outcompete human potential and that organizations will be left with a portfolio of resources that lack emotional value, empathy, and human spirit.

Delving into the discussions by the authors of this book, fundamental questions arise as to whether AI can be treated as a unique form of IC? How tolerable is the substitutability of IC with AI? How can human knowledge be protected to avoid losing human authenticity? How dangerous is the loss of human spirituality in the era of AI? How can we address and possibly solve the ethical issues arising from the interplay between IC and AI?

There is no doubt that AI, along with other emerging technologies, is having a disruptive effect on IC. However, it is not yet clear which forms of IC are most susceptible to the disruptive nature of AI and how we should balance between the desire to create greater added value and the loss of authenticity of IC.

The book chapters bring together culturally diverse perspectives, spanning from the Japanese "ba" to the German "companionship." This diversity raises a new and interesting question for future research on how diverse cultures impact the understanding of the opportunities, risks, and ethical issues of AI integration in business and economies. In future regional research, the question will undoubtedly need to be answered as to what impacts different AI adoption rates will have on countries' national IC. In addition, we need to ask what impacts they will have on the overall performance of the regions.

Returning to the multilevel aspect of IC that is frequently highlighted in the chapters, it becomes important to understand whether the same AI-related trade-offs apply across the different IC layers—the individual, organizational, national, regional, and societal layers. What knowledge in the multilevel IC ecosystem are we at risk of losing in the era of AI? Who is responsible for acting as an IC safeguard and protecting IC on different layers from harmful exploitation?

Finally, the theme of value, which is also central to this book, demands special attention when IC faces the new realities of AI. The questions here are these: Who owns the value created by AI-based IC? Who will benefit from it? Can we distinguish between human and machine-based values? And how can we ensure sustainable and fair sharing of risk and value added in the modern world? These and questions related to intellectual resource replacement, more effective management, loss, and synergy in the interface of AI raised in this book deserve the attention of future IC researchers and are likely to be addressed as important in IC theory in the near future.

2.6 Humans and Culture at the Core of IC

For value creation, however that value may be understood, the essential factor is what humans do—or don't do: whether and how they use information systems and AI, the extent to which they share their knowledge, apply it in their productive activities, and integrate it with others. In addition, organizational IC cannot be fully comprehended by focusing only on systems and processes. Humans and their interactions remain at the core of IC. The human capital dimension has always been at the heart of the IC movement (cf. Edvinsson & Malone, 1997; Sveiby, 1997), and this seems to be unchanged in our current times. However, the humanizing of IC takes different forms according to the needs of the specific socio-historical context.

The Future of Jobs Report by the World Economic Forum (WEF, 2023) offers a glimpse into human skills and abilities that are likely to matter most in the near future. According to this report, analytical and creative thinking are the most critical employee skills for the future, followed by resilience, flexibility, and agility; motivation and self-awareness; and curiosity and lifelong learning. This points to the future importance of the human ability to adapt to disrupted environments. Moreover, the WEF report emphasizes the essential role of human empathy in the age of AI and points out that investing in learning, reskilling, and upskilling will become a priority for everyone in the global ecosystem. We also propose self-leadership (Neck & Houghton, 2006; Kianto et al., 2023) to be one such crucial skill to develop across the workforce. These recommendations certainly pave the way for future IC research and practice.

The chapters in this book also emphasize that collective features of the work environment, such as organizational culture and leadership approaches, will be crucial facets of IC in the future. The social environment where IC is embedded, created, exerted, and appropriated must be recognized if the field is to provide valid understandings and actionable insights on IC-based value creation. Related deepening topics to explore include not only the development of knowledge-friendly "ba" and organizational cultures and establishment and valuation of transformative, servant, and ethical leadership behaviors and philosophies but also the intersection of IC and work well-being and happiness.

2.7 Non-rational and Non-technological Dimensions of IC and IC Management

The new perspectives opened in this book also suggest that it may be useful to deeply and critically examine what we really mean by IC and what kind of facets we expect it to consist of. As long as we are addressing how humans handle knowledge in organizations, which exist within cultures, the emotional, intuitive, and spiritual facets of knowing, deciding, and taking action will prevail alongside rational, data-driven, and evidence-based elements (Nonaka, 1994; Nonaka et al., 2000). Chapters in this book have provided pioneering discussions of such deeper layers of IC.

The chapters of the book point toward the future of IC, which—perhaps rather curiously in this age of the IT and AI boom—emphasizes the nature and role of human beings as prime actors in value creation, for whom technology may be a more or less applicable tool for achieving their goals. Rather than homo ecologicus, they imply homo sociologus—the social human being. This is the conception of individuals in their socio-historical context, where they are influenced by and simultaneously influence the social structures they are embedded in.

A conception of human nature not addressed in the chapters is homo ludens (Huizinga, 1938/1998), the playful human being. This alternative perspective teases out some enticing questions related to the role of creativity, playfulness, and divergent thinking in the IC realm.

2.8 Interdisciplinarity

As has been seen throughout IC history and in this book, the question of how knowledge produces value and what can be done to support this can and indeed has been approached from many perspectives. It is also crucial for future IC theory and practice to integrate knowledge and insights from different disciplines, such as economics, psychology, sociology, political economy, engineering and technology, environmental science, neuroscience, art, human resource management, and accounting, to provide a more holistic understanding of the complex nature of IC, its management, and its valuation. IC, seen as a complex and dynamic ecosystem, spans from individual to societal levels and covers different disciplines. Therefore, IC research must go beyond a single discipline.

This book is an invitation to open the doors for new explorations crossing disciplines and to integrate insights from various fields to address complex, real-world challenges, including the sustainability crisis, climate change, public health, social equality, global peace, and well-being, that cannot be solved by any single discipline alone. Only interdisciplinary research that fosters collaboration, knowledge sharing, continuous learning, and innovation may reveal hitherto invisible solutions and opportunities to fully translate IC into value and global societal well-being.

3 Instead of a Conclusion: The IC Journey Continues

The journey of futurizing IC is ongoing and never ending. The potential for IC-based value creation is boundless. As a response to environmental and socio-economic changes, as well as global geopolitics in the world, conceptual knowledge is constantly being rethought and redesigned. Facing the new realities of a changing world requires new perspectives and approaches. The insights provided in this book are a step forward in the discussion of the future of IC theory, bringing researchers together and creating a new energy charge for future companionships.

The interlinks between the past, present, and future are important for understanding human and collective experience, continuity, and growth. As we stand at the intersection of technological advancement and human ingenuity, we face many issues that bring new complexities to the IC arena. We hope this book will serve as a comprehensive guide for IC scholars and professionals to understand and navigate the complexities of the rapidly evolving world and its implications. Let it serve as a source of direction, insight, and inspiration in an increasingly dynamic world, encouraging new ideas, thinking, and debates.

The Editors

Appendix: Table of Author Provided Chapter Highlights

Part	Title	Author(s)	Theoretical contributions	Practical recommendations
Part I. Intellectual Capital in Flux: Navigating Complexity				
1	A Complexity Framework for Understanding Intellectual Capital	Constantin Bratianu	1. Adopting a complexity perspective of the IC that opens new directions for research. The future research of IC should extend beyond the borders of a given organization and embrace a larger perspective based on the complexity approach 2. Adopting a nonlinear approach for understanding much better the nature of IC. Intellectual capital is nonlinear because it is composed of intangible resources which are nonlinear. Therefore, it is necessary to change the linear models used so far into nonlinear models 3. Adopting a dynamics approach that challenges the potential view of IC and shows its transformation into kinetic IC as a result of KM action. The future IC should be understood as being composed of two components which have the capability of transforming one into another: the potential IC, and the kinetic IC. The transformation is moderated by the knowledge management 4. Proposing a multi-scale framework for IC to offer solutions for IC building up from the individual level to organizational level and beyond. Future IC models should incorporate different framework scales and mechanisms of scaling up the individual IC 5. Identifying the kernel of the similarity property of being composed of the three basic IC fields: rational IC, emotional IC, and spiritual IC. These components result from the processing the three basic knowledge fields: rational knowledge, emotional knowledge, and spiritual knowledge. Therefore, the future of IC should be based on the theory of knowledge fields and knowledge dynamics that has a thermodynamics support	1. Aligning the IC model to the practical multilevel structure of management. In practice, management is structured on different levels: self-management at the individual level, middle management at the team level, and top management at organizational level. Therefore, the future of IC should be considered at the same structural levels 2. Aligning the IC model to the needs of nonlinear organizational processes. The new business environment induces nonlinear phenomena like change, learning, resilience, and employees' wellbeing which act on the potential IC 3. Managing the dynamics of IC. Knowledge management acts on the potential IC to transform it into kinetic IC, like a generic force that transforms potential energy into kinetic energy of a given body 4. Designing a better motivational system and creating a dynamic organizational culture. The future IC model based on the knowledge fields and knowledge dynamics theory contains the rational, emotional, and spiritual intellectual capital components and the dynamics between them 5. The new model opens new directions for designing new measurement systems. There is a need for new measuring models which are capable of reflecting the intangibility and nonlinearity of IC

(continued)

Part	Title	Author(s)	Theoretical contributions	Practical recommendations
2	Unleashing Intellectual Capital: Toward Dynamic Theory through the Humanization of Intellectual Capital	Noboru Konno	1. Relationship between IC and Knowledge Assets (KA): Utilizing an accounting analogy, the eq. IC + Intellectual Debt = KA is proposed to provide a framework for understanding the contribution of IC to an organization's KA 2. Concept of "Ba": The concept of "ba" (a shared context or space) is integral to the activation of IC and the facilitation of knowledge creation (KC). "Ba" is considered a component of IC, aiding in the transformation of KA into tangible value during the knowledge creation process	1. Dynamic nature of IC: IC should be conceptualized not as a static asset but as a dynamic and vital resource essential for enhancing competitiveness and ensuring long-term success. The effective management and utilization of IC and KA are critical drivers of innovation 2. IC in ecosystems: The significance of IC within ecosystems is increasingly recognized. As organizations collaborate within ecosystems, the relevance of IC and value creation in these contexts becomes apparent. "Ba" plays a crucial role in connecting internal and external ecosystems, thereby facilitating knowledge sharing among diverse participants 3. Humanization of IC: The future of IC management should incorporate more humanized aspects, including emotional and subjective elements. The emotional dimensions of IC, which are connected to human physical sensations and instincts, will become increasingly important, particularly with the rise of artificial intelligence (AI)
3	Intellectual Capital as a Basis for Cash Flow and Renewal	Tomi Hussi and Aino Kianto	1. IC is not only relevant for organizational renewal but also for the ability to generate cash flow 2. Both cash flow and renewal can be understood with an IC-based value creation model that consists of knowledge assets dynamics through knowledge flows 3. A new terminology for knowledge assets is provided: Cash flow and renewal can both be approached from the perspective of three types of knowledge assets: energy, demand, and platform 4. Knowledge flows are clarified alongside with knowledge assets, adding to the so far relatively neglected understanding of the dynamic dimension of IC: Both cash flow and renewal are energized by the three knowledge flows that put the assets in motion: reflection, dialogue, and offering	1. The current terminology within IC is too academic and difficult to understand by the practitioners. Increasing flexibility in terminology could enhance the adoption of IC framework in business management practices 2. The introduction of the cash flow dimension of IC makes it more inviting to the C-suite manager as they are mainly evaluated by the short-term performance of an organization 3. The process of renewal based on knowledge assets and knowledge flows supports the innovativeness of an organization 4. Clarified understanding of the business model based on IC-related cash flow can increase the motivation and commitment of the employees

(continued)

Part	Title	Author(s)	Theoretical contributions	Practical recommendations
4	Individual-Level Intellectual Capital—A Framework for Future Management and Reflection	Sanna Mari Alppivuori and Aino Kianto	1. For understanding IC, it is crucial to better acknowledge its individual dimension and to examine it from the perspective of individuals at work 2. This chapter deepens the analysis of individual-level intellectual capital 3. Individual IC (IIC) consists of human, structural, relational, renewal, and emotional intellectual capitals 4. Emotional IC is an important completely new dimension of (I) IC that has been neglected in previous studies 5. Our chapter provides a model that can be used for identifying and assessing IIC	1. From the managerial perspective, the chapter supports understanding the holistic nature of employee IIC and its contribution to firm-level IC 2. The model presented in the chapter enables an improved assessment of employee IIC in recruitment and personnel development 3. From the employee perspective, the chapter provides a framework for reflecting on one's own IIC
5	The Liability of Tacitness in Intellectual Capital: Overcoming Research Challenges with Grounded Theory Designs	Carla Curado and Tiago Gonçalves	Future IC research should engage in: 1. Dense theory development emerging from adequate match of tacit IC research gap-spotting and GT features 2. Theory creation resulting from tacit IC literature review process and data analysis integration supported by suitable GT approaches 3. Tacit IC research coding processes and matching GT approaches promoting theoretical clarification and new theoretical drivers in tacit IC 4. Tacit IC research goals and appropriate GT data coding rationales and thus providing strong theoretical development of the field	Forthcoming tacit IC practices will offer new support for sustainable competitive advantage: 1. Tacit IC governance development in organizations will rise after the identification of emerging types of tacit IC components. The challenges of digital and remote environments for tacit IC management will be softened 2. Tacit IC auditing will flourish when using the appropriate performance measures for tacit IC. The different organizational, ethical, and sustainable options will press the creation of distinct measures 3. Tacit IC retention will result from the finding of adequate strategies and practices to retain tacit IC in organizations, by turning individual forms into collective forms of tacit knowledge. Particular attention should be given to industrial context when designing the strategic actions and management procedures to capture, keep, and develop the maximum value of tacit IC
Part II. Smart Societal Growth: Intellectual Capital in Sustainable Ecosystems				

(continued)

Part	Title	Author(s)	Theoretical contributions	Practical recommendations
1	IC as Intellectual Companionship	Günther M. Szogs	1. IC-companionship rediscovers IC as an intellectual attitude beyond IC as a label for a profession 2. IC-companionship connects to arts and divers other actors via intrinsic intellectual activity thus enhancing meaningful outcome 3. IC-companionship uses humanistic holistic sources to reconnect research with others not just as quantitative add-on but as qualitative integral transformation	1. IC-companionship is as well IC compassion-ship. It focusses on interdependencies of disciplines and areas of interconnectivity like SDG 17 2. IC-companionship adopts, reinforces, and adjusts IC navigating tools like intellectual balance sheets not for static mechanical comparisons but for interactive monitoring of well-balanced societal innovation 3. IC-companionship honors all necessary intellectual specialization but tries to transcend categories like human, structural, and relational capital to a broader scope of beneficial potentials
2	Sustainable National Intellectual Capital (SNIC) and Its Applications	Carol Y.Y. Lin	1. Proposing an IC ecosystem for a more comprehensive IC field of research 2. Conducting interdisciplinary IC research helps tackle problems in an increasingly sophisticated world 3. Crossing levels (e.g., organizational IC + national IC) IC studies enables proper context positioning	1. The SNIC model provides a guideline for utilizing SNIC data to enhance national intangible assets 2. Government can prioritize and achieve better national investment through SNIC trend analysis 3. SNIC trend analysis assists international business to make better international expansion decisions
3	Relevance and the Future of Intellectual Capital Management in the Public Sector	Harri Laihonen and Paula Pusenius	1. In the public sector, IC theory or IC management practices may not only consider the organizational goals of efficiency, cost minimization, or profit maximization; they must also consider aspects such as fairness, accessibility, and benefits to society 2. The complexity of the institutional framework compels a change in the unit of analysis in public sector IC management from individual organizations to hybrid networks and ecosystems, combining the IC of public, private, and the third and fourth sectors 3. Changes in both the expectations toward public services and the ways of organizing these services call for a more profound understanding of administrative capabilities enabling the accumulation and utilization of IC	1. By systematically managing IC and effectively leveraging intangible resources, public organizations can enhance their capability to address societal challenges and deliver valuable services 2. Public organizations can play a decisive role as platforms or ecosystems pooling national, regional, and local IC to enhance collaboration and create public value 3. There are many IC management frameworks, practices, and tools available for the use of public managers to explore and develop administrative capabilities
Part III. Intellectual Capital Meets Artificial Intelligence: Reimagining the IC Landscape				

(continued)

Part	Title	Author(s)	Theoretical contributions	Practical recommendations
1	Intellectual Capital and the Era of Raising AI	Bror Salmelin	1. The focus in this chapter is to give a snapshot on the challenges intellectual capital and fast developing AI bring to organizational operations. Knowledge management is the key when building intellectual capital, and AI leads to high risks in developing the structural, human, and relational capital. The corruption of information together with deepfake technologies sets high demand on understanding and developing and protecting the IC assets and use of them in any organization 2. It is essential to interlink the different functionalities and relationships between these components of the IC when AI enables harvesting of large amounts of information faster, but with quite poor quality control of the output, and also the relational capital being jeopardized by new AI-based application which enables, e.g., deepfake connections 3. From a theoretical perspective, we need methods to assess the risks of poor quality information and connections and to ensure where possible to use high-quality data, often internal to the organization to teach the AI system and users. This will lead to the immediate need of new skills in any given organization using AI tools	1. AI develops fast, and to have organizations grow into the use of it requires a clear development strategy for the take-up. When we understand the operative principles of AI systems and tools, we simultaneously will understand the role of verifying the quality of the AI implies in IC of organizations, being a powerful tool to speed up the processes of using the multilayer IC in a safe(r) manner

(continued)

Part	Title	Author(s)	Theoretical contributions	Practical recommendations
2	From a Data-driven to Information-driven Management Paradigm: Reflections on Generative AI and Intellectual Capital Management	Henri Hussinki and Josh Morton	1. Gen AI is a catalyst in IC value creation, contributing to the organization's IC and augmenting the organizational capabilities to efficiently utilize its intellectual capital, drive its key processes, and create value 2. Structural capital has an emphasized role in the information-driven paradigm, as organizations can process all their accumulated text-based data and augment their human and other organizational capabilities with Gen AI 3. Gen AI enables an organization's personnel to know everything about an organization's proprietary information through this new technology, bolstering its human capital 4. The emergence of Gen AI is likely to affect the relationships through which organizations access and gather information from extra-organizational sources. However, information accessed through customers, suppliers, distributors, partners, supply chains, markets, and so on will remain at the core of an organization's relational capital	1. Organizations must identify and harness their critical human, structural, and relational capital resources for the proprietary Gen AI model, as the technology itself cannot integrate to these key organizational resources 2. Efficient Gen AI utilization sets demand for new employee skills, such as information engineering for Gen AI specialists and Gen AI literacy for all employees, having implications for human capital management. For instance, organizations should develop and retain the ambidextrous experts who possess a deep understanding of this new technology and the context in which Gen AI is used 3. Contemporary, information-driven organizations seek actionable insights from unstructured data, such as text documents created by humans or information systems. This emphasizes the role of controlled generation of new information and the design and maintenance of adaptable information systems 4. Gen AI value creation requires collaboration between the context experts who can identify valuable information and the Gen AI experts who can establish robust data pipelines and information system architectures that enable the efficient collection, cleaning, storage, and use of relevant data 5. Organizations should be prepared to participate in the emerging market of commercialized information products and services, whether it is in the form of a provider or customer

(continued)

Part	Title	Author(s)	Theoretical contributions	Practical recommendations
3	IC Related Risks and AI—Friends and Foes!	Susanne Durst	1. This chapter advances intellectual capital (IC) theory by stressing the relevance of considering positive and negative risks associated with the three IC dimensions 2. The risks associated with human capital (HC), structural capital (SC), and relational capital (RC) are presented with regard to the increasing use of artificial intelligence (AI)-based tools and are embedded in a small firm environment In particular, the IC theory for small companies is strengthened and expanded 3. Looking at risks from both the positive (opportunity) and the negative (threat) side and AI as a complementary resource and as a substitute enables a more differentiated understanding of IC in general and its most important dimensions	1. This chapter advances intellectual capital (IC) practice by stressing the relevance of considering positive and negative risks associated with the three IC dimensions 2. The risks associated with human capital (HC), structural capital (SC), and relational capital (RC) are presented with regard to the increasing use of artificial intelligence (AI)-based tools and are embedded in a small firm environment 3. Viewing AI from the perspective of a complementary resource and a substitute opens up scope for different IC practice 4. The results could help decision-makers in smaller companies to better understand the importance of rigorous IC management in order to be better equipped for current and future change and adversity. This in turn could improve IC practice
Part IV. Reenvisioning Intellectual Capital: Rethinking Economic Models, Value, and Progress in the Knowledge Era				

(continued)

Part	Title	Author(s)	Theoretical contributions	Practical recommendations
1	Considerations Towards the Development of a Foundational Theory of Intellectual Capital	Anthony K.P. Wensley and M. Max Evans	1. Currently there is no foundational Theory of Intellectual Capital (IC). However, research in IC, Knowledge Management (KM), and Economics (i.e., Theories of the Firm) demonstrate important considerations that need to be reflected on in the development of such a theory. Presently no theory adequately incorporates the varied characteristics of organizational knowledge or the rich variety of organizational forms that create, manage, and share IC 2. At present, there is no adequate theory that explains the process by which organizational knowledge underpins the creation of organizational value. This is largely rooted in an inability to fully operationalize and measure organizational knowledge or IC. Ultimately, this makes it difficult to establish the relative importance of individual sub-components of IC or explain how they influence organizational performance. To develop a theory of IC, it will be necessary, at minimum, to be able to articulate the manner that IC and its subcomponents create value in any organizational setting 3. Any theory also must be able to provide an explanation for the multiplicity of organizational forms involved in the creation, sharing, and articulation of IC and provide some explanation/ prediction with respect to their evolution	1. It is important to systematically revise knowledge and remove inaccurate and false knowledge. This works best when the organization has a culture where continual questioning is encouraged because organizational knowledge needs to be recognized as being uncertain, revisable, and even false 2. There is a need to look to the future to identify organizational knowledge needed for operational and strategic planning, especially knowledge that is not currently possessed. One of the best ways to do this is to recruit individuals who have general organizational knowledge and specific domain knowledge (when it can be identified). If one element is missing, provide them with an environment which proactively encourages them to acquire the skills. A proactive environment will be one that combines appropriate values, rewards, and infrastructure for them to be successful. Increasingly they should become better judges of what skills to develop and what knowledge to acquire and share 3. There is a need to create a culture where the value of existing knowledge is constantly reviewed in the light of changes in the micro- and macro-organizational environments

(continued)

Part	Title	Author(s)	Theoretical contributions	Practical recommendations
2	Futurizing Intellectual Capital: New Economic Models and the Venue of AI Requests for an Update	Günter Koch	1. ICR taking into account Natural Capital Accounting (NCA) as a source of additional financial and non-financial data to be entered in an ICR 2. Open question if objects generated by an AI system/AI algorithms are to be valuated as knowledge objects and in case they are: how will they be emancipated to be entered in an ICR?	1. Alternative economics models – Degrowth (or post-growth) economy: proponents argue for a shift toward sustainable and equitable forms of economic organization that prioritize human well-being and ecological sustainability over GDP growth – Solidarity Economy: emphasizes solidarity, cooperation, and social justice as central principles for organizing economic activities – Economy for the Common Good (ECG): redefining the goals and metrics of economic activity to prioritize the well-being of people and the planet over mere financial profit. The ECG offers a reference model motivating enterprises ethical enterprise mgt Conclusion: none of these models will replace the currently predominant "capitalistic model" in a near future 2. The two dimensions of any model as required by Europe's Green Deal Green Deal and "Double Materiality": It emphasizes the interconnectedness of financial performance (financial materiality) and environmental, social, and governance (ESG) factors (non-financial materiality) 3. Natural Capital Accounting Natural Capital Accounting (NCA) as defined in ISO 14054 involves incorporating the value of natural resources and environmental impacts into the financial accounting of companies

(continued)

Part	Title	Author(s)	Theoretical contributions	Practical recommendations
3	The Future of Intellectual Capital in the Era of Artificial Intelligence: Analysis from the Perspective of Value Creation	Ante Pulic	1. IC is placed in a new theoretical framework. Namely, there was no place for IC in the mainstream economy, either at the micro- or macro-level. This new environment represents Complexity Economics, which in all its characteristics corresponds to what IC is. On the other hand, treating IC as an integral part of that contemporary economic framework not only complements Complexity Economics but becomes its driving force 2. What can be called "capital" is precisely explained. Only that which fulfills three conditions: that it is measurable, that it can be expressed in money, and that it can be collateral 3. Division of SC into passive and active parts. In the following years and especially in the next decade, AI will be increasingly used in business, so it is very important to monitor its role in value creation. It is precisely the division of structural capital into passive and active parts that opens up the possibility of calculating AI's contribution to added value	1. Measurement of HC efficiency in processes. This is essential for wider application in practice and increasing business efficiency. The level of business processes is crucial in the analysis of value creation because business processes are the place where value and entropy are created 2. Introducing the concept of entropy into everyday business. Namely, entropy is all around us; it accompanies us even when we cook dinner and when we drive a car. That is why it is important to know that he is with us in business as well. You should have knowledge about the level of entropy in business processes and the company in order to increase the responsibility of management 3. Treatment of gig and freelance work. Now this type of work is treated as a cost, so it does not enter into the added value even though it creates it. This creates the wrong picture of the achieved business efficiency, i.e., it shows it higher than what it would be if it were treated as HC. That is why expenses for gigs and freelance work should be treated as temporary HC of the company

(continued)

Part	Title	Author(s)	Theoretical contributions	Practical recommendations
4	Effective Intellectual Capital Management as the Enabler of Future Value and Success in a Knowledge Economy	Stefan Güldenberg	1. This paper aims to challenge our outdated and backward-looking understanding of value and success by linking the IC framework with the attention-based view of the firm, system dynamics, organizational learning, and sensemaking 2. Organizations exist today not because they are more efficient than the market but because they are more intelligent. Intelligent organizations therefore attract intelligent people, which ideally increases the overall organizational intellectual capital 3. In intelligent organizations, in contrast to traditional industrial organizations, almost every employee is directly or indirectly involved in the decision-making process. Therefore, in contrast to the past, the strategy must also be communicated to all these employees. This places enormous demands on strategic performance measurement and control 4. This contribution tries to redefine strategic performance management for today's companies as a central component of strategic thinking, learning, and action in a knowledge economy. In doing so, the weaknesses of financial performance measurement tools have been outlined, and the need for action toward IC measurement and management has been highlighted. At the same time, the limitations of existing IC measurement frameworks have been critically discussed 5. In a nutshell this contribution develops a research agenda of IC measurement and management based on a system dynamics perspective	1. A mindshift among our leaders is needed: Intellectual capital measurement and management require an important mindshift of our leaders from a backward to a forward-looking approach, from a focus on financial metrics to non-financial metrics, from a view of the organization as a money-making machine to a view of the organization as a brain and living organism 2. At the core of IC measurement and management systems lies the idea to develop a strategic map that shows the path to be taken into the future and at the same time provides orientation for all stakeholders 3. As a conclusion five principles have been proposed that should guide the implementation of IC measurement and management tools in order to improve the existing strategic performance management in organizations 4. Properly applied, IC can not only help to accelerate the necessary sustainable transformation of our businesses and society but also redefine what we teach in business schools about corporate value, role models, and successful careers for the next generation 5. If we stop defining value and success in financial terms only, we will open the doors to many more opportunities to shape our own destiny and the future viability and resilience of organizations and our society at large

(continued)

Part	Title	Author(s)	Theoretical contributions	Practical recommendations
5	Being Critical About Intellectual Capital in 2024: Chocolate as a Manifesto for Social Change	John Dumay	1. Provides a case study based on fifth-stage IC research that shows how research is worthwhile and connected to improving society and the environment 2. Questions the morality of the shared value business model 3. Demonstrates how researchers must consider the three traditional IC elements alongside financial, manufactured, and natural capital to form a more complete analysis of a particular context	1. Demonstrates how emphasizing financial capital above other capital can have a detrimental effect on human and natural capital 2. Demonstrates how financial capital is not equitably shared using the shared value business model due to the excess power of companies over individuals (farmers) in the supply chain 3. Demonstrates how it is possible to change business models to positively impact people's lives (human capital) and the environment (natural capital), and this is certainly worthwhile

References

Alvino, F., Di Vaio, A., Hassan, R., & Palladino, R. (2021). Intellectual capital and sustainable development: A systematic literature review. *Journal of Intellectual Capital, 22*(1), 76–94.

Anderson, M. H., & Sun, P. Y. (2017). Reviewing leadership styles: Overlaps and the need for a new 'full-range' theory. *International Journal of Management Reviews, 19*, 76–96.

Bratianu, C. (2023). Knowledge dynamics: Exploring its meanings and interpretations. *Management Dynamics in the Knowledge Economy, 11*(2), 100–111.

Brown, M. E., & Treviño, L. K. (2006). Ethical leadership: A review and future directions. *The Leadership Quarterly, 17*(6), 595–616.

Cabrilo, S., & Dahms, S. (2018). How strategic knowledge management drives intellectual capital to superior innovation and market performance. *JKM, 22*(3), 621–648.

Edvinsson, L., & Malone, M. S. (1997). *Intellectual capital: Realizing your company's true value by finding its hidden brainpower*. Harper Business.

Huizinga, J. (1938/1998). *Homo Ludens: A study of play-element in culture*. Taylor & Francis.

Januškaitė, V., & Užienė, L. (2018). Intellectual capital as a factor of sustainable regional competitiveness. *Sustainability, 10*(12).

Kianto, A. (2007). What do we really mean by the dynamic dimension of intellectual capital? *International Journal of Learning and Intellectual Capital, 4*(4), 342–356.

Kianto, A., Cabrilo, S., & Hussinki, H. (2023). Futurizing the intellectual capital theory to uncover pertinent and unexplored horizons. In C. Bratianu, M. Handzic, & E. Bolisani (Eds.), *The future of knowledge management: Reflections from the 10th anniversary of the International Association of Knowledge Management (IAKM)* (pp. 67–90). Springer.

Kumar, S., Sahoo, S., Lim, W. M., Kraus, S., & Bamel, U. (2022). Fuzzy-set qualitative comparative analysis (fsQCA) in business and management research: A contemporary overview. *Technological Forecasting and Social Change, 178*. Article 121599.

Neck, C., & Houghton, J. (2006). Two decades of self-leadership theory and research, past developments, present trends, and future possibilities. *Journal of Managerial Psychology, 21*(4), 270–295.

Nonaka, I. (1994). A dynamic theory of organizational knowledge creation. *Organization Science, 5*(1), 14–37.

Nonaka, I., Toyama, R., & Konno, N. (2000). SECI, Ba and leadership: A unified model of dynamic knowledge creation. *Long Range Planning, 33*(1), 5–34.

Ragin, C. C. (2008). *Redesigning social inquiry: Fuzzy sets and beyond.* University of Chicago Press.
Sveiby, K. E. (1997). *The new organizational wealth: Managing & measuring knowledge-based assets*. Berrett-Koehler Publishers.
World Economic Forum. (2023). The future of jobs report.

D.Sc. Aino Kianto is Full Professor of Knowledge Management at the LUT Business School, Lappeenranta-Lahti University of Technology (LUT), Finland. She is the leader of the LUT Knowledge Management Team, one of the world's leading academic laboratories working on knowledge-related management topics and executing the Master Programme on Knowledge Management and Leadership since 2001. Prof. Kianto's research focuses on knowledge management, intellectual capital, innovation, resilience, and organizational renewal. Her research on these topics has been published widely and acknowledged with several international awards. Her papers have appeared in, for example, *Journal of Business Research*, *Technovation*, *R&D Management*, *Human Resource Management Journal*, *Journal of Knowledge Management*, *Journal of Intellectual Capital*, and *Accounting, Auditing and Accountability Journal*. Prof. Kianto has delivered keynote speeches and acted as a track chair in many international conferences and currently serves in the editorial board of four academic journals. She promotes the transfer of research-based insights to work life by collaborating with companies and public organizations in research projects and consulting, press interviews, lectures in industry events, and teaching MSc and MBA courses. In the intellectual capital field, she is especially known for advancing the dynamic dimension of intellectual capital and her studies addressing the intersection of intellectual capital and knowledge management, innovation, and organizational performance.

D.Sc. Slađana Čabrilo is a Full Professor of Management in the Department of International Business Administration, I-Shou University, Taiwan. She holds degrees in technology, engineering, and management from the University of Novi Sad, Serbia. Her research focuses on intellectual capital, knowledge management, innovation, digital transformation, and international business. She published in highly ranked journals such as *Journal of Business Research*, *Industrial Marketing Management*, *European Management Review*, *Management Decision*, *Review of Managerial Science*, *Journal of Intellectual Capital*, and *Journal of Knowledge Management*. Her experience includes participation in scientific and industry-related projects; publishing academic articles, books, and book chapters; holding lectures and presentations worldwide; and serving on editorial boards of academic journals and conferences. She is known in the field of intellectual capital for insights from emerging economies and recently for using complexity theory, configurational analysis, and fuzzy set qualitative comparative analysis (fsQCA) techniques to uncover complex relationships and patterns between intellectual capital and organizational performance. Her research has been awarded and recognized as "most prestigious across knowledge clusters" in ranked journals. Through her work she contributed to both academic literature and practical applications, offering insights that help knowledge-intensive organizations navigate the challenges of the digital age.

D.Sc. Lina Užienė is an Associate Professor at Kaunas University of Technology (KTU), School of Economics and Business, Lithuania. She holds a PhD in Business and Administration from Kaunas University of Technology. Her scientific research focuses on intellectual capital, knowledge management, digital transformation, societal innovation, and national policy development based on efficient management of intangible resources and innovation-oriented infrastructures. She acts as a national and international expert on knowledge and intellectual capital management. She is an author of numerous academic publications, a consultant, a research project manager, and a speaker to promote the knowledge economy and intellectual capital development via public forums and platforms. She is the vice president of The New Club of Paris which is an agenda developer for the knowledge economy in Europe and worldwide aiming to support nations, cities, communities, and organizations in their transition into a knowledge society. She is also a member of different scientific committees and bodies responsible for the development of methodologies and the transfer of knowledge from educational systems to business practice. Her recent research and consulting activities focus on emerging technologies, societal transformation, and the development of ecosystems based on intellectual resources and innovation.

The manufacturer's authorised representative in the EU is Springer
Nature Customer Service Centre GmbH, Europaplatz 3, 69115 Heidelberg,
Germany. If you have any concerns regarding our products, please
contact ProductSafety@springernature.com

Printed and bound by CPI Group (UK) Ltd, Croydon, CR0 4YY
30/09/2026
02225599-0016